# Work and Sleep

# WORK AND SLEEP

*Research Insights for the Workplace*

Edited by

Julian Barling

Christopher M. Barnes

Erica L. Carleton

*and*

David T. Wagner

OXFORD
UNIVERSITY PRESS

# OXFORD
UNIVERSITY PRESS

Oxford University Press is a department of the University of Oxford. It furthers
the University's objective of excellence in research, scholarship, and education
by publishing worldwide.Oxford is a registered trade mark of Oxford University
Press in the UK and certain other countries.

Published in the United States of America by Oxford University Press
198 Madison Avenue, New York, NY 10016, United States of America.

© Oxford University Press 2016

First Edition published in 2016

Library of Congress Cataloging-in-Publication Data
Names: Barling, Julian, editor.
Title: Work and sleep : research insights for the workplace / edited by Julian Barling, Christopher
    M. Barnes, Erica L. Carleton, David T. Wagner.
Description: New York : Oxford University Press, 2016.
Identifiers: LCCN 2015035592
Subjects: LCSH: Psychology, Industrial. | Job stress. | Sleep.
Classification: LCC HF5548.8.W647 2016 | DDC 158.7—dc23 LC record available at http://lccn.
    loc.gov/2015035592
ISBN 978-0-19-021766-2

9 8 7 6 5 4 3 2 1
Printed by Sheridan, USA

# CONTENTS

**PART III: Management and Educational Implications**

# CONTRIBUTOR LIST

**Peter Bamberger**
Department of Organizational
  Behavior
School of Business Administration
Tel Aviv University
Ramat Aviv, Israel

**Larissa K. Barber**
Department of Psychology
Northern Illinois University
DeKalb, Illinois

**Julian Barling**
Department of Organizational
  Behavior and Psychology
Smith School of Business
Queen's University
Ontario, Canada

**Christopher M. Barnes**
Department of Management and
  Organization
Foster School of Business
University of Washington
Seattle, Washington

**Christopher J. Budnick**
Department of Psychology
Northern Illinois University
DeKalb, Illinois

**Rona Cafri**
Department of Organizational Behavior
School of Business Administration
Tel Aviv University
Ramat Aviv, Israel

**Erica L. Carleton**
Ian O. Ihnatowycz Institute for
  Leadership
Ivey Business School
Western University
London, Ontario

**Anne Casper**
Department of Psychology
University of Mannheim
Mannheim, Germany

**Philip Cheng**
Sleep Research Laboratory
Henry Ford Hospital
Sleep Disorders and Research Center
Novi, Michigan

**Tori Crain**
Department of Psychology
Colorado State University
Fort Collins, Colorado

**Christopher Drake**
Sleep Research Laboratory
Henry Ford Hospital
Sleep Disorders and Research Center
Novi, Michigan

**Helen S. Driver**
Sleep Disorders Laboratory and EEG/
  EMG Department
Kingston General Hospital and Queen's
  University
Kingston, Ontario, Canada

**Charlotte Fritz**
Department of Industrial and
   Organizational Psychology
Portland State University
Portland, Oregon

**J. Jeffrey Gish**
Lundquist College of Business
University of Oregon
Eugene, Oregon

**E. Kevin Kelloway**
Department of Psychology
Saint Mary's University
Halifax, Nova Scotia, Canada

**Chak Fu Lam**
Sawyer Business School
Suffolk University
Boston, Massachusetts

**Alistair W. MacLean**
Department of Psychology
Queen's University
Kingston, Ontario, Canada

**Anna Sophia Pinck**
Department of Psychology
University of Mannheim
Mannheim, Germany

**Maartje E. Schouten**
Rotterdam School of Management
Erasmus University Rotterdam
Rotterdam, The Netherlands;
Eli Broad College of Business
Michigan State University
East Lansing, Michigan

**Sabine Sonnentag**
Department of Psychology
University of Mannheim
Mannheim, Germany

**Gretchen M. Spreitzer**
Department of Business
   Administration, and Management &
   Organizations
Ross School of Business
University of Michigan
Ann Arbor, Michigan

**Evelyn van de Veen**
Amsterdam, The Netherlands

**David T. Wagner**
Department of Management
Lundquist College of Business
University of Oregon
Eugene, Oregon

**Jennifer H. K. Wong**
Department of Psychology
Saint Mary's University
Halifax, Nova Scotia, Canada

# PART I
*Sleep and Work, Work and Sleep*

# CHAPTER 1

# Work and Sleep

*Looking Back, and Moving Forward*

JULIAN BARLING, CHRISTOPHER M. BARNES,
ERICA L. CARLETON, AND DAVID T. WAGNER

## WORK AND SLEEP: LOOKING BACK, AND MOVING FORWARD

The interdependence of work and sleep has a long history, but the scientific study of their interdependence has a much shorter past. This was all very much of a nonissue until those fateful years of 1878 and 1879 when Thomas Edison first invented and experimented with a mass-produced light bulb, and then in 1880, received a patent for his invention. Prior to this, night work was almost unheard of, save for those few people involved in policing or security. Then, all of sudden, work became possible during the dark hours of night on a much larger scale than was ever thought possible before Edison's invention. Quite simply, the structure and timing of work changed dramatically and forever with the advent of what was to be called "shift work." Today, just under 30% of all employed people in the United States are involved in some form of shift work (Alterman, Luckhaupt, Dahlhamer, Ward, & Calvert, 2013)

In those early times in which safety standards, unions, and government regulation were still very much in the future, very elementary work schedules were established, usually consisting of two large groups of employees who would work 12-hour shifts, changing between nights and days every few weeks. Behind the scenes, academic research aimed at understanding the effects of shift work on sleep and performance was already underway shortly after the turn of the twentieth century. And almost 100 years later, the findings from this early research will not be surprising. For example, after subjecting volunteer college students to 50 hours of continued wakefulness, Herbert Laslett (1924) found that cognitive functioning declined (and in a few cases hallucinations occurred). Based on further experimentation, 4 years later Laslett concluded that "An individual's normal amount of sleep cannot be curtailed or eliminated without loss of efficiency" (1928, p. 370).

Not surprisingly, research intensified over the next several decades, with increasing nuance and sophistication in what was being learned about very different work shift systems (Parkes, 2015) and their effects on employees' work performance, which is reflected in Chapter 2 by Philip Cheng and Christopher Drake. As Alistair W. MacLean shows in Chapter 8, hazardous occupations have received considerable attention in research on the effects of sleep on performance and safety. Thus, we have known for several decades that work, safety, and health are all optimized when shift schedules are compatible with nonwork lives, and rotate in a forward (day-to-night), stable, and predictable fashion (Sauter, Murphy, & Hurrell, 1990), and when employees have a voice in the shift schedules on which they work (Barton, 1994). In addition, it is clear that working shifts also affects the well-being of employees' spouses or partners and children (Barling, 1990).

Although the study of the effects of shift work on sleep was historically crucial, the focus has now broadened. The amount of time devoted to work, whether through weekly overtime or through night-based overtime, significantly influences sleepiness at work (e.g., Son, Kong, Koh, Kim, & Härmä, 2008). But the effects go beyond sleepiness: Using archival data and an experience sampling study in two different samples, Barnes, Wagner, and Ghumman (2012) showed that there was a negative and nonlinear relationship between time spent working and time spent sleeping: As can be seen in Figures 1.1 and 1.2, which reflect findings from both samples, the negative effects on sleep are worse the more time spent working. Thus, as the authors cogently note, because time is a finite resource, people "borrow" time from sleep to meet increasing work (and family) demands.

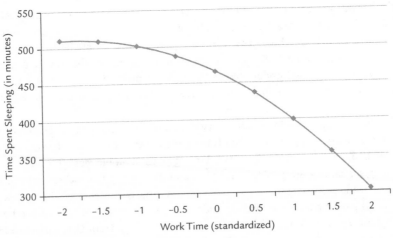

**Figure 1.1.**
Nonlinear effect of time spent working on sleep (sample 1).
Data for both figures are from Barnes et al. (2012).

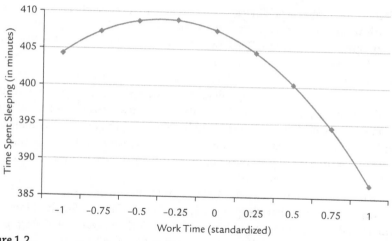

**Figure 1.2.**
Nonlinear effect of time spent working on sleep (sample 2).

If so much has been known for so long, you might justifiably ask: Why the need for a book on work and sleep? Has anything changed? In short, we suggest that with respect to our understanding of work and sleep, almost everything has changed. An appreciation of what has changed so much provides the perfect introduction to this book.

First and foremost, the contemporary scholarly community whose expertise is understanding the "work" facet of work and sleep is very different from its counterparts of yesteryear. Historically, the scholars most interested in "work" brought with them an expertise in either the cognitive and physical aspects of work performance or safety performance. Not surprisingly, their narrow focus shaped and limited the research that was conducted and the knowledge that was generated.

This is important, because just how much the scholars involved shape and limit a field is also evident from the study of the interdependence of work and family. Until the early 1980s, scholars interested in this topic were primarily developmental and family psychologists and sociologists who brought with them a nuanced approach to the understanding of "family," although at the same time their appreciation of work was rudimentary (Barling, 1990). Indeed, at that time work was conceptualized in research as parents either being employed or not, or through the number of hours worked per week. It was only when organizational psychologists became interested in work and family in the mid-1980s that the research benefitted from a sophisticated appreciation of the broad nature and subjective experience of work (rather than the presence/absence or amount of work).

Today, the scholars involved in studying work and sleep have a broad background in organizational behavior and/or industrial and organizational psychology, and consequently the focus of research now extends beyond the narrow effects of sleep on either task performance or safety. Instead, as will be seen from the chapters in this book, we now have a vastly different literature available, one that involves a very broad understanding of the nature and experience of work and its interdependence with sleep.

Second, very few topics investigated by academic researchers have received as much public interest as has the study of sleep.[1] As but one example, Ariana Huffington's (2010) TED talk "How to succeed? Get more sleep" has already been watched by no fewer than three million people![2]

Third, although the amount of sleep people need has remained unchanged over decades, the amount of time people devote to sleep each night has not. The average sleep duration for adults in the United States has decreased over the past 30 years, with most of the decline occurring by 2004. Moreover, the number of adults who sleep less than the minimum recommended (>7 hours per night) or more than the maximum recommended (<9 hours per night) has increased over the same period (Ford, Cunningham, & Croft, 2015).

Fourth, the sheer prevalence of sleep problems in the general population has raised awareness that sleep is an issue (Ferrie Kumari, Singh-Manoux, & Kivimaki, 2011). Exacerbating this is the fact that the prevalence of sleep problems and clinical sleep disorders (as described in Chapter 3 by Helen S. Driver) is likely to increase given increasing work pressures (e.g., Barnes et al., 2012) and the pervasive and insidious reach of smart phones into what was once sacrosanct sleep routines. In turn, these sleep disorders will continue to affect workplace behaviors.

Fifth, the decades-old knowledge that decreased sleep and interrupted sleep were major contributing factors to automobile and transportation incidents is by no means new, and was responsible for public policy initiatives, such as regulations in many jurisdictions restricting excessive hours of work in occupations that could compromise public safety (e.g., airline pilots, heavy duty truck drivers). Add to this the growing awareness that sleep problems also compromise people's own health. For example, research now shows that being at risk for or being diagnosed as having a sleep disorder such as sleep apnea or insomnia is associated with an increased risk for a variety of cardiovascular diseases and type 2 diabetes (Newman et al., 2000) as well as obesity and metabolic disturbance (Spiegel, Leproult, & Van Cauter, 1999; Wolk & Somers, 2007). Poor sleep quality also affects daily physical well-being in the form of muscle pain, headaches, and gastrointestinal problems (Kuppermann et al., 1995).

Last, dramatic developments in the measurement of aspects of sleep over the past several decades have been very important in stimulating the study of work and sleep. This is clearly evidenced in the proliferation of sleep clinics, which invariably specialize in the physiological assessment of sleep disorders as well as their treatment; it would not have been unusual to see nonmedical sleep researchers use such facilities for their research. What has changed most recently, however, is the accessibility of sophisticated assessment devices for sleep via apps on smart phones or through mass-marketed wearable technologies (e.g., fitness trackers) that have enabled organizational and psychological researchers with modest research budgets, who are interested in the interdependence of work and sleep, to collect sleep data that were formerly difficult to obtain at best.

## Conceptual and Methodological Advances

As already noted, organizational scholars involved in the study of work and sleep are no longer content to limit their focus to task performance and/or safety. The range of workplace behaviors already investigated reflects many of the major workplace behaviors routinely subject to scrutiny. Thus, researchers have focused their attention on sleep, mood, and emotions (see Chapter 6 by J. Jeffrey Gish and David T. Wagner), occupational safety (see Chapter 9 by Jennifer H. K. Wong and E. Kevin Kelloway), and work withdrawal (see Chapter 10 by Erica Carleton and Julian Barling). Larissa K. Barber and Christopher J. Budnick show in Chapter 7 how insufficient sleep indirectly affects unethical behaviors at work. Consistent with the major emphasis on the spillover between work and family in the organizational literature (e.g., Grzywacz & Butler, 2008), Charlotte Fritz and Tori Crain in Chapter 4 help to unravel the link between nonwork experiences and sleep.

Research over the past decade has also shown that organizational scholars have been willing to apply a range of conceptual theories, models, and approaches in their attempt to understand how these work experiences affect sleep. This is witnessed in studies that have used self-regulation and ego depletion (Wagner, Barnes, Lim, & Ferris, 2012), mindfulness (Hülsheger et al., 2014), emotional labor (Diestel, Rivkin, & Schmidt, 2015), and organizational justice (Hietapakka et al., 2013) theories to explain the connections between work and sleep.

Even a cursory examination of the fields of organizational behavior or organizational psychology would point to the major methodological advances that have taken place over the past decades, and these advances have benefited the study of work and sleep. Thus, for example, we now see multiple different experimental approaches used to study the interdependence of work and sleep, such as daily studies (Barnes, Lucianetti, Bhave, & Christian, 2015), interventions (Greenberg, 2006), laboratory research (e.g., Wagner et al., 2012), longitudinal studies (see Van Laethem, Beckers, Kompier, Dijksterhuis, & Geurts, 2013), multilevel studies (Berkman et al., 2015), and the use of archival data (Barnes & Wagner, 2009).

Together, this has expanded the causal questions asked, such that scholars are now equally interested in whether and how work affects sleep and whether and how sleep affects work (see Chapter 5 by Sabine Sonnentag, Anne Casper, and Anna Sophia Pinck).

## Work and Sleep: Moving Forward

Though the authors of the different chapters in this book collectively make it clear just how far research has come in a short period of time, nothing in this book suggests that we have reached an endpoint in knowledge generation. Instead, we see this book as a platform for advancing evidenced-based knowledge, management education, and practice regarding work and sleep. Although only fools would look backward while trying to predict where they are headed, we suggest that several directions are already discernible.

Perhaps the easiest prediction is that research on the topic of work and sleep will continue to flourish and develop in different directions as new questions are asked. For example, with researchers beginning to investigate the work and sleep experiences of older workers (see Chapter 11 by Peter Bamberger and Rona Cafri), can research on the work and sleep experiences of younger workers be far behind? Similarly, increasing numbers of people are now forced to work more than one job—what of their work and sleep? In a different area, research has begun to focus on the effects of poor sleep on destructive leadership (Barnes et al., 2015). To what extent might sufficient sleep and quality sleep enhance high-quality leadership?

Second, as Christopher M. Barnes, Maartje E. Schouten, and Evelyn van de Veen make clear in Chapter 13, discussions to date about the effects of sleep on work and work on sleep have been largely absent from management education. We suspect that this will change in the future for several reasons. (1) Research findings on work and sleep now regularly find their way into scholarly management journals with a volume that will be difficult if not impossible to ignore for management educators. (2) The interest displayed by management practitioners (and to some extent policymakers) will make it more likely that the topic of work and sleep finds its way into management curricula. (3) Popular media coverage in outlets such as the *Wall Street Journal, Huffington Post*, and the *Harvard Business Review* blog (https://hbr-blogs.wordpress.com/), and books such as this, will make current evidenced-based knowledge easily accessible to management educators, enhancing the likelihood that work and sleep will be included in management education in the future.

Finally, organizations are beginning to take findings from research on work and sleep very seriously. For example, the U.S. Federal Aviation Association now mandates that pilots must have 10 hours of rest between 8- and 9-hour shifts ("Pilot rest rules," 2014). It is also not uncommon to find that major professional sports teams, including basketball (McCauley, 2015) and football (Clark, 2012) in the United States and the world-famous soccer team Real Madrid (Fenn, 2015), all have experts advising them on optimal conditions for sleep, and optimal sleep duration, for their players. In addition, some "traditional" companies (e.g., Huffington Post, Google) regularly encourage positive sleep hygiene. As organizations look for a competitive edge to help them thrive, and as evidenced-based knowledge becomes more accessible, organizations are more likely to proactively implement interventions, such as those based on positive organizational scholarship (see Chapter 12 by Gretchen M. Spreitzer, Charlotte Fritz, and Chak Fu Lam) or even napping, the benefits of which have long been apparent both from empirical research (Taub, Tanguay, & Clarkson, 1976) and from those on the front lines of leadership: As Robert Sutton (2012) notes in his widely read book *Good Boss, Bad Boss*, when Sir Peter Parker, a former chief executive with British Rail, was asked for management advice, he would respond: take an afternoon nap!

To conclude, our hope is that this book will capture the current state of the literature on work and sleep, and help bring that knowledge back into management education. We also look forward to this book serving as a launch point for more research on this issue of vital organizational and social importance, and to seeing the results of these endeavors find their way into organizations, thereby enhancing management practice and employee well-being and performance.

## NOTES

1. Exceptions would include topics such as the study of leadership.
2. Information accessed on May 17, 2015.

## REFERENCES

Alterman, T., Luckhaupt, S. E., Dahlhamer, J. M., Ward, B. W., & Calvert, G. M. (June 2013). Prevalence rates of work organization characteristics among workers in the U.S.: Data from the 2010 National Health Interview Survey. *American Journal of Industrial Medicine, 56*, 647–659.

Barling, J. (1990). *Employment, stress and family functioning.* Oxford, UK: Wiley.

Barnes, C. M., Lucianetti, L., Bhave, D., & Christian, M. (2015). You wouldn't like me when i'm sleepy: Leader sleep, daily abusive supervision, and work unit engagement. *Academy of Management Journal, 58*, 813–845.

Barnes, C., & Wagner, D. T. (2009). Changing to daylight saving time cuts into sleep and increases workplace injuries *Journal of Applied Psychology, 94*, 1305–1317.

Barnes, C. M., Wagner, D. T., & Ghumman, S. (2012). Borrowing from sleep to pay work and family: Expanding time-based conflict to the broader nonwork domain. *Personnel Psychology, 65*, 789–819.

Barton, J. (1994). Choosing to work at night: A moderating influence on individual tolerance to shift work. *Journal of Applied Psychology, 79*, 449–454.

Berkman, L. F., Liu, S. Y., Hammer, L., Moen, P., Klein, L. C., Kelly, E., . . . Buxton, O. M. (2015). Work–family conflict, cardiometabolic risk, and sleep duration in nursing employees. *Journal of Occupational Health Psychology, 20*, 420–433. http://dx.doi.org/10.1037/a0039143.

Clark, K. (2012, November 14). NFL: Sleep your way to the top. http://www.wsj.com/articles/SB10001424127887324556304578117112742606502. Accessed April 14, 2015.

Diestel, S., Rivkin, W., & Schmidt, K-H. (2015). Sleep quality and self-control capacity as protective resources in the daily emotional labor process: Results from two diary studies. *Journal of Applied Psychology, 100*, 809–827.

Fenn, A. (2015, April 21). *How Gareth Bale and Real Madrid sleep their way to the top.* http://www.bbc.com/sport/0/football/32276547. Accessed April 23, 2015.

Ferrie, J. E., Kumari, M., Singh-Manoux, A., & Kivimaki, M. (2011). Sleep epidemiology—a rapidly growing field. *International Journal of Epidemiology, 40*, 1431–1437.

Ford, E. S., Cunningham, T. J., & Croft, J. B. (2015). Trends in self-reported sleep duration among US adults from 1985 to 2012. *Sleep, 38*, 829–832A.

Greenberg, J. (2006). Losing sleep over organizational injustice: Attenuating insomniac reactions to underpayment inequity with supervisory training in interactions injustice. *Journal of Applied Psychology, 91*, 58–69.

Grzywacz, J. G., & Butler, A. B. (2008). Work-family conflict. In J. Barling & C. L. Cooper (Eds.), *The SAGE handbook of organizational behavior, Vol. 1: Micro processes* (pp. 451–468). Thousand Oaks, CA: Sage Publications.

Hietapakka, L., Elovainio, M., Heponiemi, T., Presseau, J., Eccles, M., Aalto, A-M., . . . Sinervo, T. (2013). Do nurses who work in a fair organization sleep and perform better and why? Testing potential psychosocial mediators of organizational justice. *Journal of Occupational Health Psychology, 18,* 481–491

Huffington, A. (2010). *How to succeed? Get more sleep.* http://www.ted.com/talks/arianna_huffington_how_to_succeed_get_more_sleep?language=en. Accessed May 17, 2015.

Hülsheger, U. R., Lang, J. W. B., Depenbrock, F., Fehrmann, C., Zijlstra, F. R. H., & Alberts, H. J. E. M. (2014). The power of presence: The role of mindfulness at work for daily levels and change trajectories of psychological detachment and sleep quality. *Journal of Applied Psychology, 99,* 1113–1128.

Kuppermann, M., Lubeck, D. P., Mazonson, P. D., Patrick, D. L., Stewart, A. L., Buesching, D. P., & Filer, S. K. (1995). Sleep problems and their correlates in a working population. *Journal of General Internal Medicine, 10,* 25–32.

Laslett, H. R. (1924). An experiment of the effects of loss of sleep. *Journal of Experimental Psychology, 7,* 45–58.

Laslett, H. R. (1928). Experiments on the effects of the loss of sleep. *Journal of Experimental Psychology, 11,* 370–396.

McCauley, J. (2015, March 12). Warriors seek sleep advice to keep an edge. http://www.nba.com/2015/news/03/12/warriors-edge-sleep-advice.ap/Accessed March 17, 2015.

Newman, A. B., Spiekerman, C. F., Enright, P., Lefkowitz, D., Manolio, T., Reynolds, C. F., & Robbins, J. (2000). Daytime sleepiness predicts mortality and cardiovascular disease in older adults. *Journal of the American Geriatrics Society, 48,* 115–123.

Parkes, K. R. (2015). Shift rotation, overtime, age, and anxiety as predictors of offshore sleep patterns. *Journal of Occupational Health Psychology, 20,* 27–39.

Pilot Rest Rules: Preventing sleepy pilots. (2014, January 7). *The Economist.* http://www.economist.com/blogs/gulliver/2014/01/pilot-rest-rules. Accessed May 17, 2015.

Sauter, S. L., Murphy, L. R., & Hurrell, J. R., Jr. (1990). Prevention of work-related psychological disorders: A National Strategy proposed by the National Institute for Occupational Safety and Health (NIOSH). *American Psychologist, 45,* 1146–1158.

Son, M., Kong, J-O., Koh, S-B., Kim, J., & Härmä, M. (2008) Effects of long working hours and the night shift on severe sleepiness among workers with 12-hour shift systems for 5 to 7 consecutive days in the automobile factories of Korea. *Journal of Sleep Research, 17,* 385–394.

Spiegel, K., Leproult, R., & Van Cauter, E. (1999). Impact of sleep debt on metabolic and endocrine function. *The Lancet, 354,* 1435–1439.

Sutton, R. I. (2012). *Good boss, bad boss: How to be the best . . . and learn from the worst.* New York, NY: Business Plus.

Taub, J. M., Tanguay, P. E., & Clarkson, D. (1976). Effects of daytime naps on performance and mood in a college student population. *Journal of Abnormal Psychology, 85,* 210–217.

Van Laethem, M., Beckers, D. G. J., Kompier, M. A. J., Dijksterhuis, A., & Geurts, S. A. E. (2013). Psychosocial work characteristics and sleep quality: A systematic review of longitudinal and intervention research. *Scandinavian Journal of Work, Environment & Health, 39,* 535–549.

Wagner, D. T. Barnes, C. M. Lim, V. K. G., & Ferris, D. L. (2012). Lost sleep and cyberloafing: Evidence from the laboratory and a daylight saving time quasi-experiment. *Journal of Applied Psychology, 97,* 1068–1076.

Wolk, R., & Somers, V. K. (2007). Sleep and metabolic syndrome. *Experimental Physiology, 92,* 67–78.

CHAPTER 2

# Shift Work and Work Performance

PHILIP CHENG AND CHRISTOPHER DRAKE

## SHIFT WORK AND WORK PERFORMANCE

As the workforce becomes more globalized, the demand for 24-hour consumer service has resulted in an increasing number of individuals engaging in shift work. Shift work may encompass any work schedules that deviate from the traditional day shift (typically starting between 7 am and 10 am), such as night, early morning, late afternoon/evening shifts, or rotating shifts. Large deviations from the traditional work schedule inevitably require shift workers to work during their typical time of sleep and sleep during the daytime. The reversal of typical sleep and wake schedules often is at odds with the worker's endogenous sleep/wake rhythms (often referred to as "circadian rhythms"), which are regulated by a biological clock located in the hypothalamus of the brain. Although some individuals are able to adapt accordingly, a significant number of shift workers experience functional impairments due to the misalignment between their biological sleep schedule and their work schedule, often in combination with a genetic vulnerability to sleepiness during nocturnal hours (Drake et al., 2015). This lack of adaptation, termed shift work disorder, can result in compromised work performance, which is exacerbated by fragmented daytime sleep. Understanding the consequences of circadian misalignment in the workplace is important not only for improving workplace productivity but also for safety, as exemplified by the infamous Chernobyl and Three Mile Island incidents, both of which occurred during the night shift.

### Sleep/Wake Systems

Sleep and wakefulness are governed by two biological processes that work in tandem (Borbély, 1982). The first process is often referred to as the sleep-dependent process (Process S), and builds pressure for sleep with wakefulness, and dissipates

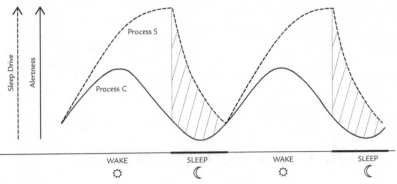

**Figure 2.1.**
Two process model of sleep.

with sleep. As such, sleepiness may occur as a result of an excessive buildup of sleep pressure from prolonged wakefulness, or inadequate dissipation of sleep pressure due to curtailed sleep. The second process is referred to as the sleep-independent circadian process (Process C), which is reflected by a rhythmic variation of sleep propensity that is governed by a circadian oscillator (Borbély, 1982). This process is relatively unaffected by sleep or sleeplessness, which explains why individuals undergoing total sleep deprivation often report a period of restored energy the following morning despite a total lack of sleep. Importantly, this circadian process is calibrated/syncronized by a series of environmental cues, the most important of which is natural sunlight or bright artificial light.

Under normal circumstances, both processes are aligned so that workers are going to bed when their sleep pressure is high, and their circadian rhythms for alertness are low, as illustrated in Figure 2.1. However, employees working outside of the day shift may experience misalignment between their endogenous circadian rhythms and their scheduled work times. Using the example of the night shift, workers are often attempting sleep at a time when their circadian rhythms are promoting increasing alertness, thereby resulting in fragmented sleep as well as difficulties falling and staying asleep (see Figure 2.2). Moreover, night shift workers

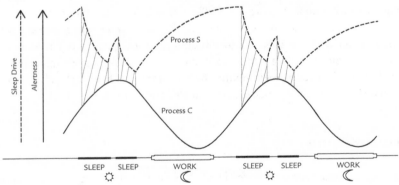

**Figure 2.2.**
Example of circadian misalignment in a night-shift worker.

are also likely to be starting work when their circadian alerting signal is dissipating and melatonin secretion is rising, resulting in increased difficulties in maintaining a functional level of alertness, and therefore impaired task performance. Task performance deficits across various domains are further compounded by the fact that these workers are likely experiencing heightened sleep drive from inadequate time for sleep or disturbed sleep prior to work.

### Prevalence

The seasonally adjusted estimate of the total working population in the United States is approximately 147.3 million (Bureau of Labor Statistics, 2014). The prevalence of shift work varies based on the specific definitions of shift work and the region studied. However, of the total workforce, an estimate of between 17.7% and 25.9% worked shifts that fell at least partially outside the day shift (McMenamin, 2007). Of the common alternate work shifts, the most common is the early morning shift, which is classified as starting between 4 am and 7 am (American Academy of Sleep Medicine, 2014). The percentage of early morning shift workers is estimated at 12.4% (United States Department of Commerce, Bureau of the Census, & United States Department of Labor, 2004). Night shift work begins between 6 pm and 4 am and constitutes approximately 4.3% of the total U.S. workforce. The evening/afternoon shift begins between 2 pm and 6 pm, and also makes up 4.3% of the total U.S. workforce. Finally, some workers are considered to have a rotating shift, in which work times change at varying rates in both directions (i.e., shifts that progress with earlier versus later start times). Start times can shift as rapidly as multiple rotations within a week, or as slow as four or more weeks per shift schedule. As might be expected, the consequences of shift work also vary between types of shifts, rate of rotation, and direction of rotation.

"Fixed" or permanent night shifts appear to be common, especially in North America, likely because of its perceived stability relative to rotating shifts. Often, new (and usually younger) shift workers are assigned fixed night shifts, and are later offered the opportunity to move to earlier shifts based on years of experience and seniority. For example, newer employees usually begin as night shift workers, move to a fixed evening shift following a number of years of night work, and finally end with a fixed morning shift. This progression may be related to the natural phenomenon of circadian delay in teen and young adults, resulting in a tendency toward later sleep and wake times (Crowley, Acebo, & Carskadon, 2007). Prior studies have also shown that older adults report more difficulties coping with shift work (Foret, Bensimon, Benoit, & Vieux, 1981; Härmä, Hakola, Akerstedt, & Laitinen, 1994).

## CONSEQUENCES OF SHIFT WORK

As the demand for shift work grows, so does the importance of understanding the adverse consequences of shift work. Many of the negative consequences relate to the effects of impaired sleep and have a substantially negative impact on work performance. Moreover, a notable portion of shift work involves safety-sensitive operations such as transportation, healthcare, and first-responders, which further emphasizes the importance of understanding the consequences of shift work in order to inform interventions.

## Consequences for Sleep

### Sleep Duration

Due to the fact that shift workers are often attempting sleep during the day when the active circadian signal for wakefulness occurs, it is not uncommon for shift workers to report fragmented and reduced sleep. Shift workers frequently report decreased total sleep time compared to day workers. Studies find that shift workers report an average decrease of 30 to 60 minutes of sleep, based on both self-report data as well as electroencephalography and actigraphy-verified data (Mitler, Miller, Lipsitz, Walsh, & Wylie, 1997; Park, Matsumoto, Seo, Cho, & Noh, 2000; Pilcher, Lambert, & Huffcutt, 2000). Furthermore, there is also evidence that curtailment of sleep in shift workers occurs immediately following the onset of shift work, and workers show little or slow adaptation to the shift work schedule (Foret & Benoit, 1978). An early study examining abrupt shifts from night to day sleep in oil refinery operators demonstrated limited adjustments in sleep time across four consecutive nights. Another study also examining transitions to night shift work found decreased sleep progress across the transition, with individuals losing an additional 0.8 hours of sleep over 6 days, following an initial loss of 1.1 hours (Wilkinson, 1992).

The extent to which sleep is curtailed also differs by type of shift work. Though sleep duration averaged across rotating shifts appears comparable to that of fixed night shifts, research comparing sleep between different phases of rotating shifts (i.e., evening, night, and morning shifts) finds important differences (Pilcher et al., 2000). In comparison to day workers, rotating shift workers working the night shift exhibit a decrease of sleep duration of almost one full standard deviation, which is approximately 1.1 hours. Workers rotating through the morning shift also exhibited a decrease in sleep compared to day workers (0.34 standard deviations less, ~37 minutes), though to a lesser extent when compared to sleep during the night shift rotation. Interestingly, shift workers rotating through evening shifts exhibited longer sleep durations than day workers, with an average of 0.85 standard deviations more (~56 minutes). The data on permanent evening shift workers also show similar results, suggesting that evening shifts may provide an advantage for sleep duration as compared to other shifts (Pilcher et al., 2000). This is likely due to a combination of two factors. The first is that the evening shift schedule may still allow for sleep initiation during the dark, which is intensified by additional sleep drive. The second is that the average individual possesses a circadian rhythm that is slightly longer than 24 hours, which increases the ease for circadian delay, especially with limited light exposure following sleep time.

Apart from biological impediments to achieving adequate sleep, shift workers may also curtail sleep in order to meet family and social obligations. In a qualitative study conducted in a large Midwestern metropolitan area, interviews suggested that shift workers often shortened their sleep time in anticipation of the physical and emotional needs of their family members (Maume, Sebastian, & Bardo, 2010). This was particularly apparent in women, as they were often the designated "default parent," who may have had to shorten sleep time in order to prepare her children for school, care for sick children, or prepare meals for the family. Similarly, shift workers may also need to change sleeping arrangements to utilize services that operate on the traditional work schedule, such as banking and postal services. Finally, shift workers may also opt to reduce sleep in order to maintain social relationships with individuals who work traditional day shifts.

### Sleep Quality

In addition to reduced sleep time, shift workers may also experience other sleep difficulties, such as falling and staying asleep, or poor sleep quality. In fact, shift work may serve as a precipitating factor for sleep difficulties, or may exacerbate preexisting symptoms of insomnia. According to a large epidemiological study of the greater Detroit area, 18.5% of night workers reported clinically significant sleep difficulties, which was more than twice the reported rate in day workers (Drake, Roehrs, Richardson, Walsh, & Roth, 2004). Clinically significant sleep disturbance (e.g., insomnia or shift work disorder) has a significant impact on workplace performance, often through absenteeism, reduced work productivity, and increased workplace injuries. On average, workers with insomnia miss three more workdays in a year than those without insomnia and utilize more services for a range of comorbidities common with insomnia (Kleinman, Brook, Doan, Melkonian, & Baran, 2009). Together, the annual workplace cost of insomnia-related incidents in the U.S. civilian labor force totals between $15 and $17.7 billion a year (Kleinman et al., 2009), which would be comparable to 1% of the social security tax revenue estimated for 2015.

## Adjustment of Sleep and Circadian Rhythms to Shift Work

Numerous studies have compared permanent night shift work to rotating shifts in an attempt to establish one as less impairing to sleep duration, and therefore less detrimental to work performance. Permanent night shifts have been purported to provide the opportunity for full circadian adjustment, whereas rotating shifts do not. If night workers can adjust their circadian rhythm to match their work schedule, workers could experience the benefit of minimized cognitive and health impairments associated with circadian misalignment. However, evidence for the occurrence of circadian adjustment in permanent night workers appears to be mixed. Previous research has indicated that permanent night workers show less decrement in sleep duration than shift workers rotating through the night shift

(Pilcher et al., 2000), suggesting that night workers may show partial circadian adjustment. Though this may initially suggest that permanent night shifts are less detrimental to sleep than rotating shifts, there are reasons why this may not necessarily be the case. First, recall that evening shifts provide the advantage of increased sleep duration, even relative to day workers. This indicates that workers on a rotating shift have the opportunity for recovery sleep, whereas this reprieve would not be readily available to permanent night workers. This is especially important when considering that sleep debt accumulates over time, suggesting the possibility that chronically accumulating sleep loss, albeit to a lesser extent when examined daily, could have more adverse consequences.

Second, there is also evidence that a significant majority of night workers revert to night time sleep on their off-shift days (Petrov et al., 2014), which may also prevent individuals from achieving significant and stable circadian adjustment to the night shift.

Third, it is possible that the longer duration of sleep in permanent night workers may have less to do with circadian adjustment, but rather may reflect a state of heightened homeostatic sleep drive. To parse this out, research examining the timing of melatonin secretion was conducted because it is considered the most valid index of endogenous circadian rhythm. In a review of such research, Folkard (2008) found that only a very small minority of permanent night workers (less than 3%) show full circadian adjustment to their work schedule. Even when considering partial adjustments, less than 25% of individuals exhibit the degree of circadian adjustment required to result in cognitive and health benefits. In light of this research, it is plausible that the degree of circadian misalignment in permanent night workers is being masked by an increase in sleep drive. This is an important distinction because daytime functioning is not only related to the amount of sleep achieved, but is also regulated by the individual's endogenous circadian pacemaker; therefore processes such as attention and alertness may still be impaired in night workers despite only modest decrements in sleep duration.

## Consequences to Work Performance

### Sleepiness

Sleepiness is a major consequence of shift work that permeates across multiple areas of functioning, and is a natural consequence of curtailment of sleep duration, poor quality sleep, or misalignment of circadian rhythms. In the medical literature, sleepiness is generally distinguished from "fatigue" in that it refers specifically to a homeostatic drive for sleep, not unlike hunger or thirst. As previously described, decreased sleep quantity is common in shift work (with the exception of evening shift workers). Similarly, shift workers also report poor quality sleep indexed by a decreased sleep efficiency, which indicates more and/or longer bouts of wakefulness during their designated sleep period (Drake et al., 2004). Finally, sleepiness can also occur as a function of the endogenous circadian pacemaker, which normally provides a wake-promoting signal during the daytime, when shift workers are often attempting to sleep, and a lack thereof during the night shift when alertness is critical.

Though the prevalence of sleepiness varies based on the operational definition, most studies find that at least 75% of shift workers report excessive sleepiness during shift work (Åkerstedt & Wright, 2009). This is particularly notable in comparison to excessive sleepiness in day workers, which is generally found to occur in 7.7% of workers (Roehrs, Carskadon, Dement, & Roth, 2011). Although sleepiness may reduce work performance across multiple domains, involuntary sleeping on the job effectively halts performance altogether. Naturally, increased sleepiness during shift work also leads to increased accidental sleeping during work. For example, a study comparing nurses working various shifts reported that as many as 35.3% of nurses working nights reported accidentally falling asleep. This is notably higher compared to only a 2.7% rate of accidental sleeping reported in nurses working days (Gold et al., 1992). Similarly, a study in train drivers found that 11% admitted to regularly falling asleep while operating the train during night trips, and an additional 59% percent reported falling asleep at least once during night trips (Åkerstedt, Torsvall, & Fröberg, 1983).

Research has also examined self-awareness of sleepiness, particularly because awareness of increased sleepiness may be used as a signal for intervention prior to involuntary sleep bouts intruding into wakefulness (e.g., falling asleep at the wheel). Unfortunately, early studies in train operators indicated that although individuals were able to recognize their struggle to remain alert, they were not able to perceive a definite and final admonition of an imminent dozing-off event (Åkerstedt et al., 1983). Furthermore, it was not uncommon for train drivers to have no recognition of accidental dozing, despite both observed and physiologically verified sleep onset (Åkerstedt et al., 1983; O'Hanlon & Kelley, 1977). Qualitative data in extended driving even demonstrated that drivers have difficulty believing or accepting that they had fallen asleep. This further indicates that sleepy workers not only have trouble recognizing the onset of dozing, but also may not recall the occurrence of dozing after it has occurred. This was further experimentally confirmed in healthy individuals (Herrmann et al., 2010) who were asked to explicitly indicate the onset of sleepiness following one night of sleep deprivation. Despite being rewarded monetarily for accurate reporting, 60% of individuals failed to report sleepiness prior to dozing-off. Moreover, posttask interviews revealed that only one individual reported underestimating her subjective sleepiness; the others continued to report no perception of sleepiness prior to dozing-off. Together, these data indicate that shift workers are unlikely to be able to autonomously intervene through a perception of their own sleepiness.

One of the most dangerous situations for accidental sleeping involves driving. Numerous studies have shown that night and morning shift workers are at increased risk for motor vehicle accidents, such as doctors driving after being on call or medical residents after long work shifts. As previously described, night workers tend to experience chronic short sleep durations, indicating that many of them are constantly sleep deprived. In addition to sleep deprivation, night shift workers are generally commuting following the end of their shift, which likely occurs during the early morning hours. In individuals whose circadian rhythms are not fully adjusted to the night shift, this will likely coincide with the lowest point in the regulation of several cognitive and physiological functions (e.g., alertness), and therefore they will be at increased risk for motor vehicle accidents. Similarly, morning shift workers are likely commuting to work during the same period, which is also compounded by both sleep deprivation and sleep inertia (a period of 10–30 minutes of grogginess following awakening).

### Cognitive Functioning

When shift workers are able to remain awake, a myriad of evidence points to deficits in cognitive performance.

**Errors.** Perhaps the most indicative of reduced cognitive performance is rates of error. In a classic study of shift workers in a Swedish gas company, error rates for manual calculating and logging of gas use were examined across 20 years and compared between day, afternoon, and night shifts (Bjerner, Holm, & Swensson, 1955). Results revealed that error rates of both commission and omission peaked during the night shifts, and were almost three times more prevalent as compared to error rates during the day shift. Research examining errors in the medical setting have also found that shift work in interns is related to increased serious diagnostic and medication errors (errors in ordering or administration of pharmaceutical agents, intravenous fluids, or blood products), as well as increased rates of patient death (Barger et al., 2006; Landrigan et al., 2004). Similarly, another study comparing nurses on rotating shifts and day or evening shifts found that rotators were twice as likely to commit work-related accidents or errors and 2.5 times more likely to have near-miss accidents (Gold et al., 1992). Moreover, there is also evidence suggesting that shift workers may exhibit impairments not only for error detection, but also for reduced capacity for error correction (Hsieh, Tsai, & Tsai, 2009).

**Vigilance.** Research has documented reduced brain activation, indexed by hypometabolism of brain glucose, following sleep loss, suggesting that several domains of task performance would be affected. Perhaps the most reliably demonstrated impairment is related to decreased vigilance, which would contribute significantly to increased error demonstrated in shift workers (Dinges et al., 1997; Van Dongen & Dinges, 2005). Vigilance is commonly tested using the "Psychomotor Vigilance Test" (PVT), in which participants are placed in front of a monitor and asked to press a button as soon as they see a flash of a small dot on the screen. The dot appears at varying intervals of several seconds, which required sustained attention. Outcome measures include both lapses in attention (i.e., no button press following the flash of the dot) and reaction time (i.e., how quickly the participant responded with the button press to the dot). Performance on the PVT is predictive of task performance in the real world, such as performance on motor vehicle operation (Dinges et al., 1997; Jewett, Dijk, Kronauer, & Dinges, 1999; Van Dongen & Dinges, 2005). In fact, a study examining PVT lapses greater than 30 seconds found that performance deficits across the day were similarly distributed to roadway crashes, which further evinces the ecological validity of performance on the PVT (Konowal, Van Dongen, Powell, Mallis, & Dinges, 1999). Not surprisingly, individuals who are under alcohol intoxication show notable deficits in this task. Accordingly, one study compared performance on the PVT during simulated shift work and alcohol intoxication (Lamond et al., 2004). Results demonstrated that individuals working the simulated night shift exhibited lapses in attention comparable to alcohol intoxication at a blood alcohol concentration level of 0.10% (above the legal limit in the United States) on the first night of the study, and that vigilance appeared to improve with more days of simulated shift work. Another study using the PVT in rotating shift workers found that performance on the night shift showed slower reaction times during the night shift compared to the day shift, and also showed a significantly greater decrease in reaction time between the start and end of the night shift (Härmä et al., 2006).

**Processing speed.** Other research examining circadian variation in a range of cognitive processes has also found differences in processing speed, logical reasoning, and short-term memory (Monk et al., 1997). To measure processing speed, a visual search task was performed in which individuals were asked to locate a specific letter in a string of letters, and the accuracy and response times were recorded. Results showed that response times increased across the period that coincides with night shift work. Consistent with the previous discussions of increased errors, individuals also showed a higher error rate with this visual search task. Similar results were also found using a sample of shift workers completing the Digit Symbol Substitution task, in which the speed of translating symbols to digits based on a legend was recorded (Rouch, Wild, Ansiau, & Marquié, 2005). Together, the evidence suggests that shift workers may require more time to complete the same tasks as day workers.

**Logical reasoning.** Logical reasoning has also been shown to vary throughout the circadian period, and thus is impacted during shift work. This was demonstrated with a reasoning task in which individuals were presented with a statement describing the sequence of two letters (e.g., "M follows C"), which is then followed by the presentation of the two letters (e.g., "MC"). The individual responds with "True" or "False" based on whether the two letters follow the sequence described by the preceding statement. In the example presented, the correct answer would be "False" because the letter "M" did not come after "C" as stated. The statements vary by active and passive voice, and are stated both positively and negatively. When compared across 24 hours, accuracy declined starting at approximately 1 am and reached a low point at 5 am (Monk et al., 1997). Response times also followed a similar trend, with time for trial completion increasing at approximately 1 am and the longest response times occurring in the morning hours between 6 am and 8 am. This suggests that night shift workers may take longer to make decisions involving reasoning, and may also be more prone to reasoning errors during their shift.

**Categorization.** Though much of the research indicates performance deficits across multiple domains of cognitive functioning, there is also evidence suggesting that not all domains are uniformly impacted. Research examining differential neurocognitive mechanisms employed in categorization suggests that rule-based categorization is disproportionately impacted by sleep loss compared to information-integration categorization (Maddox et al., 2009). A rule-based strategy for categorization utilizes explicit decisional rules that can be verbalized, such as categorization based on size (i.e., smaller objects in category 1, larger objects in category 2). An information-integration strategy for categorization relies on predecisional integration of multiple stimulus dimensions, and its occurrence is generally automatized below the level of conscious awareness.

Categorization is a particularly relevant cognitive process because it often distinguishes one optimal response from other less optimal or even harmful responses. For example, categorization of chest pain by a medical emergency responder may lead to life or death depending on the accurate categorization as a heart attack, as opposed to inaccurately categorizing it as indigestion. Categorization is also relevant to safety-sensitive operations, such as threat detection completed by Transportation Security Administration officers at the airport. Because threat objects, such as guns, knives, or explosives, vary widely by shapes, sizes, or materials, categorization of such items requires integration of information along multiple physical dimensions. Although falling back on rule-based categorization may capture a portion of threat objects (e.g., detection of pointed objects for knives), this strategy is suboptimal because other threat objects may be missed. Not surprisingly, a study of performance in a luggage-screening task completed during simulated night shifts found that accurate categorization of threat objects was significantly impacted during the night shift compared to the day shift (Basner et al., 2008).

### Adaptive Flexibility

Another important factor in work performance includes versatility in learning to perform novel tasks. This is especially so with a dynamically changing work environment. Not surprisingly, poor sleep has been found to also impair requisite skills for flexibility, such as memory and learning. Prior studies have demonstrated that performance on new tasks improves following sleep, whereas performance tested following the same amount of time in wakefulness shows no improvement, or even deterioration. This has been demonstrated with both declarative memory (e.g., recall of previously memorized words) and procedural memory (e.g., a novel motor task) (Plihal & Born, 1997). This suggests that new items encoded into memory may be rehearsed and consolidated during sleep. However, there is also evidence suggesting that sleep may go beyond memory consolidation, and may even allow for the development of pattern recognition and insight. In a widely cited study in which performance on a novel task was tested, volunteers were randomized into three conditions: 8 hours of nocturnal sleep, nocturnal wakefulness, or daytime wakefulness (Wagner, Gais, Haider, Verleger, & Born, 2004). The task employed was one that conferred gradual improvements in performance following practice, but also had the potential for abrupt and significant improvements if a hidden abstract rule was discovered. Volunteers were not informed of the existence of this short-cut. Results showed that twice as many individuals in the nocturnal sleep condition spontaneously demonstrated insight into the short-cut as compared to both conditions of wakefulness. In combination, the research demonstrates the value of sleep in effective learning, suggesting that shift workers may also experience impaired learning of novel tasks.

***Creativity.*** Creativity is also often important in successful work performance, and requires cognitive flexibility. In a study of shift workers diagnosed with shift work disorder, use of armodafinil significantly improved performance on the Remote Associates Test (RAT), which is a task measuring creativity (Drake, Gumenyuk, Roth, & Howard, 2014). In the RAT, participants are tested on their ability to make meaningful connections or associations between seemingly unrelated words or ideas. Each item presents three words, such as "speak," "money," and "street," and the subject has to come up with a fourth word that will meaningfully relate to all three words. In this example, the fourth word could be "easy" because it relates to each of the three words: "speakeasy," "easy money," and "easy street." Results of improved creativity following use of armodafinil suggest that night workers who are not appropriately adjusted suffer deficits in cognitive flexibility that detract from creative thinking. Similar findings were also produced using other tasks measuring creativity, such as the Torrance Tests of Creative Thinking (Walsh, Randazzo, & Schweitzer, 2004).

Together, the implications of these results suggest that shift workers are also more likely to experience difficulties in adapting to new job demands, perhaps due to employment of more rigid learning strategies during training. In particular, performance in contexts that require adaptability may be most affected, such as emergencies or crises, because they require decision making under conditions that are (1) changing dynamically, and (2) are likely to be uncommon circumstances that are less practiced. Because of the reduced sleep duration and quality, cognitive performance during shift work is likely less fluid, less innovative, and less adaptable.

### Psychomotor Functioning

Research has also demonstrated circadian variation in psychomotor control, which can impact performance in shift workers requiring manual labor or complex psychomotor tasks, such as surgery and driving. A prior study examining circadian variation in manual dexterity found that performance decreased after 11 pm and reached a nadir at approximately 5 am (Monk et al., 1997), which also coincides with the circadian nadir indexed by core body temperature. This suggests that shift workers may be at increased risk for manual errors or even injuries related to equipment operation. Not surprisingly, this was confirmed in another study examining percutaneous injuries in first year interns working various shifts (Ayas et al., 2006). Results from this study revealed that interns were at higher risk of self-injury from used needles during the night compared to day shifts. Percutaneous injuries are especially dangerous because lacerations from used needles can result in exposure to blood-borne pathogens, such as hepatitis and human immunodeficiency viruses, and therefore have significant implications for occupational health. Specifically, results from this study indicated an overall two-fold increase in risk for percutaneous injuries during the night shift, with the risk increasing to as high as four and five times in delivery rooms and emergency rooms, respectively. Furthermore, of all percutaneous injuries with at least one contributing factor cited, fatigue was implicated in 56% of incidents, and lapses in attention were implicated in 62% (Ayas et al., 2006).

### Affective and Social Functioning

It has long been established that sleep and emotional health are intimately related, as is evident by the heightened risk of psychopathology following the development of insomnia. Affective functioning is an important construct in workplace psychology because it often guides decision making and impacts workplace morale and relationships. Research has demonstrated that sleep loss results in compromised brain functioning in areas responsible for affect and affect regulation. In particular, sleep loss is related to increased negative affect, such as hostility, and decreased positive affect, such as cheerfulness or joviality (Scott & Judge, 2006). As a result, individuals experiencing chronic sleep loss may appear cantankerous, and in turn experience a reduction of positive relations with others. Additionally, neuroimaging research found that sleep loss reduces brain function in areas responsible for affect and affective regulation, indicating that sleep-deprived brains are less able to regulate emotions, particularly with negatively valenced emotions (Yoo, Gujar, Hu, Jolesz, & Walker, 2007). In other words, shift workers, due to a curtailment of their sleep, may experience stress more intensely, which is further exacerbated by impaired stress management due to sleep difficulties.

Sleep-deprived shift workers may also experience difficulties in social functioning due to distortions in affective processing. Effective social functioning allows individuals to work effectively in teams to accomplish larger goals, and therefore is especially important in organizations. Prior research demonstrated that sleep-deprived individuals have more difficulty recognizing happy and angry facial expressions of low to moderate intensity compared to non-sleep-deprived individuals (van der Helm, Gujar, & Walker, 2010). This is relevant because facial expressions serve as an important cue for appropriate social behavior, and can have damaging consequences if misconstrued. For example, failure to repair ruptures in relationships with co-workers can lead to brewing discontentment and decreased workplace morale. Similarly, failure to share in a colleague's celebrations or happiness can also lead to ruptures in rapport. Research in sleep deprivation have also found that sleep loss leads to increased mistrust in others, as indexed by behaviors on an economic game involving bargaining and trust (Anderson & Dickinson, 2010). Furthermore, evidence also suggests that decreased sleep quantity is also predictive of reduced citizenship behavior directed toward the individual's organization, such as offering ideas in meetings to benefit the functioning of the organization.

Sleep-dependent changes in affect can also influence work decisions. In particular, sleepy or sleep-deprived individuals may have increased sensitivity to reward and decreased aversion to punishment (Chuah et al., 2010). As such, individuals experiencing sleep loss may show increased impulsivity, or increased propensity for high-risk/high-reward behaviors. In fact, night workers report engaging in more impulsive behaviors as compared to day workers. Combined with impairments to reasoning skills, these behaviors may result in significant long-term negative outcomes. For example, in a Stop-Light task in which individuals respond to traffic light signals, sleepy individuals are more likely to make risky decisions during the yellow light for monetary reward compared to alert individuals (Roehrs, Greenwald, & Roth, 2004). This suggests that sleepy shift workers may be prone to impulsive driving or otherwise behaving more recklessly.

## Duration of Consequences

Most research examining the consequences of shift work is focused on the acute deleterious effects. However, recent studies have also suggested that stable shift work may also lead to chronic effects on cognition. In a longitudinal study examining large cohorts of shift workers over a period of 10 years, results revealed that individuals who have worked rotating shifts for 10 or more years demonstrated more cognitive decline than those who were exposed to rotating shifts for less than 10 years (Marquié, Tucker, Folkard, Gentil, & Ansiau, 2015). Cognitive decline was measured using a global index consisting of a battery of cognitive tests, including word recall, processing speed tests, and tests of selective attention. The amount of cognitive decline was equivalent to age-related decline over 6.5 years. Another analysis comparing cognitive performance in current and previous shift workers to day workers showed that deficits in cognitive performance remained significant in workers who had terminated shift work within the past 5 years. Previous shift workers showed recovery in cognitive performance only following more than 5 years of non-shift work (Marquié et al., 2014). Together, these results suggest that chronic shift work can have cumulative effects on cognitive performance, and that cognitive recovery from shift work can take at least 5 years.

## INTERVENTIONS

Given the myriad of performance deficits that stem from sleep difficulties and circadian misalignment occurring with shift work, there is a need for a better understanding of effective interventions to improve task performance and health in shift workers. Interventions can be affected at multiple levels, such as changes at the organizational level, changes in behaviors at the individual level, and change at the molecular level via medications.

## Adjustments in Shift Scheduling

Cognitive and performance deficits in shift workers can often be mitigated via adjustments to shift schedules. Permanent night shifts are commonly perceived or even prescribed as more benign due to greater stability; however, there appears to be mixed evidence for this. Although evidence suggests that permanent night workers get more sleep on average compared to shift workers rotating through the night shift, permanent night workers lack the opportunity to rotate through the evening shift, which may provide an opportunity for some recovery sleep. This indicates that permanent night workers are experiencing chronic sleep loss, for which the effects are cumulative and can lead to long-term consequences.

Adjustments to shift schedules can also be particularly beneficial to rotating shift workers. Changes can be made to both the direction of the rotation as well as the rate at which the shift rotates. Due to the fact that the human circadian pacemaker usually runs slightly longer than 24 hours, forward rotating shifts are generally thought to be more adaptable. Evidence for this can be seen in studies in which light exposure is prevented, and individuals are allowed to sleep freely in the absence of bioactive light (Czeisler et al., 1999). Under this "free running" condition, sleep onset is delayed each night because each endogenous cycle runs slightly longer than 24 hours (see Figure 2.3). Due to this natural delay, forward rotating shifts are thought to be more adaptable for most individuals. Supporting evidence suggests that sleep quantity and quality also appear to be better in forward compared to backward rotating shifts (Tucker, Smith, Macdonald, & Folkard, 2000).

Adjustments to the speed of rotation can also be beneficial. Based on research examining recovery from jet lag, evidence suggests that a mean shift of 1 to 1.5 hours of circadian adjustment per day can be expected (Aschoff, Hoffmann, Pohl, & Wever, 1975). This suggests that slower rotating shifts may be less impairing to psychological functioning than rapidly rotating shifts. There is some evidence to support this, as curtailment of sleep during the night rotation is twice as much in rapid (less than 4 days on each shift) compared to slower rotations (greater than 4 days on each shift) (Pilcher et al., 2000). This was also tested in a large factory in which a portion of workers was adjusted from weekly rotations to 21-day rotations (Czeisler, Moore-Ede, & Coleman, 1982). Results showed that workers on the 21-day rotation reported

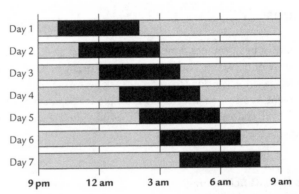

**Figure 2.3.**
Example of a free running sleep in the absence of light (sleep indicated by black bars). Sleep onset is later each night because the human circadian pacemaker generally runs slightly longer than 24 hours.

a 70% drop in complaints about shift changes, increased shift satisfaction, improvements in health, and reductions in personnel turnover. Furthermore, manufacturing productivity also increased significantly in the 21-day rotation group.

## Improving Sleep

Interventions in shift work can also target the improvement of sleep, both in quantity and quality. The use of light-blocking shades, comfortable eye masks, and ear plugs may aid in creating an environment that is more conducive for daytime sleep. However, interventions may also include additional behavioral approaches that may increase sleep opportunity in ways that also allow for personal, social, and familial obligations to be met. This can sometimes be achieved via the use of two separate sleep periods. The first "anchor" sleep period lasts for approximately 4 hours, and occurs at the same time each day, even on nonwork days. The second sleep period also lasts for another 3–4 hours, and can be taken at irregular times based on work schedule and other obligations. The use of this two sleep period system aids in stabilizing circadian rhythm and also increases sleep duration for a given 24-hour period (Minors & Waterhouse, 1983). In cases in which the sleep disturbance is of clinical significance (i.e., impairments meet the criteria for Shift Work Disorder), seeking behavioral interventions from healthcare professionals may be warranted.

The use of exogenous melatonin or melatonin agonists in conjunction with controlled exposure to bright light can also improve daytime sleep. Studies show that doses of melatonin as low as 0.3 mg can increase total sleep time during the day, as does doses between 1 and 10 mg (Hughes & Badia, 1997; Rajaratnam et al., 2009). Use of prescription sleep medication has also been shown to improve sleep. One study examining the use of the benzodiazepine triazolam in volunteers in a simulated shift work paradigm demonstrated an increase of 30–60 minutes in daytime sleep duration, though individuals did not report related improvements in alertness (Walsh, Schweitzer, Anch, Muehlbach, & others, 1991). Other studies using newer benzodiazepines have also demonstrated similar results (for a review, see Liira et al., 2014).

## Circadian Adjustment

The use of deliberate and appropriate timing of bright light exposure (~10,000 lux at the cornea) has gained empirical support in shifting circadian rhythms. Due to the fact that the circadian pacemaker is predominately calibrated by bright light, this can be harnessed via the use of artificial bright light. Exposure to bright light close to bedtime can induce a phase delay of the internal clock, whereas exposure to bright light approximately 2 hours before habitual wake time, or closely after the habitual wake time, can induce a phase advance. When used appropriately, each hour of exposure to bright light should incur a 30-minute shift in the biological clock. Alternatively, the use of light-blocking goggles can also be helpful, such as during instances when shift workers need to run errands during daylight shortly before their scheduled sleep time. This was demonstrated in a simulated shift work study in which some individuals were provided with exposure to specifically timed bright light as well as dark goggles when they went outside in daylight. Results showed that individuals who were exposed to bright light and dark goggles reported less fatigue, less mood disturbances, more vigor, and longer sleep duration (Eastman, Stewart, Mahoney, Liu, & Fogg, 1994). The use of dark or blue-blocking glasses has also been shown to effectively suppress melatonin production (Sasseville, Paquet, Sévigny, & Hébert, 2006) as well as change melatonin secretion profiles when used in conjunction with bright light (Figueiro, Plitnick, & Rea, 2014).

### Improving Alertness and Performance

Studies have also shown that naps prior to the start of shift work may be an effective countermeasure that improves alertness and performance during the shift, as this would allow for some dissipation of sleep pressure prior to work. Other studies have also found that naps in combination with caffeine use can also reduce workplace sleepiness and improve work performance (Schweitzer, Randazzo, Stone, Erman, & Walsh, 2006). On the other hand, alerting medications such as modafinil and armodafinil can also be used to improve various outcomes in shift work, including creativity, sleepiness while driving, psychomotor vigilance, as well as objectively defined sleepiness based on the Multiple Sleep Latency Test (Drake et al., 2014).

## CONCLUSIONS

As discussed in this chapter, shift workers may experience impairments to work performance due to chronic sleep disruption and circadian misalignment. The negative effects of shift work can impact a range of cognitive processes, including vigilance, attention, and decision making. Psychomotor and affective functioning can also be adversely affected. Together, these impairments lead not only to decreased productivity, but also to increased rates of error and accidents. Interventions may include changes in shift scheduling that take into account a range of information, including chronobiology as well as social and contextual factors. Interventions may also make use of light exposure, melatonin, and sleep aids.

REFERENCES

Åkerstedt, T., Torsvall, L., & Fröberg, J. E. (1983). A questionnaire study of sleep/wake disturbances and irregular work hours. *Sleep Research, 12,* 358.
Åkerstedt, T., & Wright, K. P. (2009). Sleep loss and fatigue in shift work and shift work disorder. *Sleep Medicine Clinics, 4*(2), 257–271. http://doi.org/10.1016/j.jsmc.2009.03.001.

American Academy of Sleep Medicine. (2014). *The international classification of sleep disorders: Diagnostic and coding manual.* Darien, IL: American Academic of Sleep Medicine.

Anderson, C., & Dickinson, D. L. (2010). Bargaining and trust: The effects of 36-h total sleep deprivation on socially interactive decisions. *Journal of Sleep Research, 19*(1-Part-I), 54–63. http://doi.org/10.1111/j.1365-2869.2009.00767.x.

Aschoff, J., Hoffmann, K., Pohl, H., & Wever, R. (1975). Re-entrainment of circadian rhythms after phase-shifts of the Zeitgeber. *Chronobiologia, 2*(1), 23–78.

Ayas, N., Barger, B., Cade, B., Hashimoto, D., Rosner, B., Cronin, J. W., . . . Czeisler, C. A. (2006). Extended work duration and the risk of self-reported percutaneous injuries in interns. *JAMA, 296*(9), 1055–1062. http://doi.org/10.1001/jama.296.9.1055.

Barger, L. K., Ayas, N. T., Cade, B. E., Cronin, J. W., Rosner, B., Speizer, F. E., & Czeisler, C. A. (2006). Impact of extended-duration shifts on medical errors, adverse events, and attentional failures. *PLoS Medicine, 3*(12), e487. http://doi.org/10.1371/journal.pmed.0030487.

Basner, M., Rubinstein, J., Fomberstein, K. M., Coble, M. C., Ecker, A., Avinash, D., & Dinges, D. F. (2008). Effects of night work, sleep loss and time on task on simulated threat detection performance. *Sleep, 31*(9), 1251–1259.

Bjerner, B., Holm, A., & Swensson, A. (1955). Diurnal variation in mental performance: A study of three-shift workers. *British Journal of Industrial Medicine, 12*(2), 103.

Borbély, A. (1982). A two process model of sleep regulation. *Human Neurobiology, 1*(3), 195–204.

Bureau of Labor Statistics. (2014). *Employment situation summary* (Report No. USDL 14-2037). Washington, DC: U.S. Government Printing Office.

Chuah, L. Y. M., Dolcos, F., Chen, A. K., Zheng, H., Parimal, S., & Chee, M. W. L. (2010). Sleep deprivation and interference by emotional distracters. *Sleep, 33*(10), 1305.

Crowley, S. J., Acebo, C., & Carskadon, M. A. (2007). Sleep, circadian rhythms, and delayed phase in adolescence. *Sleep Medicine, 8*(6), 602–612. http://doi.org/10.1016/j.sleep.2006.12.002.

Czeisler, C. A., Duffy, J. F., Shanahan, T. L., Brown, E. N., Mitchell, J. F., Rimmer, D. W., . . . Kronauer, R. E. (1999). Stability, precision, and near-24-hour period of the human circadian pacemaker. *Science, 284*(5423), 2177–2181. http://doi.org/10.1126/science.284.5423.2177.

Czeisler, C. A., Moore-Ede, M. C., & Coleman, R. H. (1982). Rotating shift work schedules that disrupt sleep are improved by applying circadian principles. *Science, 217*(4558), 460–463.

Dinges, D. F., Pack, F., Williams, K., Gillen, K. A., Powell, J. W., Ott, G. E., . . . Pack, A. I. (1997). Cumulative sleepiness, mood disturbance and psychomotor vigilance performance decrements during a week of sleep restricted to 4-5 hours per night. *Sleep, 20*(4), 267–277. Retrieved from http://psycnet.apa.org.proxy.lib.umich.edu/psycinfo/1997-06077-003.

Drake, C., Belcher, R., Howard, R., Roth, T., Levin, A. M., & Gumenyuk, V. (2015). Length polymorphism in the Period 3 gene is associated with sleepiness and maladaptive circadian phase in night-shift workers. *Journal of Sleep Research, 24*(3), 254–261. Retrieved from http://onlinelibrary.wiley.com.proxy.lib.umich.edu/doi/10.1111/jsr.12264/full.

Drake, C., Gumenyuk, V., Roth, T., & Howard, R. (2014). Effects of armodafinil on simulated driving and alertness in shift work disorder. *Sleep, 37*, 1987–1994.

Drake, C., Roehrs, T., Richardson, G., Walsh, J. K., & Roth, T. (2004). Shift work sleep disorder: Prevalence and consequences beyond that of symptomatic day workers. *Sleep, 27*(8), 1453–1462.

Eastman, C. I., Stewart, K. T., Mahoney, M. P., Liu, L., & Fogg, L. (1994). Dark goggles and bright light improve circadian rhythm adaptation to night-shift work. *Sleep*, *17*(6), 535–543. Retrieved from http://psycnet.apa.org.proxy.lib.umich.edu/psycinfo/1995-36063-001.

Figueiro, M. G., Plitnick, B., & Rea, M. S. (2014). The effects of chronotype, sleep schedule and light/dark pattern exposures on circadian phase. *Sleep Medicine*, *15*(12), 1554–1564. http://doi.org/10.1016/j.sleep.2014.07.009.

Folkard, S. (2008). Do permanent night workers show circadian adjustment? A review based on the endogenous melatonin rhythm. *Chronobiology International*, *25*(2-3), 215–224. http://doi.org/10.1080/07420520802106835.

Foret, J., & Benoit, O. (1978). Shiftwork: The level of adjustment to schedule reversal assessed by a sleep study. *Waking & Sleeping*, *2*, 107–112. Retrieved from http://psycnet.apa.org.proxy.lib.umich.edu/psycinfo/1980-20411-001.

Foret, J., Bensimon, G., Benoit, O., & Vieux, N. (1981). Quality of sleep as a function of age and shift work. In A. Reinberg, N. Vieux, & P. Andlaur (Eds.), *Aspects of human efficiency* (pp. 273–282). London, UK: English University Press.

Gold, D. R., Rogacz, S., Bock, N., Tosteson, T. D., Baum, T. M., Speizer, F. E., & Czeisler, C. A. (1992). Rotating shift work, sleep, and accidents related to sleepiness in hospital nurses. *American Journal of Public Health*, *82*(7), 1011–1014.

Härmä, M. I., Hakola, T., Akerstedt, T., & Laitinen, J. T. (1994). Age and adjustment to night work. *Occupational and Environmental Medicine*, *51*(8), 568–573. http://doi.org/10.1136/oem.51.8.568.

Härmä, M. I., Tarja, H., Irja, K., Mikael, S., Jussi, V., Anne, B., & Pertti, M. (2006). A controlled intervention study on the effects of a very rapidly forward rotating shift system on sleep–wakefulness and well-being among young and elderly shift workers. *International Journal of Psychophysiology*, *59*(1), 70–79. http://doi.org/10.1016/j.ijpsycho.2005.08.005.

Herrmann, U. S., Hess, C. W., Guggisberg, A. G., Roth, C., Gugger, M., & Mathis, J. (2010). Sleepiness is not always perceived before falling asleep in healthy, sleep-deprived subjects. *Sleep Medicine*, *11*(8), 747–751. http://doi.org/10.1016/j.sleep.2010.03.015.

Hsieh, S., Tsai, C.-Y., & Tsai, L.-L. (2009). Error correction maintains post-error adjustments after one night of total sleep deprivation. *Journal of Sleep Research*, *18*(2), 159–166. http://doi.org/10.1111/j.1365-2869.2008.00730.x.

Hughes, R. J., & Badia, P. (1997). Sleep-promoting and hypothermic effects of daytime melatonin administration in humans. *Sleep*, *20*(2), 124–131.

Jewett, M. E., Dijk, D.-J., Kronauer, R. E., & Dinges, D. F. (1999). Dose-response relationship between sleep duration and human psychomotor vigilance and subjective alertness. *Sleep*, *22*, 171–179. Retrieved from http://psycnet.apa.org.proxy.lib.umich.edu/psycinfo/1999-13085-002.

Kleinman, N. L., Brook, R. A., Doan, J. F., Melkonian, A. K., & Baran, R. W. (2009). Health benefit costs and absenteeism due to insomnia from the employer's perspective: A retrospective, case-control, database study. *The Journal of Clinical Psychiatry*, *70*(8), 1098–1104. http://doi.org/10.4088/JCP.08m04264.

Konowal, N., Van Dongen, H., Powell, J. W., Mallis, M., & Dinges, D. F. (1999). Determinants of microsleeps during experimental sleep deprivation. *Sleep*, *22*(Suppl. 1), S328–S329.

Lamond, N., Dorrian, J., Burgess, H. J., Holmes, A. L., Roach, G. D., McCulloch, K., . . . Dawson, D. (2004). Adaptation of performance during a week of simulated night work. *Ergonomics*, *47*(2), 154–165. http://doi.org/10.1080/00140130310001617930.

Landrigan, C. P., Rothschild, J. M., Cronin, J. W., Kaushal, R., Burdick, E., Katz, J. T., . . . Czeisler, C. A. (2004). Effect of reducing interns' work hours on serious medical errors in intensive care units. *New England Journal of Medicine*, *351*(18), 1838–1848.

Liira, J., Verbeek, J. H., Costa, G., Driscoll, T. R., Sallinen, M., Isotalo, L. K., & Ruotsalainen, J. H. (2014). Pharmacological interventions for sleepiness and sleep disturbances caused by shift work. In *Cochrane database of systematic reviews*. New York, NY: John Wiley. Retrieved from http://onlinelibrary.wiley.com.proxy. lib.umich.edu/doi/10.1002/14651858.CD009776.pub2/abstract.

Maddox, W. T., Glass, B. D., Wolosin, S. M., Savarie, Z. R., Bowen, C., Matthews, M. D., & Schnyer, D. M. (2009). The effects of sleep deprivation on information-integration categorization performance. *Sleep, 32*(11), 1439.

Marquié, J.-C., Tucker, P., Folkard, S., Gentil, C., & Ansiau, D. (2015). Chronic effects of shift work on cognition: Findings from the VISAT longitudinal study. *Occupational and Environmental Medicine, 72*, 258–264..

Maume, D. J., Sebastian, R. A., & Bardo, A. R. (2010). Gender, work-family responsibilities, and sleep. *Gender & Society, 24*(6), 746–768. http://doi.org/10.1177/0891243210386949.

McMenamin, T. (2007). A time to work: Recent trends in shift work and flexible schedules. *Monthly Labor Reviews, 130*(3), 3–15.

Minors, D. S., & Waterhouse, J. M. (1983). Does "anchor sleep" entrain circadian rhythms? Evidence from constant routine studies. *The Journal of Physiology, 345*(1), 451–467. http://doi.org/10.1113/jphysiol.1983.sp014988.

Mitler, M. M., Miller, J. C., Lipsitz, J. J., Walsh, J. K., & Wylie, C. D. (1997). The sleep of long-haul truck drivers. *New England Journal of Medicine, 337*(11), 755–762. http://doi.org/10.1056/NEJM199709113371106.

Monk, T., Buysse, D., Reynolds, C., Berga, S., Jarrett, D., Begley, A., & Kupfer, D. (1997). Circadian rhythms in human performance and mood under constant conditions. *Journal of Sleep Research, 6*(1), 9–18. http://doi.org/10.1046/j.1365-2869.1997.00023.x.

O'Hanlon, J. F., & Kelley, G. R. (1977). Comparison of performance and physiological changes between drivers who perform well and poorly during prolonged vehicular operation. In R. R. Mackie (Ed.), *Vigilance: Theory, operational performance, and physiological correlates* (pp. 87–109). New York, NY: Plenum Press. Retrieved from http://link.springer.com.proxy.lib.umich.edu/chapter/10.1007/978-1-4684-2529-1_6.

Park, Y. M., Matsumoto, K., Seo, Y. J., Cho, Y. R., & Noh, T. J. (2000). Sleep–wake behavior of shift workers using wrist actigraph. *Psychiatry and Clinical Neurosciences, 54*(3), 359–360. http://doi.org/10.1046/j.1440-1819.2000.00714.x.

Petrov, M. E., Clark, C. B., Molzof, H. E., Johnson, R. L., Cropsey, K. L., & Gamble, K. L. (2014). Sleep strategies of night-shift nurses on days off: Which ones are most adaptive? *Sleep and Chronobiology, 5*, 277. http://doi.org/10.3389/fneur.2014.00277.

Pilcher, J. J., Lambert, B. J., & Huffcutt, A. I. (2000). Differential effects of permanent and rotating shifts on self-report sleep length: A meta-analytic review. *Sleep, 23*(2), 155–163.

Plihal, W., & Born, J. (1997). Effects of early and late nocturnal sleep on declarative and procedural memory. *Journal of Cognitive Neuroscience, 9*(4), 534–547. http://doi.org/10.1162/jocn.1997.9.4.534.

Rajaratnam, S. M., Polymeropoulos, M. H., Fisher, D. M., Roth, T., Scott, C., Birznieks, G., & Klerman, E. B. (2009). Melatonin agonist tasimelteon (VEC-162) for transient insomnia after sleep-time shift: Two randomised controlled multicentre trials. *The Lancet, 373*(9662), 482–491. http://doi.org/10.1016/S0140-6736(08)61812-7.

Roehrs, T., Carskadon, M. A., Dement, W. C., & Roth, T. (2011). Daytime sleepiness and alertness. In M. Kryger, T. Roth, & W. C. Dement (Eds.), *Principles and practice of sleep medicine* (5th ed., pp. 784–798). Philadelphia, PA: Saunders.

Roehrs, T., Greenwald, M., & Roth, T. (2004). Risk-taking behavior: Effects of ethanol, caffeine, and basal sleepiness. *Sleep, 27*(5), 887–894.

Rouch, I., Wild, P., Ansiau, D., & Marquié, J.-C. (2005). Shiftwork experience, age and cognitive performance. *Ergonomics, 48*(10), 1282–1293. http://doi.org/10.1080/00140130500241670.

Sasseville, A., Paquet, N., Sévigny, J., & Hébert, M. (2006). Blue blocker glasses impede the capacity of bright light to suppress melatonin production. *Journal of Pineal Research, 41*(1), 73–78. http://doi.org/10.1111/j.1600-079X.2006.00332.x.

Schweitzer, P. K., Randazzo, A. C., Stone, K., Erman, M., & Walsh, J. K. (2006). Laboratory and field studies of naps and caffeine as practical countermeasures for sleep-wake problems associated with night work. *Sleep, 29*(1), 39–50.

Scott, B. A., & Judge, T. A. (2006). Insomnia, emotions, and job satisfaction: A multilevel study. *Journal of Management, 32*(5), 622–645.

Tucker, P., Smith, L., Macdonald, I., & Folkard, S. (2000). Effects of direction of rotation in continuous and discontinuous 8 hour shift systems. *Occupational and Environmental Medicine, 57*(10), 678–684.

United States Department of Commerce, Bureau of the Census, & United States Department of Labor. (2004). Current Population Survey, May 2004: Work Schedules and Work at Home Supplement.

van der Helm, E., Gujar, N., & Walker, M. P. (2010). Sleep deprivation impairs the accurate recognition of human emotions. *Sleep, 33*(3), 335.

Van Dongen, H., & Dinges, D. F. (2005). Sleep, circadian rhythms, and psychomotor vigilance. *Clinics in Sports Medicine, 24*(2), 237–249.

Wagner, U., Gais, S., Haider, H., Verleger, R., & Born, J. (2004). Sleep inspires insight. *Nature, 427*(6972), 352–355. http://doi.org/10.1038/nature02223.

Walsh, J. K., Randazzo, A. C., & Schweitzer, P. K. (2004). Modafinil improves alertness, vigilance, and executive function during simulated night shifts. *Sleep, 27*(3), 434–439.

Walsh, J. K., Schweitzer, P. K., Anch, A. M., Muehlbach, M. J., & others. (1991). Sleepiness/alertness on a simulated night shift following sleep at home with triazolam. *Sleep, 14*, 140–146. Retrieved from http://psycnet.apa.org.proxy.lib.umich.edu/psycinfo/1991-32712-001.

Wilkinson, R. T. (1992). How fast should the night shift rotate? *Ergonomics, 35*(12), 1425–1446. http://doi.org/10.1080/00140139208967412

Yoo, S. S., Gujar, N., Hu, P., Jolesz, F. A., & Walker, M. P. (2007). The human emotional brain without sleep—a prefrontal amygdala disconnect.*Current Biology, 17*(20), R877-R878

# CHAPTER 3

# Sleep Disorders at Work

HELEN S. DRIVER

## SLEEP DISORDERS AT WORK

When people report difficulty with their sleep, the main presenting symptom is generally that which causes them the most functional impairment. Sleep complaints usually fall into two broad categories of either sleeping too little or too much. Complaints of insomnia encompass difficulty initiating and maintaining sleep, while hypersomnia includes excessive sleepiness particularly during the day. As descriptions of symptom presentation along with relevant physiological measures and scientific research has advanced, so too have standard definitions and classification systems. We use classification systems with standardized definitions and diagnostic criteria in order to differentiate among a set of related disorders. However, it is important to recognize that classification systems evolve with advances in scientific knowledge and clinical experience. One consequence of an evolving classification system is evident in epidemiologic studies where the use of different diagnostic criteria may contribute to the range in reported prevalence rates.

Sleep disorders and poor sleep health are recognized as a major public health concern (e.g., Alattar, Harrington, Mitchell, & Sloane, 2007; Colten & Altevogt, 2006; Daley et al., 2009a; Leger, Poursain, Neubauer, & Uchiyama, 2008; Luyster, Strollo, Zee, & Walsh, 2012; Sarsour, Kalsekar, Swindle, Foley, & Walsh, 2011; Uehli et al., 2014). For example, in 2006 the Institute of Medicine in the United States of America, estimated that 50–70 million people in America, or about 1 in 6, have a chronic disorder of sleep that adversely impacts their daily functioning and health (Colten & Altevogt, 2006). A study in Finnish workers found significant associations between insomnia-related symptoms, early morning awakening, being more tired than others of the same age, use of sleeping pills, and probable sleep apnea with sickness absences from work (Lallukka et al., 2014).

A recent meta-analysis of 27 observational studies, published between 1982 and 2011, that included 268,332 workers found that about 13% of work injuries (of any severity leading to physical or mental harm occurring in the course of work and excluding commuting accidents) could be attributed to sleep problems (Uehli et al., 2014). Workers with a sleep problem of any duration or frequency had a 1.62 times higher risk of being injured than workers without sleep problems (RR: 1.62, 95% CI: 1.4–1.84). The highest relative work injury risks were noted for individuals who used sleep medication or had breathing-related sleep problems, followed by multiple symptoms.

Sleep problems, and obstructive sleep apnea (OSA) in particular, have been reported to cause a two- to seven-fold increased risk of traffic accidents (Hartenbaum et al., 2006). Untreated sleep disorders have also been shown to adversely impact productivity and cognitive function, and increase work absenteeism (Fulda & Schulz, 2001; Leger, 2012; Sivertsen, Björnsdóttir, Øverland, Bjørvatn, & Salo, 2013) as will be described in more detail in this chapter. Following an overview of sleep disorders, two of the more prevalent sleep disorders, namely, insomnia and OSA, will be described, including their impact on work.

## Classification Systems of Sleep Disorders

Sleep medicine as a clinical specialty has evolved since the 1970's along with an increased awareness of the adverse impact of sleep disorders (Edinger & Morin, 2012). In 1977 the World Health Organization (WHO) included sleep disorders in the International Classification of Diseases (ICD). Sleep disorders have also been included in the *Diagnostic and Statistical Manual of Mental Disorders (DSM)* of the American Psychiatric Association (APA), indicating the importance of sleep for mental health. For specialists in sleep medicine, the first classification system was developed by associations and societies involved in sleep research as well as physicians practicing sleep medicine as a clinical discipline and published in 1979. Subsequent revisions of the system for sleep specialists appeared as the International Classification of Sleep Disorders (ICSD) through the American Academy of Sleep Medicine (AASM) published in 1990, with a second edition in 2005 and the third edition (ICSD-3) in 2014.

Thus three different nosologies for the classification of sleep disorders have evolved over the last 45 years—one by the WHO, another by specialists in mood disorders, and a third by sleep specialists, namely ICD-10 (World Health Organization, 2011), *DSM-5*, and ICSD-3. In an effort to simplify the classification of sleep-wake disorders for non-sleep specialists in the current systems there has been a convergence of categories based on pathophysiology and an aggregation of diagnoses under broad labels (Table 3.1). From this the six common categories of sleep disorders that have emerged are Insomnia, Sleep-Related Breathing Disorders (Apnea), Hypersomnia, Circadian Rhythm Disorders, the Parasomnias, and Sleep-Related Movement Disorders. The ICSD-3 includes 64 highly specific sleep disorders under these six categories. The category with the most disorders listed is that of sleep

**Table 3.1.** SLEEP DISORDER CLASSIFICATION

| 2013: DSM-5 | 2014: ICSD-3 |
|---|---|
| 1. Insomnia Disorder | 1. Insomnia (3 disorders) |
| 2. Hypersomnolence Disorder | 2. Sleep-Related Breathing (19 disorders) |
| 3. Narcolepsy |    5 subcategories |
| 4. Breathing-Related Sleep Disorder |    a. Obstructive sleep apnea (adult and pediatric) |
| 5. Circadian Rhythm Sleep–Wake Disorders |    b. Central sleep apnea syndromes (8 disorders) |
| 6. Parasomnias |    c. Hypoventilation (6 disorders) |
| 7. Restless Legs Syndrome (RLS) |    d. Hypoxemia |
| 8. Substance/Medication-induced Sleep Disorder |    e. Isolated symptoms and normal variants (2 disorders) |
| Other and Unspecified | 3. Central Disorders of Hypersomnia (8 disorders) |
| | 4. Circadian Rhythm Sleep Disorders (7 disorders) |
| | 5. Parasomnias (14 disorders) 3 subcategories |
| |    a. NREM (4 disorders) |
| |    b. REM (3 disorders) |
| |    c. Other (6 disorders) |
| |    d. Isolated (1 disorder)—sleep talking |
| | 6. Sleep-Related Movement Disorders (10 disorders) |
| |    a. Isolated symptoms that are apparently normal variants and unresolved issues (3 disorders) |
| |    Other sleep disorders |

Classification in the current versions of the *Diagnostic and Statistical Manual of Mental Disorders (DSM)* by the American Psychiatric Association (APA) published in 2013 and the *International Classification of Sleep Disorders (ICSD) Diagnostic & Coding Manual* by the American Academy of Sleep Medicine (AASM) published in 2014.

related breathing disorders, which is a reflection of advances in research and technology in this field, as well as the high prevalence, increased awareness and impact of OSA in particular.

The diagnosis of a sleep disorder often requires determining the etiology of the presenting symptom/s as there may be a number of possible causes or contributing factors leading to the complaint. For example, as show in Figure 3.1, an overlap in presenting complaints of excessive daytime sleepiness (EDS) or unrefreshing sleep may be attributable to factors including insufficient sleep, sleep disruption by external factors, a circadian misalignment, behavioral issues, or an intrinsic sleep disorder.

## Epidemiology of Sleep Disorders

Estimates of the population of people with sleep disorders has mostly been derived from self-report via questionnaires, phone interviews and surveys. The interpretation of data on prevalence rates have been complicated by the use of different definitions and methodologies. What is clear is that complaints of poor

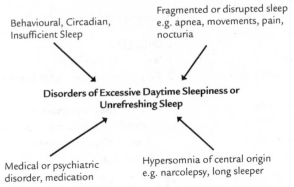

**Figure 3.1.**
Conditions associated with excessive daytime sleepiness and unrefreshing sleep.

sleep are common in the general population. An estimated 52-64% of people seen through primary healthcare practices have sleep complaints (Simon & VonKorff, 1997; Terzano et al., 2004). Depending on the syndrome, the prevalence of sleep complaints across five primary healthcare practices in North Carolina has been reported to be between 13% and 55% (Alattar et al., 2007). Patients with hypertension, pain syndromes, and depression had a significantly increased risk for all sleep complaints. A survey mailed to 20–60 year olds in the general population in Sweden found a 3-month prevalence of poor sleep of 35% and for insomnia of 8% (Linton & Bryngelsson, 2000). These findings were similar to a survey of the general population in the United States in 1991 where one-third reported a sleep problem and 9% had a chronic problem (Ancoli-Israel & Roth, 1999).

An Australian study conservatively estimated that in 2004 more than 6% of the Australian population had a chronic sleep disorder (Hillman, Murphy, Antic, & Pezzullo, 2006). The most common disorder was chronic insomnia at 5%, OSA at 4%, periodic limb movement disorder 3.9% and narcolepsy at less than 0.05%. They estimated the total cost of sleep disorders at $7.5 billion, based on direct healthcare and indirect costs (associated work-related accidents, motor vehicle accidents, and other productivity losses; and nonfinancial costs of burden of disease), when the population of Australia was 20.1 million representing 0.8% of Australian gross domestic product (GDP) (Hillman et al., 2006). The societal cost of chronic sleep disorders is significant considering that according to the World Bank, total healthcare expenditure (public and private) in 2004 and 2012 in Australia was 8.6% of the GDP in 2004 up to 9.1% in 2012, in the USA 15.7% and 17.9%, and in Canada 9.8% to 10.9%. Given that insomnia and OSA are two of the most prevalent sleep disorders, in the next section these will be examined in more detail.

### Insomnia

Insomnia is dissatisfaction with sleep quality and/or duration experienced as an inability to fall asleep, stay asleep or poor quality sleep described as "unrefreshing" or non-restorative sleep. An isolated or occasional sleepless night that becomes a recurring issue can lead to significant distress. Insomnia may be triggered by a stressful life event or changes in sleep schedules that should usually remit once the precipitating event has subsided. Indeed, insomnia can be a situational problem, for example, sleeping in a strange environment, it can be recurrent and intermittent, or a persistent problem. Even people with chronic insomnia experience variability across nights, a good night of sleep may be interspersed between several poor ones. The type of sleep difficulty may change over the course of insomnia. Difficulty falling asleep is more common early on in the course of insomnia and problems maintaining sleep, possibly still with onset difficulties, are more common with persistent insomnia (Morgan, 2012; Morin et al., 2011). Furthermore, many people suffer with insomnia for years without obtaining effective relief (Morin et al., 2009).

**Definition.** In the ICSD-3 (American Academy of Sleep Medicine, 2014), some form of daytime impairment is included in the definition of insomnia syndrome, which is defined as a persistent difficulty with sleep initiation, duration, consolidation, or quality that occurs despite adequate opportunity and circumstances for sleep. The duration of insomnia is a key factor in two of the three diagnostic categories of insomnia. A diagnosis of insomnia is applicable to patients with and without other medical or psychiatric conditions regardless of whether those comorbidities are viewed as potentially sleep disruptive. The three categories include:

1. Chronic insomnia disorder: Difficulty with sleep onset and/or sleep maintenance associated with daytime impairment that occur at least three-times per week and is present for at least three months.
2. Short-term insomnia disorder: Clinically significant sleep dissatisfaction or waking impairment that fails to meet the minimal frequency (three times per week) and duration (for 3 months) criteria of chronic insomnia disorder.
3. Other insomnia disorder: Sufficient symptoms of insomnia to warrant clinical attention but that do not meet criteria for short-term insomnia disorder.

**Prevalence.** The description of insomnia in epidemiological studies has largely focused on the symptoms of insomnia—disorders initiating or maintaining sleep, early morning awakenings, non-restorative sleep or sleep dissatisfaction. More recent studies tend to have captured the presence of daytime sleepiness and the frequency (number of nights per week) and persistence/duration (number of months) for insomnia disorder also called insomnia syndrome. Insomnia is highly prevalent in the general population. Women, middle-aged and older adults, people with a relative who has insomnia, and individuals with high caffeine intake, poor self-rated physical or psychological mental health or lower socioeconomic status are more likely to experience insomnia (Dauvilliers et al., 2005; Linton & Bryngelsson, 2000; Morgan, 2012; Morin et al., 2011; Singareddy et al., 2012). Despite variability in definitions and methodology used, approximately 20-40% of adults report some insomnia symptoms and about 10–13% meet criteria for an insomnia disorder (Morgan, 2012; Morin et al., 2011; Ohayon, 2005). A recent survey of workers in the USA estimated a higher prevalence of insomnia syndrome at 23% (Kessler et al., 2011). For an estimated 10–14% of people seen through primary healthcare practices their insomnia is severe and interferes with daytime functioning (Simon & VonKorff, 1997; Terzano et al., 2004). Daytime dysfunction as a consequence of insomnia includes fatigue, decreased mood, irritability, general malaise and cognitive impairment.

**Comorbidity.** The high prevalence of insomnia is in part due to the co-existence with other medical disorders such as pain, depression, anxiety, congestive heart failure and angina, hypertension, diabetes, obesity, medication effects or another sleep disorder (Katz & McHorney, 1998; Pearsons et al., 2006; Singareddy et al., 2012; Suka et al., 2003). The comorbidity of insomnia with psychiatric disorders is particularly high with anxiety, mood, and substance abuse disorders (Pearson et al., 2006; Roth et al., 2006; Singareddy et al., 2012). Furthermore, the inter-connectedness of insomnia with mood is evident in that individuals with insomnia were five times more likely to present with anxiety or depression than people without insomnia in the 2002 US National Health Interview Survey (Pearson et al., 2006). Although insomnia can be a symptom of another medical (e.g., pain) or psychiatric (e.g., anxiety) disorder, should insomnia persist and go untreated, it can also exacerbate the concurrent condition.

**Impact.** People with insomnia report significant impairment in their sense of vitality, health perception and their perceived ability to carry out everyday physical activities (Katz & McHorney, 2002; Linton & Bryngelsson, 2000). In addition to the individual, adverse societal effects have been documented including psychosocial, occupational, economic, and public safety, as summarized in Table 3.2 (Daley et al., 2009a, 2009b; Kucharczyk, Morgan, & Hall, 2012; Moul et al., 2002; National Institutes of Health, 2005; Roth et al., 2006; Simon & VonKorff, 1997; Sivertsen et al., 2009).

*Table 3.2.* THE ADVERSE EFFECTS OF CHRONIC INSOMNIA COVER
A RANGE OF DOMAINS

| Domain | Effect |
| --- | --- |
| Behavior and psychosocial | Increased fatigue, reduced vitality, impaired concentration and memory, nervousness, reduced quality of life |
| Mood disturbance | Irritability, depression, anxiety, increased risk for substance abuse |
| Clinical consequences | Cardiovascular morbidity, headaches, gastrointestinal (GI) symptoms |
| Public safety | Impaired vigilance and attention, more prone to make errors, increased accident risk, impaired driving |
| Work | Reduced productivity, reduced motivation, lower job satisfaction, increased disability, absenteeism (odds ratio 2:1), accidents |
| Economic | Increased healthcare utilization, permanent work disability (odds ratio of 4.5) |

The impairment in behaviors and psychosocial function with insomnia include problems with attention and memory, mood disturbances, lower ratings of enjoyment of interpersonal relationships, and more days unable to work or to carry out normal activities (Fortier-Brochu, Beaulieu-Bonneau, Ivers, & Morin, 2012; Roth et al., 2006; Simon & VonKorff, 1997). Furthermore, impaired cognitive skills as a consequence of insomnia include attention, memory and vigilance, and may contribute to significant functional impairments at home, at work, or while driving a motor-vehicle. The odds ratios from large epidemiologic studies for non-vehicular accidents associated with insomnia is around 2.4 and for reduced productivity at work is around 4.8 (Daley et al., 2009a; Leger, Guilleminault, Bader, Levy, & Paillard, 2002). Industrial accidents have also been reported to be higher for severe insomniacs than good sleepers (Kucharczyk et al., 2012; Leger et al., 2002). Insomniacs also report lower job satisfaction and energy at work than good sleepers (Leger, Massuel, Metlaine, and the SISYPHE Study Group, 2006).

*Cognitive performance.* A recent meta-analysis of 24 studies for a total of 639 individuals with insomnia and 558 normal sleepers reported that insomnia is associated with reliable (though of small to moderate magnitude) cognitive impairments involving working memory, episodic memory and problem solving, which all rely to some extent on the integrity of the prefrontal cortex (Fortier-Brochu et al., 2012). Comparable performance between people with insomnia and normal sleepers was found for other aspects of attention (alertness, divided attention, sustained attention and vigilance), perceptual and psychomotor processes, verbal functions, procedural memory and some aspects of executive functioning (verbal fluency, flexibility) as well as on general cognitive functioning. The cognitive impairments noted are in concordance with complaints of difficulty concentrating or making decisions and with memory problems reported by people with insomnia. Therefore some of the cognitive deficits reported in insomnia could account for workplace errors and poor decision-making particularly when these activities require executive control. For example, people with insomnia consistently report having to reread or redo tasks, or making mistakes ranging from minor (e.g., errors in documenting date of birth) to major mistakes (e.g., near-miss vehicular accident) (Kyle, Espie, & Morgan, 2010).

*Absenteeism.* More frequent absences from work have been reported by individuals with insomnia disorder at about 4 days annually due to insomnia, as well as greater reduction of productivity reported by 41% compared to 12% of good sleepers (Daley et al., 2009b). Finnish workers who reported frequent insomnia-related symptoms had about 5.6 days more sickness absence per working year compared to those matched for age without insomnia (Lallukka et al., 2014). In a Swedish survey, being off-work during the past week was reported by 28% of people with insomnia, and by 13% of people who reported poor sleep compared to 7% of the good sleepers (Linton & Bryngelsson, 2000). Severe insomniacs missed twice as many workdays during the previous year than good sleepers in a French study of 240 insomniacs and 391 good sleepers matched for professional activities and work schedules (Leger et al., 2002). Similar findings were obtained in a survey of 369 pairs of full-time workers with insomnia disorder matched with good sleepers and excluding depression/anxiety (Leger et al., 2006). Insomniacs showed almost twice the absenteeism rate as good sleepers, particularly for blue-collar workers (OR = 3.0), women (OR = 2.31) and for managers (OR = 2.29). For this group of matched-pairs, days off work was significantly higher for insomniacs at 5.8 days ± 1.1 per year per employee, compared with 2.4 days ± 0.5 for good sleepers, and their absences lasted longer (Godet-Cayré et al., 2006). With an odds ratio for absenteeism from work for insomnia at almost 2 to 4:1 in comparison to good sleepers, it is evident that the struggle with insomnia is severe enough to prevent people from reporting to work.

*Accidents.* Although absenteeism and accidents cannot always be linked exclusively to sleep difficulties, they represent one of the main determinants of help-seeking among individuals with insomnia (Morin, LeBlanc, Daley, Grégoire, & Mérette, 2006). The risk of accidents is increased in cases of excessive daytime sleepiness and sleep deprivation. The cause of "fall-asleep accidents" is multifactorial, including extended work hours resulting in sleep deprivation and sleep disorders, such as OSA as described in more detail below.

*Cost.* In Canada, the cost of insomnia disorder has been estimated at $5,000 per person per year compared to $424 for good sleepers (Daley et al., 2009a). These costs associated with insomnia included direct expenses of healthcare consultations and products used to promote sleep, including prescribed and over-the-counter medications and alcohol, as well as indirect costs resulting from loss of resources such as absenteeism and reduced productivity. Having insomnia was associated with 27.6 days per year of insomnia-related lost productivity compared to 2.6 days per year for good sleepers. In a U.S.-based study of 138,820 adults (age 18–64 years), direct and indirect costs for six months before a diagnosis of insomnia were calculated to be about $1,253 more than for people without insomnia who had similar demographics, location, health plan type, comorbidities, and drug use patterns (Ozminkowski, Wang, & Walsh, 2007). Direct costs included inpatient, outpatient, pharmacy, and emergency room costs for all diseases; the indirect costs were related to absenteeism from work and the use of short-term disability programs (Ozminkowski et al., 2007).

Another U.S.-based study of healthcare claims data from 2,086 members found that total healthcare costs were 75% higher in those with moderate and severe insomnia compared to those with no insomnia at $1,323 versus $757 and mean lost productivity costs were 72% higher at $1,739 versus $1,013 (Sarsour, Kalsekar, Swindle, Foley, & Walsh, 2011). A survey of 7,428 employed health plan subscribers in the United States with insomnia syndrome (at least three-times per week for at least one month) including daytime impairment reported individual-level decrements in annual work performance at $3,274 before controlling for comorbidity and $2,280 after controlling for comorbidity (Kessler et al., 2011). This study included "presenteeism," i.e., being present at work but with compromised productivity, as well as absenteeism to estimate human capital loss due to insomnia.

Overall, the indirect costs of insomnia, estimated as lost resources, was ten-times higher than the direct costs spent for treating insomnia. Aside from lost productivity, health-related costs of insomnia include more frequent utilization of health-care services and hospitalizations, more medications particularly for cardiovascular, central nervous system (CNS), gastrointestinal and genitourinary disorders (Leger et al., 2002). Chronic diseases more often linked to severe insomnia include depression (odds ratio 8.2), congestive heart failure (CHF) (odds ratio 2.5), obstructive airway disease and prostate problems (odds ratios 1.6) (Katz, & McHorney, 1998). The consequences of persistent insomnia on quality of life, functioning, psychiatric risk, workplace disability and healthcare utilization are considerable.

## SLEEP-RELATED BREATHING DISORDERS (APNEA)

In the ICSD-3 (American Academy of Sleep Medicine, 2014) the sleep-breathing disorders are grouped into (1) OSA disorders, (2) central sleep apnea (CSA) disorders, (3) sleep-related hypoventilation disorders, and (4) sleep-related hypoxemia disorder. Many patients meet diagnostic criteria for more than one of these groups. Diagnosis is often based on which disorder predominates, although this may vary from night-to-night, and over time. There is also overlap in pathophysiology for these breathing disorders. Isolated symptoms and normal variants include (1) snoring—typically occurs on inspiration but may also occur on expiration, and (2) catathrenia—a sleep-related groaning that appears to be associated with prolonged expiration. The most common of these sleep related breathing disorders, obstructive sleep apnea, will be reviewed below and then followed by a brief description of the three other types of breathing disorders during sleep.

## OBSTRUCTIVE SLEEP APNEA

*Definition.* Obstructive sleep apnea is characterized by repetitive episodes of complete (apnea) or partial (hypopnea) upper airway obstruction occurring during sleep. These events often result in reductions in blood oxygen saturation and are usually terminated by brief arousals from sleep. Obstructive sleep apnea syndrome (OSAS), which includes obstructive sleep apnea hypopnea syndrome and the upper airway resistance syndrome (UARS) is associated with the classic symptoms of snoring, pauses in breathing during sleep, unrefreshing sleep and daytime sleepiness. Other common symptoms are morning headaches and dry mouth. Apneas, hypopneas, and snoring may be exacerbated following the ingestion of alcohol, use of sedating medications prior to sleep, or following an increase in body weight (Caples, Gami, & Somers, 2005).

OSAS can be effectively treated by applying continuous positive airway pressure (CPAP) via a mask during sleep, other therapies include positional therapy (avoid sleeping in the supine position), an oral appliance or surgical interventions where appropriate. The gold standard treatment modality for OSA is CPAP.

***Prevalence.*** Estimates of OSA in the adult population have been reported at 24% for men and 9% for women and with those meeting the criteria for OSAS, which includes excessive daytime sleepiness at 4% of men and 2% of women; estimates increase with age (Caples et al., 2005; Young et al., 1993; Young, Peppard, & Gottlieb, 2002). Based on a survey conducted in 2009 by the Public Health Agency of Canada, an estimated 22% (5.4 million) of Canadian adults have diagnosed sleep apnea (3%) or are at high risk of having OSA (19%) (Evans et al., 2014; Statistics Canada, 2009).

***Comorbidity.*** Obstructive sleep apnea is associated with other chronic conditions including obesity, hypertension (Peppard, Young, Palta, & Skatrud, 2000), type-2 diabetes (Kendzerska, Gershon, Hawker, Tomlinson, & Leung, 2014; Reichmuth, Austin, Skatrud, & Young, 2005; Vgontzas, Bixler, & Chrousos, 2005), chronic obstructive pulmonary disease (COPD) and asthma (Ezzie, Parsons, & Mastronarde, 2008; Mohsensin, 2007; Prasad, Sharmilee, Nyenhuis, & Weaver, 2014), cardiovascular disease (McNicholas, Bonsignore, and the Management Committee of EU COST ACTION B26, 2007; Shahar et al., 2001) including coronary artery disease, congestive heart failure (CHF) and stroke (Yaggi et al., 2005) and depression (Peppard, Szklo-Coxe, Hla, & Young, 2006). People with severe OSA also have 2 to 4 times higher odds of complex arrhythmias (such as atrial fibrillation, ventricular ectopy) than those without OSA (Mehra et al., 2006). COPD is the fourth leading cause of death in the United States and is caused largely by cigarette smoking (Mohsensin, 2007). Given the high prevalence of both COPD and OSA particularly in the middle-aged population, they may co-occur by chance, called "overlap syndrome," and result in exacerbation of poor gas exchange. Likewise, undiagnosed or inadequately treated OSA may adversely affect control of asthma and vice versa (Prasad et al., 2014).

Epidemiological studies have shown that type-2 diabetes is often associated with OSAS and snoring (Kendzerska et al., 2014; Reichmuth et al., 2005; Vgontzas et al., 2005). In a recent study of a large clinical cohort of people diagnosed with OSA but without diabetes at baseline, over a median follow-up of 67 months, 11.7% (1,017 of 8,678) developed diabetes (Kendzerska et al., 2014). Controlling for multiple confounders, initial OSA severity predicted risk for incident diabetes—patients with severe OSA had a 30% higher risk of developing diabetes compared with those without OSA. The OSAS-related factors that may contribute to metabolic dysregulation include increased sympathetic activity, sleep fragmentation and intermittent hypoxia (McNicholas et al., 2007; Vgontzas et al., 2005) which may cause metabolic disturbances including insulin resistance independently of other known risk factors. In patients with the metabolic syndrome, the incidence of OSA is high with higher prevalence in obese patients with diabetes and people with morbid obesity (Drager, Togeiro, Polotsky, & Lorenzi-Filho, 2013). As reviewed by Drager et al. (2013), studies of patients who are adherent to CPAP therapy have reported reductions in several components of the metabolic syndrome including blood pressure, visceral adiposity and triglyceride level. These findings support the concept that OSA exacerbates the cardio-metabolic risk attributed to obesity and the metabolic syndrome. There is increased evidence that OSAS is an independent risk factor for hypertension, ischemic heart disease, and probably stroke, which can be alleviated for CPAP therapy (Drager et al., 2013; McNicholas et al., 2005).

**Impact.** In addition to OSA symptoms of snoring and excessive daytime sleepiness, people report impaired concentration or memory, personality changes and deterioration of quality of life, more bodily pain and depression (Al Lawati, Patel, & Ayas, 2009; Baldwin et al., 2001; Lee, Nagubadi, Kryger, & Mokhlesi, 2008; Young et al., 2002). OSA has also been shown to be associated with impaired cognitive function (alertness, vigilance, vitality) that interferes with activities of daily living and increased work disability (Baldwin et al., 2001; Lee et al., 2008; Sjösten et al., 2009; Young et al., 2002). A clear relationship between excessive sleepiness and decreased work productivity was found in 428 people referred for suspected sleep-disordered breathing, with improvements in a sub-sample who were followed-up on therapy (Mulgrew et al., 2007). Work limitations with OSA and sleepiness were observed for time management, mental-interpersonal relationships and work output. Interestingly, the relationship between OSA severity and work limitation was dependent on job type—OSA severity did not appear to affect work performance in white-collar workers, whereas associations were noted in blue-collar workers for time management and output (Mulgrew et al., 2007). An interesting review of sleepiness highlighted white-collar sleepiness due to OSA in the judicial system (Grunstein & Banerjee, 2007). In the index case of judicial sleepiness, the judge was found to have OSA and his driver's license was withdrawn, despite official acknowledgement of effective treatment of sleep apnea.

**Cognitive performance.** A recent meta-analysis of executive function reported medium to very large impairments with OSA that was independent of age and disease severity (Olaithe & Bucks, 2013). This meta-analysis was based on 35 studies that included adults, average age 50 years, with 551 healthy controls and 1,010 people with OSA including daytime sleepiness, examined across five domains of executive function (Olaithe & Bucks, 2013). People with OSA were found to have difficulty *shifting* between tasks or mental sets as well as *updating* and monitoring working memory, and *inhibiting* dominant or automatic responses (an internally generated act of control). They were also found to struggle with *generating* new information without external input or efficiently accessing long term memory, and they had significant problems with *fluid reasoning* or problem solving. Furthermore, improvements in these five domains of executive function were found with CPAP treatment for OSA.

**Absenteeism.** Obstructive sleep apnea syndrome has been associated with an increased risk of both sickness absence and disability pension (Lallukka et al., 2014; Omachi, Claman, Blanc, & Eisner, 2009; Siverstein et al., 2013; Sjösten et al., 2009). In a study of patients referred for suspected OSA, those with a combination of OSA and daytime sleepiness were at higher risk of both recent work disability [adjusted odds ratio (OR), 13.7; 95% CI, 3.9–48] and longer-term work duty modification (OR, 3.6; CI, 1.1–12) (Omachi et al., 2009). A Finnish study examined national registers for all (>9 days) or very long-term (>90 days) sickness absences and for disability pensions (Sjösten et al., 2009). They found that OSAS was associated with a 1.7 to 2.7 fold increased risk of work disability in men and women (higher for women) during approximately six years after the OSAS diagnosis compared to controls after adjustments for sociodemographic factors. In a recent study that examined effects of insomnia and apnea on subsequent sickness absence among Norwegian employees, both apnea and insomnia were independently and jointly associated with sickness absence (Siverstein et al., 2013). As an indicator of burnout syndrome, higher levels of emotional exhaustion have been reported by patients with OSAS (Guglielmi, Jurado-Gámez, Gude, & Buela-Casal, 2014). The presence of subjective sleepiness and poor sleep quality rather than the diagnosis of OSAS were determining factors of perceived job stress and burnout.

**Accidents.** Reports indicate that patients with OSA are two to seven times more likely to have a motor vehicle collision, are more likely to have multiple motor vehicle collisions, and of greater severity compared to controls (Hartenbaum et al., 2006; Sassani et al., 2004). The risk of driving accidents can be mitigated with successful treatment of OSA and education (George, 2007; Sassani et al., 2004). Other costs of OSA include the impact on the patient's family, decreased work productivity and work related and transportation related accidents (Wittmann & Rodenstein, 2004). In men, average age 50 years, with a diagnosis of moderate-to-severe OSA, CPAP therapy has been demonstrated to reduce the average number of lifetime motor vehicle collisions and lifetime risk of cardiovascular events; treatment with CPAP was estimated to reduce the 10-year risk of motor vehicle collisions (fatal and non-fatal) by 52% (Pietzsch, Garner, Cipriano, & Linehan, 2011).

For many years prior to diagnosis, people with OSA are at two to three-times greater risk for work place accidents and increased healthcare expenditures (Ronald et al., 1999; for review see Uehli et al., 2014). Given the increased risk of motor vehicle collisions by people with OSA compared to the general population, physicians are mandated to assess risk and ability to drive in many patients with sleep apnea, which has significant implications for patients (George, 2007).

**Costs.** The economic cost of sleep apnea has recently been reviewed (Léger, Bayon, Laaban, & Philip, 2012) and showed higher healthcare expenditure prior to and leading up to a diagnosis and a reduction following effective therapy (Albarrack *et al.*, 2005). In a Canadian study, during the 10 years prior to their initial diagnostic evaluation for apnea, OSAS patients used approximately twice as many healthcare services (as defined by physician claims and overnight stays in hospital) (Ronald et al., 1999). These cost differences increased over the years approaching the time of diagnosis, especially for the last three years prior to diagnosis. A study of adults with sleep apnea living in Washington State, found that healthcare costs during the year preceding the formal diagnosis of OSA was about twice the costs for controls even after adjustment for the "chronic disease score," a global measure of chronic disease status (Kapur et al., 1999). In their review, Wittman and Rodenstein (2004) summarized that undiagnosed sleep apnea carries an increase in healthcare costs, the excess cost is directly related to disease severity at the time of diagnosis, that the excess cost increases with time, and that the excess cost might decrease with an adequate treatment if well adhered to. CPAP therapy has been found to be an efficient use of healthcare rescources when the cost of therapy, improved daytime sleepiness, motor vehicle collisions, and quality of life were considered (Ayas et al., 2006). Another Canadian retrospective study found that treatment of OSAS with

CPAP therapy reversed the increasing healthcare utilization in men with OSAS for the five years prior to diagnosis and five years of treatment compared with matched controls (Albarrack *et al.,* 2005).

Along with obstructive sleep apnea there are three other disorders classified as sleep-related breathing disorders.

## CENTRAL SLEEP APNEA (CSA) SYNDROMES

These syndromes are characterized by reduction or cessation of airflow due to absent or reduced respiratory effort. Central apnea or hypopnea may occur in a cyclical (waxing and waning) or intermittent fashion also called periodic breathing pattern. Patients with central sleep apnea of various etiologies may also exhibit OSA. This pattern of breathing disorder is seen in CHF, less commonly this breathing pattern following stroke or in association with other neurological disorders. Central sleep apnea due to high altitude periodic breathing is generally acute, as long-time residents of high altitude locations adapt. Central sleep apnea may be due to a medication or substance. CSA due to a medical reason is usually due to a structural lesion in the central nervous system. In central sleep apnea due to drug or substance, CSA is secondary to the effects of potent opioids or other respiratory depressants on respiratory control centers. Treatment-emergent central sleep apnea is a change in apnea-type when placed on positive airway pressure (PAP) treatment from predominantly obstructive events to apneas that are central in origin.

## SLEEP RELATED HYPOVENTILATION DISORDERS

These disorders are characterized by an abnormal increase in levels of carbon dioxide ($CO_2$) during sleep. With increasing rates of obesity in the Western population, the incidence of Obesity Hypoventilation Syndrome (OHS) has increased.

## SLEEP RELATED HYPOXEMIA DISORDER

This is when oxygen saturation ($SpO_2$) during sleep is low at levels equal to or below 88% in adults.

### Hypersomnias

In modern society, daytime sleepiness affects 10–25% of the population (see Miglis & Kushida, 2014). As described earlier (Figure 3.1), excessive daytime sleepiness may be a consequence of reduced or disturbed sleep, a sleep or medical or psychiatric disorder, or it might be an inherent disorder of central (brain) origin. Excessive daytime sleepiness is a cardinal symptom of narcolepsy, which is characterized by irresistible episodes of sleep attacks, sleep paralysis, hallucinations (either at sleep onset—hypnopompic, or at sleep offset—hypnagogic), cataplexy (skeletal muscle weakness with preservation of consciousness that is trigged by emotions, usually laughter or anger), and automatic behaviors. Not all symptoms occur in all individuals and they can occur in any combination although daytime sleepiness must be present.

The ICSD-3 lists eight disorders of central hypersomnia, including two types of narcolepsy type 1 with cataplexy and narcolepsy type 2 without cataplexy and one normal variant being long sleeper. The other hypersomnia disorders include Kleine-Levin syndrome, hypersomnia due to a medical disorder, hypersomnia due to medication or substance, hypersomnia associated with psychiatric disorder, and insufficient sleep syndrome.

## Circadian Rhythm Disorders

The timing of wake and sleep is regulated across a 24-hour period with the major sleep period in humans occurring when it is dark. This 24-hour or circadian (about a day) periodicity is mediated by light and synchronized with an internal pacemaker located in the brain—the suprachiasmatic nucleus (SCN). The SCN is linked to the retina so that light falling on the eye mediates entrainment with the environment. The circadian rhythm disorders refer to changes in the timing of sleep and wake due to a disruption or misalignment of the body's internal clock and the external 24-hour environment. This misalignment can lead to complaints of insomnia or excessive daytime sleepiness or both. People subjected to circadian misalignment report impairment in mental, physical, social, educational and occupational performance and functioning (for a review see Bittencourt, Santos-Silva, De Mello, Andersen, & Tufik, 2010; Dodson & Zee, 2010).

The following circadian rhythm disorders are listed in the ICSD-3 (American Academy of Sleep Medicine, 2014):

1. Delayed Sleep-Wake Phase Disorder: The habitual timing of sleep and wake is delayed, usually by more than two hours, relative to conventional or socially acceptable timing with difficulty awakening for example in time for school, that is present for at least three months. This delayed timing is more prevalent in adolescents and young adults.
2. Advanced Sleep-Wake Phase Disorder: The timing of the major sleep episode is earlier (advanced), typically by two or more hours prior to the required or desired times, with associated complaints of early morning or maintenance insomnia and excessive evening sleepiness. The prevalence of advanced timing increases with age and is more evident in the elderly.
3. Irregular Sleep-Wake Rhythm Disorder: Episodes of sleep and wake are disorganized and variable throughout the 24-hour cycle. Depending on the time of day and their particular sleep-wake pattern, individuals have symptoms of insomnia and/or excessive sleepiness. Irregular sleep-wake schedules are more

commonly observed in neurodegenerative disorders, such as dementia, and in children with developmental disorders.

4. Non-24-Hour Sleep-Wake Rhythm Disorder: Often found in totally blind individuals when no clearly defined rhythm of sleep and wake is evident across the 24-hour period.

5. Shift Work Disorder: Complaints of insomnia or excessive sleepiness that occur in association with work hours that occur during the usual sleep episode or part thereof.

6. Jet Lag Disorder: A change in time zone causes a temporary mismatch between the timing of sleep from the habitual to the new local environment with complaints of disturbed sleep, sleepiness and fatigue, and impaired daytime function. Symptom severity and duration is dependent on a number of factors including the number of time zones traveled, tolerance, duration of travel and the ability to sleep while travelling, exposure to time-cues (in particular sunlight), and the direction of the travel. Eastward travel, which requires an advance in circadian rhythms and sleep-wake hours (going to bed earlier than habitual time), is usually more difficult to adjust to than westward travel.

7. Circadian Sleep-Wake Disorder Not Otherwise Specified (NOS)

## Parasomnias

Unusual behaviors or physical events during sleep are called parasomnias. With parasomnias a dissociated experience and behavioral expression—movement and behavior, occurs when the brain remains largely asleep. This is a mixed state with both complex motor behaviors of wakefulness and the lack of conscious awareness of sleep. The majority of these disorders are categorized according to the stage of sleep [non-rapid eye movement (NREM) or rapid eye movement (REM)] from which they occur (American Academy of Sleep Medicine, 2014; Schenck & Mahowald, 2010).

NREM parasomnias typically arise during abrupt, partial arousals from deep NREM sleep (i.e., slow-wave sleep or N3). They include confusional arousals (i.e., waking and being confused), sleepwalking, sleep terrors and sleep related eating disorders. The NREM parasomnias may share a common pathophysiology in that they have a comparable response to the same pharmacotherapies and share a strong familial-genetic predisposition. NREM parasomnias peak in childhood, though they are not uncommon in adults, with a prevalence range between 1% and 4% (Modi, Camacho, & Valerio, 2014).

REM related parasomnias arise during REM sleep and include REM Sleep Behavior Disorder (RBD), recurrent isolated sleep paralysis and nightmare disorder. RBD is a behavioral and dream disorder of REM sleep (Schenck & Mahowald, 2010). RBD predominantly affects middle-aged and older men who usually enact vivid dreams that feature confrontation, aggression, and violence. Vigorous and violent behaviors of RBD are enacted with the eyes closed and without awareness of the bedside environment, and commonly result in injury either to themselves or to their bed-partner. For patients experiencing RBD and nightmares, awakening from a dream-episode typically results in rapid alertness, orientation, and detailed dream recall, which is typical of most awakenings from REM sleep and is in contrast to the confusional arousals from slow-wave sleep (deep NREM sleep) found with sleep-walking and sleep terrors.

Other parasomnias include exploding head syndrome, sleep related hallucinations, sleep enuresis (bed-wetting), parasomnias due to a medical disorder, parasomnias due to a medication or substance. A normal variant of parasomnia is sleep talking. Parasomnias often occur with other sleep disorders, particularly sleep-related breathing disorders, RLS, and narcolepsy. The therapeutic strategy for managing parasomnias therefore is first to treat any comorbid condition/s and then to reassess if additional, specific therapy is warranted for the parasomnia.

## Sleep-Related Movement Disorders

The movements during sleep that characterize these sleep disorders are usually simple but stereotypical movements that disturb sleep or the onset of sleep (American Academy of Sleep Medicine, 2014; Lapointe & Frenette, 2014). Restless legs syndrome (RLS), also known as Willis-Ekbom disease, is included under these disorders even though it is a wake phenomenon of leg discomfort occurring in the evenings or at night. With RLS, in order to reduce the leg discomfort and unpleasant sensations, people often have to walk or move. In European and North American population-based studies the overall prevalence of RLS has been estimated at 5–10%, lower in Asian countries; it is twice as prevalent in women as men and increases with age up to 60–70 years. RLS is also closely associated with periodic limb movements (PLMs). Typically the PLMs are extension of the big toe in combination with partial flexion of the ankle, sometimes involving the knee and even the hip. These stereotypical movements occur in a series. For a diagnosis of periodic leg movement disorder (PLMD) the PLMs occur during sleep (PLMS), and are associated with clinical sleep disturbance or fatigue that cannot be accounted for by another primary sleep disorder or other etiology. Similar considerations relate to the distinction between rhythmic movement disorder and the presence of rhythmic movements, which include sleep related leg cramps, bruxism (tooth grinding), rhythmic movement disorder, sleep related movement disorders due to a medical disorder as well as due to medication or substance.

## CONCLUSIONS

As previously described, there are a number of different sleep disorders and these disorders affect approximately one in five people in the working population. As well as incurring adverse effects on the physical and mental well-being of the individual, the burden of poor sleep has an inevitable impact on work and on society, for example, 13% of work injuries can be attributed to sleep problems. As outlined in a recent document published by the American Academy of Sleep Medicine and Sleep Research Society (Luyster et al., 2012): *"Sleep deficiency (defined as a state of inadequate or mistimed sleep) unrelated to a primary sleep disorder, associated with biological, social, environmental and lifestyle factors, is a growing and underappreciated determinant of health status. The consequences to society are enormous, including disease and accident risk, longevity, and elevated direct medical costs and indirect costs related to work absenteeism and property damage."* Recognizing and treating sleep disorders, including insomnia, sleep apnea, RLS/PLM, as well as optimizing sleep duration and quality, should be recommended as standard occupational health practice.

## REFERENCES

Alattar, M., Harrington, J. J., Mitchell, M., & Sloane, P. (2007). Sleep problems in primary care: A North Carolina Family Practice Research Network (NC-FP-RN) study. *Journal of American Board Family Medicine, 20,* 365–374.

Al Lawati, N. M., Patel, S. R., & Ayas, N. T. (2009). Epidemiology, risk factors, and consequences of obstructive sleep apnea and short sleep duration. *Progress in Cardiovascular Diseases, 51,* 285–293.

Albarrak, M., Banno, K., Sabbagh, A. A., Delaive, K., Walld, R., Manfreda. J., et al. (2005) Utilization of healthcare resources in obstructive sleep apnea syndrome: a 5-year follow-up study in men using CPAP. *Sleep* 28:1306–11

American Academy of Sleep Medicine. (2014). *International classification of sleep disorders (ICSD-3): Diagnostic and coding manual, 3rd ed.* Westchester, IL: American Academy of Sleep Medicine.

American Psychiatric Association. (2013). *Diagnostic and statistical manual of mental disorders, 5th ed. (DSM-5).* Washington, DC: American Psychiatric Association.

Ancoli-Israel, S., & Roth, T. (1999). Characteristics of insomnia in the United States: Results of the 1991 National Sleep Foundation survey. *Sleep, 22*(Suppl. 2), s347–s353.

Ayas, N. T., FitzGerald, J. M., Fleetham, J. A., White, D. P., Schulzer, M., Ryan, C. F. et al. (2006). Cost-effectiveness of continuous positive airway pressure therapy for moderate to severe obstructive sleep apnea/hypopnea. *Archives of Internal Medicine, 166,* 977–984.

Baldwin, C. M., Griffith, K. A., Nieto, F. J., O'Connor, G. T., Walseben, J. A., & Redline, S. (2001). The association of sleep disordered breathing and sleep symptoms with quality of life in the Sleep Heart Health Study. *Sleep, 24,* 96–105.

Bittencourt, L. R. A., Santos-Silva, R., De Mello, M. T., Andersen, M.L., & Tufik, S. (2010). Chronobiological disorders: Current and prevalent conditions. *Journal of Occupational Rehabilitation, 20,* 21–32.

Caples, S. M., Gami, A. S., & Somers, V. K. (2005). Obstructive sleep apnea. *Annals of Internal Medicine, 142,* 187–197.

Colten, H. R., & Altevogt, B. M. for the Institute of Medicine. (2006). *Sleep disorders and sleep deprivation: An unmet public health problem.* Washington, DC: National Academies Press.

Daley, M., Morin, C. M., LeBlanc, M., Grégoire, J. P., & Savard, J. (2009a). The economic burden of insomnia: Direct and indirect costs for individuals with insomnia syndrome, insomnia symptoms, and good sleepers. *Sleep, 32,* 55–64.

Daley, M., Morin, C. M., LeBlanc, M., Gregoire, J. P., Savard, J., & Baillargeon, L. (2009b). Insomnia and its relationship to health-care utilization, work absenteeism, productivity and accidents. *Sleep Medicine, 10,* 427–438.

Dauvilliers, Y., Morin, C. M., Cervena, K., Carlander, B., Touchon, J., Besset, A., et al. (2005). Family studies in insomnia. *Journal of Psychosomatic Research, 58*, 271–278.

Dodson, E. R., & Zee, P. C. (2010). Therapeutics for circadian rhythm sleep disorders. *Sleep Medicine Clinics, 5*, 701–715.

Drager, L. F., Togeiro, S. M., Polotsky, V. Y., & Lorenzi-Filho, G. (2013). Obstructive sleep apnea: A cardiometabolic risk in obesity and the metabolic syndrome. *Journal of the American College of Cardiology, 62*(7), 569–576.

Edinger, J. D., & Morin, C. M. (2012). Sleep disorders classification and diagnosis. In C. M. Morin & C. A. Espie (Eds.), *The Oxford handbook of sleep and sleep disorders* (pp. 361–395). New York, NY: Oxford University Press.

Evans, J., Skomro, R., Driver, H. S., Graham, B., Mayers, I., McRae, L., . . . Fleetham, J. (2014) Sleep laboratory testing referrals in Canada: Sleep Apnea Rapid Response Survey. *Canadian Respiratory Journal, 21*, e4–e10.

Ezzie, M. E., Parsons, J. P., & Mastronarde, J. G. (2008). Sleep and obstructive lung diseases. *Sleep Medicine Clinics, 3*, 505–515.

Fortier-Brochu, E., Beaulieu-Bonneau, S., Ivers, H., & Morin, C. M. (2012). Insomnia and daytime cognitive performance: A meta-analysis. *Sleep Medicine Reviews, 16*, 83–94.

Fulda, S., & Schulz, H. (2001). Cognitive dysfunction in sleep disorders. *Sleep Medicine Reviews, 5*, 423–445.

George, C. F. (2007). Sleep apnea, alertness, and motor vehicle crashes. *American Journal of Respiratory and Critical Care Medicine, 176*, 954–956.

Godet-Cayré, V., Pelletier-Fleury, N., Le Vaillant, M., Dinet, J., Massuel, M. A, & Léger, D. (2006). Insomnia and absenteeism at work. Who pays the cost? *Sleep, 29*, 179–184.

Grunstein, R. R., & Banerjee, D. (2007). The case of "judge nodd" and other sleeping judges–media, society, and judicial sleepiness. *Sleep, 30*(5), 625–632.

Guglielmi, O., Jurado-Gámez, B., Gude, F., & Buela-Casal, G. (2014). Job stress, burnout, and job satisfaction in sleep apnea patients. *Sleep Medicine, 15*, 1025–1030.

Hartenbaum, N., Collop, N., Rosen, I. M., Phillips, B., George, C. F. P, Rowley, J. A., . . . American College of Chest Physicians, the American College of Occupational and Environmental Medicine, and the National Sleep Foundation. (2006). Sleep apnea and commercial motor vehicle operators: Statement from the joint task force of the American College of Chest Physicians, the American College of Occupational and Environmental Medicine, and the National Sleep Foundation. *Chest, 130*, 902–905.

Hillman, D. R., Murphy, A. S., Antic, R., & Pezzullo, L. (2006). The economic cost of sleep disorders. *Sleep, 29*, 299–305.

Kapur, V., Blough, D. K., Sandblom, R. E., Hert, R., de Maine, J. B., Sullivan, S. D., & Psaty, B. M. (1999). The medical cost of undiagnosed sleep apnea. *Sleep, 22*, 749–755.

Katz, D. A., & McHorney, C. A. (1998). Clinical correlates of insomnia in patients with chronic illness. *Archives of Internal Medicine, 159*, 1099–1107.

Katz, D. A., & McHorney, C. A. (2002). The relationship between insomnia and health-related quality of life in patients with chronic illness. *The Journal of Family Practice, 51*, 229–235.

Kendzerska, T., Gershon, A. S., Hawker, G., Tomlinson, G., & Leung, R. S. (2014). Obstructive sleep apnea and incident diabetes: A historical cohort study. *American Journal of Respiratory and Critical Care Medicine, 190*(2), 218–225.

Kessler, R. C., Berglund, P.A., Coulouvrat, C., Hajak, G., Roth, T., Shahly, V., . . . Walsh, J. K. (2011). Insomnia and the performance of US workers: Results from the America Insomnia Survey. *Sleep, 34*, 1161–1171.

Kucharczyk, E. R., Morgan, K., & Hall, A. P. (2012). The occupational impact of sleep quality and insomnia symptoms. *Sleep Medicine Reviews, 16*, 547–559.

Kyle, S. D., Espie, C. A., & Morgan, K. (2010). " . . . not just a minor thing, it is something major, which stops you from functioning daily": Quality of life and daytime functioning in insomnia. *Behavioral Sleep Medicine, 8*, 123–140.

Lallukka, T., Kaikkonen, R., Härkänen, T., Kronhelm, E., Partonen, T., Rahkonen, O., & Koskinen, S. (2014). Sleep and sickness absence: A nationally representative register-based follow-up study. *Sleep, 37*, 1413–1425.

Lapointe, E., & Frenette, E. (2014). Periodic or rhythmic movements during sleep. *Sleep Medicine Clinics, 9*, 523–536

Lee, W., Nagubadi, S., Kryger, M. H., & Mokhlesi, B. (2008). Epidemiology of obstructive sleep apnea: A population-based perspective. *Expert Review of Respiratory Medicine, 2*, 349–364.

Leger, D. (2012). A socioeconomic perspective of sleep disorders (insomnia and obstructive sleep apnea). In C. M. Morin & C. A. Espie (Eds.), *The Oxford handbook of sleep and sleep disorders* (pp. 324–347). New York, NY: Oxford University Press.

Léger, D., Bayon, V., Laaban, J. P., & Philip, P. (2012). Impact of sleep apnea on economics. *Sleep Medicine Reviews, 16*(5), 455–562.

Leger, D., Guilleminault, C., Bader, G., Levy, E., & Paillard, M. (2002). Medical and socio-professional impact of insomnia. *Sleep, 25*, 621–625.

Léger, D., Massuel, M. A., Metlaine, A., and the SISYPHE Study Group. (2006). Professional correlates of insomnia. *Sleep, 29*, 171–178.

Leger, D., Poursain, B., Neubauer, D., & Uchiyama, M. (2008). An international survey of sleeping problems in the general population. *Current Medical Research & Opinion, 24*, 307–317.

Linton, S. J., & Bryngelsson, L. (2000). Insomnia and its relationship to work and health in a working-age population. *Journal of Occupational Rehabilitation, 10*, 169–183.

Luyster, F. S., Strollo, P. J., Zee, P. C., & Walsh, J. K. (2012). Sleep: A health imperative. *Sleep, 35*, 727–734.

McNicholas, W. T., Bonsignore, M. R., and the Management Committee of EU COST ACTION B26. (2007). Sleep apnoea as an independent risk factor for cardiovascular disease: Current evidence, basic mechanisms and research priorities. *European Respiratory Journal, 29*, 156–178.

Mehra, R., Benjamin, E. J., Shahar, E., Gottlieb, D. J., Nawabit, R., Kirchner, H. L., . . . Redline, S. (2006). Association of nocturnal arrhythmias with sleep-disordered breathing: The sleep heart health study. *American Journal of Respiratory and Critical Care Medicine, 173*(8), 910–916.

Miglis, M. G., & Kushida, C. A. (2014). Daytime sleepiness. *Sleep Medicine Clinics, 9*, 491–498.

Modi, R. R., Camacho, M., & Valerio, J. (2014). Confusional arousals, sleep terrors, and sleepwalking. *Sleep Medicine Clinics, 9*, 537–551.

Mohsenin, V. (2007). Sleep in chronic obstructive pulmonary disease. *Sleep Medicine Clinics, 2*, 1–8.

Morgan, K. (2012). The epidemiology of sleep. In C. M. Morin & C. A. Espie (Eds.), *The Oxford handbook of sleep and sleep disorders* (pp. 303–323). New York, NY: Oxford University Press.

Morin, C. M., Bélanger, L., LeBlanc, M., Ivers, H., Savard, J., Espie, C. A., . . . Grégoire, J. P. (2009). The natural history of insomnia: A population-based 3-year longitudinal study. *Archives of Internal Medicine, 169*, 447–453.

Morin, C. M., LeBlanc, M., Bélanger, L., Ivers, H., Mérette, C., & Savard, J. (2011). Prevalence of insomnia and its treatment in Canada. *Canadian Journal of Psychiatry. Revue Canadienne de Psychiatrie, 56*, 540–548.

Morin, C. M., LeBlanc, M., Daley, M., Grégoire, J. P., & Mérette, C. (2006). Epidemiology of insomnia: Prevalence, self-help treatments, consultations, and determinants of help-seeking behaviors. *Sleep Medicine, 7*, 123–130.

Moul, D. E., Nofzinger, E. A., Pilkonis, P. A., Houck, P. R., Mielwald, J. M., & Buysse, D. J. (2002). Symptom reports in severe chronic insomnia. *Journal of Sleep Research, 25*, 548–558.

Mulgrew, A. T., Ryan, C. F., Fleetham, J. A., Cheema, R., Fox, N., Koehoorn, M., . . . Ayas, M. T. (2007). The impact of obstructive sleep apnea and daytime sleepiness on work limitation. *Sleep Medicine, 9*, 42–53.

National Institutes of Health. (2005). National Institutes of Health State of the Science Conference statement on Manifestations and Management of Chronic Insomnia in Adults, June 13-15, 2005. *Sleep* 28, 1049–1057.

Ohayon, M. M. (2005). Prevalence and correlates of non-restorative sleep complaints. *Archives of Internal Medicine, 165*, 35–41.

Olaithe, M., & Bucks, R. S. (2013). Executive dysfunction in OSA before and after treatment: A meta-analysis. *Sleep, 36*, 1297–1305.

Omachi, T. A., Claman, D. M., Blanc, P. D., & Eisner, M. D. (2009). Obstructive sleep apnea: A risk factor for work disability. *Sleep, 32*, 791–798.

Ozminkowski, R. J., Wang, S., & Walsh, J. K. (2007). The direct and indirect costs of untreated insomnia in adults in the United States. *Sleep, 30*, 263–273.

Pearson, N. J., Johnson, L. L., & Nahin, R. L. (2006). Insomnia, trouble sleeping, and complementary and alternative medicine: Analysis of the 2002 national health interview survey data. *Archives of Internal Medicine, 166*, 1775–1782.

Peppard, P. E., Szklo-Coxe, M., Hla, K. M., & Young, T. (2006). Longitudinal association of sleep-related breathing disorder and depression. *Archives of Internal Medicine, 166*, 1709–1715.

Peppard, P. E., Young, T., Palta, M., & Skatrud, J. (2000). Prospective study of the association between sleep-disordered breathing and hypertension. *New England Journal of Medicine, 342*, 1378–1384.

Pietzsch, J. B., Garner, A., Cipriano, L. E., & Linehan, J. H. (2011). An integrated health-economic analysis of diagnostic and therapeutic strategies in the treatment of moderate-to-severe obstructive sleep apnea. *Sleep, 34*, 695–709.

Prasad, B., Sharmilee M., Nyenhuis S. M., & Weaver T. E. (2014). Obstructive sleep apnea and asthma: Associations and treatment implications. *Sleep Medicine Reviews, 18*, 165–171.

Reichmuth, K. J., Austin, D., Skatrud, J. B., & Young, T. (2005). Association of sleep apnea and type II diabetes: A population-based study. *American Journal of Respiratory and Critical Care Medicine, 172*, 1590–1595.

Ronald, J., Delaive, K., Roos, L., Manfreda, J., Bahammam, A., & Kryger, M. H. (1999). Health care utilization in the 10 years prior to diagnosis in obstructive sleep apnea syndrome patients. *Sleep, 22*, 225–229.

Roth, T., Jaeger, S., Jin, R., Kalsekar, A., Stang, P. E., & Kessler, R. C. (2006). Sleep problems, comorbid mental disorders, and role functioning in the national comorbidity survey replication. *Biological Psychiatry, 60*, 1364–1371.

Sarsour, K., Kalsekar, A., Swindle, R., Foley, K., & Walsh, J. K. (2011). The association between insomnia severity and healthcare and productivity costs in a health plan sample. *Sleep, 34*, 443–450.

Sassani, A., Findley, L. J., Kryger, M., Goldlust, E., George, C., & Davidson, T. M. (2004). Reducing motor-vehicle collisions, costs, and fatalities by treating obstructive sleep apnea syndrome. *Sleep, 27*, 453–458.

Schenck, C. H., & Mahowald, M. W. (2010). Therapeutics for parasomnias in adults. *Sleep Medicine Clinics, 5*, 689–700.

Shahar, E., Whitney, C. W., Redline, S., Lee, E. T., Newman, A. B., Nieto, F. J., . . . Samet, J. M. (2001). Sleep-disordered breathing and cardiovascular disease: Cross-sectional results of the sleep heart health study. *American Journal of Respiratory and Critical Care Medicine, 163*(1), 19–25.

Simon, G. E., & VonKorff, M. (1997). Prevalence, burden, and treatment of insomnia in primary care. *American Journal of Psychiatry, 154*, 1417–1423.

Singareddy, R., Vgontzas, A. N., Fernandez-Mendoza, J., Liao, D., Calhoun, S., Shaffer, M. L., & Bixler, E. O. (2012). Risk factors for incident chronic insomnia: A general population prospective study. *Sleep Medicine, 13*, 346–353.

Sivertsen, B., Björnsdóttir, E., Øverland, S., Björvatn, B., & Salo, P. (2013). The joint contribution of insomnia and obstructive sleep apnoea on sickness absence. *Journal of Sleep Research, 22*, 223–230.

Sivertsen, B., Overland, S., Pallesen, S., Bjorvatn, B., Nordhus, I. H., Maeland, J. G., & Mykletun, A. (2009). Insomnia and long sleep duration are risk factors for later work disability. The Hordaland Health Study. *Journal of Sleep Research, 18*, 122–128.

Sjösten, N., Kivimäki, M., Oksanen, T., Salo, P., Saaresranta, T., Virtanen, M., . . . Vahtera, J. (2009). Obstructive sleep apnoea syndrome as a predictor of work disability. *Respiratory Medicine, 103*, 1047–1055.

Statistics Canada. (2009). *The Canadian community health survey: Rapid response on sleep apnea survey*. Centre for Chronic Disease Prevention: Public Health Agency of Canada. Retrieved from http://www.statcan.gc.ca/daily-quotidien/091208/dq091208d-eng.htm.

Suka, M., Yoshida, K., & Sugimori, H. (2003). Persistent insomnia is a predictor of hypertension in Japanese male workers. *Journal of Occupational Health, 45*, 244–250.

Terzano, M. G., Parrino, L., Cirignotta, F., Ferini-Strambi, L., Gigli, G., Rudelli, G., & Morfeo, S. (2004). Insomnia in primary care, a survey conducted on the Italian population. *Sleep Medicine, 5*, 67–75.

Uehli, K., Mehta, A. J., Miedingern, D., Hug, K., Schindler, C., Holsboer-Trachsler, E., . . . Künzli, N. (2014). Sleep problems and work injuries: A systematic review and meta-analysis *Sleep Medicine Reviews, 18*, 61–73.

Vgontzas, A. N., Bixler, E. O., & Chrousos, G. P. (2005). Sleep apnea is a manifestation of the metabolic syndrome. *Sleep Medicine Reviews, 9*, 211–224.

Wittmann, V., & Rodenstein, D. O. (2004). Health care costs and the sleep apnea syndrome. *Sleep Medicine Reviews, 8*, 269–279.

World Health Organization. (2011). *ICD-10 international classification of diseases and health related problems*, 4th ed., 10th revision (Vol. 2). Geneva, Switzerland: World Health Organization. Retrieved from http://www.who.int/classifications/icd/ICD10Volume2_en_2010.pdf?ua=1.

Yaggi, H. K., Concato, J., Kernan, W. N., Lichtman, J. H., Brass, L. M., & Mohsenin, V. (2005). Obstructive sleep apnea as a risk factor for stroke and death. *New England Journal of Medicine, 353*, 2034–2041.

Young, T., Palta, M., Dempsey, J., Skatrud, J., Weber, S., & Badr, S. (1993). The occurrence of sleep-disordered breathing among middle aged adults. *New England Journal of Medicine, 328*, 1203–1205.

Young, T., Peppard, P. E., & Gottlieb, D. J. (2002). Epidemiology of obstructive sleep apnea: A population health perspective. *American Journal of Respiratory and Critical Care Medicine, 165*, 1217–1239.

## PART II

## *Sleep and Work Experiences*

CHAPTER 4

# Recovery from Work and Employee Sleep

*Understanding the Role of Experiences and Activities Outside of Work*

CHARLOTTE FRITZ AND TORI CRAIN

## RECOVERY FROM WORK AND EMPLOYEE SLEEP: UNDERSTANDING THE ROLE OF EXPERIENCES AND ACTIVITIES OUTSIDE OF WORK

Generally, time away from work allows employees to recover and unwind from work-related demands. While sleep is one process by which employees can recover from demands and restore their performance capacity, specific experiences and activities during nonwork time may impact the quality and quantity of employee sleep. With this in mind, we first briefly discuss several relevant theoretical frameworks that help us understand the relationship between nonwork experiences and sleep, and then organize past research into a three-process model differentiating between time-based, thought-based, and arousal-based processes.

## THEORETICAL FRAMEWORKS

Many employees experience a "cycle of work and rest" (Zijlstra & Sonnentag, 2006) in which times for rest and recovery (including sleep) from work are often primarily determined by working times rather than by employees' need for rest. The Effort-Recovery Model describes recovery as a process during which demands and stressors (Meijman & Mulder, 1998) are reduced or removed so that load reactions (i.e., accumulated strain resulting from demands and stressors) decrease. Similarly, the Cognitive Activation Theory of Stress (Meurs & Perrewe, 2011; Ursin & Eriksen, 2010) proposes that activation or arousal necessary for detecting and handling stressors is associated with increased strain over time if opportunities for rest and recovery are not available. More specifically, insufficient recovery from stressors may play a role in the development of more chronic strain due to extended periods of activation. Accordingly, the Allostatic Load Model (Ganster & Rosen, 2013; McEwen, 1998) assumes that the chronic overactivation of allostatic (e.g., cardiovascular, neuroendocrine, and other) regulatory systems is associated with impaired psychological and physical well-being and decreased performance capacity. Furthermore, Ganster and Rosen (2013) suggest that sleep disturbance is one of the early psychosomatic indicators of allostatic load.

Dealing with workplace demands and stressors requires effort and self-control and therefore depletes self-regulatory resources. According to the Ego-Depletion Model (Muraven & Baumeister, 2000) all acts of self-regulation draw on the same resource. As a result, resource restoration can occur only when people disengage from self-regulatory efforts for some time. Although research on recovery from work indicates that specific experiences during nonwork time can help replenish self-regulatory resources and increase well-being (see Sonnentag & Fritz, 2015), Barnes (2012) extends the idea to the experience of sleep suggesting that sleep allows for the restoration of self-regulatory capacity.

Espie (2002) proposes a psychobiological model of good sleep. Specifically, the model suggests that physiological and cognitive dearousal as well as affect regulation are important factors contributing to good sleep. Based on the theoretical frameworks described above, there are numerous mechanisms through which nonwork experiences might impact employee sleep. In this chapter we will draw on these frameworks focusing on three specific processes—time-based, thought-based, and arousal-based processes—and their relationship to employee sleep.

## NONWORK EXPERIENCES AND ACTIVITIES

When studying recovery from work, we can focus on specific activities that employees engage in during nonwork time (e.g., exercise, housework), or the psychological experiences themselves (e.g., relaxation). Whereas nonwork activities refer to particular behaviors, experiences focus on the perceptions and psychological processes associated with those behaviors. Sonnentag and Fritz (2007) proposed four core recovery experiences, namely psychological detachment from work, relaxation, mastery, and control. *Psychological detachment* can be defined as mental disengagement from work during nonwork time. This includes refraining from work-related activities (e.g., work-related emails), work-related thoughts (e.g., ruminating about a work-related conflict, brainstorming to solve a work-related problem), and work-related emotions (e.g., anxiety about an upcoming performance evaluation). *Relaxation* refers to the experience of low physical and mental activation and reduced effort and self-regulation. Relaxation can come along with activities such as meditation, taking a bath, or listening to music. In contrast, *mastery experiences* require a certain level of self-regulation and provide opportunities to learn and broaden our horizon (e.g., through learning a new hobby or travel). Finally, *control* during nonwork time refers to a sense of autonomy over which activities to pursue during nonwork time as well as when and how to pursue them. Research indicates that these four experiences are positively related, but conceptually and empirically distinct (Sonnentag & Fritz, 2007). Other nonwork experiences that have been examined are positive and negative work reflection during nonwork time (e.g., Fritz & Sonnentag, 2006) and social connectedness (e.g., Fritz & Sonnentag, 2005). Whereas research relating specific recovery experiences and employee sleep is still limited, we propose that the three processes that we will describe in more detail below are associated with recovery (or lack thereof) and implications for employee sleep. In the next sections of this chapter we will first describe the three processes (time-, thought-, and arousal-based processes) that may unfold during nonwork time that can impact employee sleep quality or quantity and then review past research in that area.

## PROCESSES UNDERLYING RELATIONSHIPS BETWEEN NONWORK EXPERIENCES AND EMPLOYEE SLEEP

One of the most frequently mentioned reasons for a lack of good sleep is insufficient time. Work responsibilities, nonwork responsibilities, and leisure activities take up a considerable amount of employees' time each day, leaving too little time for sleep (Figure 4.1). Furthermore, worrying or ruminating about work-related or nonwork-related demands and problems can take additional time away from sleep. Accordingly, several of the theoretical frameworks introduced above (Effort-Recovery Model, Cognitive Activation Theory, Allostatic Load Model, Ego Depletion Model) implicitly assume that time needs to be allocated to recover from stressors and demands and to build or replenish personal resources. Thus, time-based processes may be able to explain the relationships between nonwork experiences and sleep. A second process relating nonwork experiences to sleep could be mental activation (i.e., a thought-based process). For example, problem solving and rumination are associated with cognitive activation that prevents employees from entering into the restful mental state that is necessary for falling asleep, staying asleep, and perceiving restfulness of sleep. Accordingly, Cognitive Activation Theory suggests that reducing mental activity is important for rest and recovery. Similarly, Espie (2002) points to mental dearousal as an important contributor to good sleep. A third process relating nonwork experiences to sleep is physiological or affective arousal (i.e., an arousal-based process). Accordingly, the Allostatic Load Model suggests that sustained arousal resulting from exposure to stressors is associated with strain symptoms including impaired sleep. Similarly, Espie (2002) suggests that physiological dearousal is a necessary prerequisite of restful sleep. In this chapter, we will review the literature related to affective (e.g., anger, anxiety, joy) and physiological (e.g., increased stress hormones) arousal acknowledging that the arousal may be a reaction to a positive (e.g., excitement over receiving a promotion at work) or a negative (e.g., worry, anxiety, or shame after failure) event. While occurring during nonwork time, the arousal can either be due to work (e.g.,

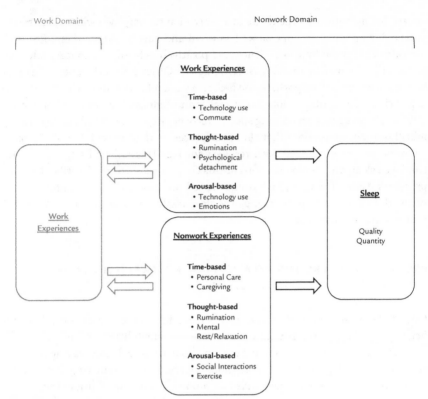

**Figure 4.1.**
Processes underlying relationships between nonwork experiences and employee sleep.

increased stress hormones and anger due to a conflict at work) or due to nonwork (e.g., physiological arousal due to exercising late in the day, engaging interactions with others). Although the studies we review mostly focus on either affective, or physiological arousal, we acknowledge that both types of arousal often go hand in hand. Furthermore, physiological and affective arousal often cooccur with mental activation (e.g., ruminating about a conflict). However, for this chapter, we will report research regarding thought-related processes and sleep in a separate section.

## Time-Based Processes and Employee Sleep

The first of the three processes mentioned above focuses on the role of time engaged in certain activities during nonwork time on employee sleep. Although the concept of time-based conflict between work and other life domains is well established (e.g., Edwards & Rothbard, 2000), few studies to date have examined in detail how individuals distribute their time among work, nonwork, and sleep. Given that time is a finite resource, increased time spent on one activity (e.g., work, chores, or hobbies) requires less time spent on another activity (e.g., sleep). Accordingly,

Barnes, Wagner, and Ghumman (2012) suggested that individuals borrow time from sleep in order to accommodate both work and nonwork demands. Their formative research indicates that both work time and family time have an increasingly powerful and interactive effect on time spent sleeping. In light of these findings, we discuss specific work- and nonwork-related activities and experiences that take place in the nonwork domain that influence the amount of time available for sleep. Specifically, we will focus on technology use, commuting, personal care, caregiving, and leisure activities since they have been studied most extensively so far.

## Work-Related Technology Use

One way for employees to borrow from sleep time is by engaging in work-related activities after their regular work hours. In many jobs, technology allows employees to take care of work-related tasks after hours (e.g., typing up a report and emailing it off to your supervisor, making a quick phone call to exchange information regarding an ongoing work project). According to Gradisar et al. (2013), nine out of 10 Americans report using some type of technology in the hour before bed. Thus, sleep time may be traded for technology use. Such technology use can include work-related tasks, such as checking email or talking on the phone to colleagues, which can decrease the amount of time spent sleeping and the quality of sleep. Although some research has examined work-related technology use in relation to psychological detachment from work (e.g., Derks, van Mierlo, & Schmitz, 2014), few studies have examined time spent using a smartphone for work purposes in relation to sleep. In a recent exception, Lanaj, Johnson, and Barnes (2014) found that sleep quantity mediated the effect of work-related smartphone use (minutes used after 9 pm) on next morning depletion. Research by Schieman and Young (2013) suggests that work-related communication in the nonwork domain (e.g., cell phone calls, text messages, or emails) is positively associated with sleep problems. In addition, Barber and Jenkins (2014) found that psychological detachment from work during nonwork time mediated the effect of work-related technology use on sleep duration, quality, and consistency, but only for those individuals who possessed low boundaries around technology use. This initial research suggests that technology use, and smartphone use specifically, is an important target for interventions aiming to increase sleep quantity and quality. Furthermore, organizations may be able to assist employees in creating boundaries around the amount of time technology is used at home so that time will not be borrowed from sleep.

## Commuting

Commuting can be described as a work-related activity outside of paid work hours that can impact the duration and quality of sleep. Interestingly, although organizational scholars have suggested that commuting can be used as a means to detach from the workplace allowing for beneficial health and well-being outcomes (e.g.,

Fritz, Yankelevich, Zarubin, & Barger, 2010), sleep scholars have focused more heavily on the detrimental impact of commuting time on sleep time. For example, results based on nationally representative samples from the American Time Use Survey indicate that commuting time is reciprocally related to sleep duration (Basner et al., 2007; Basner, Spaeth, & Dinges, 2014). Although these data are cross-sectional, the authors suggest that individuals trade sleep time for commuting time. Therefore, other sleep researchers have pointed to the potential value of telecommuting for increasing sleep duration (e.g., Hale, 2014).

## Personal Care

Personal care activities may take the form of grooming (e.g., shaving, putting on makeup), health-related self-care (e.g., yearly dentist appointment), travel related to personal care (e.g., drive to and from a doctor's office), and other personal activities (e.g., getting a haircut). Research by Basner and colleagues (2007) indicates that time devoted to personal care is associated with less sleep on both weekdays and weekends. Basner et al. (2014) further found that grooming time was associated with short sleep durations, with short sleepers grooming earlier in the morning than those individuals who obtained normal amounts of sleep during both weekdays and weekends. In contrast, long sleepers spent less time grooming in general, and started their grooming activities later in the morning. Because this research is based solely on cross-sectional data, other scholars (e.g., Hale, 2014) have noted that it is unclear whether personal care actually influences sleep time, or whether individuals who engage in more personal care also tend to wake up earlier, have shorter sleep durations, and choose to spend a larger portion of their morning routine on grooming.

## Caregiving

Caregiving roles for both children and/or aging adults may also prevent individuals from obtaining adequate sleep quantity and quality. Research by Basner et al. (2007) has found that time spent caring for a nonhousehold or household member was negatively associated with sleep time on weekdays and weekends. Not surprisingly, these findings also suggest that individuals with two or more children in the home are less likely to be long sleepers than those without children on both weekdays and weekends.

Alternatively, some studies have focused specifically on special caregiving roles, such as those of new parents and those who care for children and family members with disabilities or chronic illness. New mothers report less total sleep time, less efficient sleep, and more wake time after sleep onset postpartum (e.g., Kang, Matsumoto, Shinkoda, Mishima, & Seo, 2002), and obtain less sleep during the night and more sleep during the day, compared to new fathers who maintain consistent sleep patterns before and after the birth of their child (Gay, Lee, & Lee,

2004). However, both parents experienced more sleep disruptions following the birth than during the pregnancy, and in general, fathers obtained less total sleep than mothers overall. Emphasis in the literature has also been placed on sleep in parents of children with disabilities and chronic illness indicating shorter total sleep times and earlier wake times, in addition to more sleep disruptions and poorer sleep quality (Meltzer, 2008; Meltzer & Moore, 2008). Aside from parents, sleep of caregivers of aging parents has also been examined. Castro et al. (2009) find that women providing care to a family member with dementia are likely to have objectively-measured sleep durations highly similar to those they are caring for, in addition to a comparison group of noncaregiver women with mild to moderate sleep impairment. In summary, these findings suggest that the role played within the family system is associated with particular caregiving demands that are likely to influence the amount of time allocated toward sleep.

### Leisure Activities

In addition to personal care and family responsibilities, different aspects of leisure time prevent employees from obtaining adequate amounts of quality sleep. For example, research indicates that time spent socializing, relaxing, and enjoying leisure activities is associated with shorter sleep (Basner et al., 2007, 2014). Tucker, Dahlgren, Akerstedt, and Waterhouse (2008) implemented an experimental design to test the effect of leisure activities on sleep outcomes. Specifically, participants were instructed to pursue quiet leisure activities at home, engage in active leisure activities, or do additional work for four consecutive evenings of a regular work day. Results indicate no differences in self-reported or objective sleep duration or quality among the three conditions. However, satisfaction with the activity engaged in was associated with better sleep quality and activities characterized by lower mental effort were associated with better sleep in general. Thus, although initial research evidence suggests that employees borrow from sleep time to engage in leisure activities, the findings of Tucker et al. (2008) indicate that time is not the only process linking activities and experiences during nonwork time to employee sleep quality and quantity. We continue to examine these additional processes in the next section.

Technology, even when used for leisure activities, can impact employee sleep. For example, Custers and Van den Bulck (2012) found that television viewing is associated with later weekend bedtimes, but that there is no significant association between having a television in the bedroom and sleep duration. Furthermore, both weekday and weekend bedtimes and rise times are later for those who have internet access in the bedroom and use the internet to a greater extent. In contrast, Gradisar et al. (2013) did not find any association between technology use and later bedtimes, which the authors suggest is the result of including caffeine, bedroom lighting, and napping behavior as covariates. This study also finds that the use of interactive technologies preceding bedtime, such as computers, cell phones, and video game consoles, is associated with difficulties falling asleep and reports of sleep being unrefreshing. Accordingly, a large body of research indicates that light, such as short-wavelength blue light emitted by technological devices, can suppress melatonin, a hormone that aids in the onset of sleep and the entrainment of circadian rhythms (e.g., West et al., 2010). In this way, technology use before bed can lead to shorter sleep durations and can disrupt sleep during the night. In summary, these studies propose that technology use for leisure can cut into employees' sleep time. However, a lack of time does not seem to be the only explanation for impaired sleep. Rather, mental, physiological, and emotional arousal may also contribute to the relationship between leisure activities and sleep.

Taking time to exercise (one common leisure activity) on a regular basis is important for everyday well-being but may reduce the amount of time available for sleep, especially for employees with long work hours or high caregiving demands. Meta-analytic evidence suggests that exercise has a positive effect on total sleep time (e.g.,Youngstedt, O'Connor, & Dishman, 1997). However, recent time use data suggest otherwise, namely that time spent engaging in sports, exercise, or recreation (including attending sporting or recreational events) is negatively associated with sleep duration on both weekdays and weekends (Basner et al., 2007). Basner et al. (2014) found that long sleepers spend less time engaging in sports, exercise, or recreation on both weekdays and weekends, as compared to short and normal sleepers. Although these studies provide insight into time use for exercise and sleep, other studies have examined associations between exercise and sleep from an arousal perspective. These studies will be discussed in greater detail in later sections of this chapter.

Volunteering outside of paid work time is a common practice within the United States (Bureau of Labor Statistics, 2011). Although volunteering has been associated with beneficial outcomes for employees (e.g., Rodell, 2013), little research so far has investigated whether time spent volunteering is exchanged for sleep time and additionally impacts sleep quality. In a recent exception, Basner et al. (2007) found that volunteering was significantly and negatively associated with sleep time on weekdays, but positively and significantly associated with sleep time on the weekends. Furthermore, Basner et al. (2014) have found that long sleepers tend to spend less time volunteering than normal sleepers on both weekdays and weekends, whereas short sleepers tend to spend more time volunteering on weekends. As a result of these preliminary findings, future research should continue to investigate the associations among paid work, volunteering, and sleep.

## Thought-Based Processes and Employee Sleep

As proposed earlier in this chapter, mental activation during nonwork time can impact sleep quality and quantity. This mental activation may be due to work-related thoughts or thoughts referring to experiences and plans outside of work. In either case, these thoughts can be adaptive or maladaptive and unpleasant or pleasant. Cognitive Activation Theory—focusing on reactions to experienced stress—suggests that sustained mental activation is associated with strain symptoms, which could include impaired sleep. More specifically, Espie (2002) suggests that cognitive dearousal is important for good sleep. Specifically, active information processing drastically declines right before sleep onset. In contrast, problem solving, ruminating about issues, and other types of mental activation inhibit sleep onset and can impair sleep in general. Below we will summarize findings regarding relationships between mental activation during nonwork time and employee sleep.

### Work-Related Thoughts

Several studies have focused on negative work-related thoughts (e.g., rumination/worry about work, negative work reflection) and their relationships with employee sleep. Berset et al. (2011) examined the relationship between work-related rumination and employee sleep in two different samples and found that based on the resulting cross-sectional data, rumination was associated with impaired sleep reported through a variety of indicators such as self-reported sleep onset difficulties, impaired sleep maintenance, early morning awakening, sleep dissatisfaction, and daytime dysfunction. Similarly, Rodriguez-Munoz, Notelaers, and Moreno-Jimenez (2011) found that work-related worry during nonwork time was associated with lower sleep quality.

Cropley, Dijk, and Stanley (2006) examined a group of school teachers using a daily-diary design. Their findings indicate associations between work-related rumination during the evening of a workday and sleep quantity and quality reported the following morning. However, Pereira, Meier, and Elfering (2013) found no relationship between work-related worries and employee sleep. Specifically, using a daily-diary design, self-reported worries during the evening of a workday were not associated with activity-based sleep assessments using actigraphy or sleep quality reported the following morning. Finally, Vahle-Hinz, Bamberg, Dettmers, Friedrich, and Keller (2014) used a daily-diary design to examine the relationship between work-related rumination in the evening and restful sleep as indicated by reported levels of tiredness the following morning. Surprisingly, results from between-person analyses indicate no relationship during the work week. However, rumination on Saturday was associated with higher tiredness Sunday morning. Thus, within a workday, findings regarding relationships between work-related rumination and sleep seem to be inconsistent so far.

Querstret and Cropley (2012) took a more fine grained approach by examining three aspects of work-related rumination during nonwork time: affective rumination (e.g., being troubled by work-related problems), problem-solving pondering (e.g., thinking about ways to improve work performance), and detachment (e.g., the ability to stop thinking about work-related problems). Results based on 719 working adults indicate a negative relationship with sleep quality for affective rumination and problem-solving pondering, and a positive relationship for detachment.

More generally, being engaged in work-related thoughts during nonwork time is one indicator of low psychological detachment from work (Sonnentag & Fritz, 2014). Research, although still limited, so far supports the notion of a positive relationship between psychological detachment and sleep quality and quantity. Specifically, Sonnentag and Fritz (2007), using a cross-sectional design, found positive relationships between psychological detachment from work during nonwork time and sleep quality. Similarly, Barber and Jenkins (2014) found that psychological detachment during nonwork time was associated with higher self-reported sleep quantity and quality and lower sleep inconsistency. Findings from a daily-diary study during the work week found positive relationships between psychological detachment in the evening and sleep quality reported the following morning (Hülsheger et al., 2014). Using activity-based assessments of sleep, Pereira and Elfering (2014) found some support for a positive relationship on Sunday, but not Saturday. Finally, Hahn, Binnewies, Sonnentag, and Mojza (2011) used a quasiexperimental study design including a training group and a waitlist-control group to examine the effects of a recovery from work training (including a training component focusing on psychological detachment) on employee recovery experiences and well-being outcomes including sleep. Findings indicate a significant increase in psychological detachment from before to after the training. In addition, psychological detachment was positively associated with self-reported sleep quality.

In contrast to research linking rumination and other negative work-related thoughts to sleep, studies of positive work-related thoughts (e.g., related to a recent professional achievement) thus far are still scarce. One possibility is that such thoughts might lead to positive mental activation, which could have distinct influences on employee sleep. We assume that this kind of activation often accompanies affective arousal, such as excitement or joy, and therefore included these results in the section below on affective arousal.

### Nonwork-Related Thoughts

When considering potential effects of nonwork-related thoughts on employee sleep, we may need to qualify these thoughts according to their pleasantness and functionality. Pleasant nonwork-related thoughts not only impact mental activation, but also affective arousal, which we will discuss later. Furthermore, during time outside of work, employees may specifically aim at reducing mental activation (work-related or not) to rest and regain performance capacity. This is especially important considering that any kind of mental or affective effort and self-regulation draws on the same psychological resource (Muraven & Baumeister, 2000). Therefore, one way to conceptualize reduced mental activation could be through activities that require low mental effort, are related to high levels of relaxation, or are associated with a sense of mindfulness. In contrast, mental activation during nonwork time may be operationalized as household chores, leisure activities, or social interactions that require mental engagement. Below we review the limited research that has examined the relationships between nonwork-related mental activation and employee sleep.

### Worry/Rumination

Over the past decade, research pointing to the association between cognitive activation and sleep has been conducted in a variety of populations (Åkerstedt et al.,

2007; Espie, 2002; Harvey, 2000, Rodriguez-Munoz et al., 2011). Many studies, however, still lack a specific focus on employee samples and assess mental activation in general terms rather than differentiating between work-related and nonwork-related thoughts. In such studies, mental activation is often defined or operationalized as cognitive hyperarousal (Espie, 2002), presleep cognitive activity (Harvey & Espie, 2004), or general worries (Åkerstedt et al., 2007). Findings from these studies indicate that mental activation is associated with a variety of sleep difficulties, especially when activation immediately before bedtime is high (Åkerstedt et al., 2007; Castro et al., 2009; Harvey, 2000; Harvey & Espie, 2004; Meltzer & Moore, 2008).

### Mental Rest and Relaxation

In general terms, a state of mental relaxation (i.e., reduced brain activity) is a prerequisite for sleep onset and may also beneficially influence sleep duration, consistency, and quality (Espie, 2002; Harvey, 2000; Harvey & Espie, 2004). For example, Sonnentag and Fritz (2007) found a positive relationship between relaxing recovery experiences and sleep quality, and Tucker et al. (2008) found that engaging in activities that involve lower mental effort leads to better self-reported sleep. One way to mentally "down-regulate" is meditation and mindfulness practices (e.g., Kabat-Zinn, 1990). Not surprisingly, research suggests that these practices reduce sleep disturbances and that mindfulness practices (Howell et al., 2008) and trait mindfulness (Allen & Kiburz, 2012) generally lead to a variety of indicators of sleep quality. Despite these findings, research specifically focusing on employee mindfulness and sleep is still scarce, suggesting a fruitful avenue for future research.

### Arousal-Based Processes and Employee Sleep

As a stress response, affective and physiological arousal can indicate chronic over-activation or allostatic load (Ganster & Rosen, 2013; McEwen, 1998). Two strain-related emotions associated with high arousal are anger and anxiety, whereas positive emotions with high arousal could include excitement and energy (Watson, 2000). Accordingly, research indicates that negative work emotions mediate the relationships between work demands and emotions during nonwork time (Ilies et al., 2007). Thus, physiological arousal in and of itself as well as the experienced emotions associated with it can impact employee sleep. More specifically, we propose that in a state of high arousal, employees will have a hard time falling asleep and maintaining sleep throughout the night as well as being less likely to experience their sleep as restful. Accordingly, Espie (2002) suggests that physiological dearousal and minimal affect are important contributors to good sleep. As such, in the following sections, we describe both work-related and nonwork-related activities and experiences during nonwork time that elicit an arousal response and can impact sleep quality and quantity. Specifically, we will focus on technology use, social interactions, and exercise, as they have been studied most extensively so far.

### Technology Use

There is building evidence that technology use during nonwork time can influence employee sleep quality and quantity. However, studies around technology use and sleep so far have rarely examined the underlying processes of these relationships. In earlier sections we described the role of time and mental activation in this relationship. However, we additionally propose that technology use during nonwork time influences sleep by triggering affective and/or physiological arousal (e.g., through their interactive nature or exposure to blue light; Cajochen, 2007; Gradisar et al., 2013). These studies have found that technology use during nonwork time (work-related or not) is related to well-being outcomes (e.g., Derks et al., 2014). Focusing on technology use during nonwork time in general, findings from Gradisar et al. (2013) indicate that using interactive technologies (i.e., computers, cell phones) in the hour before bedtime, as opposed to more passive technologies (e.g., television, music players), is associated with difficulty initiating sleep and experiencing less refreshing sleep. Custers and Van den Bulck (2012) found that time to bed and time to rise are later for those individuals who have internet access in their bedroom and have a higher volume of internet use, and bedtimes are later on weekends for those individuals who watch more television. When interpreting the findings regarding technology use, we should take into account that most research has not differentiated between work-related and nonwork-related technology use. However, one study that focused on technology used for work-relevant phone calls, text messages, or emails found positive relationships with sleep problems (Schieman & Young, 2013).

### Social Interactions

Social experiences during nonwork time can help or hinder employee sleep. Specifically, they can be a source of emotional support, joy and humor, as well as confrontation or conflict, all of which can be associated with physiological and affective responses that impact sleep. For example, social support from a nonwork source (e.g., family member) has been found to be associated with better sleep (Nordin, Westerholm, Alfredsson, & Akerstedt, 2012). In contrast, experienced negative affect partially mediates the link between interpersonal conflict and sleep disturbances the following night (Brisette & Cohen, 2002).

Troxel, Robles, Hall, and Buysse (2007) presented a theoretical model linking relationship functioning in partners to sleep. Specifically, they suggest that healthy relationships promote sleep (through increased oxytocin, positive emotions, and a sense of closeness), whereas unhealthy relationships impair sleep (through vigilance and negative emotions). Accordingly, marital happiness has been associated with increased sleep quality (e.g., Troxel, Buysse, Hall, & Matthews, 2009). In contrast, other research finds that women's exposure to intimate partner violence is associated with sleep disturbances and insomnia (e.g., Pigeon et al., 2011; Rauer & El-Sheikh, 2012). Thus, positive and negative aspects of relationships can be expected to influence sleep, in large part through their influence on physiological and affective arousal.

### Exercise

Exercise has been the subject of much attention in relation to sleep. Engaging in exercise may have beneficial effects on sleep as exercise can reduce stress hormones, subsequently reducing our negative affective and physiological arousal at bedtime. Studies find that aspects of sleep are generally improved for individuals engaging in exercise (e.g., Kredlow, Capozzoli, Hearon, Calkins, & Otto, 2015). When interpreting these results, it is necessary to take into account a potential reciprocal relationship (e.g., Kline, 2014) in that poor sleep can result in decreased daytime activity, but that a physically active lifestyle also can improve sleep quality. Some scholars have cautioned against exercising immediately before sleep because of its arousing effects (e.g., an increase in endorphins and a sense of energy; van Straten & Cuijpers, 2009). Meta-analytic evidence points to the moderating effects of time of day on the relationship between exercise and sleep, with exercising within 3 hours of bedtime actually leading to some improved aspects of sleep (Kredlow et al., 2015). Thus, there is a need for continuing research on the association between the activating and/or relaxing effects of exercise on sleep, particularly in employee samples.

## IMPLICATIONS FOR RESEARCH AND PRACTICE

In the sections above we have highlighted the role of nonwork experiences for employee sleep. Based on the review of the literature, in the next sections we will turn our attention toward the theoretical and practical implications that emerge from this research.

### Implications for Research

Although our review of the literature seems to indicate relationships between employees' nonwork activities and experiences and sleep outcomes, many questions remain unanswered. One limitation of past research is that the focus is not specifically on working adults, but often on clinical samples. In addition, many studies do not explicitly examine activities and experiences during nonwork time. Even those studies that focus on nonwork activities and experiences rarely differentiate between work-related and nonwork-related phenomena (an exception is the research regarding work-related rumination and psychological detachment from work during nonwork time). Furthermore, study designs vary between cross-sectional designs and daily-diary designs, and sleep is assessed in a variety of ways. As a result, it is not surprising that some of the findings are inconsistent across studies. Below we list implications for research and suggestions for future research based on the three different processes discussed throughout the chapter.

### Time-based processes

Our review of the literature indicates that by engaging in a variety of activities during nonwork time, individuals may borrow time from sleep (e.g., Basner et al., 2007, 2014). Although the study samples were large and nationally representative, analyses were based on cross-sectional data. Thus, there is a need for future research to examine some of these specific activities in more detail and over time. For example, does commuting time truly influence sleep? Drawing on the recovery literature, under what conditions is commuting time beneficial or detrimental (e.g., type of transportation, activity engaged in during commute)? We also agree with Hale's (2014) sentiments that qualitative inquiries may be very helpful in determining underlying mechanisms of the relationships among time use activities and sleep duration. For example, how do individuals decide where to allocate time and how does an understanding of the importance of sleep play into those decisions? What are some strategies that prevent time from being borrowed from sleep? Thorough investigations into these processes will help to better design effective individual- and organizational-level interventions aimed at improving recovery from work, including sleep. Lastly, there is a need for an investigation of the conditions under which socializing, relaxing, and leisure activities are beneficial or detrimental to sleep. For example, a recent meta-analysis conducted on the relationship between exercise and sleep has pointed to moderators such as sex, age, levels of activity at baseline, type of exercise, time of day exercise is engaged in, exercise duration, and adherence (e.g., Kredlow et al., 2015). Furthermore, the time-based research reviewed suggests that sleep time is traded for time spent socializing with others (e.g., Basner et al., 2007). Future studies may examine this trade-off of sleep time for sleep quality that results from time spent with others.

### Thought-based processes

Although there is general research support for the notion that cognitive activation is associated with impaired sleep, future research should explore this relationship in more detail. Specifically, because some of the findings around rumination are inconsistent, future research should take a closer look at the actual content and valence of these work-related thoughts. Querstret and Cropley (2012) already took a first step in this direction by differentiating between affective rumination, problem-solving pondering, and detachment. Future research may expand on these findings by more explicitly assessing positive mental activation or repetitive thought and employee sleep. Furthermore, research should more explicitly assess how nonwork-related thoughts (e.g., making plans, reflecting on our relationships with others) impact employee sleep. In addition, we suggest that future research assess employee sleep in more depth. For example, it would be helpful to understand whether mental activation mostly impacts sleep onset that night or sleep consistency and sleep quality. Furthermore, research may examine to what extent mental activation during nonwork time not only impacts employees that night but may impact sleep the following nights, potentially creating a "spiraling" or "accumulation" effect. When examining the role of mental activation in employee sleep, cognitive and affective arousal may be closely linked in many cases. Furthermore, both aspects of activation go along with physiological arousal and brain activation that may be able to explain the effects on sleep in more depth. Therefore, we suggest that future research assess these different aspects of activation together to better understand how they interact to predict employee sleep.

### Arousal-based processes

Future research on activities in the nonwork domain that influence sleep quality through an activation-inducing process may involve an investigation into different mediators, such as those that pertain to different types of arousal. For example, perhaps information from a co-worker in a late night text message influences sleep quality through an emotional activation pathway, while checking emails influences sleep quality because of exposure to blue light levels. The extent to which the arousal pathway shares overlapping variance with a mental activation pathway is also a fruitful avenue for future research. Additionally, our literature review indicates that technology use during nonwork time is a primary variable of interest to both sleep and organizational scholars. However, so far, few studies differentiate between work-related and nonwork-related technology use and their specific outcomes for employees. There is also a need to uncover the steps that can be taken to mitigate the effect of technology use during nonwork time, if it cannot be avoided. For example, what is the effect of dimming our screen on a laptop or smartphone? Furthermore, our literature review suggests that social interactions with friends and family can be either beneficial (e.g., social support) or detrimental (e.g., conflict) for sleep quality. Further investigation is needed to determine how individuals' engagement in multiple roles is associated with sleep quality. For example, does social support or other positive interactions with friends or family buffer the effect of roles that tend to be disadvantageous for obtaining quality sleep? Finally, future research will benefit from further disentangling the relationship between exercise and sleep. Both activities are key factors in overall health and include important opportunities for recovery from work demands. Therefore, it is important to understand how both activities can enhance (rather than inhibit) each other.

## Practical Implications

### Scheduling of work

It is clear that work schedules influence sleep. However, the extent to which schedules are flexible has significant implications not only for sleep, but also for how well individuals are able to accommodate nonwork demands, which in turn can affect sleep. Flexible schedules can be organized in terms of the timing of work, the location of work, the amount of work, and the continuity of work (see Kossek & Michel, 2011 for a review). Results from both cross-sectional and longitudinal studies suggest that employees' control over work time is associated with improved sleep quality (e.g., Salo et al., 2014). Furthermore, some research shows that for each hour that work starts later, individuals obtain approximately 20 minutes more sleep (Basner et al., 2014). Thus, organizations, to the extent possible, should provide employees with discretion over when and where they work in order to optimize not only employee work/nonwork balance, but also sleep. Although flexible scheduling practices are ideal, organizations within certain industries are increasingly moving toward 24–7 operations with extended work shifts, irregular rotations, and night and evening shifts. These types of schedules, which are seen in industries such as communications, transportation, healthcare, and retail, are not optimal for sleep or managing nonwork responsibilities. It is well established that shift work is associated with detriments to both physical and psychological functioning, especially nightwork (e.g., Smith, Folkard, Tucker, & Evans, 2011). Therefore, organizations should seek to implement shift systems that represent a compromise between employer goals, employee recommendations, and guidelines for shiftwork (Knauth, 1997), thereby optimizing health and performance. Such efforts would also address employees' experiences of time-based work–family conflict, as time will less likely be borrowed from sleep if work and family demands can be more easily met. Additionally, organizations should be aware of, and follow, the national regulations around timing of work and duty hour limitations.

### Organizational support for recovery from work

While work schedules create an infrastructure for opportunities to recover from work demands including sleep, organizations can develop additional strategies to support their employees. For example, recent research indicates that supervisor support for employees' family demands is associated with better employee sleep (Berkman, Buxton, Ertel, & Okechukwu, 2010). Although supervisors can engage in a variety of behaviors that help employees create more time for recovery and sleep, one particularly helpful behavior may be role-modeling. Specifically, supervisors can model positive behaviors around recovery from work and sleep. But supervisors can impact employee sleep even further by creating a workgroup climate around work–nonwork boundaries. For example, supervisors can help reduce the expectations around work-related technology use during nonwork time (e.g., answering emails late at night; Barber & Santuzzi, 2015; Park, Fritz, & Jex, 2011), which can reduce work-related rumination and increase psychological detachment from work, both of which impact employee sleep.

### Sleep hygiene

In addition to addressing scheduling, organizations can potentially help improve employee functioning in both the work and nonwork domain by providing training on sleep hygiene. Sleep hygiene represents those guidelines based on sleep physiology and pharmacology that allow for sufficient quality and adequate quantity of sleep. Such guidelines include practices around health (e.g., good diet, adequate exercise, stress management, avoidance of caffeine, nicotine, and alcohol), environmental factors (e.g., light, temperature, noise), in addition to individuals' behaviors that are related to sleep itself (e.g., consistency and regularity of sleep schedule, activities individuals engage in prior to bedtime, efforts to initiate sleep; Yang, Lin, Hsu, & Cheng, 2010). It should be noted that research on sleep hygiene interventions so far has mostly been conducted with clinical samples and findings are somewhat inconsistent (Irish, Kline, Gunn, Buysse, & Hall, 2015). Results from both epidemiological and experimental studies indicate a beneficial effect of sleep hygiene recommendations on sleep outcomes; however, these studies are limited in number. Thus, moving forward, sleep hygiene training may be a promising and practical tool for improving employee sleep. Our review of the literature points to a few specific applications of sleep hygiene practices that may be especially effective in improving employee sleep. For example, work-related and nonwork-related technology use may be a primary target for future sleep hygiene interventions, considering that devices such as smartphones use blue light, which has been found to suppress melatonin (e.g., West et al., 2010) delaying sleep onset and disrupting sleep. Furthermore, time spent utilizing technological devices can lead to less time available for sleeping and their noises can disrupt sleep, while the content of emails, phone calls, and texts can also elicit cognitive activation and emotional arousal. The emphasis on stress management in sleep hygiene practices also suggests that efforts should be made to decrease stressful work experiences close to bedtime. For example, work should not be conducted in bed and workspaces should not be located in the bedroom. Lastly, because sleep schedules should be regulated to the extent possible, individuals should work with other family members, such as bed partners and children, to establish consistent sleep schedules. Given that time is borrowed from sleep to accommodate work and family demands (Barnes et al., 2012), families may be less likely to push back bedtimes if everyone is on the same schedule and holding each other accountable.

## CONCLUSIONS

In this chapter we provided an overview of the literature on employee nonwork experiences and sleep. Specifically, we presented time-based, thought-based, and arousal-based (affective and physiological) processes during nonwork time and their relationships to sleep quality and quantity. We reported research including self-reports and objective assessments of sleep. Research appears to indicate relationships between all three processes and employee sleep, thereby allowing for a better understanding of processes predicting employee sleep as well as providing input for potential interventions to improve employee sleep. In addition, our review of the literature indicates inconsistencies among findings from different studies as well as avenues for future research. Overall, the reviewed literature points to the important role of activities and experiences during employees' nonwork time for sleep quality and quantity. Although more and more research indicates that sleep is a key player in employee recovery from work, specific recovery experiences and processes help or hinder good sleep. Because the nonwork domain is most proximal in time and experience to employee sleep, it may be the most influential, and therefore we encourage future research to more explicitly examine the relationship between activities and experiences during nonwork time and employee sleep.

## REFERENCES

Åkerstedt, T., Kecklund, G., & Axelsson, J. (2007). Impaired sleep after bedtime stress and worries. *Biological Psychology, 76*, 170–173. doi:10.1016/j.biopsycho.2007.07.010

Allen, T. D., & Kiburz, K. M. (2012). Trait mindfulness and work–family balance among working parents: The mediating effects of vitality and sleep quality. *Journal of Vocational Behavior, 80*, 372–379. doi:10.1016/j.jvb.2011.09.002

Barber, L. K., & Jenkins, J. S. (2014). Creating technological boundaries to protect bedtime: Examining work-home boundary management, psychological detachment and sleep. *Stress and Health, 30*, 259–264. doi:10.1002/smi.2536

Barber, L. K., & Santuzzi, A. M. (2015). Please respond ASAP: Workplace telepressure and employee recovery. *Journal of Occupational Health Psychology, 20*, 172–189. doi:10.1037/a0038278

Barnes, C. M. (2012). Working in our sleep: Sleep and self-regulation in organizations. *Organizational Psychology Review, 2*, 234–257. doi:10.1177/2041386612450181

Barnes, C. M., Wagner, D. T., & Ghumman, S. (2012). Borrowing from sleep to pay work and family: Expanding time-based conflict to the broader nonwork domain. *Personnel Psychology, 65*, 789–819. doi:10.1111/peps.12002

Basner, M., Fomberstein, K. M., Razavi, F. M., Banks, S., William, J. H., Rosa, R. R., & Dinges, D. F. (2007). American time use survey: Sleep time and its relationship to waking activities. *Sleep, 30*, 1085–1095. Retrieved from http://www.journalsleep.org/ViewAbstract.aspx?pid=26930.

Basner, M., Spaeth, A. M., & Dinges, D. F. (2014). Sociodemographic characteristics and waking activities and their role in the timing and duration of sleep. *Sleep, 37*, 1899–1906L. doi:10.5665/sleep.4238

Berkman, L. F., Buxton, O., Ertel, K., & Okechukwu, C. (2010). Managers' practices related to work–family balance predict employee cardiovascular risk and sleep duration in extended care settings. *Journal of Occupational Health Psychology, 15*, 316–329. doi:10.1037/a0019721

Berset, M., Elfering, A., Lüthy, S., Lüthi, S., & Semmer, N. K. (2011). Work stressors and impaired sleep: Rumination as a mediator. *Stress and Health, 27*, e71–e82. doi:10.1002/smi.1337

Brisette, I., & Cohen, S. (2002). The contribution of individual differences in hostility to the associations between daily interpersonal conflict, affect, and sleep. *Personality and Social Psychology Bulletin, 28,* 1265–1274. doi:10.1177/01461672022812011

Bureau of Labor Statistics. (2011). Volunteering in the United States—2010. http://www.bls.gov/news.release/volun.toc.htm. Accessed December 16, 2014.

Cajochen, C. (2007). Alerting effects of light. *Sleep Medicine Reviews, 11,* 453–464. doi:10.1016/j.smrv.2007.07.009

Castro, C. M., Lee, K. A., Bliwise, D. L., Urizar, G. G., Woodward, S. H., & King, A. C. (2009). Sleep patterns and sleep-related factors between caregiving and non-caregiving women. *Behavioral Sleep Medicine, 7,* 164–179. doi:10.1080/15402000902976713

Cropley, M., Dijk, D.-J., & Stanley, N. (2006). Job strain, work rumination, and sleep in school teachers. *European Journal of Work and Organizational Psychology, 15*(2), 181–196. doi:10.1080/13594320500513913

Custers, K., & Van den Bulck, J. (2012). Television viewing, internet use, and self-reported bedtime and rise time in adults: Implications for sleep hygiene recommendations from an exploratory cross-sectional study. *Behavioral Sleep Medicine, 10,* 96–105. doi:10.1080/15402002.2011.596599

Derks, D., van Mierlo, H., & Schmitz, E. B. (2014). A diary study on work-related smartphone use, psychological detachment and exhaustion: Examining the role of the perceived segmentation norm. *Journal of Occupational Health Psychology, 19,* 74–84. doi:10.1037/a0035076

Edwards, J. R., & Rothbard, N. P. (2000). Mechanisms linking work and family: Clarifying the relationship between work and family constructs. *Academy of Management Review, 25,* 178–199. doi:10.5465/amr.2000.2791609

Espie, C. A. (2002). Insomnia: Conceptual issues in the development, persistence, and treatment of sleep disorder in adults. *Annual Review of Psychology, 53,* 215–243. doi:10.1146/annurev.psych.53.100901.135243

Fritz, C., & Sonnentag, S. (2005). Recovery, health, and job performance: Effects of weekend experiences. *Journal of Occupational Health Psychology, 10,* 187–199. doi:10.1037/1076-8998.10.3.187

Fritz, C., & Sonnentag, S. (2006). Recovery, well-being, and performance-related outcomes: The role of workload and vacation experiences. *Journal of Applied Psychology, 91,* 936–945. doi:10.1037/0021-9010.91.4.936

Fritz, C., Yankelevich, M., Zarubin, A., & Barger, P. (2010). Happy, healthy, and productive: The role of detachment from work during nonwork time. *Journal of Applied Psychology, 95,* 977–983. doi:10.1037/a0019462

Ganster, D. C., & Rosen, C. C. (2013). Work stress and employee health: A multidisciplinary review. *Journal of Management, 5,* 1085–1122. doi:10.1177/0149206313475815

Gay, C. L., Lee, K. A., & Lee, S. Y. (2004). Sleep patterns and fatigue in new mothers and fathers. *Biological Research for Nursing, 5,* 311–318. doi:10.1177/1099800403262142

Gradisar, M., Wolfson, A. R., Harvey, A. G., Hale, L., Rosenberg, R., & Czeisler, C. (2013). The sleep and technology use of Americans: Findings from the National Sleep Foundation's 2011 Sleep in America Poll. *Journal of Clinical Sleep Medicine, 9,* 1291–1299. doi:10.5664/jcsm.3272

Hahn, V. C., Binnewies, C., Sonnentag, S., & Mojza, E. J. (2011). Learning how to recover from job stress: Effects of a recovery training program on recovery, recovery-related self-efficacy, and well-being. *Journal of Occupational Health Psychology, 16,* 202–216. doi:10.1037/a0022169

Hale, L. (2014). Inadequate sleep duration as a public health and social justice problem: Can we truly trade off our daily activities for more sleep? *Sleep, 37,* 1879–1880. doi:10.5665/sleep.4228

Harvey, A. G. (2000). Pre-sleep cognitive activity: A comparison of sleep-onset insomniacs and good sleepers. *British Journal of Clinical Psychology, 39*, 275–286. doi:10.1348/014466500163284

Harvey, K. J., & Espie, C. A. (2004). Development and preliminary validation of the Glasgow Content of Thoughts Inventory (GCTI): A new measure for the assessment of pre-sleep cognitive activity. *British Journal of Clinical Psychology, 43*, 409–420. doi:10.1348/0144665042388900

Howell, A. J., Digdon, N. L., Buro, K., & Sheptycki, A. R. (2008). Relations among mindfulness, well-being, and sleep. *Personality and Individual Differences, 45*, 773–777. doi:10.1016/j.paid.2008.08.005

Hülsheger, U. R., Lang, J. W., Depenbrock, F., Fehrmann, C., Zijlstra, F. R., & Alberts, H. J. (2014). The power of presence: The role of mindfulness at work for daily levels and change trajectories of psychological detachment and sleep quality. *Journal of Applied Psychology, 99*, 1113–1128. doi:10.1037/a0037702

Ilies, R., Schwind, K. M., Wagner, D. T., Johnson, M. D., DeRue, D. S., & Ilgen, D. R. (2007). When can employees have a family life? The effects of daily workload and affect on work-family conflict and social behaviors at home. *Journal of Applied Psychology, 92*, 1368–1379. doi:10.1037/0021-9010.92.5.1368

Irish, L. A., Kline, C. E., Gunn, H. E., Buysse, D. J., & Hall, M. H. (2015). The role of sleep hygiene in promoting public health: A review of empirical evidence. *Sleep Medicine Reviews, 22*, 23–36. doi:10.1016/j.smrv.2014.10.001

Kabat-Zinn, J. (1990). *Full catastrophe living: Using the wisdom of your body and mind to face stress, pain, and illness.* New York, NY: Bantam Dell. doi:10.1037/032287

Kang, M. J., Matsumoto, K., Shinkoda, H., Mishima, M., & Seo, Y. J. (2002). Longitudinal study for sleep–wake behaviours of mothers from pre-partum to post-partum using actigraph and sleep logs. *Psychiatry and Clinical Neurosciences, 56*, 251–252. doi:10.1046/j.1440-1819.2002.00992.x

Kline, C. E. (2014). The bidirectional relationship between exercise and sleep: Implications for exercise adherence and sleep improvement. *American Journal of Lifestyle Medicine, 8*, 375–379. doi:10.1177/1559827614544437

Knauth, P. (1997). Changing schedules: Shiftwork. *Chronobiology International, 14*, 159–171. doi:10.3109/07420529709001153

Kossek, E. E., & Michel, J. S. (2011). Flexible work schedules. In S. Zedeck (Ed.), *APA handbook of industrial and organizational psychology* (pp. 535–572). Washington, DC: American Psychological Association. doi:10.1037/12169-017

Kredlow, M. A., Capozzoli, M. C., Hearon, B. A., Calkins, A. W., & Otto, M. W. (2015). The effects of physical activity on sleep: A meta-analytic review. *Journal of Behavioral Medicine, 38*, 427–449. doi:10.1007/s10865-015-9617-6

Lanaj, K., Johnson, R. E., & Barnes, C. M. (2014). Beginning the workday yet already depleted? Consequences of late-night smartphone use and sleep. *Organizational Behavior and Human Decision Processes, 124*, 11–23. doi:10.1016/j.obhdp.2014.01.001

McEwen, B. S. (1998). Stress, adaptation, and disease: Allostasis and allostatic load. *Annals of the New York Academy of Sciences, 840*, 33–44. doi:10.1111/j.1749-6632.1998.tb09546.x

Meijman, T. F., & Mulder, G. (1998). Psychological aspects of workload. In P. J. D. Drenth & H. Thierry (Eds.), *Handbook of work and organizational psychology, Vol. 2: Work psychology* (pp. 5–33). Hove, England: Psychology Press.

Meltzer, L. J. (2008). Brief report: Sleep in parents of children with autism spectrum disorders. *Journal of Pediatric Psychology, 33*, 380–386. doi:10.1093/jpepsy/jsn005

Meltzer, L. J., & Moore, M. (2008). Sleep disruptions in parents of children and adolescents with chronic illnesses: Prevalence, causes, and consequences. *Journal of Pediatric Psychology, 33*, 279–291. doi:10.1093/jpepsy/jsm118

Meurs, J. A., & Perrewé, P. L. (2011). Cognitive Activation Theory of Stress: An integrative theoretical approach to work stress. *Journal of Management, 37,* 1043–1068. doi:10.1177/0149206310387303

Muraven, M., & Baumeister, R. F. (2000). Self-regulation and depletion of limited resources: Does self-control resemble a muscle? *Psychological Bulletin, 126,* 247–259. doi:10.1037/0033-2909.126.2.247

Nordin, M., Westerholm, P., Alfredsson, L., & Akerstedt, T. (2012). Social support and sleep. Longitudinal relationships from the WOLF-Study. *Psychology, 3,* 1223–1230. doi:10.4236/psych.2012.312A181

Park, Y., Fritz, C., & Jex, S. M. (2011). Relationships between work-home segmentation and psychological detachment from work: The role of communication technology use at home. *Journal of Occupational Health Psychology, 16,* 457–467. doi:10.1037/a0023594

Pereira, D., & Elfering, A. (2014). Social stressors at work and sleep during weekends: The mediating role of psychological detachment. *Journal of Occupational Health Psychology, 19,* 85–95. doi:10.1037/a0034928

Pereira, D., Meier, L. L., & Elfering, A. (2013). Short-term effects of social exclusion at work and worries on sleep: Social exclusion, worries, sleep. *Stress and Health, 29,* 240–252. doi:10.1002/smi.2461

Pigeon, W. R., Cerulli, C., Richards, H., He, H., Perlis, M., & Caine, E. (2011). Sleep Disturbances and their association with mental health among women exposed to intimate partner violence. *Journal of Women's Health, 20,* 1923–1929. doi:10.1089/jwh.2011.2781

Querstret, D., & Cropley, M. (2012). Exploring the relationship between work-related rumination, sleep quality, and work-related fatigue. *Journal of Occupational Health Psychology, 17,* 341–353. doi:10.1037/a0028552

Rauer, A. J., & El-Sheikh, M. (2012). Reciprocal pathways between intimate partner violence and sleep in men and women. *Journal of Family Psychology, 26,* 470–477. doi:10.1037/a0027828

Rodell, J. B. (2013). Finding meaning through volunteering: Why do employees volunteer and what does it mean for their jobs? *Academy of Management Journal, 56,* 1274–1294. doi:10.5465/amj.2012.0611

Rodríguez-Muñoz, A., Notelaers, G., & Moreno-Jiménez, B. (2011). Workplace bullying and sleep quality: The mediating role of worry and need for recovery. *Behavioral Psychology, 19,* 453–468. Retrieved from http://www.psicologiaconductual.com/PDFenglish/2011/art03.2.19.pdf.

Salo, P., Ala-Mursula, L., Rod, N. H., Tucker, P., Pentti, J., Kivimäki, M., & Vahtera, J. (2014). Work time control and sleep disturbances: Prospective cohort study of Finnish public sector employees. *Sleep, 37,* 1217–1255. doi:10.5665/sleep.3842

Schieman, S., & Young, M. C. (2013). Are communications about work outside regular working hours associated with work-to-family conflict, psychological distress and sleep problems? *Work & Stress, 27,* 244–261. doi:10.1080/02678373.2013.817090

Smith, C. S., Folkard, S., Tucker, P., & Evans, M. S. (2011). Work schedules, health, and safety. In J. C. Quick & L. E. Tetrick (Eds.), *Handbook of occupational health and safety* (pp. 185–204). Washington, DC: American Psychological Association.

Sonnentag, S., & Fritz, C. (2007). The Recovery Experience Questionnaire: Development and validation of a measure assessing recuperation and unwinding from work. *Journal of Occupational Health Psychology, 12,* 204–221. doi:10.1037/1076-8998.12.3.204

Sonnentag, S., & Fritz, C. (2014). Recovery from job stress: The stressor-detachment model as an integrative framework. *Journal of Organizational Behavior, 35,* S72–S103. doi:10.1002/job

Sonnentag, S., & Fritz, C. (2015). Recovery from job stress: The stressor-detachment model as an integrative framework. *Journal of Organizational Behavior, 36,* S72-S103. doi:10.1002/job.1924

Troxel, W. M., Buysse, D. J., Hall, M., & Matthews, K. A. (2009). Marital happiness and sleep disturbances in a multi-ethnic sample of middle-aged women. *Behavioral Sleep Medicine, 7,* 2–19. doi:10.1080/15402000802577736

Troxel, W. M., Robles, T. F., Hall, M., & Buysse, D. J. (2007). Marital quality and the marital bed: Examining the covariation between relationship quality and sleep. *Sleep Medicine Reviews, 11,* 389–404. doi:10.1016/j.smrv.2007.05.002

Tucker, P., Dahlgren, A., Akerstedt, T., & Waterhouse, J. (2008). The impact of free-time activities on sleep, recovery and well-being. *Applied Ergonomics, 39,* 653–662. doi:10.1016/j.apergo.2007.12.002

Ursin, H., & Eriksen, H. R. (2010). Cognitive activation theory of stress (CATS). *Neuroscience and Biobehavioral Review, 34,* 877–881. doi:10.1016/j.neubiorev.2009.03.001

Vahle-Hinz, T., Bamberg, E., Dettmers, J., Friedrich, N., & Keller, M. (2014). Effects of work stress on work-related rumination, restful sleep, and nocturnal heart rate variability experienced on workdays and weekends. *Journal of Occupational Health Psychology, 19,* 217–230. doi:10.1037/a0036009

van Straten, A., & Cuijpers, P. (2009). Self-help therapy for insomnia: A meta-analysis. *Sleep Medicine Reviews, 13,* 61–71. doi:10.1016/j.smrv.2008.04.006

Watson, D. (2000). *Mood and temperament.* New York, NY: Guilford Press. doi:10.1017/s1352465801213125

West, K. E., Jablonski, M. R., Warfield, B., Cecil, K. S., James, M., Ayers, M. A., . . . Brainard, G. C. (2010). Blue light from light-emitting diodes elicits a dose-dependent suppression of melatonin in humans. *Journal of Applied Physiology, 110,* 619–626. doi:10.1152/japplphysiol.01413.2009

Yang, C.-M., Lin, S.-C., Hsu, S.-C., & Cheng, C.-P. (2010). Maladaptive sleep hygiene practices in good sleepers and patients with insomnia. *Journal of Health Psychology, 15,* 147–155. doi:10.1177/1359105309346342

Youngstedt, S. D., O'Connor, P. J., & Dishman, R. K. (1997). From wake to sleep: The effects of acute exercise on sleep: A quantitative synthesis. *Sleep, 20,* 2013–2014. Retrieved from http://www.journalsleep.org/

Zijlstra, F. R. H., & Sonnentag, S. (2006). After work is done: Psychological perspectives on recovery from work. *European Journal of Work and Organizational Psychology, 15,* 129–138. doi:10.1080/13594320500513855

## CHAPTER 5

# Job Stress and Sleep

SABINE SONNENTAG, ANNE CASPER,
AND ANNA SOPHIA PINCK

## INTRODUCTION

Sleep is essential for human functioning. For instance, it is crucial for memory and brain plasticity (Walker & Stickgold, 2006), and it protects health via adaptive and innate immune responses (Irwin, 2015). In recent years, fields such as organizational psychology and organizational behavior have started to acknowledge the relevance of sleep (Barnes, 2012), and substantial attention has been directed to the detrimental effects of impaired sleep. It has been shown that poor sleep compromises job performance and stimulates deviant behavior at the workplace (Barnes, Schaubroeck, Huth, & Ghumman, 2011; Christian & Ellis, 2011; Mullins, Cortina, Drake, & Dalal, 2014). However, experiences at the workplace and their affective consequences may also be associated with sleep. In this chapter, we address the relationship between job stress and indicators of poor sleep. Specifically, we review empirical evidence that stressful job conditions (job stressors) as well as experienced strain symptoms are related to impaired sleep. We discuss neurobiological and cognitive arousal as potential mediators of this relationship. Moreover, we address factors that play a moderating role in the relationship between job stress and sleep problems. Figure 5.1 shows our conceptual framework.

The chapter is organized as follows: First, we describe core job-stress concepts potentially relevant for sleep. Specifically, we introduce job stressors and strain symptoms often subsumed under *job stress* as an umbrella term. Next, we review empirical research that examined a direct association between job stress and sleep, covering cross-sectional and longitudinal studies as well as studies that took within-person variability in job stress and sleep into account. The sections that follow discuss mediators and moderators of the job stress–sleep relationship. In the final section of this chapter we highlight the most important empirical findings and point to unanswered questions that need to be addressed in future research.

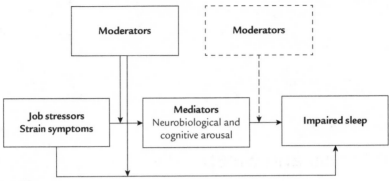

**Figure 5.1.**
Conceptual model.

## Core Concepts

Job stress is a broad concept that covers the conditions in a person's job environment, the cognitive, affective, and physiological reactions to these conditions, as well as the interplay between conditions and reactions. To avoid this ambiguity inherent in the job-stress concept, researchers call the conditions that potentially evoke cognitive, affective, and physiological reactions "stressors" and the reactions "strain" (cf. Kahn & Byosiere, 1992).

A broad range of different job conditions can turn into stressors when taxing or exceeding a person's capacity. Major stressor categories include task-related stressors (e.g., time pressure, overload, hassles), role stressors (e.g., role conflict, role ambiguity, illegitimate tasks), social stressors (e.g., interpersonal conflicts, injustice, harassment, incivility), stressors related to working time (e.g., shift work, long working hours), career-related stressors (e.g., job insecurity, underemployment), traumatic stressors (e.g., exposure to major accidents or disasters), and physical stressors (e.g., noise, heat) (Sonnentag & Frese, 2012).

With respect to stressors of a specific workplace, we can distinguish between chronic and more acute stressors. Chronic stressors refer to more or less enduring conditions that are present during longer periods of time (e.g., months or even years); acute stressors refer to more short-term events that are present on specific days or weeks. This distinction between chronic and acute stressors is reflected in the designs of empirical studies: Most cross-sectional and longitudinal panel designs address chronic stressors, whereas most day-level and week-level studies focus on acute stressors.

When facing job stressors, employees can develop acute strain symptoms within a short period of time (seconds to hours), including physiological arousal, negative affect, and increased levels of fatigue (Ilies, Dimotakis, & de Pater, 2010; Rodell & Judge, 2009; Zohar, Tzischinski, & Epstein, 2003). In addition, when experiencing job stressors, many employees tend to react with repetitive thought processes such as rumination and worry (Wang et al., 2013). Although these short-term reactions to stressors cease after some time, exposure to chronic stressors can have longer-term implications. For instance, empirical research has shown that experiencing a high level of job stressors is associated with an increase in strain symptoms over time (Ford et al., 2014). Typical strain symptoms associated with job stressors include physical as well as psychological reactions. Physical reactions comprise symptoms such as backache or gastrointestinal problems (Nixon et al., 2011). With respect to psychological reactions, burnout has received substantial attention during recent decades (Maslach, Schaufeli, & Leiter, 2001). Burnout is characterized by emotional exhaustion, cynicism, and inefficacy. Other psychological reactions to job stressors include depression (Schmidt, Roesler, Kusserow, & Rau, 2014) or irritation (Dormann & Zapf, 2002). Also sleep problems can be seen as a typical strain symptom (e.g., Nixon et al., 2011). In this chapter we will present empirical evidence that job stressors are indeed associated with an increased likelihood of suffering from impaired sleep. Moreover, we will examine whether other strain symptoms (e.g., burnout) are related to sleep problems.

## Cross-Sectional Evidence

Cross-sectional research has provided evidence that job stressors are associated with poor sleep. Specifically, studies addressed task-related stressors, role stressors, social stressors, stressors related to working time, career-related stressors, traumatic stressors, environmental stressors, and physical demands.

*Task-related stressors.* A number of studies found that task-related stressors such as high job demands (e.g., workload, time pressure) are related to impaired sleep (Berset, Elfering, Lüthy, Lüthi, & Semmer, 2011; Stenfors et al., 2013; Winwood & Lushington, 2006). When differentiating between various indicators of poor sleep, researchers found that employees facing high job demands reported difficulty initiating sleep, difficulty maintaining sleep, and difficulty waking up (Åkerstedt et al., 2002; Knudsen, Ducharme, & Roman, 2007). In addition to quantitative job demands, other demands are related to poor sleep: For instance, Stenfors et al. (2013) found a significant—albeit weak—positive correlation between emotional demands at work and sleep disturbances. Barber and Santuzzi (2015) reported that workplace telepressure (i.e., preoccupation with and perceived necessity to respond quickly to electronic messages), as a recently emerged job demand, relates positively to poor sleep quality, but not to reduced sleep quantity. This overall finding of a positive association between job demands and poor sleep is also reflected in meta-analytical findings presented by Nixon et al. (2011). These authors reported a weighted correlation of $r = 0.14$ between workload and sleep disturbances. In addition to workload, organizational constraints as another type of task-related stressors are related to sleep disturbances (weighted correlation $r = 0.17$).

*Role stressors.* Findings on the association between role stressors and impaired sleep are mixed. In the meta-analysis of Nixon et al. (2011), role conflict showed a significant, but weak correlation with sleep disturbances (weighted correlation $r = 0.13$); role ambiguity was not related to sleep disturbances (weighted correlation $r = 0.04$).

***Social stressors.*** Social stressors such as interpersonal conflicts (Winwood & Lushington, 2006) and the experience of injustice (Hietapakka et al., 2013) are associated with poor sleep. When contrasting ongoing conflicts with finished conflicts, Stenford et al. (2013) detected a larger effect size for ongoing than for finished conflicts, suggesting that the effects of social conflicts on sleep might be rather short-lived and decrease once the conflicts are resolved. Compared to other job stressors, meta-analytical evidence suggests a comparably large effect size for the association between interpersonal conflicts and disturbed sleep (weighted correlation $r = 0.22$; Nixon et al., 2011). With respect to workplace bullying, (i.e., an ongoing, systematic hostile and unethical communication directed by one or more toward an individual; Niedhammer et al., 2009) as a specific social stressor, Nielsen and Einarsen (2012) reported a nonsignificant meta-analytical correlation of $r = -0.10$ between bullying and sleep quality indicators, spanning a large range of effect sizes. Possibly, also here the temporal proximity of the stressor plays an important role: It could be that experiencing ongoing bullying at work is associated with poor sleep, but having experienced bullying in the past is not.

***Working time.*** Sleep problems can result from stressors related to working time. There is a large literature showing that shift work is associated with poor sleep (Åkerstedt, 2003; Drake, Roehrs, Richardson, Walsh, & Roth, 2004; Pilcher, Lambert, & Huffcutt, 2000). With respect to long working hours and overtime, findings are inconsistent: Some studies report a positive relationship between long working hours and overtime on the one hand and impaired sleep quality on the other hand (Nakashima et al., 2011; Rau & Triemer, 2004), whereas others do not (Åkerstedt et al., 2002; Dahlgren, Kecklund, & Åkerstedt, 2006). It seems that it is primarily sleep duration that is affected by long working hours (Dahlgren et al., 2006; Parkes, 2015); however, other sleep complaints occur, particularly at very high levels of overtime (Kanazawa et al., 2006; Nakashima et al., 2011). This mixed pattern of results is reflected in Nixon et al.'s (2011) meta-analytical finding of a small—albeit significant—weighted correlation of $r = 0.05$ between work hours and disturbed sleep.

***Career-related stressors.*** Stressors associated with a person's career have rarely been examined with respect to sleep problems—although it is highly plausible that people who experience threats to their career suffer from poor sleep. Among the few studies that did address career-related stressors in relationship to sleep, Burgard and Ailshire (2009) found a concurrent relationship between job insecurity and poor sleep quality. Stenford et al. (2013) reported that being overqualified revealed a weak positive association with disturbed sleep.

***Traumatic stressors.*** Experiencing traumatic stressors at work is associated with impaired sleep. For instance, in a study with emergency room nurses, Adriaenssens, de Gucht, and Maes (2012) found that frequency of exposure to traumatic events is related to sleep problems. Moreover, there is evidence that combat exposure is related to insomnia in soldiers (Piccioni et al., 2010; Wright, Britt, Bliese, & Adler, 2011).

***Environmental stressors and physical demands.*** Additionally, environmental stressors such as hazardous chemicals, climate, and noise have been found to be associated with impaired sleep (Lallukka, Rahkonen, Lahelma, & Arber, 2010). Finally, Winwood and Lushington (2006) reported a positive zero-order correlation between physical demands (e.g., having a physically very strenuous job) and poor sleep; in a multiple-regression approach, however, only psychological demands were associated with sleep problems. It might be that not the physical demands per se, but the associated psychological strain is responsible for impaired sleep.

**Conclusions.** Taken together, cross-sectional research identified associations between job stressors and disturbed sleep. The size of the correlations varies somewhat between the various types of stressors. The largest effect sizes have been observed for social stressors (e.g., interpersonal conflicts), possibly because these stressors threaten employees' well-being in a fundamental way (Baumeister & Leary, 1995). Importantly, the cross-sectional associations between perceived job stressors and poor sleep do not warrant any conclusions about causality. For instance, employees who suffer from poor sleep may perceive a higher level of job stressors. In addition, third variables (e.g., personality, socioeconomic status) might also influence the cooccurrence of job stressors and poor sleep.

## Longitudinal Research

Longitudinal studies have attempted to shed more light on the causal relationship between stressful experiences on the job and impaired sleep. Although longitudinal research does not provide evidence about causality in a strict sense, well-designed studies at least can rule out some alternative explanations. Specifically, when controlling for the baseline level of impaired sleep, longitudinal studies can answer the question of whether job stress predicts change in sleep over time.

Van Laethem, Beckers, Kompier, van Dijksterhuis, and Geurts (2013) reviewed 16 longitudinal studies on workplace factors and sleep quality, with three studies categorized as high-quality studies. The type of job stressor that received the most attention in these 16 studies was high job demands (e.g., high workload and high time pressure). Van Laethem et al. (2013) reported strong evidence that job demands were negatively related to sleep quality over time. For instance, in one of the high-quality studies, de Lange et al. (2009) found that a high level of job demands predicted sleep complaints 1 year later when controlling for earlier sleep complaints. A more recent review including 24 studies resulted in a similar finding; it reported a significant association between high job demands and future sleep disturbances (Linton et al., 2015). The same review found a significant association between high job strain (i.e., high demands combines with low job control) and future sleep disturbances. The effect sizes in this review, however, were relatively small.

Other stressful job experiences were related to poor sleep quality in longitudinal studies. Van Laethem et al. (2013) found moderately strong evidence for a longitudinal relationship between effort–reward imbalance (i.e., experiencing that effort invested into work exceeds the rewards received; Siegrist, 1996) and sleep quality (Ota et al., 2009). Linton et al. (2015) reported a significant, albeit small odds ratio to experience sleep disturbances in employees with a high effort–reward imbalance compared to employees with a small effort–reward imbalance. Similarly, organizational injustice was found to predict poor sleep quality in some of the studies reviewed by van Laethem and her co-workers (Elovainio, Kivimäki, Vahtera, Keltikangas-Järvinen, & Virtanen, 2003). A recent study not included in the review of van Laethem et al. points to a similar process. In a sample of managers, Ng and Feldman (2013) examined how breach of the psychological contract predicted insomnia over time. They found that managers who realized that their psychological contract with the organization had been broken (for instance, the organization did not fulfill its promises) reported symptoms of insomnia 8 months later. Findings on the longitudinal association between bullying and sleep disturbances are mixed. Linton et al. (2015) reported a significantly increased probability of having sleep disturbances after having experienced or observed bullying. A large-scale primary study not included in the review of Linton et al. (2015), however, points to a more differentiated picture (Hansen, Hogh, Garde, & Persson, 2014). This study also found that experiencing bullying at work predicted sleep disturbances and poor sleep quality 2 years later. When controlling for sleep at baseline, the association between bullying and sleep 2 years later became insignificant. This finding suggests that bullying may have an immediate effect on employees' sleep and these sleep problems may persist over time, but a delayed reaction seems to be rather unlikely.

Taken together, these longitudinal studies suggest that employees who face a high level of job stressors such as high job demands or injustice tend to develop sleep problems over time. Underlying mediating processes might be physiological arousal and repetitive thought. We will discuss these mediators later in this chapter.

Other studies looked at longitudinal relationships between strain symptoms resulting from stressful on-the-job experiences and sleep problems. Armon, Shirom, Shapira, and Melamed (2008) examined how burnout predicts an increase in insomnia over a period of 18 months in a sample of apparently healthy employees. Analysis showed that burnout at baseline predicted insomnia 18 months later, when controlling for baseline insomnia, baseline depression, and a range of other variables. Interestingly, insomnia at baseline also predicted an increase in burnout over time, pointing to a reciprocally reinforcing process between burnout and insomnia. Another longitudinal study using a time lag of 1 year found that depression at baseline, but not burnout, predicted an incidence of insomnia over time (Jansson-Fröjmark & Lindblom, 2010). To sum up, there is empirical evidence that strain symptoms associated with job stress predict sleep problems later on; in addition, sleep problems seem to contribute to a worsening of strain symptoms over time, suggesting a potential reciprocal relationship between strain symptoms and sleep problems.

### Day-Level and Week-Level Studies

A person's sleep—as a response to chronic stressors encountered on the job—does not change only over longer periods of time (e.g., months or years). It also fluctuates within shorter periods of time. Most obviously, sleep duration often differs substantially between weekdays and weekends (Basner et al., 2007; Hale, 2005), particularly in persons with an evening chronotype (i.e., persons preferring late sleep timing; Roepke & Duffy, 2010). Along with sleep duration, sleep quality also fluctuates over the week. Using diary data, van Hooff, Geurts, Kompier, and Taris (2006) reported that self-reported sleep complaints decreased from Monday to Friday. Including subjective sleep-quality data assessed on the weekend, Rook and Zijlstra (2006) demonstrated that sleep quality was particularly high on Saturday nights, but declined substantially on Sunday nights—probably because respondents anticipated the upcoming workweek.

Although multiple factors may influence both sleep duration and sleep quality, job stress may contribute substantially to this within-person variability of sleep over the course of the week. Research has examined whether the experience and/ or anticipation of job stressors and job strain predict poor sleep. Studies focusing specifically on within-person variability of job stressors and sleep have analyzed whether highly stressful days or weeks are followed by impaired sleep (Dahlgren, Kecklund, & Åkerstedt, 2005; Jones & Fletcher, 1996). More specifically, day-level studies have examined whether experiencing job stressors on a specific day is related to sleep problems in the night following the stressful day. Overall, there is some evidence that this is indeed the case. For instance, in a diary study using actigraph methodology to assess sleep parameters, Pereira, Meier, and Elfering (2013) found that after workdays during which employees experienced social exclusion, sleep was more fragmented (i.e., a greater number of awakenings occurred during the night). Social exclusion, however, was not related to sleep onset latency (i.e., time needed until falling asleep after having gone to bed), sleep efficiency (i.e., percentage of time spent sleeping after sleep onset and last awakening before getting up), or self-reported sleep quality. In another study, Pereira, Semmer, and Elfering (2014) focused on illegitimate tasks (i.e., tasks that employees perceive as unreasonable or unnecessary). Analysis showed that experiencing illegitimate tasks during the day at work predicted increased sleep fragmentation and sleep onset latency, but not sleep efficiency or sleep duration at night. Interestingly, day-specific time pressure was unrelated to sleep parameters. This result mirrors findings from an earlier study by Jones and Fletcher (1996) in which day-specific job demands were not related to day-specific subjective sleep quality. Although the nonsignificant findings in the study by Jones and Fletcher (1996) might be attributed to a rather small sample size, the overall pattern of results suggests that—at least at the day level—not all types of stressors are equally detrimental for subsequent sleep. The results from the research of Pereira et al. (2013, 2014) suggest that in particular stressors that threaten a person's self (i.e., social exclusion, illegitimate tasks) impair sleep during the night following the stressful experience.

In addition to this line of research that focused on job stressors, other studies looked at psychological strain as a predictor of poor sleep. Åkerstedt, Orsini, et al. (2012) collected diary data on sleep parameters, stress during the day, and worries at bedtime from a sample of 50 adults (70% employed) over a period of 42 days. In univariate analyses, both average stress during the day and worries at bedtime predicted poor sleep quality during the following night. In multivariate analyses, worries at bedtime were the most important predictor, suggesting a mediating effect from stress during the day on sleep via worries at bedtime. A study by Wagner, Barnes, and Scott (2014) demonstrated that even strain experienced earlier in the day can impair sleep: On those days when bus drivers experienced anxiety during the afternoon, they were more likely to suffer from insomnia at night than on days when afternoon anxiety was low.

Some studies focused on the possibilities that not only the past experience of a stressful day, but the anticipation of a stressful day might impair sleep quality as well. For instance, Kecklund and Åkerstedt (2004) asked a sample of cabin-crew staff and truck drivers at bedtime about their momentary mood and their expectations for the next day. Sleep recordings were taken during the night. Analysis showed that when expecting a difficult day—as opposed to a pleasant day—study participants reported higher bedtime stress and anxiety and had lower sleep quality (i.e., a lower percentage of Stage 2 sleep, a lower percentage of slow wave sleep, and less absolute time spent in slow wave sleep).

Åkerstedt, Kecklund, and Axelsson (2007) examined whether bedtime worries when anticipating a stressful day were related to impaired sleep during the night. Indeed, when employees worried a lot at bedtime (when anticipating a presumably high-stress day) they had lower sleep efficiency, had a higher amount of time being awake between sleep onset and final awakening, and needed more time to get to a deep-sleep stage after sleep onset. In addition, a study by Pereira and Elfering (2014) suggests that the anticipation of job stress impairs sleep quality. More specifically, in an ambulatory-assessment study Pereira and Elfering (2014) examined how social stressors at work are related to sleep during the weekend. They found that experiencing social stressors at work—as reported at the end of the work week—predicted a change in sleep variables on Sunday night, but not on Saturday night. Specifically, social stressors were related to an increase in sleep onset latency, an increase in sleep fragmentation, and a decrease in sleep duration (but not to any change in sleep efficiency). The finding that sleep was impaired on Sunday night, but not on Saturday night, suggests that sleep problems were not primarily a reaction to the social stressors experienced during the past week, but may have resulted from anticipating social stressors during the upcoming workweek. Taken together, day-level studies suggest that sleep is impaired when experiencing stress, either as a reaction to stressors that have occurred on the job or as a result of anticipating a stressful day.

Some researchers have extended the day-level perspective to a week-level approach. For instance, Dahlgren, Kecklund, and Åkerstedt (2005) found that during weeks when employees experienced a high level of stress at work, total sleep time—measured by activity monitors—decreased. Sleep efficiency, however, remained unaffected by the experienced stress level.

Over a period of 5 weeks, Syrek and Antoni (2014) surveyed employees on Friday afternoons (asking about job stressors during the past work week) and Monday mornings (asking about sleep during the weekend). Analyses showed that unfinished tasks, but not time pressure during the week, predicted self-reported sleep disturbances over the weekend. In a study with student workers, Park and

Sprung (2015) found that during weeks in which working students experienced a high level of work–school conflict (i.e., experiencing that work interferes with school demands) they reported poor sleep quality. Overall, these week-level studies mirror findings from day-level studies: During particularly stressful times, sleep quality tends to be impaired.

## Mediating Processes

Researchers have suggested that the link between the experience of stressors and strain can be explained by prolonged activation, that is neurophysiological arousal that follows or precedes a stressor (Ursin & Eriksen, 2004). In turn, it has been proposed that hyperarousal contributes to symptoms of insomnia (Bonnet & Arand, 2010; Riemann et al., 2010). For example, Riemann and his co-workers (2010) indicated that hyperarousal manifests itself at the neurobiological and the cognitive–behavioral level. In the following, we will discuss neurobiological and cognitive–behavioral arousal as two possible pathways linking job stressors to subsequent sleep impairment.

**Neurobiological arousal.** With respect to the neurobiological level, researchers argued that not only genetic, electrophysiological and neurophysiological factors, but also autonomic, neuroendocrine, and neuroimmunological processes can contribute to sleep problems (Riemann et al., 2010). There is some evidence that symptoms of autonomic arousal such as increased heart rate (particularly during the night) and low heart rate variability are associated with insomnia (Spiegelhalder et al., 2011). For instance, Farina et al. (2013) reported that compared to a healthy control group insomnia patients had reduced heart rate variability (i.e., a higher arousal level) before sleep and during early sleep stages. Similarly, it has been reported that specific diurnal cortisol patterns are associated with sleep disturbances (Kumari et al., 2009).

To date, findings on the associations between autonomic, neuroendocrine, and neuroimmunological factors and sleep are not unequivocal in empirical studies and questions about causality are far from being resolved (Balbo, Leproult, & Van Cauter, 2010; Riemann et al., 2010). Nevertheless, the hyperarousal hypothesis is particularly promising when looking at the relationship between job stress and sleep. Job stress is associated with indicators of hyperarousal such as poor autonomic functioning (Vrijkotte, van Doornen, & de Geus, 2000) and endocrinological dysregulation (Bellingrath & Kudielka, 2008; Qi et al., 2014). These manifestations of neurobiological hyperarousal may be an important pathway from job stress to poor sleep. Future studies may want to directly address autonomic and neuroendocrinological processes as a possible mediating mechanism between job stress and sleep.

**Cognitive–behavioral arousal.** Brosschot, Pieper, and Thayer (2005) argued that the underlying mechanism in prolonged activation following or preceding a stressor is of a cognitive nature. More precisely, they suggested that it is the active cognitive representation of stressors in the form of repetitive thought processes that causes the stress response to be extended. Repetitive thought has been defined as "the process of thinking attentively, repetitively, or frequently about oneself and one's world" (Segerstrom, Stanton, Alden, & Shortridge, 2003, p. 1) and refers to thought processes such as rumination and worry (Segerstrom et al., 2003; Watkins, 2008). In line with this perspective, past research suggests that *not* thinking about work during off-job time—i.e., psychologically detaching from work—might be a protective factor in the stressor–strain process (Sonnentag, Binnewies, & Mojza, 2010). Psychological detachment can be described as a "sense of being away from the work situation" and includes "refraining from work-related activities (. . .) *and* not thinking about job related issues" (Sonnentag, 2012, p. 1) during leisure time. As shown in several studies, the experience of stressors at work is negatively related to psychological detachment during nonwork time (e.g., Nicholson & Griffin, 2015; Sonnentag & Fritz, 2007). We will start by summarizing empirical evidence on the associations between cognitive–behavioral arousal and poor sleep; then we will review studies that explicitly tested cognitive–behavioral arousal as a mediator in the relationship between job stressors and poor sleep.

**Bivariate associations between cognitive–behavioral arousal and sleep.** Many studies report associations between repetitive thought processes or low psychological detachment on the one hand and impaired sleep on the other hand. We will present evidence from cross-sectional, longitudinal, and day-level research.

*Cross-sectional research.* Åkerstedt and colleagues (2002) reported that the inability to stop thinking about work during leisure time was a risk indicator for self-reported sleep disturbances. Moreover, when taking persistent thoughts about work into account, the association between quantitative workload and impaired sleep was no longer significant, suggesting that persistent thoughts might be a mediator in the relationship between quantitative workload and sleep. As well, in two other cross-sectional studies, worry and rumination were positively associated with insomnia (Mitchell, Mogg, & Bradley, 2012) and negatively associated with sleep quality (Querstret & Cropley, 2012).

*Longitudinal research.* Åkerstedt, Nordin, Alfredsson, Westerholm, and Kecklund (2012) reported that mental preoccupation with work-related thoughts was associated with a higher risk of the onset of sleep impairment during the following 5 years.

*Day-level research.* With regard to within-person associations, Loft and Cameron (2014) reported findings from a diary study. In this study, presleep arousal (i.e., being kept awake by thoughts) predicted a longer time to get to sleep as well as fewer hours of sleep. Additionally, presleep arousal was negatively associated with a global index of sleep quality including information about sleep quality, time of lights out, sleep duration, time to get to sleep, as well as time of waking. In another diary study, Hülsheger and her colleagues (2014) examined psychological detachment as a mediator in the relationship between mindfulness at work and self-reported sleep quality. In this study, direct effects of psychological detachment on self-reported sleep quality were found both at the within-person and the between-person level of analysis, suggesting that both a person's general level of detachment as well as the daily level of detachment are associated with sleep quality. More precisely, persons who generally showed higher detachment from work during off-job time also reported higher levels of sleep quality. Additionally, on days when a person detached more from work than usual, sleep quality was higher.

In sum, repetitive thought and low psychological detachment have been shown to be associated with impaired self-reported sleep quality in studies with both between-person and within-person designs. Additionally, repetitive thought was prospectively associated with the onset of sleep impairment. These results suggest that the experience of repetitive thought or low psychological detachment during leisure time might be a mediating mechanism in the relationship between job stressors and sleep.

***Cognitive–behavioral arousal as a mediator between job stressors and sleep.*** Some studies directly addressed the question of whether cognitive–behavioral arousal mediates the relationship between job stressors and sleep. In the following, we will summarize research from cross-sectional and day-level studies.

*Cross-sectional research.* Berset, Elfering, Lüthy, Lüthi, and Semmer (2011) examined rumination as a mediator of the relationship between job stressors and self-reported sleep quality. In two samples, rumination fully mediated the relationship between time pressure and sleep quality. More precisely, higher levels of time pressure were associated with higher levels of rumination, which in turn predicted poorer sleep quality. The same pattern emerged for effort–reward imbalance in one of the two samples. In the other sample, rumination partially mediated the relationship between effort–reward imbalance and poor sleep quality while the direct effect also remained significant. In another cross-sectional study, worry was found to mediate the relationship between social stressors at work and self-reported sleep quality (Rodríguez-Muñoz, Notelaers, & Moreno-Jiménez, 2011). In one of two samples, worry fully mediated the association between workplace bullying and sleep quality, whereas there was no significant relationship between bullying and worry in the other sample. In both samples, however, worry was significantly negatively related to sleep quality.

*Day-level research.* Using a within-person perspective, Cropley, Dijk, and Stanley (2006) reported findings from a diary study with a sample of schoolteachers. In this study, schoolteachers who reported higher levels of daily job strain (i.e., a combination of high job demands, low job control, and low skill utilization) also reported higher levels of rumination during the following evening as compared to teachers who reported low levels of job strain. This study revealed negative direct effects of both daily job strain and rumination on self-reported sleep quality. However, the indirect effect of daily job strain on sleep quality via rumination remained insignificant. In the previously described study, Pereira, Meier, and Elfering (2013) examined the role of work-related worries on the relationship between social exclusion during the workday and sleep during the subsequent night. Work-related worries during the evening were significantly associated with higher sleep fragmentation and lower sleep efficiency, but not with sleep onset latency. Importantly, work-related worries did not mediate the relationship between social exclusion and sleep problems. Possibly other mediators such as neurobiological arousal play a mediating role here.

With regard to psychological detachment, no study thus far has investigated detachment as a mediator of the relationship between job stressors and impaired sleep. However, Barber and Jenkins (2014) examined the relationship between work-related information and communication technology use at home and self-reported sleep quality, quantity, and consistency in a cross-sectional study. In this study, psychological detachment mediated the relationship between work-related technology use at home and all of the three sleep measures.

Taken together, indirect effects of job stressors on self-reported sleep via repetitive thought have been found in several cross-sectional studies. At the within-person level, most studies reported direct effects of repetitive thought on sleep. However, indirect effects of job stressors on self-reported sleep quality via repetitive thought remained insignificant at the within-person level. With regard to more objective measures of sleep quality, evidence is mixed: Main effects of repetitive thought were found for some measures (i.e., sleep fragmentation and sleep efficiency) but not for others (i.e., sleep onset latency). These results could imply that chronic job stress and repetitive thought are more relevant to the occurrence of sleep impairment than the experience of acute stressors and repetitive thought on a daily basis. However, within-person mediations have so far been examined in only two studies focusing on specific measures of job stress (i.e., social exclusion and job strain). It might therefore be premature to conclude that the association between acute stressors and sleep impairment is not mediated by daily cognitive processes. More research is needed with regard to within-person processes; in addition, more research using objective measures of sleep quality is needed.

## Moderator Effects

The previous section described potential mediating mechanisms for the relationship between job stressors and sleep. In the following section, we shed light on factors that act as moderators for this relationship. Most of these studies tested the moderator effects on the direct relationship between job stress and sleep; very few studies looked at moderators of the mediation processes (for an exception see Barber & Jenkins, 2014). Moderators that have been examined comprise job-related factors such as social support, job control, interactional justice, and performance expectations as well as factors at the work–home boundary.

With regard to job-related factors, Gadinger et al. (2009) found social support as well as job control to be moderators of the relationship between job demands and sleep quality in a sample of German-speaking executives. Testing for a three-way interaction, they found a strong negative relationship between job demands and sleep quality when both job control and social support where low; for all other combinations of job control and social support, job demands were unrelated to sleep quality.

These findings are corroborated by Niedhammer et al. (2009). In their cross-sectional study of 7,694 employees, they investigated the relationship between workplace bullying and sleep disturbances. Niedhammer et al. (2009) identified social support as a buffer of the relationship between workplace bullying and sleep disturbances in men, but not in women.

Greenberg (2006) found interactional justice to be an additional job factor moderating the relationship between job stressors and sleep. Greenberg investigated the role of interactional justice on the association between underpayment and insomnia among nurses by using a repeated measurement design. He showed that a reduction of pay was associated with greater insomnia. However, the detrimental effect of this underpayment on insomnia was weaker for nurses whose supervisor had received training in interactional justice, suggesting a buffering effect of interactional justice on the relationship between underpayment and insomnia. Interestingly, this effect could still be observed 6 months after the training of the supervisors.

Another moderating factor related to the work context refers to the leader's performance expectations. In their week-level study over a 5-week period, Syrek and Antoni (2014) showed that unfinished tasks resulted in rumination and impaired sleep on the weekend. Looking at perceived leader expectations as a moderator, they reported that when these expectations were perceived to be high, the effect of unfinished tasks on rumination and sleep was stronger.

Finally, there are studies that examined the moderating role of factors at the work–home boundary. Barnes, Wagner, and Ghumman (2012) investigated the effects of time spent working and time spent on family demands on time spent sleeping. By utilizing a hierarchical linear model, they found a negative interaction effect of time spent working and time spent with the family on time spent sleeping. Interestingly, the negative effect of time spent working on sleep time occurred only at high levels of family time; there was no significant relationship between time spent working and time spent sleeping when time spent with family was low.

In their cross-sectional study of the relationship between work-related information and communication technology (ICT) use at home and sleep indicators, Barber and Jenkins (2014) examined boundary creation (i.e., deliberately setting boundaries between work and home) as a moderator. They found that the indirect effect of increased boundary crossing through the use of ICT on sleep quantity through psychological detachment was moderated by boundary creation: ICT use at home was negatively related to psychological detachment only for those individuals who set low boundaries around their work-related ICT use at home.

In sum, these studies provide evidence that experiences on the job as well as factors at the work–home boundary act as moderators of the relationship between job stress and sleep.

## DISCUSSION

Research reviewed in this chapter clearly shows that stressors at work are related to impaired sleep. Employees who are encountering more job stressors tend to have more sleep problems than employees in less stressful jobs. Moreover, during time periods (e.g., days and weeks) when employees face more job stressors, their sleep tends to be more impaired than during times when no stressors are present. It is important to note that this relationship between job stressors and sleep problems is dependent on the different time frames and different types of stressors. We will discuss the specific patterns of findings below.

With respect to the mediating mechanisms, arousal seems to be a major pathway linking job stressors to sleep impairment. More precisely, neurobiological and mainly cognitive–behavioral arousal (e.g., worry and rumination) seem to play a role in this relationship. With respect to moderators, it turned out that job resources (i.e., job control, social support), interactional justice, as well as factors at the work–home interface (e.g., boundary creation) buffer the relationship between job stressors and impaired sleep. Although explicitly tested in only a few studies (e.g., Barber & Jenkins, 2014; Syrek & Antoni, 2014), probably all these moderators impact the relationship between job stressors and arousal as a mediator, but not the relationship between the mediator and sleep outcomes.

It is important to distinguish between impaired sleep as a short-term reaction to job stressors and as a longer-term consequence. When looking at the short-term reaction—as done in day-level or week-level studies—it becomes obvious that particularly self-relevant stressors such as social exclusion and illegitimate tasks are associated with poor sleep (Pereira et al., 2013, 2014). Other job stressors such as a high workload or time pressure are not reflected in impaired sleep at the day or week level (Jones & Fletcher, 1996; Pereira et al., 2014; Syrek & Antoni, 2014). Interestingly, Vahle-Hinz, Bamberg, Dettmers, Friedrich, and Keller (2014) reported that a high day-specific workload was related to feelings of fatigue during the next morning. Although this finding could imply that workload negatively affected sleep, it might also be that workload has an effect on fatigue in the morning, irrespective of sleep quality.

There are at least two explanations for the finding that predominantly self-relevant stressors, but not quantitative demands, are related to poor sleep at the day level. First, self-relevant stressors are highly worrisome. For instance, social stressors are particularly troublesome for employees because they threaten their sense of belonging and social embeddedness at work. Other stressors—albeit often unpleasant—are less fundamentally disturbing and therefore can be overcome more easily during a recovery period in the evening before going to sleep. Second, these other stressors such as workload and time pressure require a high level of effort investment and therefore lead to a high level of fatigue (Zohar et al., 2003). This high level of fatigue—as a deactivated state—might help individuals find restorative sleep. Social stressors, however, are predominantly associated with a high level of negative activated affect (Ilies, Johnson, Judge, & Keeney, 2011) and rumination (Wang et al., 2013) that in turn are associated with poor sleep (Kalmbach, Pillai, Roth, & Drake, 2014; Stoia-Caraballo et al., 2008). In addition, it might be easier to leave high workload at work when leaving the workplace in the evening, whereas social stressors more likely intrude into an employee's private life (Martinez-Corts, Demerouti, Bakker, & Boz, 2015). In addition, when being at home employees might talk more intensely about social stressors than about a high workload, maintaining high arousal after work.

Studies of sleep problems as a longer-term consequence of job stressors mainly identified job demands (i.e., workload and time pressure) as predictors of impaired sleep (Van Laethem et al., 2013). Social stressors predicted sleep problems over time, but lost their predictive power when controlling for the initial level of sleep problems and other confounding variables (Hansen et al. 2014; Lallukka, Rahkonen, & Lahelma, 2011). These results—along with the findings from day-level studies—suggest that employees react to social stressors rather immediately, but social stressors do not seem to contribute to an increase in impaired sleep over time: Once social conflicts have been settled, sleep problems are ameliorated (Stenfors et al., 2013). Other job stressors (e.g., job demands), however, contribute to an increase in sleep problems over time (de Lange et al., 2009). Accumulative exhaustion processes could be an underlying mechanism that impairs sleep quality over time (Armon et al., 2008).

Until now, most studies have looked at social stressors versus other stressors such as job demands in isolation (for an exception, cf. Eriksen, Bjorvatn, Bruusgaard, & Knardahl, 2008). To identify the specificities of social stressors versus other job stressors, we need research that examines the diverse set of stressors within the same studies, using identical study designs and time lags.

Effect sizes for the relationship between job stressors and sleep problems are relatively small. For instance, cross-sectional research found weighted correlations ranging from $r = 0.04$ to $r = 0.22$ between job stressors and sleep disturbances. When interpreting these effect sizes, we have to keep in mind that sleep is a complex process, influenced by many different factors including genetic factors (Genderson et al., 2013), personality (Hintsanen et al., 2014), and the family situation (Peng & Chang, 2013). The workplace is just one of several life domains that influence a person's sleep. Therefore, it is noteworthy that job stressors predict sleep beyond other factors (e.g., health behaviors; Lallukka et al., 2010).

Moreover, moderators might attenuate the relationship between job stressors and sleep problems. For instance, job resources such as job control and social support (Gadinger et al., 2009) as well as deliberate boundary creation (Barber & Jenkins, 2014) have been identified as buffers between job stressors and sleep impairment. Thus, it seems that factors that attenuate the relationship between job stressors on the one hand and negative physiological arousal and repetitive job-related thoughts on the other hand are powerful moderators in the relationship between job stressors and sleep problems: For instance, Ilies et al. (2011) have shown that job control and organizational support buffer the relationship between workload and elevated blood pressure. Although not yet addressed in many studies, additional factors might play a moderating role. Sonnentag and Fritz (2015) have proposed that shifting attention away from the job while being at home weakens the association between job stressors and poor psychological detachment from work; a high level of psychological detachment from work, in turn, should reduce cognitive arousal. Thus, these factors that buffer the relationship between job stressors and physiological as well as cognitive arousal may have a positive impact on sleep.

In past decades there has been an intense debate as to whether sleep hygiene behaviors (e.g., going to bed at regular times, avoiding alcohol and caffeine before going to sleep) help to avoid sleep problems (Irish et al., 2015; Stepanski & Wyatt, 2003). Thus, it could be that sleep hygiene behaviors also help employees to maintain good sleep quality when facing job stressors.

In this review we have focused on the potential impact of job stressors on sleep indicators. In addition to this causal pathway from job stressors to sleep, another possible causal pathway warrants attention: Sleep may have an effect on perceived job stressors. It is well documented that poor sleep quality and quantity can have an impact on subsequent cognitive and affective states (Mullins et al., 2014). Importantly, sleepiness resulting from disturbed sleep impairs information processing, including long response times and attentional deficits (Mullins et al., 2014). These problems undermine task-accomplishment processes, leaving less cognitive capacity to deal with job stressors, and might therefore contribute to the experience that work is more stressful. Moreover, sleep deficits increase negative affect and decrease positive affect (Scott & Judge, 2006; Sonnentag, Binnewies, & Mojza, 2008). High negative affect, in turn, will increase the likelihood of being aware of stressors in the work environment, and as a consequence the overall level of job stressors appears to be higher.

In addition, the potential impact of sleep on job stress might be limited not only to the *perception* of job stressors. Research on job crafting and so-called i-deals (i.e., individualized agreements between employees and their employers) has emphasized that employees can proactively shape their own job situation (Rousseau, Ho, & Greenberg, 2006; Wrzesniewski & Dutton, 2001). When being less energetic because of poor sleep, people may be less able to envision a better job for themselves and therefore may be less inclined and less successful in crafting their jobs and negotiating better i-deals (cf. Lu, Wang, Lu, Du, & Bakker, 2014). Thus, over time, employees who sleep better may have a greater chance of creating better and less stressful jobs for themselves.

Although this potential causal pathway from poor sleep to job stress has not received much attention in empirical research yet (for exceptions see De Lange et al., 2009; Magnusson Hanson et al., 2011), we should not take it for granted that it is the job stressors that have an impact on sleep: Sleep could also have an impact on (perceived) job stressors. To disentangle these complex, potentially reciprocal processes we need studies that capture both short-term and longer-term changes in sleep and job stress.

In terms of practical implications, our review suggests several starting points on how to improve sleep in employees. First, organizations may directly address job stressors. It seems that it is particularly important to remain focused on long-term job demands as well as self-relevant stressors. Second, employees can be empowered to actively address their job stressors, for instance by teaching them effective coping strategies (Richardson & Rothstein, 2008). Third, it seems promising to encourage employees to reduce neurobiological and cognitive arousal during after-hours, for instance by deliberate relaxation or mindfulness exercises (De Niet, Tiemens, Lendemeijer, & Hutschemaekers, 2009; Hülsheger et al., 2014) and by minimizing the use of information technology before going to bed. Such a practice could be supported by an organizational culture that does not expect emails to be answered at night. Finally, sleep hygiene might help to stabilize healthy sleep patterns—which is particularly important when facing job stressors (Irish et al., 2015).

## REFERENCES

Adriaenssens, J., de Gucht, V., & Maes, S. (2012). The impact of traumatic events on emergency room nurses: Findings from a questionnaire survey. *International Journal of Nursing Studies, 49*, 1411–1422. doi:10.1016/j.ijnurstu.2012.07.003

Åkerstedt, T. (2003). Shift work and disturbed sleep/wakefulness. *Occupational Medicine, 53*, 89–94. doi:10.1093/occmed/kqg046

Åkerstedt, T., Kecklund, G., & Axelsson, J. (2007). Impaired sleep after bedtime stress and worries. *Biological Psychology, 76*, 170–173. doi:10.1016/j.biopsycho.2007.07.010

Åkerstedt, T., Knutsson, A., Westerholm, P., Theorell, T., Alfredsson, L., & Kecklund, G. (2002). Sleep disturbances, work stress and work hours: A cross-sectional study. *Journal of Psychosomatic Research, 53*, 741–748. doi:10.1016/S0022-3999(02)00333-1

Åkerstedt, T., Nordin, M., Alfredsson, L., Westerholm, P., & Kecklund, G. (2012). Predicting changes in sleep complaints from baseline values and changes in work demands, work control, and work preoccupation—The WOLF-project. *Sleep Medicine, 13*, 73–80. doi:10.1016/j.sleep.2011.04.015

Åkerstedt, T., Orsini, N., Petersen, H., Axelsson, J., Lekander, M., & Kecklund, G. (2012). Predicting sleep quality from stress and prior sleep: A study of day-to-day covariation across six weeks. *Sleep Medicine, 13*, 674–679. doi:10.1016/j.sleep.2011.12.013

Armon, G., Shirom, A., Shapira, I., & Melamed, S. (2008). On the nature of burnout-insomnia relationships: A prospective study of employed adults. *Journal of Psychosomatic Research, 65*, 5–12. doi:10.1016/j.jpsychores.2008.01.012

Balbo, M., Leproult, R., & van Cauter, E. (2010). Impact of sleep and its disturbances on hypothalamo-pituitary-adrenal axis activity. *International Journal of Endocrinology, 2010*, 1–15. doi:10.1155/2010/759234

Barber, L. K., & Jenkins, J. S. (2014). Creating technological boundaries to protect bedtime: Examining work–home boundary management, psychological detachment and sleep. *Stress and Health: Journal of the International Society for the Investigation of Stress, 30*, 259–264. doi:10.1002/smi.2536

Barber, L. K., & Santuzzi, A. M. (2015). Please respond ASAP: Workplace telepressure and employee recovery. *Journal of Occupational Health Psychology, 20*, 172–189. doi:10.1037/a0038278

Barnes, C. M. (2012). Working in our sleep: Sleep and self-regulation in organizations. *Organizational Psychology Review, 2*, 234–257. doi:10.1177/2041386612450181

Barnes, C. M., Schaubroeck, J., Huth, M., & Ghumman, S. (2011). Lack of sleep and unethical conduct. *Organizational Behavior and Human Decision Processes, 115*, 169–180. doi:10.1016/j.obhdp.2011.01.009

Barnes, C. M., Wagner, D. T., & Ghumman, S. (2012). Borrowing from sleep to pay work and family: Expanding time-based conflict to the broader nonwork domain. *Personnel Psychology, 65*, 789–819. doi:10.1111/peps.12002

Basner, M., Fomberstein, K. M., Razavi, F. M., Banks, S., William, J. H., & Rosa, R. R. (2007). American time use survey: Sleep time and its relationship to waking activities. *Sleep, 30*, 1085–1095.

Baumeister, R. F., & Leary, M. R. (1995). The need to belong: Desire for interpersonal attachments as a fundamental human motivation. *Psychological Bulletin, 117*, 497–529. doi:10.1037/0033-2909.117.3.497

Bellingrath, S., & Kudielka, B. M. (2008). Effort-reward-imbalance and overcommitment are associated with hypothalamus-pituitary-adrenal (HPA) axis responses to acute psychosocial stress in healthy working schoolteachers. *Psychoneuroendocrinology, 33*, 1335–1343. doi:10.1016/j.psyneuen.2008.07.008

Berset, M., Elfering, A., Lüthy, S., Lüthi, S., & Semmer, N. K. (2011). Work stressors and impaired sleep: Rumination as a mediator. *Stress and Health, 27*, e71–e82. doi:10.1002/smi.1337

Bonnet, M. H., & Arand, D. L. (2010). Hyperarousal and insomnia: State of the science. *Sleep Medicine Reviews, 14*, 9–15. doi:10.1016/j.smrv.2009.05.002

Brosschot, J. F., Pieper, S., & Thayer, J. F. (2005). Expanding stress theory: Prolonged activation and perseverative cognition. *Psychoneuroendocrinology, 30*, 1043–1049. doi:10.1016/j.psyneuen.2005.04.008

Burgard, S. A., & Ailshire, J. A. (2009). Putting work to bed: Stressful experiences on the job and sleep quality. *Journal of Health and Social Behavior, 50*, 476–492.

Christian, M. S., & Ellis, A. P. J. (2011). Examining the effects of sleep deprivation on workplace deviance: A self-regulatory perspective. *Academy of Management Journal, 54*, 913–934. doi:10.5465/amj.2010.0179

Cropley, M., Dijk, D.-J., & Stanley, N. (2006). Job strain, work rumination, and sleep in school teachers. *European Journal of Work and Organizational Psychology, 15*, 181–196. doi:10.1080/13594320500513913

Dahlgren, A., Kecklund, G., & Åkerstedt, T. (2005). Different levels of work-related stress and the effects of sleep, fatigue and cortisol. *Scandinavian Journal of Work, Environment and Health, 31*, 277–285. doi:10.5271/sjweh.883

Dahlgren, A., Kecklund, G., & Åkerstedt, T. (2006). Overtime work and its effects on sleep, sleepiness, cortisol and blood pressure in an experimental field study. *Scandinavian Journal of Work, Environment and Health, 32*, 318–327. doi:10.5271/sjweh.1016

De Lange, A. H., Kompier, M. A. J., Taris, T. W., Geurts, S. A. E., Beckers, D. G. J., & Houtmon, I. L. D. (2009). A hard day's night: A longitudinal study on the relationships among job demands and job control, sleep quality and fatigue. *Journal of Sleep Research, 18*, 374–383. doi:10.1111/j.1365-2869.2009.00735.x

De Niet, G., Tiemens, B., Lendemeijer, B., & Hutschemaekers, G. (2009). Music-assisted relaxation to improve sleep quality: A meta-analysis. *Journal of Advanced Nursing, 65*, 1356–1364. doi:10.1111/j.1365-2648.2009.04982.x

Dormann, C., & Zapf, D. (2002). Social stressors at work, irritation, and depressive symptoms: Accounting for unmeasured third variables in a multi-wave study. *Journal of Occupational and Organizational Psychology, 75*, 33–58. doi:10.1348/096317902167630

Drake, C. L., Roehrs, T., Richardson, G., Walsh, J. K., & Roth, T. (2004). Shift work sleep disorder: Prevalence and consequences beyond that of symptomatic day workers. *Sleep, 27*, 1456–1462.

Elovainio, M., Kivimäki, M., Vahtera, J., Keltikangas-Järvinen, L., & Virtanen, M. (2003). Sleeping problems and health behaviors as mediators between organizational justice and health. *Health Psychology, 22*, 287–293. doi:10.1037/0278-6133.22.3.287

Eriksen, W., Bjorvatn, B., Bruusgaard, D., & Knardahl, S. (2008). Work factors as predictors of poor sleep in nurses' aides. *International Archives of Occupational and Environmental Health, 81*, 301–310. doi:10.1007/s00420-007-0214-z

Farina, B., Dittoni, S., Colicchio, S., Testani, E., Losurdo, A., & Gnoni, V. (2013). Heart rate and heart rate variability modification in chronic insomnia patients. *Behavioral Sleep Medicine, 11*, 1–17. doi:10.1080/15402002.2013.801346

Ford, M. T., Matthews, R. A., Wooldridge, J. D., Mishra, V., Kakar, U. M., & Strahan, S. R. (2014). How do occupational stressor-strain effects vary with time? A review and meta-analysis of the relevance of time lags in longitudinal studies. *Work & Stress, 28*, 9–30. doi:10.1080/02678373.2013.877096

Gadinger, M. C., Fischer, J. E., Schneider, S., Fischer, G. C., Frank, G., & Kromm, W. (2009). Female executives are particularly prone to the sleep-disturbing effect of isolated high-strain jobs: A cross-sectional study in German-speaking executives. *Journal of Sleep Research, 18*, 229–237. doi:10.1111/j.1365-2869.2008.00715.x

Genderson, M. R., Rana, B. K., Panizzon, M. S., Grant, M. D., Toomey, R., & Jacobson, K. C. (2013). Genetic and environmental influences on sleep quality in middle-aged men: A twin study. *Journal of Sleep Research, 22*, 519–526. doi:10.1111/jsr.12048

Greenberg, J. (2006). Losing sleep over organizational injustice: Attenuating insomniac reactions to underpayment inequity with supervisory training in interactional justice. *Journal of Applied Psychology, 91*, 58–69. doi:10.1037/0021-9010.91.1.58

Hale, L. (2005). Who has time to sleep? *Journal of Public Health, 27*, 205–211. doi:10.1093/pubmed/fdi004

Hansen, A. M., Hogh, A., Garde, A. H., & Persson, R. (2014). Workplace bullying and sleep difficulties: A 2-year follow-up study. *International Archives of Occupational and Environmental Health, 87*, 285–294. doi:10.1007/s00420-013-0860-2

Hietapakka, L., Elovainio, M., Heponiemi, T., Presseau, J., Eccles, M., & Aalto, A.-M. (2013). Do nurses who work in a fair organization sleep and perform better and why? Testing potential psychosocial mediators of organizational justice. *Journal of Occupational Health Psychology, 18*, 481–491. doi:10.1037/a0033990

Hintsanen, M., Puttonen, S., Smith, K., Törnroos, M., Jokela, M., Pulkki-Raback, L., . . . Keltikangas-Järvinen, L. (2014). Five-factor personality traits and sleep: Evidence from two population-based cohort studies. *Health Psychology, 33*, 1214–1223. doi:10.1037/hea0000105

Hülsheger, U. R., Lang, J. W. B., Depenbrock, F., Fehrmann, C., Zijlstra, F. R. H., & Alberts, H. J. E. M. (2014). The power of presence: The role of mindfulness at work for daily levels and change trajectories of psychological detachment and sleep quality. *The Journal of Applied Psychology, 99*, 1113–1128. doi:10.1037/a0037702

Ilies, R., Dimotakis, N., & De Pater, I. E. (2010). Psychological and physiological reactions to high workloads: Implications for well-being. *Personnel Psychology, 63*, 407–436. doi:10.1111/j.1744-6570.2010.01175.x

Ilies, R., Johnson, M. D., Judge, T. A., & Keeney, J. (2011). A within-individual study of interpersonal conflict as a work stressor: Dispositional and situational moderators. *Journal of Organizational Behavior, 32*, 44–64. doi:10.1002/job.677

Irish, L. A., Kline, C. E., Gunn, H. E., Buysse, D. J., & Hall, M. H. (2015). The role of sleep hygiene in promoting public health: A review of empirical evidence. *Sleep Medicine Reviews, 22*, 23–36. doi:10.1016/j.smrv.2014.10.001

Irwin, M. R. (2015). Why sleep is important for health: A psychoneuroimmunology perspective. *Annual Review of Psychology, 66*, 143–172. doi:10.1146/annurev-psych-010213-115205

Jansson-Fröjmark, M., & Lindblom, K. (2010). Is there a bidirectional link between insomnia and burnout? A prospective study in the Swedish workforce. *International Journal of Behavioral Medicine, 17*, 306–313. doi:10.1007/s12529-010-9107-8

Jones, F., & Fletcher, B. (1996). Taking work home: A study of daily fluctuations in work stressors, effects on moods and impacts on marital partners. *Journal of Occupational and Organizational Psychology, 69*, 89–106. doi:10.1111/j.2044-8325.1996.tb00602.x

Kahn, R. L., & Byosiere, P. (1992). Stress in organizations. In M. D. Dunnette & L. M. Hough (Eds.), *Handbook of industrial and organizational psychology* (2nd ed., Vol. 3, pp. 571–650). Palo Alto, CA: Consulting Psychologists Press.

Kalmbach, D. A., Pillai, V., Roth, T., & Drake, C. L. (2014). The interplay between daily affect and sleep: A 2-week study of young women. *Journal of Sleep Research, 23,* 636–645. doi:10.1111/jsr.12190

Kanazawa, H., Suzuki, M., Onoda, T., & Yokozawa, N. (2006). Excess workload and sleep-related symptoms among commercial long-haul truck drivers. *Sleep and Biological Rhythms, 4,* 121–128. doi:10.1111/j.1479-8425.2006.00218.x

Kecklund, G., & Åkerstedt, T. (2004). Apprehension of the subsequent working day is associated with a low amount of slow wave sleep. *Biological Psychology, 66,* 169–176. doi:doi:10.1016/j.biopsycho.2003.10.004

Knudsen, H. K., Ducharme, L. J., & Roman, P. M. (2007). Job stress and poor sleep quality: Data from an American sample of full-time workers. *Social Science and Medicine, 64,* 1997–2007. doi:10.1016/j.socscimed.2007.02.020

Kumari, M., Badrick, E., Ferrie, J., Perski, A., Marmot, M., & Chandola, T. (2009). Self-reported sleep duration and sleep disturbance are independently associated with cortisol secretion in the Whitehall II study. *The Journal of Clinical Endocrinology and Metabolism, 94,* 4801–4809. doi:10.1210/jc.2009-0555

Lallukka, T., Rahkonen, O., & Lahelma, E. (2011). Workplace bullying and subsequent sleep problems: The Helsinki health study. *Scandinavian Journal of Work, Environment and Health, 37,* 204–212. doi:10.5271/sjweh.3137

Lallukka, T., Rahkonen, O., Lahelma, E., & Arber, S. (2010). Sleep complaints in middle-aged women and men: The contribution of working conditions and work-family conflicts. *Journal of Sleep Research, 19,* 466–477. doi:10.1111/j.1365-2869.2010.00821.x

Linton, S. J., Kecklund, G., Franklin, K. A., Leissner, L. C., Sivertsen, B., & Lindberg, E. (2015). The effect of the work environment on future sleep disturbances: A systematic review. *Sleep Medicine Reviews, 23,* 10–19. doi:10.1016/j.smrv.2014.10.010

Loft, M., & Cameron, L. (2014). The importance of sleep: Relationships between sleep quality and work demands, the prioritization of sleep and pre-sleep arousal in day-time employees. *Work & Stress, 28,* 289–304. doi:10.1080/02678373.2014.935523

Lu, C.-q., Wang, H.-j., Lu, J.-j., Du, D.-y., & Bakker, A. B. (2014). Does work engagement increase person-job fit? The role of job crafting and job insecurity. *Journal of Vocational Behavior, 84,* 142–152. doi:10.1016/j.jvb.2013.12.004

Magnusson Hanson, L., Åkerstedt, T., Näswell, K., Leineweber, C., Theorell, T., & Westerlund, H. (2011). Cross-lagged relationships between workplace demands, control, support, and sleep problems. *Sleep, 34,* 1403–1410. doi:10.5665/SLEEP.1288

Martinez-Corts, I., Demerouti, E., Bakker, A. B., & Boz, M. (2015). Spillover of interpersonal conflicts from work into nonwork: A daily diary study. *Journal of Occupational Health Psychology, 20,* 326–337. doi:10.1037/a0038661

Maslach, C., Schaufeli, W. B., & Leiter, M. P. (2001). Job burnout. *Annual Review of Psychology, 52,* 397–422. doi:10.1146/annurev.psych.52.1.397

Mitchell, L., Mogg, K., & Bradley, B. P. (2012). Relationships between insomnia, negative emotionality and attention control. *Sleep and Biological Rhythms, 10,* 237–243. doi:10.1111/j.1479-8425.2012.00567.x

Mullins, H. M., Cortina, J. M., Drake, C. L., & Dalal, R. S. (2014). Sleepiness at work: A review and framework of how the physiology of sleepiness impacts the workplace. *Journal of Applied Psychology, 99,* 1096–1112. doi:10.1037/a0037885

Nakashima, M., Morikawa, Y., Sakurai, M., Nakamura, K., Miura, K., & Ishizaki, M. (2011). Association between long working hours and sleep problems in white-collar workers. *Journal of Sleep Research, 20*, 110–116. doi:10.1111/j.1365-2869.2010.00852.x

Ng, T. W. H., & Feldman, D. C. (2013). The effects of organisational embeddedness on insomnia. *Applied Psychology: An International Review, 62*, 330–357. doi:10.1111/j.1464-0597.2012.00522.x

Nicholson, T., & Griffin, B. (2015). Here today but gone tomorrow: Incivility affects after-work and next-day recovery. *Journal of Occupational Health Psychology, 20*, 218–225. doi:10.1037/a0038376

Niedhammer, I., David, S., Degioanni, S., Drummond, A., Philip, P., Acquarone, D., . . . Vital, N. (2009). Workplace bullying and sleep disturbances: Findings from a large scale cross-sectional survey in the French working population. *Sleep, 32*, 1211–1219.

Nielsen, M. B., & Einarsen, S. (2012). Outcomes of exposure to workplace bullying: A meta-analytic review. *Work & Stress, 26*, 309–332. doi:10.1080/02678373.2012.734709

Nixon, A. E., Mazzola, J. J., Bauer, J., Krueger, J. R., & Spector, P. E. (2011). Can work make you sick? A meta-analysis of the relationships between job stressors and physical symptoms. *Work & Stress, 25*, 1–22. doi:10.1080/02678373.2011.569175

Ota, A., Masue, T., Yasuda, M., Tsutsumi, A., Mino, Y., & Ohara, H. (2009). Psychosocial job characteristics and insomnia: A prospective cohort study using the Demand-Control-Support (DCS) and Effort-Reward Imbalance (ERI) job stress models. *Sleep Medicine, 10*, 1112–1117. doi:10.1016/j.sleep.2009.03.005

Park, Y., & Sprung, J. M. (2015). Weekly work-school conflict, sleep quality, and fatigue: Recovery self-efficacy as a cross-level moderator. *Journal of Organizational Behavior, 36*, 112–127. doi:10.1002/job.1953

Parkes, K. R. (2015). Shift rotation, overtime, age, and anxiety as predictors of offshore sleep patterns. *Journal of Occupational Health Psychology, 20*, 27–39. doi:10.1037/a0038164

Peng, H.-L., & Chang, Y.-P. (2013). Sleep disturbance in family caregivers of individuals with dementia: A review of the literature. *Perspectives in Psychiatric Care, 49*, 135–146. doi:10.1111/ppc.12005

Pereira, D., & Elfering, A. (2014). Social stressors at work and sleep during weekends: The mediating role of psychological detachment. *Journal of Occupational Health Psychology, 19*, 85–95. doi:10.1037/a0034928

Pereira, D., Meier, L. L., & Elfering, A. (2013). Short-term effects of social exclusion at work and worries on sleep. *Stress and Health, 29*, 240–252. doi:10.1002/smi.2461

Pereira, D., Semmer, N. K., & Elfering, A. (2014). Illegitimate tasks and sleep quality: An ambulatory study. *Stress and Health, 30*, 209–221. doi:10.1002/smi.2599

Piccioni, D., Cabrera, O. A., McGurk, D., Thomas, J. L., Castro, C. A., & Balkin, T. J. (2010). Sleep symptoms as a partial mediator between combat stressors and other mental health symptoms in Iraq war veterans. *Military Psychology, 22*, 340–355. doi:10.1080/089956052010491844

Pilcher, J. J., Lambert, B. J., & Huffcutt, A. I. (2000). Differential effects of permanent and rotating shifts on self-report sleep length: A meta-analytic review. *Sleep, 23*, 155–163.

Qi, X., Zhang, J., Liu, Y., Ji, S., Chen, Z., & Sluiter, J. K. (2014). Relationship between effort-reward imbalance and hair cortisol concentration in female kindergarten teachers. *Journal of Psychosomatic Research, 76*, 329–332. doi:10.1016/j.jpsychores.2014.01.008

Querstret, D., & Cropley, M. (2012). Exploring the relationship between work-related rumination, sleep quality, and work-related fatigue. *Journal of Occupational Health Psychology, 17*, 341–353. doi:10.1037/a0028552

Rau, R., & Triemer, A. (2004). Overtime in relation to blood pressure and mood during work, leisure, and night time. *Social Indicators Research, 67*, 51–73.

Richardson, K. M., & Rothstein, H. R. (2008). Effects of occupational stress management intervention programs: A meta-analysis. *Journal of Occupational Health Psychology, 13*, 69–93. doi:10.1037/1076-8998.13.1.69

Riemann, D., Spiegelhalder, K., Feige, B., Voderholzer, U., Berger, M., Perlis, M., & Nissen, C. (2010). The hyperarousal model of insomnia: A review of the concept and its evidence. *Sleep Medicine Reviews, 14*, 19–31. doi:10.1016/j.smrv.2009.04.002

Rodell, J. B., & Judge, T. A. (2009). Can "good" stressors spark "bad" behaviors? The mediating role of emotions in links of challenge and hindrance stressors with citizenship and counterproductive behaviors. *Journal of Applied Psychology, 94*, 1438–1451. doi:10.1037/a0016752

Rodríguez-Muñoz, A., Notelaers, G., & Moreno-Jiménez, B. (2011). Workplace bullying and sleep quality: The mediating role of worry and need for recovery. *Behavioral Psychology/Psicología Conductual: Revista Internacional Clínica Y de La Salud, 19*, 453–468

Roepke, S. E., & Duffy, J. F. (2010). Differential impact of chronotype on weekday and weekend sleep timing and duration. *Nature and Science of Sleep, 1*, 213–220. doi:10.2147/NSS.S12572

Rook, J. W., & Zijlstra, F. R. H. (2006). The contribution of various types of activities to recovery. *European Journal of Work and Organizational Psychology, 15*, 218–240. doi:10.1080/13594320500513962

Rousseau, D. M., Ho, V. T., & Greenberg, J. (2006). I-deals: Idiosyncratic terms in employment relationships. *Academy of Management Review, 31*, 977–994. doi:10.5465/AMR.2006.22527470

Schmidt, S., Roesler, U., Kusserow, T., & Rau, R. (2014). Uncertainty in the workplace: Examining role ambiguity and role conflict, and their link to depression—a meta-analysis. *European Journal of Work and Organizational Psychology, 23*, 91–106. doi:10.1080/1359432X.2012.711523

Scott, B. A., & Judge, T. A. (2006). Insomnia, emotions, and job satisfaction: A multilevel study. *Journal of Management, 32*, 622–645. doi: 10.1177/0149206306289762

Segerstrom, S. C., Stanton, A. L., Alden, L. E., & Shortridge, B. E. (2003). A multidimensional structure for repetitive thought: What's on your mind, and how, and how much? *Journal of Personality and Social Psychology, 85*, 909–921. doi:10.1037/0022-3514.85.5.909

Siegrist, J. (1996). Adverse health effects of high effort/low reward conditions. *Journal of Occupational Health Psychology, 1*, 27–41. doi:10.1037/1076-8998.1.1.27

Sonnentag, S. (2012). Psychological detachment from work during leisure time: The benefits of mentally disengaging from work. *Current Directions in Psychological Science, 21*, 114–118. doi:10.1177/0963721411434979

Sonnentag, S., Binnewies, C., & Mojza, E. J. (2008). "Did you have a nice evening?" A day-level study on recovery experiences, sleep, and affect. *Journal of Applied Psychology, 93*, 674–684. doi:10.1037/0021-9010.93.3.674

Sonnentag, S., Binnewies, C., & Mojza, E. J. (2010). Staying well and engaged when demands are high: The role of psychological detachment. *Journal of Applied Psychology, 95*, 965–976. doi:10.1037/a0020032

Sonnentag, S., & Frese, M. (2012). Stress in organizations. In N. W. Schmitt & S. Highhouse (Eds.), *Handbook of psychology. Volume 12: Industrial and organizational psychology* (2nd ed., pp. 560–592). Hoboken, NJ: John Wiley.

Sonnentag, S., & Fritz, C. (2007). The Recovery Experience Questionnaire: Development and validation of a measure for assessing recuperation and unwinding from work. *Journal of Occupational Health Psychology, 12*, 204–221. doi:10.1037/1076-8998.12.3.204

Sonnentag, S., & Fritz, C. (2015). Recovery from job stress: The stressor-detachment model as an integrative framework. *Journal of Organizational Behavior, 36*, S72–S103. doi:10.1002/job.1924

Spiegelhalder, K., Luchs, L., Ladwig, J., Kye, S. D., Nissen, C., & Voderholzer, U. (2011). Heart rate and heart rate variability in subjectively reported insomnia. *Journal of Sleep Research, 20,* 137–145. doi:10.1111/j.1365-2869.2010.00863.x

Stenfors, C. U. D., Magnusson Hanson, L., Oxenstierna, G., Theorell, R., & Nilsson, L.-G. (2013). Psychosocial working conditions and cognitive complaints among Swedish employees. *PLoS One, 8,* e60637. doi:10.1371/journal.pone.0060637

Stepanski, E. J., & Wyatt, J. K. (2003). Use of sleep hygiene in the treatment of insomnia. *Sleep Medicine Reviews, 7,* 215–225. doi:10.1053/smrv.2001.0246

Stoia-Caraballo, R., Rye, M. S., Pan, W., Brown Kirschman, K. J., Lutz-Zois, C., & Lyons, A. M. (2008). Negative affect and anger rumination as mediators between forgiveness and sleep quality. *Journal of Behavioral Medicine, 31,* 478–488. doi:10.1007/s10865-008-9172-5

Syrek, C., & Antoni, C. H. (2014). Unfinished tasks foster rumination and impair sleeping—particularly if leaders have high performance expectations. *Journal of Occupational Health Psychology, 19,* 490–499. doi:10.1037/a0037127

Ursin, H., & Eriksen, H. R. (2004). The cognitive activation theory of stress. *Psychoneuroendocrinology, 29,* 567–592. doi:10.1016/S0306-4530(03)00091-X

Vahle-Hinz, T., Bamberg, E., Dettmers, J., Friedrich, N., & Keller, M. (2014). Effects of work stress on work-related rumination, restful sleep, and nocturnal heart rate variability experience on workdays and weekends. *Journal of Occupational Health Psychology, 19,* 217–230. doi:10.1037/a0036009

van Hooff, M. L. M., Geurts, S. A. E., Kompier, M. A. J., & Taris, T. W. (2006). Work-home interference: How does it manifest itself from day to day? *Work and Stress, 20,* 145–162. doi:10.1080/02678370600915940

Van Laethem, M., Beckers, D. G. J., Kompier, M. A. J., Dijksterhuis, A., & Geurts, S. A. E. (2013). Psychosocial work characteristics and sleep quality: A systematic review of longitudinal and intervention research. *Scandinavian Journal of Work, Environment and Health, 39,* 535–549. doi:10.5271/sjweh.3376

Vrijkotte, T. G. M., Van Doornen, L. J. P., & De Geus, E. J. C. (2000). Effects of work stress on ambulatory blood pressure, heart rate, and heart rate variability. *Hypertension, 35,* 880–886. doi:10.1161/01.HYP.35.4.880

Wagner, D. T., Barnes, C. M., & Scott, B. A. (2014). Driving it home: How workplace emotional labor harms employee home life. *Personnel Psychology, 67,* 487–516. doi:10.1111/peps.12044

Walker, M. P., & Stickgold, R. (2006). Sleep, memory, and plasticity. *Annual Review of Psychology, 57,* 139–166. doi:10.1146/annurev.psych.56.091103.070307

Wang, M., Liu, S., Liao, H., Gong, Y., Kammeyer-Mueller, J., & Shi, J. (2013). Can't get it out of my mind: Employee rumination after customer mistreatment and negative mood in the next morning. *Journal of Applied Psychology, 98,* 989–1004. doi:10.1037/a0033656

Watkins, E. R. (2008). Constructive and unconstructive repetitive thought. *Psychological Bulletin, 134,* 163–206. doi:10.1037/0033-2909.134.2.163

Winwood, P. C., & Lushington, K. (2006). Disentangling the effects of psychological and physical work demands on sleep, recovery and maladaptive chronic stress within a large sample of Australian nurses. *Journal of Advanced Nursing, 56,* 679–689. doi:10.1111/j.1365-2648.2006.04055.x

Wright, K. M., Britt, T. W., Bliese, T. W., & Adler, A. B. (2011). Insomnia severity, combat exposure and mental health outcomes. *Stress and Health, 27,* 325–333. doi:10.1002/smi.1373

Wrzesniewski, A., & Dutton, J. E. (2001). Crafting a job: Revisioning employees as active crafters of their work. *Academy of Management Review, 26,* 179–201. doi:10.5465/AMR.2001.4378011

Zohar, D., Tzischinski, O., & Epstein, R. (2003). Effects of energy availability on immediate and delayed emotional reactions to work events. *Journal of Applied Psychology, 88,* 1082–1093. doi:10.1037/0021-9010.88.6.1082

## CHAPTER 6

# The Affective Implications of Sleep

J. JEFFREY GISH AND DAVID T. WAGNER

**THE AFFECTIVE IMPLICATIONS OF SLEEP**

Among the most fundamental forces driving human experience and behavior are moods and emotions. Emotions, which are intense and short lived, are generally caused by discrete events, whereas moods, typically muted and diffuse, are often caused by ambiguous or unclear stimuli. Affect is an umbrella term that encompasses both mood and emotion (Watson, 2000). Research on people from literate and preliterate cultures illustrates that the expression and experience of emotion are universal (Ekman & Friesen, 1971), suggesting that the implications of experienced affect are broadly relevant. The experience of affect serves many functions, ranging from the fundamental effects linked to happiness and well-being (e.g., Diener, Lucas, & Scollon, 2006) to the informational effects served by affect (e.g., Forgas & George, 2001; Schwarz & Clore, 1983). More germane to our current endeavor is research that highlights the connection between sleep and affect (Pilcher & Huffcutt, 1996), and work suggesting that affect and work performance are also linked (D. T. Wagner & Ilies, 2008).

To guide our discussion of the affective implications of sleep, and how these effects are relevant to the work domain, we build upon the Lazarus and Folkman (1984) tripartite model. In their model, they examine how reactions to stressful encounters influence affective, social, and physical outcomes. Given that other authors in this book deal directly with the physiological implications of sleep, we place our focus on the affective implications of sleep and sleep deprivation, closing with a discussion of the social implications of these affective reactions to sleep. We further organize our discussion by addressing outcomes construed as well-being and those more commonly interpreted as performance.

Toward this end, we first discuss research directly linking sleep to an individual's moods and emotions, examining both chronic as well as dynamic influences on these outcomes. We then discuss various moderators that range from individual differences to medication and behavioral interventions. Following this discussion of the fundamental implications of sleep for personal affect, we then discuss the implications of sleep and affect for personal well-being and performance, after which we turn to the social foils to these effects, for both social well-being and performance. Finally, we conclude with recommendations for scholars and practitioners.

## PROCESS OF SLEEP

Anecdotal evidence abounds linking a lack of sleep to negative moods. The workplace is filled with stories of employees who have lost sleep and subsequently subjected their co-workers to a cranky mood the following workday. Most workers have experience with such phenomena, and there is no dearth of academic investigation into sleep loss and resulting mood and emotional outcomes. An early study (Taub & Berger, 1976) found that when sleep is lost or shifted by 3 hours, mood and performance are both negatively affected. A logical question posed for empirical research on sleep is whether sleep influences mood or whether mood influences sleep. Berry and Webb (1985) correlated sleep and mood, measuring mood before a sleeping period, the amount of sleep that participants experienced, and mood the following day. This study provides some insight into directional effects, showing a greater correlation between the previous night's sleep and mood than between mood and subsequent sleep, suggesting that sleep plays a larger role in affecting mood than mood affects sleep.

Pilcher and Huffcutt (1996) conducted a helpful meta-analysis on literature that delves into the topic of sleep and its effect on cognition, motor skills, and mood. Their findings showed that sleep deprivation affected motor skills ($d = -0.087$), cognitive ability ($d = -1.55$), and mood ($d = -3.16$). A key conclusion of this meta-analysis was the disproportionately large effect of sleep deprivation on moods and emotions. The findings of Pilcher and Huffcutt (1996) undoubtedly spurred researchers to continue investigations into the powerful effect of sleep loss on affect.

Scholarly research continues to show sleep's dramatic influence on emotions. Although many studies contrast total sleep deprivation with control subjects, more benign changes to normal nightly sleep can also inhibit emotional regulation the next day (Wrzus, Wagner, & Riediger, 2014). Dinges et al. (1997) examined participant mood after a week of shorter-than-normal sleep and found that negative moods increase as nightly sleep suffers, and as days of consecutive sleep loss are strung together in succession, the negative effects are exacerbated. More than a decade later, Talbot, McGlinchey, Kaplan, Dahl, and Harvey (2010) delved deeper by investigating the effect of lost sleep on both positive and negative affect. They found that sleep-deprived individuals experience an increase in negative affect when experiencing negative events, and are unable to experience positive affect that would normally accompany positive experiences. Thus the emotional highs are not as high and the lows get even lower for people who get insufficient sleep.

Yoo, Gujar, Hu, Jolesz, and Walker (2007) approached the sleep and emotion question from a physiological perspective. They used functional magnetic resonance imaging (fMRI) to understand how the brain reacts to emotionally evocative stimuli when subjects are sleep deprived. Participants were placed in an fMRI scanner and presented with progressively more evocative visual stimuli. The scans analyzed the amount of activation in various regions of the brain. They found that the sleep-deprived group exhibited higher peak activation in the amygdala, with a greater percentage of total amygdala voxels activated within the sleep-deprived group. The study also noted that there was less activation in the medial prefrontal cortex (mPFC) for the sleep-deprived group, and the pathway between the amygdala and the mPFC, a conduit that they surmise is integral to emotional regulation, was almost nonexistent in those that had not slept. All this suggests that participants who had slept were more likely to utilize their higher-order mPFC to process the negative stimuli whereas the sleep-deprived group was more likely to use the primal response of the amygdala when faced with an evocative image. The authors suggest that the sleep-deprived group displayed a failure of top-down control of the primal amygdala response from the disrupted pathway between the mPFC and the amygdala; what this means is that the sleep-deprived group would be left poorly equipped to address emotionally charged situations.

One of the authors on the Yoo et al. (2007) study, Matthew Walker, continued this research on emotional regulation as it pertains to sleep loss (Walker, 2009). Walker again highlighted the disruption between the mPFC and the amygdala, citing it as an important factor for emotional regulation. Just like the Yoo et al. (2007) study, sleep-deprived individuals showed little mPFC control over heightened amygdala responses when emotional stimuli were presented. An additional contribution of Walker's (2009) paper is his theory that there is a rational chunk of memory surrounded by emotional baggage that he calls affective tone. The restorative process of sleep, especially the REM sleep cycle, helps us shed the affective tone associated with these memories, and Walker theorizes that recall is less influenced by emotion when we sleep well. In this regard, sleeping resets the ability to think logically about puzzles that we confront.

Researchers quickly put Walker's (2009) hypothesis to the test by investigating the amount of memory disruption experienced in research participants when exposed to negative and neutral picture stimuli (Chuah et al., 2010). The Chuah et al. (2010) study also used fMRI, and found that those individuals who viewed emotional pictures had more difficulty with a recall task they had been assigned to perform. Chuah et al. (2010) also observed a diminished connection between the limbic and prefrontal areas of the brain, which supported the earlier findings. The sleep-deprived individuals who experienced emotional distraction were less able to shed the emotional distraction and performed poorly on memory tests compared to those who had slept well and received the same distractors. Thus, Walker's (2009) affective tone hypothesis, which predicts that our factual and logical memories are surrounded by emotional shrouds until we shed those emotional layers through proper sleep, was supported by the Chuah et al. (2010) study.

As noted above, sleep has the ability to restore normal function of motor skills, cognition, and, most importantly for this chapter, emotional regulation. As we shed the affective tone of our memories through regular sleep, we are better able to approach life's challenges without unnecessary emotional baggage. Walker (2009) points out that our emotional baggage shields our access to logic that is located in our memories, memories that we rely on consistently for steady emotional well-being. When we sleep well, we are ready to call on the logic in those memories, and associated emotional information will have less effect on our judgment (Deliens & Peigneux, 2014). Furthermore, emotional regulation can be viewed as a limited resource (Hobfoll, 2002) that can be replenished by normal sleep. Lazarus and Folkman (1984) support the limited resource theory by conceding that positive outcomes in one emotional realm may be directly related to poor outcomes in another. If sleep is a restorative agent that replenishes our resource reserves, sleeping well gives us a better chance to react appropriately to emotional stimuli.

## CHRONIC SLEEP BEHAVIOR AND AFFECT

There is widespread support in the empirical literature that sleep deprivation, especially over long periods of time, leads to a greater incidence of negative mood and diminished positive mood. Moreover, sleep deprivation can have emotional implications: For example, Kahn-Greene and colleagues found that sleep deprivation leads to increased anxiety, paranoia, and depression (Kahn-Greene, Killgore, Kamimori, Balkin, & Killgore, 2007). Buysse et al. (2007) explain this phenomenon with the finding that consistently poor sleep negatively affects alertness, diminishes positive affect, and intensifies negative affect (see also Caldwell, Caldwell, Brown, & Smith, 2004; and Franzen, Siegle, & Buysse, 2008). This body of research suggests that sleepy humans are less able to appreciate the good events that happen during the day and are more likely to become irritated by negative events. If we think of experiencing positive affect and negative affect as riding a roller coaster, we still ride when short on sleep, experiencing ups and downs throughout the day, but the track on which we are riding is closer to the ground than it is when we sleep well.

## SEASONAL EFFECTS ON MOOD

Changing seasons influence our ability to fall asleep and stay asleep. As seasons change and days grow longer and shorter, especially for those living in extreme latitudes, the ever-changing zeitgeber of daily sunlight can wreak havoc on sleeping patterns (Friborg, Rosenvinge, Wynn, & Gradisar, 2014). Artificial adjustments to daily clocks, such as daylight saving time phase shifts, can modify sleep when other schedules remain constant (e.g., Barnes & Wagner, 2009). These phenomena have been investigated in the onset of seasonal affective disorder (SAD), suggesting that the irregularity of light, or shifting exposure to natural light, can impact moods and emotions (Lee, Rex, Nievergelt, Kelsoe, & Kripke, 2011; Murray et al., 2006). Indeed, Murray and colleagues (2006) suggested that exposing people to light when it had been a scarce resource in their life influenced their mood in the hypothesized direction, diminishing the effects of SAD, although their hypotheses did not reach traditional cutoff levels for statistical significance. In related research, Lee et al. (2011) found that individuals with delayed sleep-phase syndrome (DSPS) exhibited more waking hours at night and fewer during the day than the normal population, and those suffering from DSPS were 3.3 times more likely to report SAD compared to control groups. The authors suggest that the timing of bright light exposures in the winter season could attenuate SAD symptoms. Taken together, Murray et al. (2006) and Lee et al. (2011) support the importance of light for regular sleep and well-being.

By themselves, these findings are meaningful, but they become even more compelling when considering that those who live in extreme latitudes experience greater seasonal light changes than those who live closer to the equator. Moreover, the large seasonal fluctuations in the amount of sunlight inhabitants are exposed to correspond to shifts in seasonal temperature. These are nontrivial relationships as researchers have found that both temperature and sunlight give the human body cues about sleep that can impact our mood and well-being (Gillberg & Åkerstedt, 1982; LeGates, Fernandez, & Hattar, 2014), and people who are subjected to large oscillations in daytime sunlight and daily temperature should be aware of these effects.

## DYNAMIC EFFECTS OF SLEEP ON AFFECT

Diurnal variations in affect exist that are generalizable across populations. Whereas studies consistently point to a recognizable trend throughout the day for positive affect, very few have been able to mark a diurnal trend for negative affect (Watson, 2000). Murray, Allen, and Trinder (2002) found that positive affect follows our circadian rhythm, but negative affect does not. Watson (2000) surveyed college students over several days to investigate diurnal affective trends. Like most researchers before him, Watson (2000) did not find a significant trend in negative affect. However, he did report a trend on positive affect, which starts low in the morning, rises to a peak mid-afternoon, and begins a decline until the subjects rest again in the evening. Golder and Macy (2011) conducted a similar observation on a larger scale several years later, coding words associated with positive affect and negative affect that appeared on Twitter. Golder and Macy (2011) found a diurnal trend in positive affect, but this trend differed from the one Watson observed in college students. The Twitter observations showed peaks for positive affect just after waking and just before bed, with a small bump in positive affect mid-morning. Although the studies disagree on peak positive affect timing, both the Watson (2000) and the Golder and Macy (2011) observations recognize the restorative properties of sleep in their reports, further highlighting sleep's role in replenishing resource reserves.

The Watson (2000) and Golder and Macy (2011) studies both found diurnal trends in affect, but their peaks and valleys differed. This suggests that there may be differences in daily positive affect for different populations. Perhaps a regular Twitter user experiences daily affect different from a college student. In addition to these direct and cyclical factors linking sleep to affect, several researchers have investigated individual differences in personality and chronotype that might help explain these connections. These individual differences moderate how lost sleep affects different people in different ways, and in the next section, we identify and explain some of the moderators of lost sleep.

## MODERATORS

### Mindfulness

Hulsheger and colleagues suggest that mindfulness can help with emotional exhaustion (Hulsheger, Alberts, Feinholdt, & Lang, 2013). Mindfulness, hallmarked by a rational interpretation of evocative situations, facilitates effective management of emotional hurdles. Sleep aids the practice of mindfulness because sleep helps individuals shed affective tone associated with memories (Walker, 2009) and allows them to access rational memories without unhelpful emotional shrouds. According to Walker (2009), mindfulness can be achieved through sleep's restoration of limbic/prefrontal pathways that are important for emotional regulation (see also Yoo et al., 2007), and sleep's assistance in shedding affective tone associated with memories. It is through these pathways that proper sleep gives us a better chance to be mindful in our assessments and interactions. Greater mindfulness should yield more sensible reactions when we attempt to regulate our emotions. In this regard, sleep plays an important restorative role for physiological pathways that are integral to our regulation of emotions. So we are more likely to use top-down prefrontal management of our reactions, and recall logical portions of memories when we are well rested.

### Personality and Chronotype

There are daily trends in positive affect that will likely be affected by sleep, in other words a lack of sleep will diminish our ability to experience positive affect and amplify our experiences of negative affect (Dinges et al., 1997). Hobfoll (2002) argues that we lose emotional facilities or resources as the day goes on. However, the peaks and valleys of moods happen at different times for different people, some in the morning and some in the evening. Missing out on sleep simply does not affect mood and emotions the same way in every person, and personal traits help explain the differences. Horne and Ostberg (1976) were perhaps the first scholars to popularize the terms "lark" and "owl" for those people who function best in the morning and evening, respectively. Gunia, Barnes, and Sah (2014) recognize these morning/night patterns in their article on dynamic morality, suggesting that larks and owls have varying acrophases (cycle peaks) for moral decisions. Similarly, those who consider themselves morning people report different moods throughout the day than night owls (Horne & Ostberg, 1976). The Golder and Macy (2011) Twitter study also acknowledges that larks and night owls experience positive affect and negative affect at different times during the day. Moreover, each group in this study experienced its own independent rhythms for Twitter commentary around positive affect and negative affect, respectively, as evident in the weak correlation between the positive and negative reports ($r = -.08$).

When Watson (2000) discussed positive affect variation between larks and owls, he insisted that these individuals share the same shape of daily experience. That is, the larks and owls both have low positive affect in the morning and evening, reaching a peak sometime around mid-day; the owls just reach their peak later in the day than owls. Interestingly, the findings of Golder and Macy (2011) display a completely different trend for positive affect—almost completely opposite. One possibility is that this highlights the differences among observed samples, but it certainly calls for further research of within-individual trends in daily mood. The general consensus is that affect is moderated by individual morningness and eveningness, with lost sleep leading to decreased positive affect and heightened negative affect. Despite these findings, obtaining more sleep to ameliorate mood is not always an immediate possibility, which leads us to consider other moderators that might attenuate the effects of sleep deprivation on affective experience. We discuss these in the following sections.

## Medication

Many times a good night of sleep is not possible. There are, after all, only 24 hours in the day and many working professionals are frequently unable to fit work, leisure, family activities, and a full night of sleep into their daily lives. Because daily time is a resource that we cannot increase, one or more of these activities will have to be diminished when a daily schedule is overfilled. Research has found that sleep is often the activity to be cut first in the competition among activities (e.g., Basner & Dinges, 2009). Because sleep suffers among many busy individuals, it would be helpful if a medication were available to counteract the effects of lost sleep. Caffeine is one obvious solution to the problem. Many workers turn to caffeinated drinks such as coffee or tea to help restore their emotional and cognitive abilities. Other stimulants such as modafinil, dextroamphetamine, and pemoline have been used to counteract the noticeable effects of short sleep.

Drug moderation after sleep deprivation has received substantial attention in studies conducted by the United States military. Military training and work often call for irregular (and insufficient) sleep and military researchers are interested in mitigating the adverse effects that accompany lost sleep. Lieberman, Tharion, Shukitt-Hale, Speckman, and Tulley (2002) followed one of the most elite groups in the military, the Navy SEALs, and found that sleep loss hindered performance and mood, but that caffeine moderated these effects. Additional military studies investigated the effectiveness of the stimulant pemoline on sleep-deprived military members. For example, Kelly, Ryman, Schlangen, Gomez, and Elsmore (1997) focused mainly on cognitive performance during 64 hours of sleep deprivation, but they also included a self-assessment of mood. These researchers found suggestive evidence that pemoline use was related to diminished levels of tension compared to the no-drug control group. The differences were not statistically significant, but appeared promising since the mean effects were modified in the correct direction. In an earlier study, Babkoff et al. (1992) found that pemoline boosted alertness in sleepy military members, but did not influence emotions, suggesting the utility of pemoline in the area of cognitive performance. However, pemoline's effect on moods and emotions for sleep-deprived individuals still requires additional research to elucidate the drug's influence on emotions, if any exists.

Killgore, Rupp, et al. (2008) found that sleep-deprived individuals who ingested caffeine, modafinil, and dextroamphetamine performed better than a placebo group on psychomotor vigilance test reaction time, combined with fewer lapses in focus and better overall mood. This seems like good news for poor sleepers, but there were side effects associated with these drugs, such as nervousness, excitation, happiness, abdominal pain, and jitteriness. Additionally, stimulants can affect subsequent recovery sleep by inhibiting users' ability to fall asleep at a later point in time (Wesensten, Killgore, & Balkin, 2005). Some of these unintended consequences of stimulant use are obviously undesirable, but one side effect, namely happiness, is more ambiguous. Although seemingly positive, Killgore, Rupp, et al. (2008) suggest that side effects such as happiness and excitation increase the likelihood of addiction, making addiction or abuse a particular concern with a drug such as dextroamphetamine. Surprisingly, caffeine had the shortest duration of effect in psychomotor vigilance testing and the greatest number of side effects. However, caffeine was administered in one large dose in this study, which is not how coffee drinkers typically consume caffeine. The authors suggest that further research administering caffeine over longer durations would aid in better understanding caffeine's influence. Somewhat addressing this suggestion, Horne, Anderson, and Platten (2008) showed that caffeinated coffee can boost a subjectively reported afternoon dip in mood. In summary, stimulants such as caffeine, modafinil, dextroamphetamine, and pemoline have all shown promise in counteracting diminished mood and cognitive performance following lost sleep, but researchers warn that each drug's efficacy should be balanced with possible side effects while under the drug's influence.

## Naps

One way to combat sleep loss is very intuitive: Sleep when you can. This is the idea behind napping to supplement or replace the sleep that does not occur during normal sleeping hours. Dinges and Broughton (1989) define three different types of napping: (1) replacement napping in response to lost sleep in previous sleeping sessions, (2) prophylactic napping that supplements planned sleep loss in the future, and (3) appetitive napping for pleasure. We focus on replacement naps since the other two types are planned to achieve a future benefit. In contrast, replacement naps are a response to combat or moderate the ill effects of sleep deprivation. Empirical research on replacement naps highlights some promising benefits of napping.

One early study from Taub, Tanguay, and Clarkson (1974) investigated afternoon naps of varying lengths with college students. Taub and colleagues found self-reported mood arousal compared to the control condition, suggesting that mood can be enhanced by an afternoon nap. Many nap studies are summarized in the Milner and Cote (2009) review of adult napping, which points out that experience napping, length of nap, and time of day all influence the effectiveness of a nap's moderation of performance, self-reported sleepiness, and well-being. To elaborate on their findings: More experience with napping is better, length-of-nap "sweet spots" can be found for individuals that provide enough sleep to improve performance, but not so much sleep that nappers experience sleep inertia, as marked by grogginess or the need to return to sleep, and afternoons are better than mornings for naps. Horne et al. (2008) confirm that an afternoon nap will attenuate the dip in mood experienced when short on sleep.

What is an optimal-length nap? Researchers agree that a nap that is long enough to improve outcomes but not so long as to cause sleep inertia is ideal. Milner and Cote (2009) suggest that a 15 minute nap is better than 45 minutes or no nap, and Horne et al. (2008) indicate that 15–20 minutes is the "sweet spot." Research concurs that a nap of around 15 minutes is best for restoring depleted resources and avoiding sleep inertia.

Several studies suggest that the length of time since last sleep also contributes to a nap's effectiveness (e.g., Driskell & Mullen, 2005; Wiegand, Riemann, Schreiber, Lauer, & Berger, 1993) and Milner and Cote (2009) strongly recommend that future nap studies record length of time since last sleep in their results, supporting the theory that our cognitive and emotional resources are depleted while we are awake (Hobfoll, 2002). The more time we spend awake, the more we need the restoration that sleep provides. Sometimes a well-timed, appropriate-length nap is sufficient to restore resources before the main event of nighttime sleep. Given the practical utility of naps and the clear benefit, this is an area of emphasis on which we encourage practitioners and researchers to focus.

## PERSONAL IMPLICATIONS

Having addressed the effects of sleep on mood and emotion, as well as the factors that can mitigate or exacerbate these effects, we now shift our lens in order to highlight implications of these findings for both personal well-being and performance. In doing so, we further emphasize the relevance of these findings for individuals and the workplace.

As Hobfoll (2002) notes, we are more likely to deal well with life's puzzles if we have resource reserves. Many of life's puzzles involve effectively dealing with moods and emotions, with the result of such effective emotion management being better performance and emotional well-being. These puzzles are more efficiently solved with readily available resource reserves that can be recharged through sleep. Our emotional resource reserves, those facilities that we can access to regulate emotional response, are depleted when we are awake and replenished or reset with sleep (Dinges et al., 1997; Walker, 2009). We use resources to solve emotional puzzles, and depletion carries widespread implications for subsequent moods and emotions. Resource depletion can directly influence well-being by undercutting affect, but such depletion has additional, indirect effects on well-being (which we will discuss later in the chapter), because well-being is also contingent upon and has bearing on social interactions inside and outside the workplace. As a result, sleep quality and quantity are vital antecedents for employee well-being because when sleep suffers, so do employees' social lives (Totterdell, Reynolds, Parkinson, & Briner, 1994).

Sleep quantity is positively correlated with self-assessments of well-being (Yokoyama et al., 2008), and one possible reason for this is that we experience diminished mood when we do not get enough sleep. Empirical studies on sleep deprivation show a direct and mostly negative effect on mood (Pilcher & Huffcutt, 1996). Negative affect is amplified during sleepy periods and positive affect is diminished (Dinges et al., 1997; Talbot et al., 2010). In this regard, a lack of sleep makes bad experiences appear worse and decreases the positive effect of good experiences. Because of this, our sleep, or lack thereof, has the potential to influence various social spheres through its impact on moods and emotions.

Especially relevant to well-being in the workplace is evidence that poor sleep can decrease job satisfaction (Kroth, Daline, Longstreet, Nelson, & O'Neal, 2002; Scott & Judge, 2006), bring on additional work–family conflict (Allen & Kiburz, 2012), diminish marital satisfaction (Messmer, Miller, & Yu, 2012), and even decrease our ability to pick up on emotional cues displayed by people with whom we interact (van der Helm, Gujar, & Walker, 2010). First, we will address the construct of job satisfaction.

*Job satisfaction.* Job satisfaction is defined as "multidimensional psychological responses to one's job. These responses have cognitive (evaluative), affective (or emotional), and behavioral components. Job satisfactions refer to internal cognitive and affective states accessible by means of verbal—or other behavioral—and emotional responses" (Hulin & Judge, 2003, p. 259). There is a growing body of evidence showing that diminished sleep is associated with lower job satisfaction, likely because job satisfaction inherently includes both cognitive and affective elements. One Brazilian study of nurses (Luz, Marqueze, & Moreno, 2010) found a significant relationship between sleep quality and job satisfaction ($r = .41$). A study in Turkey (Merrey, Piskin, Boysan, & Sehribanoglu, 2013) reported that teachers who sleep poorly experience greater emotional exhaustion and a higher incidence of job burnout, with low levels of job satisfaction listed as a primary culprit. Kroth et al. (2002) conducted a cross-industry study that found a significant correlation between subjectively rated sleepiness and job satisfaction ($r = -.30$). Soderstrom, Jeding, Ekstedt, Perski, and Åkerstedt (2012) provide further evidence in a 388-participant longitudinal study that identifies 15 employees as burnout cases. When interpreting their results, Soderstrom and colleagues identified too little sleep (less than 6 hours) as the top factor in a chain of events that leads to burnout.

Insomnia's effect on job satisfaction, as mediated by emotional toll, was observed by Scott and Judge (2006) in a study that followed 45 employees over 3 weeks. They found that a sustained loss of sleep led to higher fatigue and hostility and lower joviality and attentiveness. Scott and Judge (2006) also found that job satisfaction was diminished by insomnia. Their results support the notion that emotions mediate the relationship between insomnia and job satisfaction. Guglielmi, Juardo-Gamez, Gude, and Buela-Casal (2014) replicate these findings in a similar observation of employed sleep apnea patients. These studies all find that poor sleep is associated with lower job satisfaction, with many of the studies showing evidence of emotional exhaustion and negative affect as powerful mediators. This suggests that our moods and emotions play a significant role in our attitudes about work, and the quality and quantity of our sleep will influence job satisfaction through their influence on moods and emotions. Consistent sleep loss and emotional depletion over time are associated with diminished job satisfaction and can lead to employee burnout. These empirical studies suggest that emotional reserves are valuable resources for improving job satisfaction. Most employee routines include heading home after work. When we head home, we take the emotions that we experience throughout the day with us. This becomes especially important when a family awaits our arrival after the work day.

**Work–family conflict.** Many employees are concerned with balancing their work and family time, and this balancing act results in conflict when work or family requires more time than is available. Additionally, work requiring high emotional regulation will increase the likelihood that the worker is emotionally depleted when interacting with family after work; indeed the conflict can be time or strain based. Sleep enters this conflict in several ways: directly when we need sleep but the time available to do so is scarce, and indirectly when we do not get enough sleep making it difficult to regulate our emotions the following day. Failed emotional regulation can directly hamper relationships, but can also make engaging in emotional labor necessary for employees to meet organizational display rules. As our past research has shown, engaging in surface acting at work on a given day is positively linked to work–family conflict and negatively linked to that evening's sleep (D. T. Wagner, Barnes, & Scott, 2014), suggesting that both emotional and sleep deficits can have reciprocal effects that result in continuing harm.

Effective emotional regulation at home requires effort. Allied streams of research suggest mechanisms for addressing this emotional regulation through a concept called mindfulness, or giving effort to regulate emotions, thereby responding rationally to issues that we face. Current research acknowledges that mindfulness is a tool that can assist emotional regulation, and researchers do not ignore the fact that emotional regulation can affect the use of mindfulness as well. Hulsheger et al. (2013) connect mindfulness to emotional regulation, suggesting that increased trait, state, and brief mindfulness will yield better emotional regulation, and Allen and Kiburz (2012) aid in understanding how sleep quality mediates the relationship between trait mindfulness and work–family balance. Allen and Kiburz (2012) found that employees who are mindful will report better work–life balance and higher sleep quality, and that those who sleep well are more likely to be mindful at work and at home. A well-rested person will have greater emotional reserves, will be more likely to be mindful at work and at home, and will report better work–life balance. Starting the day with inadequate sleep and an empty resource tank only decreases the likelihood that there is any emotional regulation fuel left at the end of the day when it is time to interact with family. In this regard, tired employees will experience more work–family conflict than well-rested ones.

*Emotional intelligence.* We have shown that sleep deprivation affects our emotions, but when we are low on sleep are we able to recognize our emotional shortcomings or use emotions effectively? As usual, the answer is, it depends. Some people are naturally better than others at gauging their emotional state, such that they recognize their emotional highs and lows using what is known as emotional intelligence (EQ). Killgore, Kahn-Greene, et al. (2008) found that sleep deprivation resulted in lower EQ scores compared to a group with normal sleep. Intrapersonal functioning, impulse control, and logical thinking were all reduced in the sleep deprived group. The authors suggested that these findings support neurobehavioral models that suggest mild prefrontal lobe dysfunction following sleep deprivation. These results are also congruent with fMRI evidence that suggests that the limbic–prefrontal pathway is disrupted by sleep loss (viz. Chuah et al., 2010; Walker, 2009; Yoo et al., 2007).

## Performance

### Emotional regulation.

As already noted, losing sleep diminishes our ability to regulate emotions, and poor emotional regulation can have myriad effects on performance in the workplace. Low quantity and poor quality sleep increase the likelihood that an unregulated limbic reaction will manage behavior (Walker, 2009; Yoo et al., 2007). Fortunately, proper prefrontal management of limbic portions of the brain can be restored through regular sleep, and can preempt knee-jerk regulation of emotions. Because regular prefrontal regulation of emotions should positively assist our interactions with supervisors, subordinates, and co-workers we will elaborate on the social performance implications of sleep as they relate to emotional regulation in the final section of this chapter.

*Creativity.* Several creativity studies feature a direct link between sleep and creative thought. According to Ritter, Strick, Bos, Van Baaren, and Dijksterhuis (2012), we can prime ourselves during sleep to be more creative. Ritter and colleagues

(2012) suggest that creativity tasks can be revisited while sleeping by using familiar odors, introduced during the wakeful creativity task and again when the participant is asleep. The introduction of the odor covertly reactivates the creativity task and leads to greater insight. This suggests that some of our creativity occurs when we are asleep, but lends new information to the theory that sleep improves creativity. U. Wagner, Gais, Haider, Verleger, and Born (2004) found that sleepy participants had greater difficulty in finding a nonobvious but creative solution to complete a number sequence. Well-rested participants were significantly better at finding the creative solution that sped their work to find subsequent solutions. In a separate study, Cai, Mednick, Harrison, Kanady, and Mednick (2009) used a nap paradigm that showed that sleep, especially REM sleep, boosted creative problem solving. Whereas research frequently cites cognition as an antecedent to creativity, there is a significant body of literature on emotional contributions to creativity (e.g., Averill, 1999; Lubart & Getz, 1997). The debate continues as to whether creativity is cognitively or emotionally driven, but the focus of this chapter will remain on emotional effects on creativity and whether sleep helps or hinders those effects.

Although the literature lacks a clear path linking good sleep to greater creativity through mood, several studies indicate that sleep leads directly to both of the latter outcomes. Thus, if better sleep can enhance creativity, it is plausible that moods and emotions mediate that relationship. In an early study of the effects of mood on creativity, Isen, Daubman, and Nowicki (1987) found that comedy films and candy heightened the mood of study participants and improved their performance on tasks that require creative thinking. In related research, Erez and Isen (2002) found that positive affect boosted expectancy motivation, in other words the belief that effort will result in performance, which should have a positive influence on creativity. Erez and Isen (2002) argue that positive affect has a significant influence on the initiation of this effort.

Interestingly, George and Zhou (2007) suggested that both positive and negative affect can positively influence creativity in the workplace if there is a supportive context for creativity in the work setting. George and Zhou (2007) found that supervisors could facilitate subordinates' creativity by providing a work environment that fosters trust, provides developmental feedback, and displays justice in interactions. If such supportive environments exist, employees can be creative when experiencing both positive and negative moods.

In a longitudinal study of 222 workers, Amabile, Barsade, Mueller, and Staw (2005) found that positive affect was an antecedent of creative thought, and that creative thought then influenced affect in a positive fashion. In this regard, a positive workplace would be expected to lead to creativity, which could beget incremental positive affect and morale. It is possible that sleep similarly influences this cycle.

Throughout this chapter we have shown that sleep positively influences affective outcomes. Although we still experience both positive and negative affect whether we sleep well or not, good sleep helps raise the peaks of positive affect and diminish the valleys of negative affect. Empirical research suggests that this phenomenon should assist in creative endeavors, especially when employees work in a supportive environment.

## INTERPERSONAL IMPLICATIONS

Thus far, we have shown that sleep plays a powerful role in driving individual mood and emotions, which also influence individuals' well-being and performance in different contexts. Despite the importance of these outcomes, they are only part of the narrative describing the connections between sleep and affect. To further explain the relationship between sleep and affect, we focus our final discussion on the social consequences of sleep and sleep deprivation.

In addition to the important role that sleep plays in personal mood and emotion, and in turn on individual well-being and performance, one of the fundamental presumptions of the social-functional approach to emotions (Frijda, 2000; Keltner & Haidt, 1999) is that conveyed emotions provide information to observers that then influences the behaviors in which those observers engage. Research in a broad range of settings, from leadership to negotiation to parent–child relationships, has shown these informational effects. Van Kleef (2009) elegantly consolidated these findings into the emotions as social information (EASI) model, which frames this body of research as influencing observers through two primary channels: affective reactions to the expressed emotion and inferential processes in which sense is made of the expressed emotion.

To briefly summarize these processes, we point out that affective reactions to emotional expressions can occur for various reasons. First, social interactions can be affected because expressed emotions can spread to observers through a process called emotional contagion (Ilies, Wagner, & Morgeson, 2007; Pugh, 2001; Totterdell, 2000), as when observers mimic and subsequently experience the sender's expressed emotions (Hatfield & Cacioppo, 1994). Another means by which expressed emotions influence observers is through the influence of emotions on "social intentions and relational orientations" (Van Kleef, 2009, p. 186). More specifically, the expression of certain emotions may lead an observer to feel enhanced liking or positive impressions of the individual. Such enhanced liking of the individual could then lead to several advantageous outcomes for the individual expressing the emotion, because people tend to treat those who they like more favorably.

A second way in which emotions can influence observers is through the inferences the observers make about the individual's underlying attitudes, feelings, or intentions (Keltner & Haidt, 1999; Van Kleef, 2009). For instance, anger suggests that the individual has failed to reach a goal and views another individual as the cause of this failure (Smith, Haynes, Lazarus, & Pope, 1993), whereas an expression of happiness suggests that the individual is succeeding or doing well, and sadness communicates that the individual may have experienced some sort of loss. In each of these instances, the emotion conveys information to the observer that in turn can be used to make inferences about the observer's role in these emotions (e.g., I triggered the individual's anger).

In light of these socioinformational functions of expressed emotions, it is reasonable to expect that the implications of sleep and sleep deprivation extend beyond individual outcomes to also affect social well-being and performance. In the following sections, we survey research linking sleep to these social outcomes.

## Social Well-Being

Emerging research suggests that sleep can influence critical relationships in the work domain, such as those between supervisors and subordinates. A recent study examined how supervisors' daily sleep patterns impact the manner in which their subordinates engage in their daily work. Barnes and colleagues (Barnes, Lucianetti, Bhave, & Christian, 2015) conducted a 2-week experience sampling study of Italian managers and their subordinates. Each morning of the study the supervisors reported on the quality of their sleep the prior night (operationalized as wakefulness after sleep onset) and the extent to which they were experiencing high levels of ego depletion (i.e., low levels of self-control). After work each day, subordinates reported the number of abusive behaviors in which the supervisor had engaged at work that day, as well as their own work engagement that day. These researchers found that the quality of a supervisor's sleep on a given night predicted the extent to which the supervisor engaged in abusive supervision on the following day, which in turn predicted the work engagement of subordinates that day. Not only does this provide further evidence that our sleep patterns influence leadership behaviors, but it also shows how the sleep patterns of one person impacts the work-relevant emotions of others. The implication is that after a poor night's sleep, not only will supervisors feel grumpy and exercise inadequate self-control, but they are also likely to hamper the emotional engagement of employees in their own work, signaling a cascading effect of supervisor behavior onto subordinate emotion.

Among the most important relationships in many people's lives is the one they enjoy with a spouse or partner. As we discussed earlier in this chapter, several studies have found evidence that sufficient and high-quality sleep leads people to have better attitudes about their marriages (e.g., Billman & Ware, 2002; Messmer et al., 2012). On their own, these findings might provide good enough reason for well-intentioned spouses to spend more time and make better use of their time between the sheets. However, recent research by Gordon and Chen (2014) revealed that sleep was negatively related to relationship conflict; moreover, they found that when resolving conflict, subjects who had obtained low levels of sleep before attempting to resolve conflict showed lower empathic accuracy and expressed a lower ratio of positive to negative emotions. In addition to these personal effects, Gordon and Chen (2014) also found that subjects' sleep was negatively related to their partner's empathic accuracy, which is to say that people who get insufficient sleep are more difficult to "read" emotionally.

Taken together, these studies suggest that sleep does not merely affect the person who slumbers, but also affects those with whom the individual interacts. Moreover, although the preceding studies suggest harmful consequences for outcomes that are often framed as well-being constructs, these constructs also have relevance for the individual's performance in work domains (e.g., conflict resolution, work engagement). It is to this final connection—the link between sleep and social performance—that we now turn our attention.

## Social Performance

As the chapters throughout this book emphasize, sleep has a powerful influence on a wide range of outcomes relevant to the work domain. In their meta-analysis of the effects of sleep deprivation, Pilcher and Huffcutt (1996) found that despite the powerful effect of sleep on motor function and cognitive outcomes, the impact of sleep on mood was two to three times stronger than the effects on these other types of outcomes. Given these powerful effects, we naturally seek to elaborate upon how these affective consequences impact measurables that matter to organizations. In this final section we elaborate upon the implications of sleep deprivation for performance in social contexts.

### Emotional Labor

We begin by noting that working adults who suffer from insomnia tend to view themselves as less efficient and less energetic at work (Leger, Massuel, Metlaine, & The SISYPHE Study Group, 2006). Giving particular attention to work that requires the exertion of emotional effort, this energy deficit for those who suffer from chronic low amounts of sleep might translate into poor performance for those who deliver emotional content as a core part of their work, for example, customer service (Hochschild, 1983).

Several studies linking sleep to workplace settings help us arrive at this conclusion. First, self-control is a limited resource and its use depletes the actor over the short run (Muraven, Tice, & Baumeister, 1998) and Baumeister and colleagues have posited that sleep is an important resource that can restore self-regulatory resources (Baumeister, Muraven, & Tice, 2000). Empirical research in recent years has validated this view, with researchers finding that sleep deprivation hampers the self-regulation necessary to suppress unethical and prejudicial behaviors (Barnes, Schaubroeck, Huth, & Ghumman, 2011; Ghumman & Barnes, 2013) as well as motivational behaviors such as cyberloafing (D. T. Wagner, Barnes, Lim, & Ferris, 2012). Ineffective self-regulation not only makes it difficult to keep oneself in a desired behavioral state, but leads to problems for those whose workplaces mandate service with a particular affective tone. Such requirements are called emotional display rules and provide the framework for employee performance in many service contexts. Most common among these are integrative display rules, which specify the need to suppress negative emotions and amplify positive emotions when engaging with a customer (Grandey, 2000). The result of these efforts is the prototypical "service with a smile." As we have noted, with inadequate sleep quality, people are likely to experience reduced positive and enhanced negative affective states. Because these states do not fit the display rules dictated by most organizations, employees are generally faced with one of two options. The first option is to mask emotions through a process called surface acting, in which employees fake a particular set of prescribed emotions while suppressing inconsistent emotions. The second option is to engage in deep acting, which requires employees to experience the prescribed emotions through processes such as cognitive reappraisal of the situation.

Not only does sleep deprivation place service employees in a state that is likely to be inconsistent with organizational display rules, but it also threatens the ability of employees to self-regulate in a way that allows them to satisfy the display rules. This self-regulation often requires both the suppression of emotions that are inconsistent with the display rules (Srivastava, Tamir, McGonigal, John, & Gross, 2009) as well as the often insincere expression of emotions that are aligned with the job's requirements. The consequence of this is that when employees suffer from inadequate sleep, they are likely to exhibit poor emotional performance at work because sleep deprivation places them in a poor affective state and limits the self-regulatory resources they could otherwise use to meet organizational display rules. Concern around these findings is further heightened given that efforts to meet display rules through surface acting subsequently hinders sleep (D. T. Wagner et al., 2014), which could give rise to a vicious cycle of poor sleep and poor work performance.

Further exacerbating the issues involved in emotional labor, sleep-deprived individuals have more difficulty perceiving and processing emotional signals (e.g., Gordon & Chen, 2014; Killgore, Kahn-Greene, et al., 2008; van der Helm et al., 2010), are prone to distraction by negative emotional stimuli (Chuah et al., 2010), and are less able to deal with mild stressors, which means that even typically manageable challenges can become overwhelming on inadequate sleep (Minkel et al., 2012). In summary, although direct evidence linking sleep to emotional performance is limited, related evidence indicates that inadequate sleep could hamper performance of emotion-laden roles, especially for those involved in customer relations.

### Emotion and Counterproductive Work Behavior

In addition to the implications of sleep deprivation for a narrow range of jobs that require emotional delivery as part of the product, inadequate or insufficient sleep also has implications for other pervasive workplace behaviors such as workplace deviance. For example, Christian and Ellis (2011) showed that nurses were more likely to feel higher levels of hostility and less self-regulatory strength on a day following inadequate sleep. At the end of the 12-hour work shift the nurses were asked to report on the extent to which they had engaged in workplace deviance, including interpersonal behaviors such as saying something hurtful to someone at work. Their findings revealed that sleep-deprived nurses exhibited higher levels of workplace deviance, with both self-regulation and hostility mediating the effects of sleep deprivation on deviance. In a follow-up study, Christian and Ellis (2011) found in a laboratory experiment that sleep-deprived participants were more likely to steal unearned money during the study and to treat other people poorly (interpersonal deviance via email), and that these effects were again mediated by state hostility and self-control. These findings show that the effects of sleep deprivation go beyond emotions and performance in emotion-focused jobs, and spill over into general work contexts, again through the effects on employee emotions.

## CONCLUSIONS

In this chapter we set out to describe the affective consequences of inadequate or low-quality sleep, particularly as those affective outcomes relate to work and other important life domains. We outlined how poor sleep can impact people's moods and emotions, which in turn influence valued personal outcomes such as job and marital satisfaction, work–family conflict, and performance in work contexts, such as those requiring emotional regulation or creativity. Moreover, these effects are not restricted to individual outcomes, but also have social implications (Van Kleef, 2009). Specifically, we emphasized how sleep is meaningfully tied to one's own moods as well as those of the individual's partner. Moreover, sleep appears to impact the ability of romantic partners to accurately perceive one another's emotions and to effectively resolve conflict (Gordon & Chen, 2014). Similar research primarily in the work domain has shown that supervisor sleep is a critical factor that drives employee behaviors (Barnes et al., 2015).

In addition to the harm that poor sleep causes to close relationships at work and elsewhere, we reviewed evidence linking sleep to performance in a variety of work contexts requiring self-regulation, such as jobs that often entail emotional labor. Likewise, sleep and affect appear to again join forces to drive workers to engage in the unsavory side of business, as those who are less well rested tend to exhibit deviant behavior through harmful interpersonal or monetary means (Christian & Ellis, 2011).

The connection between sleep, mood, and emotions influences everyone. This connection impacts many workplace processes, behaviors, and outcomes. Having used this chapter to establish the affective mechanisms stemming from sleep, we now segue into the remaining chapters that elaborate on the impact of sleep on work, often through the channels we have explored above.

## REFERENCES

Allen, T. D., & Kiburz, K. M. (2012). Trait mindfulness and work–family balance among working parents: The mediating effects of vitality and sleep quality. *Journal of Vocational Behavior, 80,* 372–379. doi:10.1016/j.jvb.2011.09.002

Amabile, T. M., Barsade, S. G., Mueller, J. S., & Staw, B. M. (2005). Affect and creativity at work. *Administrative Science Quarterly, 50,* 367–403. doi:10.2189/asqu.2005.50.3.367

Averill, J. R. (1999). Creativity in the domain of emotion. In T. Dalgleish & M. J. Power (Eds.), *Handbook of cognition and emotion* (pp. 765–782). Chichester, UK: Wiley. doi:10.1002/0470013494

Babkoff, H., Kelly, T. L., Matteson, L. T., Gomez, S. A., Lopez, A., Hauser, S., . . . Assmus, J. (1992). Pemoline and methylphenidate, interaction with mood, sleepiness, and cognitive performance during 64 hours of sleep deprivation. *Military Psychology, 4,* 235–265. doi:10.1207/s15327876mp0404_3

Barnes, C. M., Lucianetti, L., Bhave, D., & Christian, M. S. (2015). You wouldn't like me when I'm sleepy: Leader sleep, daily abusive supervision, and work unit engagement. *Academy of Management Journal, 58,* 813–845. doi:10.5465/amj.2013.1063

Barnes, C. M., Schaubroeck, J., Huth, M., & Ghumman, S. (2011). Lack of sleep and unethical conduct. *Organizational Behavior and Human Decision Processes, 115,* 169–180. doi:10.1016/j.obhdp.2011.01.009

Barnes, C. M., & Wagner, D. T. (2009). Changing to daylight saving time cuts into sleep and increases workplace injuries. *Journal of Applied Psychology, 94,* 1305–1317. doi:10.1037/a0015320

Basner, M., & Dinges, D. F. (2009). Dubious bargain: Trading sleep for leno and letterman. *Sleep, 32,* 747–752.

Baumeister, R. F., Muraven, M., & Tice, D. M. (2000). Ego depletion: A resource model of volition, self-regulation, and controlled processing. *Social Cognition, 18,* 130–150. doi:10.1521/soco.2000.18.2.130

Berry, D. T. R., & Webb, W. B. (1985). Mood and sleep in aging women. *Journal of Personality and Social Psychology, 49,* 1724–1727. doi:10.1037// 0022-3514.49.6.1724

Billman, S. J., & Ware, J. C. (2002). Marital satisfaction of wives of untreated sleep apneic men. *Sleep Medicine, 3,* 55–59. doi:10.1016/S1389-9457(01)00118-6

Buysse, D. J., Thompson, W., Scott, J., Franzen, P. L., Germain, A., Hall, M., . . . Kupfer, D. J. (2007). Daytime symptoms in primary insomnia: A prospective analysis using ecological momentary assessment. *Sleep Medicine, 8,* 198–208. doi:10.1016/ j.sleep.2006.10.006

Cai, D. J., Mednick, S. A., Harrison, E. M., Kanady, J. C., & Mednick, S. C. (2009). REM, not incubation, improves creativity by priming associative networks. *Proceedings of the National Academy of Sciences of the United States of America, 106,* 10130–10134. doi:10.1073/pnas.0900271106

Caldwell, J. A., Jr., Caldwell, J. L., Brown, D. L., & Smith, J. K. (2004). The effects of 37 hours of continuous wakefulness on the physiological arousal, cognitive performance, self-reported mood, and simulator flight performance of F-117A pilots. *Military Psychology, 16,* 163–181. doi:10.1207/s15327876mp1603_2

Christian, M. S., & Ellis, A. P. J. (2011). Examining the effects of sleep deprivation on workplace deviance: A self-regulatory perspective. *Academy of Management Journal, 54,* 913–934. doi:10.5465/amj.2010.0179

Chuah, L. Y. M., Dolcos, F., Chen, A. K., Zheng, H., Parimal, S., & Chee, M. W. L. (2010). Sleep deprivation and interference by emotional distractors. *Sleep, 33,* 1305–1313.

Deliens, G., & Peigneux, P. (2014). One night of sleep is insufficient to achieve sleep-to-forget emotional decontextualisation processes. *Cognition and Emotion, 28,* 698–706. doi:10.1080/02699931.2013.844105

Diener, E., Lucas, R. E., & Scollon, C. N. (2006). Beyond the hedonic treadmill: Revising the adaptation theory of well-being. *American Psychologist, 61,* 305. doi:10.1037/ 0003-066X.61.4.305

Dinges, D. F., & Broughton, R. J. (1989). *Sleep and alertness: chronobiological, behavioral, and medical aspects of napping.* New York, NY: Raven Press.

Dinges, D. F., Pack, F., Williams, K., Gillen, K. A., Powell, J. W., Ott, G. E., . . . Pack, A. I. (1997). Cumulative sleepiness, mood disturbance, and psychomotor vigilance performance decrements during a week of sleep restricted to 4–5 hours per night. *Sleep, 20,* 267–277.

Driskell, J. E., & Mullen, B. (2005). The efficacy of naps as a fatigue coutermeasure: A meta-analytic integration. *Human Factors, 47,* 360–377. doi:10.1518/0018720054679498

Ekman, P., & Friesen, W. V. (1971). Constants across cultures in the face and emotion. *Journal of Personality and Social Psychology, 17,* 124. doi:10.1037/h0030377

Erez, A., & Isen, A. M. (2002). The influence of positive affect on the components of expectancy motivation. *Journal of Applied Psychology, 87,* 1055. doi:10.1037/ 0021-9010.87.6.1055

Forgas, J. P., & George, J. M. (2001). Affective influences on judgments and behavior in organizations: An information processing perspective. *Organizational Behavior and Human Decision Processes, 86,* 3–34. doi:10.1006/obhd.2001.2971

Franzen, P. L., Siegle, G. J., & Buysse, D. J. (2008). Relationships between affect, vigilance, and sleepiness following sleep deprivation. *Journal of Sleep Research, 17,* 34–41. doi:10.1111/j.1365-2869.2008.00635.x

Friborg, O., Rosenvinge, J. H., Wynn, R., & Gradisar, M. (2014). Sleep timing, chronotype, mood, and behavior at an Arctic latitude (69 degrees N). *Sleep Medicine, 15,* 798–807. doi:10.1016/j.sleep.2014.03.014

Frijda, N. H. (2000). Emotions. In K. Pawlik & M. R. Rosenzweig (Eds.), *The international handbook of psychology* (pp. 207–222). London, UK: Sage. doi:10.4135/9781848608399.n12

George, J. M., & Zhou, J. (2007). Dual tuning in a supportive context: Joint contributions of positive mood, negative mood, and supervisory behaviors to employee creativity. *Academy of Management Journal, 50,* 605–622. doi:10.5465/AMJ.2007.25525934

Ghumman, S., & Barnes, C. M. (2013). Sleep and prejudice: A resource recovery approach. *Journal of Applied Social Psychology, 43,* E166–E178. doi:10.1111/jasp.12045

Gillberg, M., & Åkerstedt, T. (1982). Body temperature and sleep at different times of day. *Journal of Sleep Research & Sleep Medicine, 5,* 378–388.

Golder, S. A., & Macy, M. W. (2011). Diurnal and seasonal mood vary with work, sleep, and daylength across diverse cultures. *Science, 333,* 1878–1881. doi:10.1126/science.1202775

Gordon, A. M., & Chen, S. (2014). The role of sleep in interpersonal conflict: Do sleepless nights mean worse fights? *Social Psychological and Personality Science, 5,* 168–175. doi:10.1177/1948550613488952

Grandey, A. A. (2000). Emotional regulation in the workplace: A new way to conceptualize emotional labor. *Journal of Occupational Health Psychology, 5,* 95–110.

Guglielmi, O., Juardo-Gamez, B., Gude, F., & Buela-Casal, G. (2014). Job stress, burnout, and job satisfaction in sleep apnea patients. *Sleep Medicine, 15,* 1025–1030. doi:10.1016/j.sleep.2014.05.015

Gunia, B. C., Barnes, C. M., & Sah, S. (2014). The morality of larks and owls: Unethical behavior depends on chronotype as well as time-of-day. *Psychological Science, 25,* 2272–2274.

Hatfield, E., & Cacioppo, J. T. (1994). *Emotional contagion.* Cambridge, UK: Cambridge University Press. doi:10.1017/CBO9781139174138

Hobfoll, S. E. (2002). Social and psychological resources and adaptation. *Review of General Psychology, 6,* 307–324. doi:10.1037//1089-2680.6.4.307

Hochschild, A. (1983). *The managed heart:* Berkeley, CA: The University of California.

Horne, J. A., Anderson, C., & Platten, C. (2008). Sleep extension versus nap or coffee, within the context of "sleep debt." *Journal of Sleep Research, 17,* 432–436. doi:10.1111/j.1365-2869.2008.00680.x

Horne, J. A., & Ostberg, O. (1976). A self-assessment questionnaire to determine morningness-eveningness in human circadian rhythms. *International Journal of Chronobiology, 4,* 97–110.

Hulin, C. L., & Judge, T. A. (2003). Job attitudes: A theoretical and empirical review. In W. C. Borman, D. R. Ilgen, & R. J. Klimoski (Eds.), *Handbook of psychology* (Vol. 12, pp. 255–276). Hoboken, NJ: Wiley. doi:10.1002/0471264385.wei1211

Hulsheger, U. R., Alberts, H. J. E. M., Feinholdt, A., & Lang, J. W. B. (2013). Benefits of mindfulness at work: The role of mindfulness in emotion regulation, emotional exhaustion, and job satisfaction. *Journal of Applied Psychology, 98,* 310–325. doi:10.1037/a0031313

Ilies, R., Wagner, D. T., & Morgeson, F. P. (2007). Explaining affective linkages in teams: Individual differences in susceptibility to contagion and individualism-collectivism. *Journal of Applied Psychology, 92*, 1140. doi:10.1037/0021-9010.92.4.1140

Isen, A. M., Daubman, K. A., & Nowicki, G. P. (1987). Positive affect facilitates creative problem solving. *Journal of Personality and Social Psychology, 52*, 1122. doi:10.1037/0022-3514.52.6.1122

Kahn-Greene, E. T., Killgore, D. B., Kamimori, G. H., Balkin, T. J., & Killgore, W. D. (2007). The effects of sleep deprivation on symptoms of psychopathology in healthy adults. *Sleep Medicine, 8*, 215–221. doi:10.1016/j.sleep.2006.08.007

Kelly, T. L., Ryman, D. H., Schlangen, K., Gomez, S. A., & Elsmore, T. F. (1997). The effects of a single dose of pemoline on performance and mood during sleep deprivation. *Military Psychology, 9*, 213–225.

Keltner, D., & Haidt, J. (1999). Social functions of emotions at four levels of analysis. *Cognition & Emotion, 13*, 505–521. doi:10.1080/026999399379168

Killgore, W. D., Kahn-Greene, E. T., Lipizzi, E. L., Newman, R. A., Kamimori, G. H., & Balkin, T. J. (2008). Sleep deprivation reduces perceived emotional intelligence and constructive thinking skills. *Sleep Medicine, 9*, 517–526. doi:10.1016/j.sleep.2007.07.003

Killgore, W. D., Rupp, T. L., Grugle, N. L., Reichardt, R. M., Lipizzi, E. L., & Balkin, T. J. (2008). Effects of dextroamphetamine, caffeine and modafinil on psychomotor vigilance test performance after 44 h of continuous wakefulness. *Journal of Sleep Research, 17*, 309–321. doi:10.1111/j.1365-2869.2008.00654.x

Kroth, J., Daline, A., Longstreet, D., Nelson, M., & O'Neal, L. A. (2002). Sleep, dreams and job satisfaction. *Psychological Reports, 90*, 876–878. doi:10.2466/PR0.90.3.876-878

Lazarus, R. S., & Folkman, S. (1984). *Stress, appraisal, and coping.* New York, NY: Springer Publishing Company.

Lee, H. J., Rex, K. M., Nievergelt, C. M., Kelsoe, J. R., & Kripke, D. F. (2011). Delayed sleep phase syndrome is related to seasonal affective disorder. *Journal of Affective Disorders, 133*, 573–579. doi:10.1016/j.jad.2011.04.046

LeGates, T. A., Fernandez, D. C., & Hattar, S. (2014). Light as a central modulator of circadian rhythms, sleep and affect. *Nature Reviews Neuroscience, 15*, 443–454. doi:10.1038/nrn3743

Leger, D., Massuel, M.-A., Metlaine, A., & The SISYPHE Study Group. (2006). Professional correlates of insomnia. *Sleep, 29*, 171–178.

Lieberman, H. R., Tharion, W. J., Shukitt-Hale, B., Speckman, K. L., & Tulley, R. (2002). Effects of caffeine, sleep loss, and stress on cognitive performance and mood during U.S. Navy SEAL training. Sea-Air-Land. *Psychopharmacology, 164*, 250–261. doi:10.1007/s00213-002-1217-9

Lubart, T. I., & Getz, I. (1997). Emotion, metaphor, and the creative process. *Creativity Research Journal, 10*, 285–301. doi:10.1207/s15326934crj1004_1

Luz, E. M. S., Marqueze, E., & Moreno, C. (2010). Job satisfaction and sleep quality in nursing professionals. *Sleep Science, 4*, 49–51.

Merrey, Z., Piskin, M., Boysan, M., & Sehribanoglu, S. (2013). Burnout among Turkish teachers: The influence of sleep quality and job satisfaction. *Hacettepe University Journal of Education, 28*, 332–342.

Messmer, R., Miller, L. D., & Yu, C. M. (2012). The relationship between parent-infant bed sharing and marital satisfaction for mothers of infants. *Family Relations, 61*, 798–810. doi:10.1111/j.1741-3729.2012.00734.x

Milner, C. E., & Cote, K. A. (2009). Benefits of napping in healthy adults: Impact of nap length, time of day, age, and experience with napping. *Journal of Sleep Research, 18*, 272–281. doi:10.1111/j.1365-2869.2008.00718.x

Minkel, J. D., Banks, S., Htaik, O., Moreta, M. C., Jones, C. W., McGlinchey, E. L., ... Dinges, D. F. (2012). Sleep deprivation and stressors: Evidence for elevated negative affect in response to mild stressors when sleep deprived. *Emotion, 12,* 1015–1020. doi:10.1037/a0026871

Muraven, M., Tice, D. M., & Baumeister, R. F. (1998). Self-control as a limited resource: Regulatory depletion patterns. *Journal of Personality and Social Psychology, 74,* 774. doi:10.1037/0022-3514.74.3.774

Murray, G., Allen, N. B., & Trinder, J. (2002). Mood and the circadian system: Investigation of a circadian component in positive affect. *Chronobiology International, 19,* 1151–1169. doi:10.1081/CBI-120015956

Murray, G., Michalak, E. E., Levitt, A. J., Levitan, R. D., Enns, M. W., Morehouse, R., & Lam, R. W. (2006). O sweet spot where art thou? Light treatment of seasonal affective disorder and the circadian time of sleep. *Journal of Affective Disorders, 90,* 227–231. doi:10.1016/j.jad.2005.10.010

Pilcher, J. J., & Huffcutt, A. I. (1996). Effects of sleep deprivation on performance: A meta-analysis. *Sleep, 19,* 318–326.

Pugh, S. D. (2001). Service with a smile: Emotional contagion in the service encounter. *Academy of Management Journal, 44,* 1018–1027. doi:10.2307/3069445

Ritter, S. M., Strick, M., Bos, M. W., Van Baaren, R. B., & Dijksterhuis, A. (2012). Good morning creativity: Task reactivation during sleep enhances beneficial effect of sleep on creative performance. *Journal of Sleep Research, 21,* 643–647. doi:10.1111/j.1365-2869.2012.01006.x

Schwarz, N., & Clore, G. L. (1983). Mood, misattribution, and judgments of well-being: Informative and directive functions of affective states. *Journal of Personality and Social Psychology, 45,* 513–523. doi:10.1037/0022-3514.45.3.513

Scott, B. A., & Judge, T. A. (2006). Insomnia, emotions, and job satisfaction: A multilevel study. *Journal of Management, 32,* 622–645. doi:10.1177/0149206306289762

Smith, C. A., Haynes, K. N., Lazarus, R. S., & Pope, L. K. (1993). In search of the "hot" cognitions: Attributions, appraisals, and their relation to emotion. *Journal of Personality and Social Psychology, 65,* 916. doi:10.1037/0022-3514.65.5.916

Soderstrom, M., Jeding, K., Ekstedt, M., Perski, A., & Åkerstedt, T. (2012). Insufficient sleep predicts clinical burnout. *Journal of Occupational Health Psychology, 17,* 175–183. doi:10.1037/a0027518

Srivastava, S., Tamir, M., McGonigal, K. M., John, O. P., & Gross, J. J. (2009). The social costs of emotional suppression: A prospective study of the transition to college. *Journal of Personality and Social Psychology, 96,* 883. doi:10.1037/a0014755

Talbot, L. S., McGlinchey, E. L., Kaplan, K. A., Dahl, R. E., & Harvey, A. G. (2010). Sleep deprivation in adolescents and adults: Changes in affect. *Emotion, 10,* 831–841. doi:10.1037/a0020138

Taub, J. M., & Berger, R. J. (1976). The effects of changing the phase and duration of sleep. *Journal of Experimental Psychology: Human Perception and Performance, 2,* 30–41. doi:10.1037/0096-1523.2.1.30

Taub, J. M., Tanguay, P. E., & Clarkson, D. (1974). Effects of daytime naps on performance and mood in a college student population. *Journal of Abnormal Psychology, 85,* 210–217. doi:10.1037/0021-843X.85.2.210

Totterdell, P. (2000). Catching moods and hitting runs: Mood linkage and subjective performance in professional sport teams. *Journal of Applied Psychology, 85,* 848. doi:0021-9010.85.6.848

Totterdell, P., Reynolds, S., Parkinson, B., & Briner, R. B. (1994). Associations of sleep with everyday mood, minor symptoms and social interaction experience. *Sleep, 17,* 466–475.

van der Helm, E., Gujar, N., & Walker, M. P. (2010). Sleep deprivation impairs the accurate recognition of human emotions. *Sleep, 33,* 335–342.

Van Kleef, G. A. (2009). How emotions regulate social life: The emotions as social information (EASI) model. *Current Directions in Psychological Science, 18,* 184–188. doi:10.1111/j.1467-8721.2009.01633.x

Wagner, D. T., Barnes, C. M., Lim, V. K., & Ferris, D. L. (2012). Lost sleep and cyberloafing: Evidence from the laboratory and a daylight saving time quasi-experiment. *Journal of Applied Psychology, 97*, 1068–1076. doi:10.1037/a0027557

Wagner, D. T., Barnes, C. M., & Scott, B. A. (2014). Driving it home: How workplace emotional labor harms employee home life. *Personnel Psychology, 67*, 487–516. doi:10.1111/peps.12044

Wagner, D. T., & Ilies, R. (2008). Affective influences on employee satisfaction and performance. In N. M. Ashkanasy & C. L. Cooper (Eds.), *Research companion to emotion in organizations* (pp. 152–169). London, UK: Edward Elgar. doi:10.4337/9781848443778.00018

Wagner, U., Gais, S., Haider, H., Verleger, R., & Born, J. (2004). Sleep inspires insight. *Nature, 427*, 352–355. doi:10.1038/nature02223

Walker, M. P. (2009). The role of sleep in cognition and emotion. *Annals of the New York Academy of Sciences, 1156*, 168–197. doi:10.1111/j.1749-6632.2009.04416.x

Watson, D. (2000). *Mood and temperament.* New York, NY: Guilford Press.

Wesensten, N. J., Killgore, W. D. S., & Balkin, T. J. (2005). Performance and alertness effects of caffeine, dextroamphetamine, and modafinil during sleep deprivation. *Journal of Sleep Research, 14*, 255–266. doi:10.1111/j.1365-2869.2005.00468.x

Wiegand, M., Riemann, D., Schreiber, W., Lauer, C. J., & Berger, M. (1993). Effect of morning and afternoon naps on mood after total sleep deprivation in patients with major depression. *Biological Psychiatry, 33*, 467–476. doi:10.1016/0006-3223(93)90175-D

Wrzus, C., Wagner, G. G., & Riediger, M. (2014). Feeling good when sleeping in? Day-to-day associations between sleep duration and affective well-being differ from youth to old age. *Emotion, 14*, 624–628. doi:10.1037/a0035349

Yokoyama, E., Saito, Y., Kaneita, Y., Ohida, T., Harano, S., Tamaki, T., . . . Takeda, F. (2008). Association between subjective well-being and sleep among the elderly in Japan. *Sleep Medicine, 9*, 157–164. doi:10.1016/j.sleep.2007.02.007

Yoo, S. S., Gujar, N., Hu, P., Jolesz, F. A., & Walker, M. P. (2007). The human emotional brain without sleep–a prefrontal amygdala disconnect. *Current Biology, 17*, R877–878. doi:10.1016/j.cub.2007.08.007

# CHAPTER 7

# Sleep and Unethical Behavior

LARISSA K. BARBER AND CHRISTOPHER J. BUDNICK

## SLEEP AND UNETHICAL BEHAVIOR

Imagine that you are a working in a consulting firm as the manager of a project esti-mated at $100,000 based on time and direct costs. At the end of the project, you see that your actual costs were only $80,000. Your firm is not going to be pleased; end-ing a project this far under budget affects the firm's profit margin and will result in an uncomfortable conversation with your supervisor. You stare at the client billing sheet and weigh the possibilities. Should you charge the client $80,000 and deal with the firm's consequences later? Should you stay more hours to double-check your numbers, which could also mean finding an error that further lowers costs? Should you adjust your billable hours to hit the anticipated $100,000? Which strat-egy would you choose in this scenario (adapted from Allen & Davis, 1993)?

Researchers suggest that common misconceptions among managers and employees are that only some types of people ("bad apples") would choose the unethical approach in the above scenario and that making the ethical choice is easy (Treviño & Brown, 2004). However, a host of situational pressures can increase unethical behavior, even among people who are usually ethical. These pressures, such as workplace mistreatment or organizational culture (e.g., Kaptein, 2011; Treviño, den Nieuwenboer, & Kish-Gephart, 2014), may cause all employees to have unethical lapses from time to time. For example, the likelihood of "creative accounting" in the above scenario (also known as financial fraud) may increase if the employee believes that the repercussions of coming under budget are unfair or if the organizational norm is to always make adjustments.

The goal of this chapter is to explore another situational factor that may affect ethical behavior and organizations: sleep. What if the aforementioned scenario occurred late at night on a day in which you had only 3 hours of sleep? You could decide that maybe you made a mistake due to sleep deprivation, but lacked the time or capacity to check it before the budget deadline. You could rationalize that the organization's bottom line should not suffer due to your potential error. These thoughts could be tempting when you are tired, frustrated, and under pressure from deadlines. Given that ethical decisions are difficult, complex, and prone to situational influence (Treviño & Brown, 2004), sleepy workers may struggle more with ethical decision making than when they are well-rested.

The connection between sleep and ethical behavior is a compelling area of research that has received little attention to date, but has a number of possibilities for explaining why ethical lapses may occur in some people more than others (chronic sleep issues) or within individuals over time (transitory sleep issues). In this chapter, we discuss what qualifies as ethical behavior and common frameworks for explaining ethical decision making. We also discuss self-regulatory frameworks that can be used to explain unethical behavior, and draw from multiple theoretical approaches and current research findings to propose an integrated model of sleep and ethics. Finally, we close with some future directions in testing the model, including potential moderators.

## WHAT IS UNETHICAL BEHAVIOR?

Researchers define unethical behavior as any action that violates accepted societal norms of morality (Kish-Gephart, Harrison, & Treviño, 2010). These include behaviors such as lying and theft, and often have clear analogs in organizational settings in the form of "calling in sick" when you are not really ill or stealing equipment from work. Some behaviors, such as time sheet fraud, may even violate multiple societal norms with respect to lying about your work hours and "stealing" money from the organization that you did not earn. In many cases, counterproductive workplace behaviors (CWBs; Sackett, Berry, Wiemann, & Laczo, 2006) qualify as unethical behavior. Examples of these behaviors include verbal or physical abuse, sabotage, and theft.

However, there are instances in which CWBs may not necessarily qualify as unethical behavior (see Figure 7.1). Definitions of CWBs tend to focus on the violation of organizational norms, rather than on societal norms for morality (Bennett & Robinson, 2003; Kish-Gephart et al., 2010). Thus, some forms of counterproductive behaviors at work—ignoring someone or coming in late without permission—are certainly problematic to the productivity of the company, but are not necessarily considered unethical. This may also include behaviors such as gossiping about other employees (assuming the information is true or not intentionally misrepresented) or rude comments that qualify as incivility. Although these behaviors are not considered unethical per se, they are still relevant to this chapter from a self-regulatory perspective because they violate organizational standards and do not conflict with societal norms of appropriate behavior.

Alternatively, actions that violate societal norms of ethical behavior might be common practice or encouraged within an organization. An employee who lies to a customer in order to ensure a sale is violating societal norms, but lying to customers could be encouraged to increase the organization's bottom line. Other

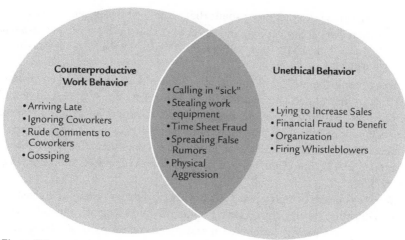

**Figure 7.1.**
Venn diagram of counterproductive work behavior and ethical behavior.

examples include financial fraud to increase the organization's profit margins and firing whistleblowers (individuals who report unethical behavior) to avoid having perceived "troublemakers" interfering with current business practices. Counterproductive ethical behaviors (i.e., whistle blowing) or organizationally sanctioned unethical behaviors (i.e., lying to increase sales) are outside of the scope of this chapter because they represent a qualitatively different situation in which there is a goal conflict in terms of societal and organizational norms. In this chapter, we will assume that "ethical" behavior for an employee in a given situation is avoiding counterproductive workplace behavior that either (1) clearly violates societal norms (i.e., theft, lying) or (2) does not conflict with societal norms and violates commonly accepted organizational norms (i.e., incivility, withdrawal).

## THEORETICAL FRAMEWORKS FOR UNETHICAL BEHAVIOR

Many frameworks have attempted to explain unethical behavior. In this chapter, we first review the most commonly referenced and researched models of moral decision making. We then present an integrative dual-process model that demonstrates how sleep factors should affect unethical behavior through self-regulation (Baumeister & Heatherton, 1996).

### Individual-Level Ethical Decision Making

Research examining individual-level ethical decision making often relies on Rest's (1986) four-stage model. In this model, moral agents must (1) be able to recognize or identify an issue as involving moral components (*moral awareness*), (2) make a judgment about that issue (*moral judgment*), (3) establish an intention (*moral motivation*), and (4) act on that intention (*moral behavior*; Kish-Gephart et al., 2010; Rest, 1986; Rest, Narvaez, Bebeau, & Thomas, 1999; Thomas, 1991).

Recognizing the ethical elements of various situations—*moral awareness*—is critical to moral decision making (Rest, 1986; Treviño, Weaver, & Reynolds, 2006). If an individual does not recognize and interpret an action or interaction as involving moral components, then that individual is unlikely to engage in moral reasoning (Rest, 1986) or judge others' morality accurately (Gino & Bazerman, 2009). Therefore, moral awareness should facilitate moral judgment (Rest, 1986).

*Moral judgments*, or individual assessments of right or wrong in a given situation, determine subsequent actions. Kohlberg's (1969) cognitive moral development theory has heavily influenced moral judgment research. Kohlberg (1969) proposed three developmental levels through which individuals progress: (1) relying on authority figures or fear of punishment (preconventional level), (2) to relying on others' expectations or formalized rules and laws (conventional level), and (3) to finally determining right from wrong based on internal standards (principled level). However, critiques of Kohlberg's theory note its overreliance on cognitive reasoning (Haidt, 2001).

An alternative view of moral judgment is the social intuitionist perspective, which proposes that moral judgment results from quick and automatic evaluations (i.e., moral intuitions; Haidt, 2001). In this model, moral reasoning typically provides post hoc rationalizations of a moral intuition/judgment. Although this model has received some support (see Greene & Haidt, 2002), moral reasoning also precedes moral judgment, at least under certain circumstances (e.g., social influence attempts). This introduces complexity when attempting to understand moral judgments, as sometimes moral judgments result from quick and intuitive processes (i.e., moral intuition) with post hoc moral reasoning providing an explanation for those judgments. At other times, moral judgments result from moral reasoning, with moral intuition having little or no impact on that process. Thus, depending on the individual and the given situation either moral intuition or moral reasoning can drive moral judgments.

Importantly, Kohlberg (1969) and Haidt (2001) fail to link moral judgments and moral behaviors, although intent is Rest's (1986) third stage. *Moral intent* (also known as moral motivation) refers to the process of weighing or prioritizing moral values relative to other values, and intending to choose the moral action. For example, take an employee who is briefly unsupervised when handling money at a cash register. The employee might know that stealing from the cash register is wrong, but is not motivated to engage in the appropriate behavior due to other (financial) concerns (low moral intent). Alternatively, the employee may decide not to yield to temptation in the future (high moral intent). Most human behavior theories acknowledge that intention precedes behavior (Ajzen, 1991; Fishbein & Ajzen, 1975; Rest, 1986), and meta-analysis suggests a medium-to-large change in our intentions contributes to a small-to-medium change in our actual behavior (Webb

& Sheeran, 2006). Thus, an individual's moral intentions should influence his or her moral behavior to some extent.

Moral behavior (Stage 4; Rest, 1986) involves acting in a manner acceptable to a given situation. However, successfully engaging any one of the Rest's (1986) prior three stages does not guarantee that subsequent stages will be engaged or successful. Concurrently, both Kohlberg's (1969; Weaver, Reynolds, & Brown, 2014) and Haidt's (2001) theories underspecify the moral reasoning and behavior relationship.

Recently, Reynolds (2006) proposed a neural connectionist decision-making model that proposes that ethical situations result in a nonconscious comparison of incoming neural network signals (i.e., sensory information) to baseline ethical prototypes. Consistent with the social intuitionist model, individuals are not consciously aware of the prototype matching process. This is evolutionarily adaptive as it quickly prepares the decision maker to adapt to or cope with the ethical situation (Reynolds, 2006). The second path relies on conscious or active reasoning (similar to Kohlberg, 1969). Active judgment processes involve analyzing, applying moral rules to, and arriving at a moral judgment about a given situation (Reynolds, 2006).

Integrating the above models, Dedeke (2013) suggested a five-stage integrative moral decision-making model, the cognitive-intuitionist model. This model suggests that when making a moral decision an individual frames the issue, preprocesses affective and cognitive information, engages in moral reflection, and then forms a behavioral intention. Common moral violations (e.g., bribery, lying) are immediately and automatically recognized and evoke an equally automatic emotional response (Dedeke, 2013). If emotional responses conflict with automatic cognitive judgments (e.g., we feel bad for a murderer with a terrible childhood, but cognitively believe that such crimes deserve capital punishment), active moral reasoning resolves that conflict (Dedeke, 2013).

Although the cognitive-intuitionist model maintains that moral judgments occur through either reflexive or active processing, it also offers a third moral judgment path that relies equally on reflexive and active reasoning. If reflexive judgment fails to solve a moral dilemma, then the individual should engage in moral reflection. Moral reflection (i.e., active reasoning) is a deliberate method of making moral decisions that consumes cognitive resources through effortful control. Therefore, self-regulatory breakdowns should affect moral decision making and behavior, which is a topic we turn to next.

## Self-Regulatory Model of Unethical Behavior

Social psychological research in the area of self-regulation views unethical behavior as self-regulatory failure that is predicted by three distinct aspects of self-regulatory success: goals or standards, monitoring, and controlling (Heatherton & Baumeister, 1996). Applied to ethics, standards represent the norms of ethical behavior in a given situation. Monitoring refers to the process of comparing our current behavior to the ethical behavioral standard, and controlling refers to the process of actually adjusting our behavior to conform to ethical standards.

The underlying assumption with this model is that engaging in ethical behavior may be an effortful process that requires ongoing monitoring and behavioral control. Additionally, the energy required for both monitoring and control is a limited resource that can easily be depleted throughout the day (Muraven & Baumeister, 2000). For example, individuals tend to have more self-regulatory failures after coping with stress late in the evening and after consuming alcohol (Baumeister & Heatherton, 1996). Therefore, individuals with depleted self-regulatory resources are most likely to demonstrate self-regulatory failure.

Using this framework, there are two primary ways in which self-regulatory failure can occur. *Underregulation* occurs when individuals do not have sufficient self-regulatory resources remaining to adjust their behavior. In other words, the individual has inadequate self-regulatory strength remaining to override unwanted or maladaptive thoughts, emotions, or behaviors (Baumeister & Heatherton, 1996). This is a breakdown of the controlling process; individuals may be aware of the behavioral standard, and that they are not adhering to it, but are unable to make adjustments to change it. Researchers have pointed to the link between self-control and unethical behavior using the underlying theory behind underregulation processes (e.g., Gailliot, Glitter, Baker, & Baumeister, 2012; Gino, Schweitzer, Mead, & Ariely, 2011).

However, the second process of *misregulation* has received less attention in the literature, at least directly. Misregulation occurs when individuals are able to exert control over their behavior, but it is not directed at the appropriate standard. Misregulation can occur by either failing to have the right standard or failing to monitor your behavior appropriately to be able to compare to the standard. Some researchers suggest that depletion of cognitive resources leads to lapses in attention needed for moral awareness, and subsequently ethical behavior (e.g., Gino et al., 2011; Street, Douglas, Geiger, & Martinko, 2001).

## Dual-Process Model of Sleep and Unethical Behavior

We propose that integrating models of ethical decision making with the self-regulatory framework approach may be a useful way of conceptualizing how sleep can impact ethical behavior in organizations. Sleep can affect self-regulatory functioning needed for ethical decision making and behavior with respect to attentional, emotional, and behavioral resources. Given that self-regulation arises from executive functioning in the brain (prefrontal cortex activities such as planning, problem solving, or reasoning), sleep may be a critical activity for replenishing self-regulatory resources needed to avoid self-regulatory failure (Muraven & Baumeister, 2000). Past research has indeed linked poor sleep to decrements in attention processes (Lim & Dinges, 2010; Van Dongen, Maislin, Mullington, & Dinges, 2003), heightened negative emotional reactivity and negative mood (Killgore, 2010; Tempesta et al., 2010), and poorer behavioral indicators

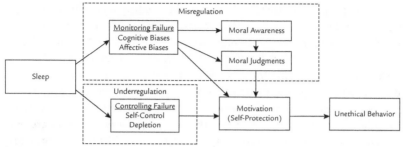

**Figure 7.2.**
Dual process model of sleep issues on unethical behavior.

of self-control (Barber & Munz, 2011; Barnes, Schaubroeck, Huth, & Ghumman, 2011; Christian & Ellis, 2011).

Current investigations into sleep and ethics rely heavily on only the behavioral component of the self-regulatory framework (underregulation), demonstrating a link between sleep and behavioral indicators of self-regulation that are required for ethical conduct (e.g., Barnes et al., 2011; Christian & Ellis, 2011). However, there is less focus in the management literature devoted to the effects of sleep on other ethical decision-making aspects such as moral awareness and judgments (misregulation; e.g., Barnes, Guina, & Wagner, 2014; Barber & Budnick, 2015). As such, we outline a dual-process model in which sleep problems affect unethical behavior through misregulation (monitoring failure) and underregulation (controlling failure), which may operate as parallel processes. Figure 7.2 outlines these two distinct processes as they relate to motivation and unethical behavior. Below, we discuss the theoretical rational for each process and associated empirical research that informs some of the anticipated relationships for each link in the model. Most of the current sleep research focuses on the link between sleep, self-control depletion, and behavior. As such, we will start with the motivation to the behavioral path, followed by the commonly studied underregulation process and less studied misregulation process.

***Motivational shifts and unethical behavior.*** The limited resources approach—or self-regulatory depletion approach—assumed in self-regulatory models is consistent with current research into how sleep factors influence subsequent self-regulation. A more recent critique of the self-regulatory depletion model argues that outcomes associated with lower self-regulatory resources (i.e., lower self-control) may be more motivational or attentional in nature than "ability" based on actual resources. This perspective suggests that depleted individuals are not devoid of exerting effortful action; instead, "ego-depletion" may instead be shifts in motivation and attention that merely prevent the application of self-control (Inzlicht & Schmeichel, 2012). This is a persuasive argument given that most demonstrations of self-regulatory depletion can be counteracted with motivational factors such as financial incentives (Muraven & Slessereva, 2003). Thus, what looks to be a lack of energy for self-control could be only a strategic withholding of effort based on low desire for exerting self-control based on the situation (Inzlicht & Schmeichel, 2012).

For example, people who are told that they will be engaging in three tasks appear "depleted" on the second task, but showed no depletion on the third. Additionally, those who were told they would be engaging in only two tasks showed no depletion effect (Muraven, Shmueli, & Burckley, 2006). However, Baumeister (2014) argues that the motivational shift (or allocation theory) perspective should be considered a complementary process alongside ego depletion rather than a replacement. Specifically, the motivation to conserve or shift resources after activities requiring self-regulatory effort itself is evidence that self-regulatory resources are limited and can be depleted. The integration of the motivational shift perspective and ego-depletion perspective also has indirect support in sleep research. Although individuals do experience decision-making decrements following short-term sleep loss, these decrements are not as large for tasks that participants find to be interesting compared to more monotonous tasks (Harrison & Horne, 2000).

Furthering this line of thought, we argue that behavioral outcomes arising from underregulation or misregulation processes are best conceptualized as antecedents of motivational shifts that lead to unethical behavior. In the first process, underregulation, sleep decreases self-control in a manner that can negatively affect the motivation to respond ethically. Thus, people may engage in unethical behavior because they are unmotivated to devote their limited resources (lower self-control) toward inhibiting ethical behavior. Thus, underregulation can be conceptualized as a shift in motivation away from the ethical behavior to conserve limited self-control resources. This can apply to common situations of interpersonal deviance or withdrawal, in which individuals know that they are being uncivil or working slowly, but are too tired to engage in the appropriate behavior. In this case, communicating professionally or paying closer attention to your work is the more effortful alternative, which is unappealing due to low self-control.

The misregulation process represents how sleep may alter individuals' cognition in a manner that leads to biases in moral awareness or moral judgments. Thus, people may engage in unethical behavior despite having intact self-regulatory resources to exert control because of two possibilities. The first possibility is that they fail to realize that there is an ethical dilemma or situation (moral awareness error) due to either a lack of recognition of the ethical standard or awareness that their behavior is not in line with the standard (i.e., attentional bias). Consequently, there is no motivational shift to ethical action because they do not perceive a need for action. The second possibility (i.e., misregulation) is that the individual is completely aware of the moral issue, but is retaliating against a perceived moral injustice (judgment error due to interpretative bias). In this case, there is a motivational shift toward unethical action because the employee believes that it is an appropriate reaction given the situation. Thus, misregulation would explain the perplexing situation in which a person is sleepy but engages in effortful regulation to engage in some types of unethical behaviors (active aggression). This is a less studied phenomenon in sleep and ethical behavior research, but is worth more investigation. However, this would be predicted by the misregulation process because individuals' motivational shift dictates that they will use their limited self-control resources to achieve unethical goals. During misregulation, the shift in motivation is either toward the wrong behavioral goal/standard or a failure to recognize the appropriate goal/standard.

Table 7.1 demonstrates how each of these processes manifests in two practical examples. The first example considers a sleep-deprived manager who sends a curse-laden email chastising his subordinates after reading the last company financial reports. The second example uses our scenario from the beginning of the chapter. Below, we provide a more in-depth discussion of research examining how sleep may lead to less motivation to engage in ethical behavior due to poor self-control, as well as how sleep affects moral awareness and judgment issues based on research on cognitive and affective biases.

**Underregulation process.** As mentioned before, the underregulation process refers to unethical behavior due to sleep through the pathway of self-control. As proposed by Muraven and Baumeister (2000), sleep quantity, quality, and consistency

*Table 7.1.* SITUATIONAL EXAMPLES OF MISREGULATION VERSUS UNDERREGULATION PATHWAYS ON MOTIVATIONAL SHIFTS

| Angry Boss | Misregulation (Awareness) | Misregulation (Judgment) | Underregulation (Self-Control) |
|---|---|---|---|
| Dual-Process Pathway | Attention to unethical behavior is biased (directed away) due to lack of awareness. Does not recognize ethical issue. | Interpretation of unethical behavior is biased due to poor judgment. | Effort is withheld from preventing unethical behavior due to poor self-control. |
| Motivational Shift in "Uncivil Email" Scenario | Believes he is merely providing immediate and "accurate" feedback to his work team. | Recognizes ethical issue, but feels that subordinates "deserve it." Thus, no need to edit email for "professional wording." | Recognizes potential ethical issue and makes a correct judgment that the behavior is wrong for this particular situation. But he sends the email anyway due to anger (motivating bias) because he does not want to edit email for "professional wording." |
| Motivational Shift in "Creative Accounting" Scenario | Believes that adjusting numbers is an appropriate course of action. | Recognizes ethical issue, but rationalized a potential mistake to adjust numbers for "fairness" to the organization. | Recognizes potential ethical issue and makes a correct judgment that the behaviors are wrong for this particular situation. But she does not want to go through the effort of double-checking (or having a potential disciplinary meeting) and adjusts numbers. |

have all been linked to decrements in both behavioral and self-reports of self-control (e.g., Barber & Munz, 2011; Barber, Barnes, & Carlson, 2013; Christian & Ellis). Thus, research in the organization sciences is increasingly adopting a self-regulatory approach to sleep and self-regulation to predict various organizational outcomes (Barnes, 2012).

Some studies to date have made a direct link between sleep and unethical behavior, as well as self-control as a mediation process. For example, self-control depletion has been documented as a mediator between lower sleep quantity and a variety of deviant behaviors directed toward the organization and individuals (Christian & Ellis, 2011; Welsh, Ellis, Christian, & Mai, 2014), such as cheating (Barnes et al., 2011) and surfing the Internet during work time (cyberloafing; Wagner, Barnes, Lim, & Ferris, 2012). Self-control has also served as a link between sleep quality and unethical behaviors with respect to abusive behaviors toward subordinates (Barnes, Lucianetti, Bhave, & Christian, 2014). In most studies to date, decreased motivation to engage in ethical behavior is assumed through low self-control, but future research may want to actually measure motivational proxies as a more comprehensive test of this theoretical model. For example, a recent study examining a minor form of unethical behavior—careless survey responding—examined all four components of the model: sleep, self-control depletion, motivation, and behavior (Barber, Barnes, & Carlson, 2013). Specifically, they found that poor sleep quality leads to careless responding behavior through decreased self-control, and in turn survey effort (a motivational proxy).

***Misregulation process.*** Compared to underregulation process research, misregulation processes have received much less attention in organizational science. Sleep has been shown to decrease the ability to anticipate moral issues in situations (Olsen, Palleson, & Espevik, 2013) and to interfere with the speed (Killgore et al., 2007; Tempesta et al., 2012) and quality of making moral judgments (Olsen, Pallesen, & Eid, 2010). We propose that the misregulation process represents a failure in monitoring ethical situations appropriately due to two sources of bias: cognitive and affective. Below, we discuss how sleep may affect these types of biases, and how biases can affect moral awareness and judgments.

***Moral awareness.*** Sleep likely affects an individuals' moral awareness due to attentional bias. Attentional bias is a type of cognitive bias that affects how individuals shift their attention to process information in the environment (see Mathews & MacLeod, 1994). Research suggests that sleep negatively affects attention, as evidenced by lower performance on vigilance tasks (e.g., Lim & Dinges, 2008). This is proposed to be due to deficits in prefrontal cortex functioning in the brain, which is important for planning and attentional control (Boonstra, Stins, Daffertshofer, & Beek, 2007). Thus, it appears that sleepy people have difficulty monitoring environmental information, especially when it calls for sustained attention.

Attentional bias for ethical awareness should work much the same way; that is, sleep likely negatively affects the ability of people to detect ethical issues in their environment. Recent research demonstrates that individuals have lower moral awareness when evaluating dilemmas when they have gotten less sleep (Barnes et al., 2015). This finding likely reflects disruptions to attentional processes that would allow individuals to recognize characteristics of a moral dilemma. More research is needed in this area to support these initial findings, as well as explorations into characteristics of the individual or moral situation that may alter the effects of sleep on moral awareness (we discuss these in more detail in the moderator section).

**Moral judgments.** Sleep may also affect moral judgments due to biases in both cognition and affect. With respect to cognition, sleepy people may be more likely to interpret a threat in their environment due to increased perceptions of vulnerability (Barber & Budnick, 2015; Budnick & Barber, 2015). That is, once they attend to information in their environment, they are more likely to err on the side of perceiving a threat. Empirical research supports the assertion that sleepy individuals have more interpretive bias toward making negative judgments when completing simple work completion tasks (Ree & Harvey, 2006) and evaluating more complex situational information (Barber & Budnick, 2015). Sleep-deprived individuals also tend to be less trusting of others in social interactions and show an increased sensitivity to issues of fairness (Anderson & Dickinson, 2010). More recent research suggests that sleepy people have a bias in fairness judgments in negative workplace situations compared to less sleepy individuals (Barber & Budnick, 2015). Given the centrality of fairness in making moral judgments (Rest, 1979), this is preliminary evidence that sleep-deprived individuals may be more cognitively disposed to perceive a moral violation, which may lead to justifying unethical behavior as an appropriate retaliation strategy.

Sleep may also affect moral judgments through affective bias. Sleep is known to negatively affect individuals' mood and emotion (Durmer & Dinges, 2005; Pilcher & Huffcutt, 1996). This effect is thought to occur due to overactivation of the amygdala (e.g., Yoo, Gujar, Hu, Jolesz, & Walker, 2007), which is important for processing emotional information when evaluating events. Moreover, research shows that compared to sleep extension (i.e., 12 hours of sleep for 6 nights), sleep restriction (4 hours a night for 6 nights) elevated evening cortisol levels and increased sympathetic nervous system activation (Spiegel, Leproult, & Van Cauter, 1999). Given that increased sympathetic activation and cortisol responses are often observed in individuals experiencing elevated levels of stress (Dickerson & Kemeny, 2004), those findings seem consistent with research showing that after sleep loss individuals have greater affective reactivity. In that study, sleep-deprived individuals were shown negatively valenced pictures. The sleep-deprived individuals exhibited greater pupil dilation than the rested individuals, suggesting heightened emotional reactivity to the negatively valenced pictures (Franzen, Siegle, & Buysse, 2008). Together these studies provide evidence that sleep loss affects the physiological components that are instrumental in the experience of negative affect, at least as broadly defined (e.g., anger, stress).

Importantly, there is evidence for a link between emotional states and social judgments. Experimental research has demonstrated that inducing negative emotional states can make individuals focus on short-term outcomes at the expense of considering long-term consequences (Gray, 1999), blame others for negative outcomes (Keltner, Ellsworth, & Edwards, 1993), and judge others more harshly

(Lerner, Goldberg, & Tetlock, 1998). Individuals may use affective information, such as anger, to make judgments about the fairness of particular situations (Scher & Heise, 1993). Thus, negative affect arising from sleep deprivation may be another mechanism through which sleep can influence judgments (Eisenberg, 2000). We suggest more research into this idea, as current work is limited for this theoretical link. Christian and Ellis (2011) suggested that sleep deprivation increases negative emotions, which go on to affect deviant behavior.

However, their study describes the hostility mechanism as an underregulation process, in which negative affect decreases the ability of individuals to regulate their reactions (due to emotion). Their study found that sleep deprivation increased unethical behavior through hostility (and self-control separately). One way to interpret this finding is that affective biases from sleep deprivation influenced moral judgments that could have affected motivation to engage in unethical behavior. However, more work clearly needs to be done in this area, as the above study did not directly assess moral judgments. In a study that did assess emotions and judgment biases (albeit not behavior), Barber and Budnick (2015) found that biases in fairness judgments due to sleep loss were not linked to affective information (i.e., there was no link to hostility or other negative emotions), suggesting a stronger case for cognitive—rather than affective—bias when it comes to judgments. Thus, one possible alternative explanation for the findings of Christian and Ellis (2011) is that affective biases due to sleep deprivation can directly decrease individuals' motivation to exert effortful control over their deviant behavior (in that study, avoiding being rude in email communications) rather than acting through moral judgments.

## POTENTIAL MODERATORS IN THE DUAL-PROCESS MODEL

Thus far we have discussed the dual-process model's main effect links, which have already garnered research attention and initial empirical support. Next, we discuss potential moderators of the underregulation and misregulation processes (see Figure 7.3). At this point, it is important to note that empirical studies of potential moderators of these links (especially those related to sleep) are only beginning to emerge. For example, Welsh and colleagues (2014) directly examined sleep factors and reported the attenuating effects of caffeine on the contribution of sleep loss to self-control depletion. After sleep loss, individuals who consumed caffeine exhibited higher levels of self-control than noncaffeinated individuals who experienced sleep loss. Moreover, researchers have observed an interaction between sleep and exercise on next-day personal resources (which can be considered relevant to managing self-regulatory processes). Individuals who slept for a greater amount of time than average on a day they exercised reported having more personal resources on the following day (Nägel & Sonnentag, 2013). Given that this is a relatively new and emerging area of research, the following section is primarily speculation concerning a number of potential moderators to the main effect paths depicted in our model. We encourage future researchers to explore and empirically validate these suggestions.

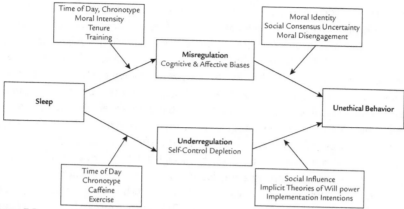

**Figure 7.3.**
Potential moderators of the dual process model of sleep issues on unethical behavior.

## Moderators of the Underregulation Process

**Sleep to self-control depletion link**. Individuals' motivation to engage in self-control is higher immediately following rest (Tyler & Burns, 2008) and wanes throughout the day (Baumeister & Heatheron, 1996). Therefore, time of day may moderate the sleep and self-control relationship. Preliminary reports show more ethical behavior earlier in the day compared to the afternoon (called the *morning morality effect*), as individuals are depleted of self-control later in the day (Kouchaki & Smith, 2014). The motivation to engage self-control seems to peak when time of day matches our circadian preference (Curtis, Burkley, & Burkley, 2014), which Gunia, Barnes, and Sah (2014) refer to as the *chronotype morality effect*. Based on previous theory and research (Curtis et al., 2015; Gunia et al., 2014) ) we suggest that a match (or mismatch) between our chronotype and the time of day might moderate the relationship between sleep loss and self-control. It seems possible that a chronotype and time of day match that facilitates peak self-control ability might attenuate the relationship between sleep loss and reduced self-control, at least to some extent. Therefore, future research should determine whether chronotype, time of day, and their interaction influence how sleep affects an individual's self-control.

Another potential moderator of the sleep and self-control depletion link is caffeine. Recent research has shown that caffeine attenuates sleep deprivation-related self-control deficits (Welsh et al., 2014). However, suggesting that organizations provide employees caffeine to manage self-control decrements due to sleep loss is premature. Identification of effective dosage levels (both amount and frequency) and the attenuation effects of caffeine tolerance are imperative for future research (Welsh et al., 2014). Failing to understand such conditions could result in detrimental employee outcomes (e.g., dependence, anxiety; Welsh et al., 2014).

Exercise may be a healthier and more sustainable way to attenuate self-control depletion effects, as a sleep by exercise interaction predicted employees' personal resources in one study (e.g., optimism, resilience; Nägel & Sonnentag, 2013). On days following *both* exercise *and* increased sleep (i.e., relative to average) employees had more personal resources, which predicted lower emotional exhaustion (Nägel & Sonnentag, 2013). Interestingly, fewer personal resources did not follow sleep loss (Nägel & Sonnentag, 2013), despite other research demonstrating self-control decrements due to sleep loss (Christian & Ellis, 2011). Arguably, self-control is a personal resource, albeit one that improves with use (Muraven, Baumeister, & Tice, 1999). Engaging in an exercise regime requires self-control as it is necessary to regulate behavior (e.g., consistently arrive on time for each session, inhibit minor pain responses) and affect (e.g., persist through fatigue), which could improve self-control. Given that getting a consistent amount of sleep (which also requires behavioral regulation) has been shown to interact with sleep quantity to predict increased self-control (e.g., Barber & Munz, 2011), future research might examine whether sleep and exercise also interact to predict self-control. Moreover, objective exercise, sleep, and self-control measures would be beneficial in subsequent studies (Nägel & Sonnentag, 2013).

**Self-control depletion-to-behavior link.** Moral judgments predict moral behavior (Reynolds & Ceranic, 2007), but social influence might moderate the depletion–to-behavior link. For example, subjective norms have predicted bribery intentions (Powpaka, 2002). Also, vehicle inspectors were observed adjusting their vehicle pass rates to conform to each local inspection site's norms in another (Pierce & Snyder, 2008). More recent findings show that negative social influence (i.e., encouraging unethical behavior) moderates the self-control depletion to the unethical behavior link. Depletion and unethical behavior were positively associated when negative social influence was present, but were unrelated without that influence (Welsh et al., 2014). Future investigations should continue to isolate moderators of the depletion to unethical behavior link while incorporating both negative and positive social influence, as the latter factor might attenuate the depletion-to-behavior link.

In addition to perceptions of what others believe (i.e., social consensus), personal beliefs seem likely to moderate the link between depletion and behavior. For instance, across four studies it was found that individuals who believed self-control (or willpower) was limited experienced ego depletion, whereas individuals who believed self-control was unlimited did not suffer ego depletion (i.e., implicit theories of willpower; Job, Dweck, & Walton, 2010). Importantly, participants' implicit theories about self-control limits predicted changes in eating behaviors, procrastination, and goal striving persistence in depleting contexts. Individuals adopting limited resource theories of self-control exhibited poorer real world (i.e., outside the laboratory) self-regulation under high regulatory demand (Job et al., 2010). Many work environments inherently involve high regulatory demand; thus, individuals' beliefs about self-control might influence how they behave in response to ethical dilemmas in those environments. Based on the above findings, employees who believe self-control is limited should exhibit a stronger link between depletion and unethical behavior. Those who do not hold such a belief should exhibit a weaker, or perhaps even a null, relationship. Future self-control investigations would likely profit from assessing both individuals' self-control beliefs and levels to determine how those beliefs alter the link between depletion levels and behavior in the workplace.

Assuming that individuals do experience ego depletion, at least in some circumstances, implementation intentions might be an inexpensive and simple method of attenuating the depletion-to-behavior link. Implementation intentions are action plans in the form of conditional statements (i.e., If cue X is present, then perform behavior Y). They remove personal volition from action initiation by delegating a predetermined behavioral response to a situational or environmental cue (for a meta-analysis, see Gollwitzer & Sheeran, 2006). Implementation intentions effectively improve goal pursuit initiation and can assist in overcoming ego depletion from self-control expenditures on relatively simple tasks (Webb & Sheeran, 2003). Therefore, implementation intentions might weaken the link between depletion and unethical behavior. Future research should examine whether implementation intentions in the form of "If I experience temptation X, then I will ignore that temptation" assist individuals in overcoming depletion to behave ethically relative to a control. With respect to the studies discussed in the above paragraph, an alternative implementation intention worth testing might be "If I am sleepy, then I will remember that self-control is unlimited."

## Moderators of the Misregulation Process

**Sleep-to-bias link.** Similar to the sleep and self-control depletion link, one potential moderator of the sleep-to-bias link is the time of day. Kouchaki and Smith (2014) report a significant linear depletion effect of time of day on moral awareness, suggesting that individual moral awareness capacity decreases over the course of normal daily activity. Unethical behavior in the afternoon was partially explained by lower moral awareness (Kouchaki & Smith, 2014). Given these findings, it is possible that the time of day exacerbates the effects of sleepiness on judgment bias. Sleepy individuals' vigilance deficits might combine with lower afternoon moral awareness to result in sleepy individuals missing larger amounts of pertinent information than when moral awareness is high. Conversely, high moral awareness in the morning might offset the detrimental effects of sleepiness. However, that moderation may depend more on the fit between the time of day and an individual's chronotype preference. The sleep-to-bias link might be stronger when there is a chronotype mismatch (i.e., morning time for evening people; evening time for morning people; Gunia et al., 2014).

Although sleepiness results in vigilance deficits, when sleepy individuals *do* perceive negative or ambiguous information they tend to interpret that information as especially threatening (Barber & Budnick, 2015; Ree & Harvey, 2006). Therefore, moral intensity might strengthen the sleep and judgment bias link. Moral intensity refers to a situation's potential for harm as reflected in the magnitude, probability, and immediacy of potential harm, as well as the proximity and number of potential victims (Jones, 1991). As threat tends to be overinterpreted when sleepy

(Barber & Budnick, 2015), high levels of moral intensity should exacerbate that tendency. Thus, when sleepy individuals encounter morally intense situations they should be especially likely to exhibit biased judgments. Not only would it be beneficial for future research to validate this suggestion, it would also likely prove beneficial to examine the unique influence of each moral intensity component on the sleep-to-bias link.

However, employees with more workplace experience might have different thresholds for (un)ethicality than employees with less experience. Given that employees with a longer tenure likely have greater experience, tenure could moderate the sleep-to-bias link. Greater exposure to a variety of moral and immoral situations or interactions over the course of time allows for a larger comparative base of prototypes. Moral intuition relies on immediate and relatively automatic judgments concerning a situation's morality (Haidt, 2001; Reynolds, 2006). Thus, having a larger prototype pool for comparison to the current circumstances could increase judgment accuracy. As such, greater experience, as reflected in longer workplace tenure, could conceivably weaken the link between sleepiness and judgment bias. Future investigations should determine how tenure length interacts with sleepiness to predict bias.

It is also likely that organizational ethics training could moderate the sleep-to-bias link. For example, Olsen et al. (2010) report that sleep deprivation increases rule-oriented ethical decision making; employees rely more on ethical schemas or norms (i.e., moral intuition) when sleepy. If those schemas and norms are strongly ethically grounded unethical decisions are unlikely. Therefore it is noteworthy that even short ethics training courses (i.e., five 75-minute ethics classes and two case study assignments; Jones, 2009) significantly improve moral reasoning. However, ethics-training research typically focuses on higher education and formal ethics classes. Less is known about organizational ethics training programs' effectiveness, as typically they are packaged with other ethics-related policies (e.g., conduct codes). Future research should isolate organizational training program components to determine which are the most influential in predicting ethical judgments and behavior (Treviño et al., 2014), as certain components might reduce the sleep and bias relationship more effectively than others might. Organizations could also directly provide employees with sleep hygiene training to improve employees' sleep practices (Brown, Buboltz, & Soper, 2006), increase self-regulation (Barber & Munz, 2011), and decrease unethical decisions and behavior (Barnes et al., 2011).

***Bias-to-behavior link.*** The next link in our model suggests that moral judgment bias should affect moral behavior; however, the strength of that association might depend in part on an individual's self-concept. For instance, moral identity is the degree to which morality is central to a person's self-definition (Reynolds & Ceranic, 2007). Research shows that moral identity interacts with moral judgment to predict moral behavior, but only under circumstances of low social consensus (Reynolds & Ceranic, 2007). However, methodological limitations (e.g., single operational definition of constructs; acceptable, but low model fit for measures) warrant further research focused on replicating this interaction with more inclusive operational definitions of moral judgment and identity and better measures (Reynolds & Ceranic, 2007).

It is noteworthy that low social consensus qualified the interactive effect in the above study, as low social consensus likely suggests disagreement concerning a situation's ethicality and therefore introduces uncertainty. It is feasible then that uncertainty unrelated to social consensus also might alter the bias-to-behavior link. For example, when an individual is newly hired and uncertain about role responsibilities, social status, and/or distinctiveness (e.g., "the rookie") the link between biased judgment and subsequent behavior is likely weaker. However, once a new hire is established within the organization, the bias-to-behavior link might strengthen due to reduced social uncertainty. Future research should examine situational moral uncertainty to determine whether moral judgments are more or less likely to facilitate moral behavior.

In addition, individuals who have an easier time altering cognitions about morally ambiguous behavior—that is, those with high *moral disengagement* levels— should have an easier time executing unethical actions. Indeed, research reports that moral disengagement predicts both unethical decisions (Detert, Treviño, & Sweitzer, 2008) and behavior (Moore, Detert, Treviño, Baker, & Mayer, 2012). Therefore, high levels of moral disengagement should strengthen the judgment to the unethical behavior link. Alternatively, low moral disengagement levels should facilitate ethical behavior following a moral judgment.

It is important to note that multiple moderators likely operate in tandem to influence the dual process model's links. For example, although moral disengagement predicts unethical behavior, this relationship might differ depending on the time of day (Kouchaki & Smith, 2014). Individuals who are low in moral disengagement tend to be ethical in the morning and unethical in the afternoon (Kouchaki & Smith, 2014). Individuals with low moral disengagement appear more susceptible to time of day effects on moral behavior, which suggests that even typically ethical individuals will behave unethically under certain conditions. However, this finding also suggests that multiple degrees of moderation are likely. For example, moral judgments could predict moral behavior differently depending on a person's moral identity or level of moral disengagement, but either of those moderating relationships might take a different form depending on a third and/or fourth factor, such as the time of day and/or chronotype. Therefore, we think that it is important for future researchers examining moderation of the bias-to behavior link (as well as other links) to consider how multiple moderators might interact to predict moral behavior for a certain individual in a particular circumstance at a given time.

## CONCLUSIONS

Contrary to the common belief that individuals who behave unethically are simply "bad apples," we reviewed research demonstrating that most individuals will behave unethically under certain circumstances. However, this review of research emphasizes that much work remains in order to understand fully how unethical behavior emerges—and can be reduced—in the workplace. Relying on sleep, self-regulation, and moral judgment/behavior research, we proposed a dual-process model of sleep and unethical behavior to guide future investigations. This model proposes that sleep can foster unethical behavior through two self-regulatory paths that shift (or override) motivation toward certain types of behavior: mis-regulation (due to affective and cognitive biases) and underregulation (due to decreased self-control). We then examined each link of this model, and presented a number of potential moderators to those links. Based on this model, we also suggested a number of research directions for researchers at the forefront of exploring the intersection of sleep, self-regulation, and ethical issues.

## REFERENCES

Allen, J., & Davis, D. (1993). Assessing some determinant effects of ethical consulting behavior: The case of personal and professional values. *Journal of Business Ethics, 12*(6), 449–458. doi:10.1007/BF01666559

Anderson, C., & Dickinson, D. (2010). Bargaining and trust: The effects of 36-h total sleep deprivation on socially interactive decisions. *Journal of Sleep Research, 19,* 54–63. doi:10.1111/j.1365-2869.2009.00767.x

Ajzen, I. (1991). The theory of planned behavior. *Organizational Behavior and Human Decision Processes, 50*(2), 179–211. doi:10.1016/0749-5978(91)90020-T

Barber, L. K., Barnes, C. M., & Carlson, K. D. (2013). Random and systematic error effects of insomnia on survey behavior. *Organizational Research Methods, 16*(4), 616–649. doi:10.1177/1094428113493120

Barber, L. K., & Budnick, C. J. (2015). Turning molehills into mountains: Sleepiness increases workplace interpretive bias. *Journal of Organizational Behavior, 36,* 360–381.

Barber, L. K., & Munz, D. C. (2011). Consistent-sufficient sleep predicts improvements in self-regulatory performance and psychological strain. *Stress and Health, 27*(4), 314–324. doi:10.1002/smi.1364

Barnes, C. M. (2012). Working in our sleep: Sleep and self-regulation in organizations. *Organizational Psychology Review, 2,* 234–257. doi:10.1177/2041386612450181

Barnes, C. M., Gunia, B. C., & Wagner, D. T. (2015). Sleep and moral awareness. *Journal of Sleep Research, 24,* 181–188. doi:10.1111/jsr.12231

Barnes, C., Lucianetti, L., Bhave, D., & Christian, M. (2015). You wouldn't like me when I'm sleepy: Leader sleep, daily abusive supervision, and work unit engagement. *Academy of Management Journal, 58*(5), 1419–1437. doi:10.5465/amj.2013.1063

Barnes, C. M., Schaubroeck, J., Huth, M., & Ghumman, S. (2011). Lack of sleep and unethical conduct. *Organizational Behavior and Human Decision Processes, 115*(2), 169–180. doi:10.1016/j.obhdp.2011.01.009

Baumeister, R. F. (2014). Self-regulation, ego depletion, and inhibition. *Neuropsychologia, 65,* 313–319. doi:10.1016/j.neuropsychologia.2014.08.012

Baumeister, R. F., & Heatherton, T. F. (1996). Self-regulation failure: An overview. *Psychological Inquiry, 7*(1), 1–15. doi:10.1207/s15327965pli0701_1

Bennett, R. J., & Robinson, S. L. (2003). The past, present, and future of workplace deviance research. In *Organizational behavior: The state of the science* (2nd ed., pp. 247–281). Mahwah, NJ: Lawrence Erlbaum Associates.

Boonstra, T. W., Stins, J. F., Daffertshofer, A., & Beek, P. J. (2007). Effects of sleep deprivation on neural functioning: An integrative review. *Cellular and Molecular Life Sciences, 64*(7–8), 934–946. doi: 10.1007/s00018-007-6457-8

Brown, F. C., Buboltz, W. C., Jr., & Soper, B. (2006). Development and evaluation of the Sleep Treatment and Education Program for Students (STEPS). *Journal of American College Health, 54,* 231–237. doi: 10.3200/JACH.54.4.231-237

Budnick, C. J., & Barber, L. K. (2015). Behind sleepy eyes: Implications of sleep loss for organizations and employees. *Translational Issues in Psychological Science, 1*(1), 89–96. doi:10.1037/tps0000014

Christian, M. S., & Ellis, A. P. J. (2011). Examining the effects of sleep deprivation on workplace deviance: A self-regulatory perspective. *Academy of Management Journal, 54*(5), 913–934. doi:10.5465/amj.2010.0179

Curtis, J., Burkley, E., & Burkley, M. (2014). The rhythm is gonna get you: The influence of circadian rhythm synchrony on self-control outcomes. *Social and Personality Psychology Compass, 8*(11), 609–625. doi:10.1111/spc3.12136

Dedeke, A. (2013). A cognitive–intuitionist model of moral judgment. *Journal of Business Ethics,* 1–21. doi:10.1007/s10551-013-1965-y

Detert, J. R., Treviño, L. K., & Sweitzer, V. L. (2008). Moral disengagement in ethical decision making: A study of antecedents and outcomes. *Journal of Applied Psychology, 93*(2), 374–391. doi: 10.1037/0021-9010.93.2.374

Dickerson, S. S., & Kemeny, M. E. (2004). Acute stressors and cortisol responses: A theoretical integration and synthesis of laboratory research. *Psychological Bulletin, 130*(3), 355–391. doi:10.1037/0033-2909.130.3.355

Durmer, J. S., & Dinges, D. F. (2005). Neurocognitive consequences of sleep deprivation. *Seminars in Neurology, 25*(1), 117–129. doi:10.1055/s-2005-867080

Eisenberg, N. (2000). Emotion, regulation, and moral development. *Annual Review of Psychology, 51,* 665–697. doi:10.1146/annurev.psych.51.1.665

Fishbein, M. & Ajzen, I. (1975). *Belief, attitude, intention and behavior: An introduction to theory and research.* Reading, MA: Addison-Wesley.

Franzen, P. L., Siegle, G. J., & Buysse, D. J. (2008). Relationships between affect, vigilance, and sleepiness following sleep deprivation. *Journal of Sleep Research, 17,* 34–41. doi:10.1111/j.1365-2869.2008.00635.x

Gailliot, M. T., Baker, M. D., Gitter, S. A., & Baumeister, R. F. (2012). Breaking the rules: Low trait or state self-control increases social norm violations. *Psychology, 3*(12), 1074–1083. doi:10.4236/psych.2012.312159

Gino, F., & Bazerman, M. H. (2009). When misconduct goes unnoticed: The acceptability of gradual erosion in others' ethical behavior. *Journal of Experimental Social Psychology, 45,* 708–719. doi:10.1016/j.jesp.2009.03.013

Gino, F., Schweitzer, M. E., Mead, N. L., & Ariely, D. (2011). Unable to resist temptation: How self-control depletion promotes unethical behavior. *Organizational Behavior and Human Decision Processes, 115*(2), 191–203. doi:10.1016/j.obhdp.2011.03.001

Gollwitzer, P. M., & Sheeran, P. (2006). Implementation intentions and goal achievement: A meta-analysis of effects and processes. *Advances in Experimental Social Psychology, 38,* 69–119. doi:10.1016/S0065-2601(06)38002-1

Gray, J. R. (1999). A bias toward short-term thinking in threat-related negative emotional states. *Personality and Social Psychology Bulletin, 25*(1), 65–75. doi:10.1177/0146167299025001006

Greene, J., & Haidt, J. (2002). How (and where) does moral judgment work? *Trends in Cognitive Sciences, 6*(12), 517–523. doi:10.1016/S1364-6613(02)02011-9

Gunia, B. C., Barnes, C. M., & Sah, S. (2014). The morality of larks and owls: Unethical behavior depends on chronotype as well as time of day. *Psychological Science, 25,* 2272–2274. doi:10.1177/0956797614541989

Haidt, J. (2001). The emotional dog and its rational tail: A social intuitionist approach to moral judgment. *Psychological Review, 108*(4), 814–834. doi:10.1037//0033-295X.108.4.814

Harrison, Y., & Horne, J. A. (2000). The impact of sleep deprivation on decision making: A review. *Journal of Experimental Psychology: Applied, 6*(3), 236–249. doi:10.1037/1076-898X.6.3.236

Inzlicht, M., & Schmeichel, B. J. (2012). What is ego depletion? Toward a mechanistic revision of the resource model of self-control. *Perspectives on Psychological Science, 7*(5), 450–463. doi:10.1177/1745691612454134

Job, V., Dweck, C. S., & Walton, G. M. (2010). Ego depletion—Is it all in your head?: Implicit theories about willpower affect self-regulation. *Psychological Science, 21,* 1686–1693. doi:10.1177/0956797610384745

Jones, T. M. (1991). Ethical decision making by individuals in organizations: An issue-contingent model. *The Academy of Management Review, 16*(2), 366–395. doi:10.2307/258867

Kaptein, M. (2011). Understanding unethical behavior by unraveling ethical culture. *Human Relations, 64*(6), 843–869. doi:10.1177/0018726710390536

Keltner, D., Ellsworth, P. C., & Edwards, K. (1993). Beyond simple pessimism: Effects of sadness and anger on social perception. *Journal of Personality and Social Psychology, 64*(5), 740–752. doi:10.1037/0022-3514.64.5.740

Killgore, W. D. S. (2010). Effects of sleep deprivation on cognition. In G. Kerkof & H. Van Dongen (Eds.), *Progress in brain research* (Vol. 185, pp.105–129). Philadephia, PA: Elsevier. doi:10.1016/B978-0-444-53702-7.00007-5

Killgore, W. D. S., Killgore, D. B., Day, L. M., Li, C., Kamimori, G. H., & Balkin, T. J. (2007). The effects of 53 hours of sleep deprivation on moral judgment. *Sleep, 30*(3), 345–352.

Kish-Gephart, J. J., Harrison, D. A., & Treviño, L. K. (2010). Bad apples, bad cases, and bad barrels: Meta-analytic evidence about sources of unethical decisions at work. *The Journal of Applied Psychology, 95*(1), 1–31. doi:10.1037/a0017103

Kouchaki, M., & Smith, I. H. (2014). The morning morality effect: The influence of time of day on unethical behavior. *Psychological Science, 25*(1), 95–102. doi:10.1177/0956797613498099

Lerner, J. S., Goldberg, J. H., & Tetlock, P. E. (1998). Sober second thought: The effects of accountability, anger, and authoritarianism on attributions of responsibility. *Personality and Social Psychology Bulletin, 24,* 563–574.

Lim, J., & Dinges, D. F. (2008). Sleep deprivation and vigilant attention. *Annals of the New York Academy of Sciences, 1129,* 305–322. doi:10.1196/annals.1417.002

Lim, J., & Dinges, D. F. (2010). A meta-analysis of the impact of short-term sleep deprivation on cognitive variables. *Psychological Bulletin, 136*(3), 375–389. doi:10.1037/a001883

Mathews, A., & MacLeod, C. (1994). Cognitive approaches to emotion and emotional disorders. *Annual Review of Psychology, 45*(1), 25–50. doi:10.1146/annurev.ps.45.020194.000325

Moore, C., Detert, J. R., Treviño, L. K., Baker, V. L., & Mayer, D. M. (2012). Why employees do bad things: Moral disengagement and unethical organizational behavior. *Personnel Psychology, 65,* 1–48. doi:10.1111/j.1744-6570.2011.01237.x

Muraven, M., & Baumeister, R. F. (2000). Self-regulation and depletion of limited resources: Does self-control resemble a muscle? *Psychological Bulletin, 126*(2), 247–259. doi:10.1037/0033-2909.126.2.247

Muraven, M., & Slessareva, E. (2003). Mechanisms of self-control failure: Motivation and limited resources. *Personality and Social Psychology Bulletin, 29*(7), 894–906. doi: 10.1177/0146167203029007008

Nägel, I. J., & Sonnentag, S. (2013). Exercise and sleep predict personal resources in employees' daily lives. *Applied Psychology. Health and Well-Being, 5*(3), 348–368. doi:10.1111/aphw.12014

Olsen, O. K., Pallesen, S., & Eid, J. (2010). The impact of partial sleep deprivation on moral reasoning in military officers. *Sleep, 33*(8), 1086–1090.

Olsen, O. K., Pallesen, S., & Espevik, R. (2013). The impact of partial sleep deprivation on military naval officers' ability to anticipate moral and tactical problems in a simulated maritime combat operation. *International Maritime Health,* *64*(2), 61–65.

Pierce, L., & Snyder, J. (2008). Ethical spill over in firms: Evidence from vehicle emissions testing. *Management Science, 54*(11), 1891–1903. doi:10.1287/mnsc.1080.0927

Pilcher, J. J., & Huffcutt, A. J. (1996). Effects of sleep deprivation on performance: A meta-analysis. *Sleep: Journal of Sleep Research & Sleep Medicine, 19*(4), 318–326.

Powpaka, S. (2002). Factors affecting managers' decision to bribe: An empirical investigation. *Journal of Business Ethics, 40,* 227–246. doi:10.1023/A:1020589612191

Ree, M. J., Pollitt, A., & Harvey, A. G. (2006). An investigation of interpretive bias in insomnia: An analog study comparing normal and poor sleepers. *Sleep, 29*(10), 1359–1362.

Rest, J. R. (1979). *Development in judging moral issues.* Minneapolis, MN: University of Minnesota Press.

Rest, J. R. (1986). *Moral development: Advances in research and theory.* New York, NY: Praeger.

Reynolds, S. J. (2006). Moral awareness and ethical predispositions: Investigating the role of individual differences in the recognition of moral issues. *Journal of Applied Psychology, 91*(1), 233–243. doi:10.1037/0021-9010.91.1.233

Reynolds, S. J., & Ceranic, T. L. (2007). The effects of moral judgment and moral identity on moral behavior: An empirical examination of the moral individual. *Journal of Applied Psychology, 92,* 1610–1624. doi: 10.1037/0021-9010.92.6.1610

Sackett, P. R., Berry, C. M., Wiemann, S. A., & Laczo, R. M. (2006). Citizenship and counterproductive behavior: Clarifying relations between the two domains. *Human Performance, 19*(4), 441–464. doi:10.1207/s15327043hup1904_7

Scher S.J., & Heise D. R (1993). Affect and the perception of injustice. *Advances in Group Processes, 10,* 223–252.

Spiegel, K., Leproult, R., & Van Cauter, E. (1999). Impact of sleep debt on metabolic and endocrine function. *Lancet, 354,* 1435–1439. doi:10.1016/S0140-6736(99)01376-8

Street, M. D., Douglas, S. C., Geiger, S. W., & Martinko, M. J. (2001). The impact of cognitive expenditure on the ethical decision-making process: The cognitive elaboration model. *Organizational Behavior and Human Decision Processes, 86*(2), 256–277. doi:10.1006/obhd.2001.2957

Tempesta, D., Couyoumdjian, A., Curcio, G., Moroni, F., Marzano, C., De Gennaro, L., & Ferrara, M. (2010). Lack of sleep affects the evaluation of emotional stimuli. *Brain Research Bulletin, 82,* 104–108. doi:10.1016/j.brainresbull.2010.01.014

Tempesta, D., Couyoumdjian, A., Moroni, F., Marzano, C., De Gennaro, L., & Ferrara, M. (2012). The impact of one night of sleep deprivation on moral judgments. *Social Neuroscience, 7*(3), 292–300. doi:10.1080/17470919.2011.614002

Treviño, L. K., & Brown, M. E. (2004). Managing to be ethical: Debunking five business ethics myths. *The Academy of Management Executive, 18*(2), 69–81. doi:10.5465/AME.2004.13837400

Treviño, L. K., Den Nieuwenboer, N. A., & Kish-Gephart, J. J. (2014). (Un)Ethical behavior in organizations. *Annual Review of Psychology, 65*(1), 635–660. doi:10.1146/annurev-psych-113011-143745

Treviño, L. K., Weaver, G. R., & Reynolds, S. J. (2006). Behavioral ethics in organizations: A review. *Journal of Management, 32,* 951–990. doi:10.1177/0149206306294258

Tyler, J. M., & Burns, K. C. (2008). After depletion: The replenishment of the self's regulatory resources. *Self and Identity, 7*(3), 305–321. doi:10.1080/15298860701799997

Van Dongen, H. P. A., Maislin, G., Mullington, J. M., & Dinges, D. F. (2003). The cumulative cost of additional wakefulness: Dose-response effects on neurobehavioral functions and sleep physiology from chronic sleep restriction to total sleep deprivation. *Sleep, 26*(2), 117–126. Retrieved from http://www.med. upenn.edu/uep/user_documents/VanDongen_etal_Sleep_26_2_2003.pdf

Wagner, D. T., Barnes, C. M., Lim, V. K., & Ferris, D. L. (2012). Lost sleep and cyberloafing: Evidence from the laboratory and a daylight saving time quasi-experiment. *Journal of Applied Psychology, 97*(5), 1068–1076. doi:10.1037/a0027557

Weaver, G. R., Reynolds, S. J., & Brown, M. E. (2014). Moral intuition: Connecting current knowledge to future organizational research and practice. *Journal of Management, 40*(1), 100–129. doi:10.1177/0149206313511272

Webb, T. L., & Sheeran, P. (2003). Can implementation intentions help overcome ego-depletion? *Journal of Experimental Social Psychology, 39*, 279–286. doi:10.1016/S0022-1031(02)00527-9

Welsh, D. T., Ellis, A. P. J., Christian, M. S., & Mai, K. M. (2014). Building a self-regulatory model of sleep deprivation and deception: The role of caffeine and social influence. *Journal of Applied Psychology, 99*, 1268–1277. doi: 10.1037/a0036202.

Yoo, S., Gujar, N., Hu, P., Jolesz, F., & Walker, M. (2007). The human emotional brain without sleep—a prefrontal amygdala disconnect. *Current Biology, 17*, 877–878. Retrieved from http://www.ncbi.nlm.nih.gov/pubmed/17956744

# CHAPTER 8

# Work, Sleep, and Driving

ALISTAIR W. MACLEAN

## WORK, SLEEP, AND DRIVING

Driving is an integral part of many work environments either as a job requirement or as a means of getting to and from the workplace. According to the Royal Society for the Prevention of Accidents (2007) driving is the most dangerous work activity that most people do. Sleepiness is the second leading cause of crashes and fatalities after drugs and alcohol. Both laboratory and field studies inform our knowledge of the causative factors underlying these events and the countermeasures necessary to prevent them.

### Driving and Crashes

World-wide more than 3,000 people die every day as a result of a vehicle crash; 20 to 50 million more sustain nonfatal injuries. The economic costs are estimated at between 1% and 3% of the Gross National Product. Barring effective action, "road traffic injuries are predicted to become the fifth leading cause of death in the world" (World Health Organization, p. 4). The United Nations General Assembly has proclaimed 2011 to 2020 a Decade of Action for road safety. Pillar 4 of the plan is "Safer road users" and one of the core indicators by which success will be measured is the "number of countries with a formal policy to regulate fatigue among commercial vehicle drivers."

### Sleepiness-Related Crashes

Estimates of the number of crashes caused by sleepiness or fatigue vary widely. The U.S. Department of Transportation (2011) reports that from 2005 to 2009, drowsy driving was responsible on average for 2.5% of fatal crashes, 2.2% of crashes in which an injury occurred, and 1.3% of all police-reported crashes. Nevertheless there is a broad spectrum of results that suggests that the proportion of sleep-related crashes is about 20% (Garbarino, Nobili, Beelke, De Carli, & Ferrillo, 2001; Horne & Reyner, 1995; Klauer, Dingus, Neale, Sudweeks, & Ransey, 2006; Tefft, 2012; Vanlaar, Simpson, Mayhew, & Robertson, 2008).

## Work-Related Driving

Three broad, and not necessarily mutually exclusive, groups of people drive in relation to their work: (1) professional drivers, (2) those who are not professional drivers but who have to travel between different locations to perform their work, and (3) commuters. Driving as a job requirement encompasses a wide range of vehicles and drivers. One difficulty of interpreting traffic statistics is that in many cases no distinction is made between different types of drivers. However, Howard et al. (2014) found that "professional drivers are just as susceptible to the effects of acute sleep loss as nonprofessional drivers, rather than being more resistant to sleep loss than other populations" (p. 136).

***1. Professional drivers.*** Clarke, Ward, Bartle, and Truman (2009) identified six classes of vehicle found to be most commonly involved in a work-related vehicle crash, which accounted for 88% of the 2,111 reports that they studied: (1) company cars, (2) vans/pickups, (3) large goods vehicles, (4) buses, (5) taxis, and (6) emergency vehicles. They found that large goods vehicle drivers had a higher proportion of fatigue-related collisions. In the United Kingdom work-related road crashes are the greatest cause of work-related accidental death and about 40% of sleepiness-related crashes involve someone driving a commercial vehicle (TUC, 2013). Smith and Williams (2014) report United States Bureau of Labor Statistics that project a 21% increase in the trucking industry by 2020, making it the "eighth highest occupation in terms of new jobs", and suggesting that sleep-related crashes may become even more important in the future if no corrective action is taken. Their data indicate "that vehicle related incidents are costly and have longer time-loss than other types of injuries" (p. 71).

Studies by the U.S.A. National Transportation Safety board reported by Philip and Åkerstedt (2006) identified sleepiness as a significant factor in crashes involving heavy vehicles; they estimate that "52% of 107 one-vehicle accidents involving heavy trucks were fatigue related" (p. 348). Philip et al. (2010) found that both professional drivers and drivers who drove more than 25,000 km/year had a higher risk of driving accidents.

***2. Jobs requiring driving.*** Drivers who are generally not regarded as professional but for whom driving is an integral part of their work include community nurses, home care workers, social workers, commercial sales representatives, and maintenance workers (TUC, 2013). Police officers appear to fall somewhere between this group and the previous one. They recognize the impact that their heavy work schedules (Vila, 2006) have on their driving (Radun, Ohisalo, Radun, & Kecklund, 2011).

**3. Commuters.** The International Labour Organisation reported that in 2002 commuting accidents had reached almost 15% of all work-related accidents in the developed countries. There are indications that this proportion has grown, particularly in developing countries such as Malaysia where in recent years 88% of accidents are reported to have occurred while commuting (Nordin, 2014). Åkerstedt, Peters, Anund, and Kecklund (2005) using a driving simulator found that workers driving after a night shift had substantially increased levels of sleepiness and decreased driving performance. Similar findings have been reported for medical professionals following shifts (Ftouni et al., 2013; Scott et al., 2007; Tornero, Ventura, Bourguet, & Poquet, 2012).

In Canada, in 2011, 45% (15.4 million people) of the population commuted to work (Statistics Canada, 2011). Private vehicles were used by 83%: of those using public transit, 64% commuted by bus. In 2011 in the United Kingdom 67% of commuters used private transport as their main means of commuting (Goodman, 2013). In the United States in recent years we have seen growth in "supercommuting," which is defined in different ways by different authors but generally involves either commutes in excess of 90 minutes in duration or 50 miles in distance; 5% of U.S. workers have long commutes and they may typically leave for work before 06:00 am (Rapino & Fields, 2013).

## Legal and Policy Implications

Legislation and policy differ among jurisdictions but responsibility and liability for vehicle crashes fall primarily on employers and drivers (Ellis & Grunstein, 2001; George, 2011; Jones, Dorrian, & Dawson, 2003; Jones, Dorrian, & Rajaratnam, 2005). Williamson and Friswell (2013) argue that occupational fatigue is unique in that people may be exposed to risks to which they would not otherwise be subject. "Responsibility to manage fatigue risk in workplaces falls directly under the general duties requirement on employers to eliminate hazards ..." (p. 89); however, they concede that "deciding how far to go in attempting to reduce workplace fatigue risk and the effects of fatigue is not clear cut" (p. 90) and, although some solutions exist, further work is required to both understand and counter fatigue. Under workers' compensation legislation employers also have liabilities for injuries to workers driving within their scope of employment. This liability may in some circumstances extend to third parties, for example, individuals injured by employees. Workloads that contravene or fail to permit compliance with hours of service guidelines may give rise to increased liability as would failure to monitor compliance (George, 2011).

In response to increasing levels of concern about occupational fatigue generally, and its effect on driving in particular, governments, industry, and unions have increasingly developed policies mandating or providing guidelines for working hours and conditions of employment. Most have provisions determining hours of work and the scheduling of work. "Yet, most around-the-clock industries still have regulations and policies that do not take the neurobiology underlying fatigue into account and therefore tend to be overly permissive (unsafe) in some situations and overly restrictive (suboptimal) in others" (Satterfield & Van Dongen, 2013, p. 127). To a greater extent organizations are adopting integrated approaches to the management of fatigue known as risk management systems. Elements of these approaches will be described below when countermeasures to sleepiness are considered.

The driver of any vehicle has a duty to operate it in a safe manner. "With respect to sleepiness, a driver with a sleep disorder or extreme sleepiness from whatever cause is at risk for a sleepiness-related accident. If that individual does not take measures to reduce this risk, then they may be guilty of dangerous driving and liable for the consequences of falling asleep while driving a motor vehicle" (George, 2011, p. 92). A crucial issue is whether the driver was aware of sleepiness or had indulged in behaviors likely to cause sleepiness. A major problem with the regulation of sleepy driving is that—unlike some other risky road behaviors such as drunk driving, speeding, and the use of seat belts—no objective measure of the level of driver sleepiness currently exists (Watling, Armstrong, & Smith, 2013). However, in one approach to this problem the State of New Jersey has enacted legislation (the Maggie McDonnell law) to the effect that a driver who has been awake for 24 or more hours can be inferred to be driving recklessly (Powell & Chau, 2010).

Although there is evidence that both the public (Williams, Davies, Thiele, Davidson, & MacLean, 2012) and some of the judiciary (Ellis & Grunstein, 2001) have been inclined to treat sleep deprivation as less culpable than alcohol intoxication, recent indications are that crashes in which the driver is judged to be culpable through lack of sleep are being dealt with severely (Cassidy, 2014; Laframboise, 2014).

## Nature of Sleepiness

Before examining further the causes, characteristics, and mitigation of sleepy driving it will be helpful to review some of the basic physiological and behavioral aspects of sleepiness. Sleep is essential, "vital for both the brain and the body" (Czeisler, 2015, p. 6). Disruption of the duration, timing, or quality of sleep produces deterioration in many aspects of bodily functioning (Czeisler, 2015) vital to effective driving. The drive to sleep is powerful and cannot be ignored. "We may struggle valiantly against this strong force but ultimately all performance will bend before it" (Webb, 1975, p. 135).

### Terminology

Although the terms sleepiness and fatigue and their synonyms are frequently used interchangeably by the general public, government agencies, clinicians, and researchers (Noy et al., 2011, p. 496; Van Dongen, Caldwell, & Caldwell, 2011, p. 36), there is some consensus that they refer to separate constructs (Drake, 2011, p. 67). Sleepiness has been defined as "a drive towards sleep" (Åkerstedt,

2011, p. 186) often due to a reduction or fragmentation of sleep (Mullins, Cortina, & Drake, 2014) and fatigue as "the reluctance to continue a task as a result of physical or mental exertion or a prolonged period of performing the same task" (Beirness, Simpson, & Desmond, 2005, p. 6). "Perhaps the main feature of fatigue, distinct from sleepiness, is that although fatigue may lead the individual to desire sleep, fatigue is often not dissipated by that sleep" (Monk, 2012). In common with most of the literature, no distinction is made between the terms in this review.

Similarly, in the literature the terms crash and accident are used interchangeably. Accident implies an event without apparent cause. Although it is clear that sleepiness is a causal factor in many crashes, and is not accidental, many sleepy drivers do not crash. For a crash to occur a confluence of circumstances must be present for some of which no clear causal chain may be present and can therefore be regarded as accidental. A driver who falls asleep briefly on a straight road may, provided a vehicle in front does not brake suddenly or some similar incident occur, survive without any harm. Unfortunately, incidents such as these may lead drivers to underestimate the degree of danger present when they are sleepy.

### Mechanisms

Although there is no universally accepted theory of sleepiness, a widely accepted hypothesis is due to the work of Carskadon and Dement (1982) who suggested the existence of both physiological and manifest sleep tendencies. MacLean, Davies, and Thiele (2003) represented this hypothesis as shown in Figure 8.1. (This also provides a useful heuristic for considering the relationship between sleepiness and driving.) Physiological sleepiness is determined by both sleep history and circadian factors. When all alerting factors are removed the physiological sleep tendency can be measured. If alerting factors are present (e.g., motivation, physical activity, caffeine) they can oppose, or mask, the underlying sleep tendency.

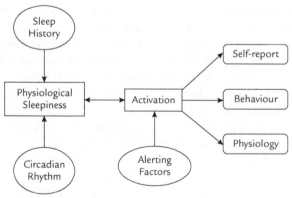

**Figure 8.1.**
Model of sleepiness.
Based on Carskadon and Dement (1982), from "The hazards and prevention of driving while sleepy" by Alistair W. MacLean, David R.T. Davies, and Kris Thiele, 2003, *Sleep Medicine Reviews, 7*, 510. Copyright 2003 by *Sleep Medicine Review*. Reprinted with permission.

The model is consistent with the two-process model proposed by Borbély (1982), which postulates a Process S (sleep history) that increases exponentially during wakefulness and declines exponentially during sleep and a Process C (circadian rhythm) that fluctuates over the 24-hour day. Folkard and Åkerstedt (1992) proposed the addition of a further Process W that integrates the emergence from sleep, also known as sleep inertia, conceived of as a saturating exponential function. More detailed accounts of these mechanisms can be found in Dijk and Lazar (2012) and Monk (2012).

The model, although one among many (e.g., Mullins et al., 2014), provides a simplified yet useful explanation both of the factors producing sleepiness and how their manipulation can increase or decrease sleepiness. The outcome of these manipulations will thus affect self-reports of sleepiness, and the behavioral outcomes of sleepiness, such as driving, and physiology. Clearly, sleep history and circadian rhythm are the major determinants of physiological sleepiness and can also be manipulated to minimize sleepiness. The presence of alerting factors can mitigate, to some extent, the effects of physiological sleepiness.

## Sleepiness and Performance

Sleepiness is commonly observed as a function of sleep loss and the relationship between sleep loss and performance has been extensively studied. Many reviews are available of studies in both laboratory and natural environments (Dinges & Kribbs, 1991; Lim & Dinges, 2010; Monk, 2012; Pilcher & Huffcutt, 1996) and the principal effects of sleep loss on performance are clear. One of the most pervasive and insidious effects is the occurrence of microsleeps—sometimes called "blocks" or "lapses"—that are described in the classic monograph of Williams, Lubin, and Goodnow (1959) as "brief periods of no response which increase in frequency and duration" (p. 1). Depending on whether tasks are paced or unpaced (Broadbent, 1953), that is, the required response is determined by the environment or is under the control of the operator, the effect of microsleeps appears as either errors or as changes in the speed of response. Monk (2012) has described this as the first pathway linking sleep deprivation to performance impairment. The other pathways he has identified as cognitive rigidity—"a lack of creativity in the way in which the task is approached" that may lead to a lack of ability to adapt to changing situations; cognitive slowing—a reduction in the speed with which information is processed; and losing motivation. This last pathway is unique as it not only has direct effects on performance but also mediates microsleeps and cognitive rigidity (pp. 99–100). Even after prolonged sleep loss individuals can, when sufficiently motivated, perform extremely well—at least for short periods of time (Gulevich, Dement, & Johnson, 1966) while otherwise they may simply stop trying (cf. the activation path in Figure 8.1).

It was early recognized that tasks particularly affected by sleepiness share certain characteristics (Wilkinson, 1992). They must be long, have a response determined by the environment, and lack motivation. However, some short tasks are also affected by sleep loss leading to the understanding that what tasks sensitive to sleepiness share is "a relentless requirement for sustained attention" (Dinges & Kribbs, 1991, p. 120). Depending on circumstances, driving shares all of these characteristics.

In addition to the direct effects of sleep loss, performance is determined by the time of day at which it is measured. Many behaviors and physiological variables continue to oscillate with a period close to 24 hours even when individuals are isolated from other time cues (Dijk & Lazar, 2012). Circadian rhythms produce periods of increased sleepiness during the nighttime hours and, to a lesser extent, in the early afternoon. Decrements in performance also occur during these periods (Monk, 2012) and this temporal pattern has been shown to be consistent with the observed patterns of a variety of incidents, accidents, and catastrophes (Mitler et al., 1988).

Much of the literature describing the effects of sleep loss on performance has focused on measures known to be sensitive to sleepiness, such as under monotonous conditions involving low motivation, and conditions known to be favorable to demonstrating the adverse effects of sleep deprivation. Until quite recently relatively little has focused on higher cognitive functions such as planning, decision making, and risk taking. In an extensive review of the impact of sleep deprivation on decision making, Harrison and Horne (2000), identified several areas in which the effect of sleep loss had been underestimated including ". . . impaired language skills--communication, lack of innovation, inflexibility of thought processes, inappropriate attention to peripheral concerns or distraction, over-reliance on previous strategies, unreliable memory for when events occurred, change in mood including loss of empathy with colleagues, and inability to deal with surprise and the unexpected" (p. 246). Sleep loss has also been shown to: increase risk taking (Harrison & Horne, 1998), impair innovative thinking and decision making (Harrison & Horne, 1999), and affect responses to moral dilemmas (Killgore et al., 2007). Many of the phenomena identified in the extensive research on sleepiness related to sleep loss are relevant to driving. For example, driving requires sustained attention, may be monotonous, may require quick decisions in a changing environment, and may take place at hours during which the driver would normally be asleep. Sleepiness, possibly accompanied by microsleeps, impairs the ability of a driver to function effectively and increases the possibility of an adverse event.

## Sleepiness and Driving

### Changes in Performance

There is a considerable body of literature describing changes in driving performance as a consequence of sleepiness. Dingus et al. (2006) draw a useful distinction between empirical data collection (test tracks and simulators), large-scale naturalistic data collection, and epidemiological data (p. xxvii). Information about sleepy drivers comes from all these sources. Observations in a controlled environment may give access to knowledge that is unobtainable in a natural environment because of ethical or practical considerations. Clearly, comparison of outcomes from controlled studies with those from a natural environment must take into account the different methods used and the context in which the data were obtained. Experiencing a crash in a simulator is very different from having one on the road. Nevertheless, with the appropriate cautions, useful generalizations may be made (Mayhew et al., 2011; Mullen, Charlton, Devlin, & Bédard, 2011; Philip, Sagaspe, Taillard, et al., 2005; Shechtman, Classen, Awadzi, & Mann, 2009; Wang et al., 2010).

There is substantial evidence that under conditions in which sleepiness can be presumed or established to be present deteriorations in driving behavior are manifested in a number of different ways including increased variability in lane position, increased variability in speed, an increased number of off-road events, and slowed reaction time (Howard et al., 2014; MacLean et al., 2003; Meng et al., 2015; Philip, Sagaspe, Moore, et al., 2005; Thiffault & Bergeron, 2003; Ting, Hwang, Doong, & Jeng, 2008).

### Driving While Sleepy

In questionnaire studies drivers report that driving while sleepy is a common phenomenon. From 14% to 77% (median 57) reported that they drive while sleepy (BaHammam et al., 2014; Beirness et al., 2005; Marcoux, Vanlaar, & Robertson, 2012; Marshall, Bolger, & Gander, 2004; Meng et al., 2015; Obst, Armstrong, Smith, & Banks, 2011; Pérez-Chada et al., 2005; Robertson, Holmes, & Vanlaar, 2009; Sagaspe et al., 2010; van den Berg & Landström, 2006; Vanlaar et al., 2008). From 14% to 39% (median 18) reported that they fell asleep while driving in the last 6 months to a year (BaHammam et al., 2014; Beirness et al., 2005; Marcoux et al., 2012; Robertson et al., 2009; Vanlaar et al., 2008). Near misses were reported by from 11% to 33% (median 30) of which from 46% to 50% were attributed to sleepiness (BaHammam et al., 2014; Obst et al., 2011; Philip et al., 2010; Sagaspe et al., 2010; Vanlaar, Simpson, Mayhew, & Robertson, 2007). From 7% to 21% (median 12) reported a crash in the previous 6 months to a year (BaHammam et al., 2014; Marcoux et al., 2012; Marshall et al., 2004; Meng et al., 2015; Philip et al., 2010; Robertson et al., 2009; Sagaspe et al., 2010).

From analyses of the 100-Car Naturalistic Driving Study, Klauer et al. (2006) reported that driving on divided highways produces a slightly greater amount of drowsiness than on undivided highways, but as traffic density increases the frequency of drowsiness decreases. Both these phenomena are probably related to the level of stimulation produced. Klauer et al. (2006) concluded "that driving drowsy is at least three times riskier than driving while alert during the same level of traffic density" (p. 53). "Driving while drowsy on either dry or wet roadways increased near-crash/crash risk by at least three times over that of driving alert on a dry or wet roadway" (p. 56).

In addition to its effects on performance, sleepiness may adversely influence other risky behaviors related to driving including consuming alcohol, speeding, distracted driving, and aggression (Watling et al., 2013).

### Driver's Perception of Risk

Although many drivers continue to drive even when they recognize that they are sleepy they are often aware of the effects of sleepiness on driving. Obst et al. (2011) found that drivers perceived the risk of driving while sleepy to be a higher risk than driving with a blood alcohol concentration in excess of 0.05. Several studies have demonstrated that driving while sleepy is as dangerous as driving with pro-scribed blood alcohol levels (Arnett, Wilde, Munt, & MacLean, 2000; Dawson & Reid, 1997; Verster, Taillard, Sagaspe, Olivier, & Philip, 2011).

### Characteristics of Sleepiness-Related Crashes

Sleepiness-related crashes are more likely to (1) occur at night or mid-afternoon, (2) involve a single vehicle running off the roadway or rear-end or head-on colli-sions, (3) occur on higher-speed roadways, (4) involve only the driver as an occu-pant, and (5) result in serious injuries (Stutts, Wilkins, & Vaughn, 1999). Sagaspe et al. (2010, p. 583) also report that "sleep-related accidents are more severe than non-sleep-related accidents." Elzohairy (2007) found that the most common errors committed by sleepy drivers included (1) following too close (59%), (2) losing control (28%), (3) improper lane change (4%), and (4) failure to yield (4%). Abe, Komada, Nishida, Hayashida, and Inoue (2010) found that short nocturnal sleep (<6 hours) and longer periods of driving were associated with rear-end collisions and single car accidents and in Ontario, Canada, police officers most commonly associated sleepy driving with rear-end and head-on collisions (69.9%), collisions happening at night (70.4%), and collisions involving a single vehicle running off the roadway (90.4%) (Robertson et al., 2009).

### Factors Increasing Likelihood of Sleepy Driving

**Restricted sleep.** Insufficient or poor quality sleep is frequently reported in rela-tion to sleepiness while driving. Contributing causes may include not enough sleep (BaHammam et al., 2014; Beirness et al., 2005; Luckhaupt, Kak, & Calvert, 2010; Meng et al., 2015; Nordbakke & Sagberg, 2007; Pérez-Chada et al., 2005; Valent, Di Bartolomeo, Marchetti, Sbrojavacca, & Barbone, 2010; van den Berg & Landström, 2006; Vanlaar et al., 2007; Wheaton, Chapman, Presley-Cantrell, Croft, & Roehler, 2013), poor quality sleep before driving (van den Berg & Landström, 2006), night or rotating shifts (Sharwood et al., 2013; Vanlaar et al., 2007), and poor work schedules (Philip et al., 2002; van den Berg & Landström, 2006). Reduced sleep quantity has also been associated with sleepiness while driving, specifically, getting less than 6 hours sleep has been reported to lead to increased sleepiness or falling asleep while driving (Wheaton et al., 2013; Wheaton, Shults, Chapman, Ford, & Croft, 2014) and increased risk of crashes (Abe et al., 2010). An interesting cultural factor relating to sleepiness while driving is reported by Al-Houqani, Eid, and Abu-Zidan (2013) who found that sleep-related crashes increased sharply during the month of Ramadan. The authors suggest that this "is due to the decrease of the nocturnal sleep duration, the delay in rising time and the absence of breakfast and caffeine intake." (p. 1054)

**Working conditions.** Drivers perceive that driving after a long, stressful work day (Nordbakke & Sagberg, 2007; Valent et al., 2010; Vanlaar et al., 2007), driving continuously for an extended period without a break (Aworemi, Abdul-Azeez, Oyedokun, & Adewoye, 2010; Meng et al., 2015; Nordbakke & Sagberg, 2007; Pérez-Chada et al., 2005; Vanlaar et al., 2007), and making many driving trips over the course of the day (Vanlaar et al., 2007) all contribute to falling asleep or nodding off at the wheel. However, 44% of drivers surveyed by Beirness et al. (2005) reported that "they had only been driving for an hour when they nodded off" (p.12) indicating that falling asleep can occur quite quickly after commencing a drive and does not occur only on long drives.

As noted above, shift work is also cited as a factor associated with greater levels of sleepiness and impaired driving performance (Di Milia, 2006; Ftouni et al., 2013). A National Sleep Foundation (2012) study found that truck drivers were significantly more likely than a control group not employed in the transportation industry to work shifts of 9 hours or more. Bus, taxi, limousine, or truck drivers were also less likely to work the same schedule each day or the same day each week than the control group and had more shifts starting between the hours of 03:30 am and 06:30 am. Consistent with the model of sleepiness shown in Figure 8.1, the greater levels of sleepiness, and hence increased risk for driving incidents, seen in shift workers are related to reduced sleep time, decreased quality of sleep, and disturbances in the circadian rhythm produced by shift work (Bajraktarov et al., 2011).

**Circadian changes.** Vehicle crashes are not equally distributed across the day. The two time periods in which most sleep-related crashes occur are 03:00 to 05:00 and 14:00 to 16:00 (see MacLean et al., 2003; H. Zhang, Yan, Wu, & Qiu, 2014) coincident with the periods of increased sleepiness during the nighttime hours and the early afternoon described above. Drivers frequently cite poor work schedules as contributing to sleepiness while driving (van den Berg & Landström, 2006). Night driving is associated with increased levels of sleepiness (Abe et al., 2010; Klauer et al., 2006; Vanlaar et al., 2007). Many drivers report that they feel most sleepy in the period from about 03:00 to 06:00 (van den Berg & Landström, 2006). A time of particular risk for commuters is the drive home, particularly from a night shift (Åkerstedt et al., 2005). Similar results have been found in studies of medical personnel (Barger et al., 2005; Scott et al., 2007) and police forces (Radun, Ohisalo, Radun, Wahde, & Kecklund, 2013). "The reason for the accident risk associated with the postnight shift commute is, most likely, the combination of the circadian low and an extended time awake . . . " (Åkerstedt et al., 2005, p. 19).

**Sleep disorders.** Working conditions, particularly shift work, can have a deleterious effect on health including sleep disorders (Bajraktarov et al., 2011). However, individuals with certain sleep disorders are more likely to be sleepy while driving either because sleepiness is a major aspect of the disorder, as in the case of obstructive sleep apnea or narcolepsy, or because they are more likely to have experienced shortened sleep length or disturbed sleep, as in the case of insomnia. In a study of 35,004 drivers Philip et al. (2010) found that 16.9% complained of at least one sleep disorder, 9.3% complained of insomnia, 5.2% complained of obstructive sleep apnea, and 0.1% complained of narcolepsy and hypersomnia. The highest risk of accidents was found in patients with narcolepsy and hypersomnia or multiple sleep disorders.

**Alcohol.** Drivers who have consumed alcohol, even at low doses, are at increased risk for sleepiness because of its exacerbating effects on sleepiness and on performance (Arnedt et al., 2000; Barrett, Horne, & Reyner, 2004; Horne, Reyner, & Barrett, 2003; Howard et al., 2007; Roehrs, Beare, Zorick, & Roth, 1994; Vakulin et al., 2007; Wilson, Fang, Cooper, & Beirness, 2006; X. Zhang, Zhao, Du, & Rong, 2014) even when that alcohol is ingested on the previous night (Nordbakke & Sagberg, 2007). Essentially, alcohol combines additively with sleep loss to increase self-reported sleepiness and decrease performance; this impairment can extend beyond the point at which blood alcohol concentrations are zero. Drivers generally underestimate the extent of their impairment.

**Drugs.** Many drugs have a side-effect of sleepiness including hypnotics, antianxiety drugs, antidepressants, antipsychotic drugs, antiepileptic drugs, and antihistamines (Hetland & Carr, 2014; Schweirzer, 2011). Bonnet et al. (2005) in a review of the use of stimulants to counteract the effects of sleep deprivation concluded that depending on a number of factors including the availability of medical supervision, limited use of stimulants may be appropriate. However, Gates, Dubois, Mullen, Weaver, and Bedard (2013) found that even the use of stimulant drugs is no guarantee of improved driving: The odds of an unsafe driving action were 78% higher for truck drivers who tested positive for stimulant use.

**Additional factors.** Young drivers have frequently been found to be more at risk than older, more experienced drivers (Abe et al., 2010; BaHammam et al., 2014; Elzohairy, 2007; Lowden, Anund, Kecklund, Peters, & Åkerstedt, 2009; Obst et al., 2011; Philip et al., 2010; Sagaspe et al., 2010; Watling, 2014; Wheaton et al., 2013, 2014). Females are less likely to drive while sleepy (Beirness et al., 2005; Elzohairy, 2007; Obst et al., 2011; Vanlaar et al., 2007; Wheaton et al., 2013, 2014). Feeling sleepy while driving is, not surprisingly, predictive of crashes (BaHammam et al., 2014; Ozer, Etcibaşı, & Oztürk, 2014; Pérez-Chada et al., 2005; Sagaspe et al., 2010) as is the occurrence of previous near misses (BaHammam et al., 2014).

## Detection and Countermeasures

### Detection of Sleepiness

**Technical approaches.** Abe, Mollicone, Basner, and Dinges (2014) identify two areas of technology that they regard as promising "for managing sleepiness/fatigue risk in human systems" (p. 74): "optimizing work schedules . . . and technologies for detecting drowsy and fatigued operators on the job" (pp. 74–75). The former will be dealt with below. The latter draws attention to an extensive literature on technologies that can be used to identify drowsy driving and implement counter-measures (Brown, Lee, Schwarz, Dary Florentino, & McDonald, 2014; Dawson, Searle, & Paterson, 2014). It nevertheless remains the case that most drivers rely on their own judgment as to when they are too sleepy to drive and make use of simple countermeasures that are available to every driver. As mentioned above, these individual strategies are increasingly being integrated into fatigue manage-ment systems that combine both individual and system-wide strategies for the mitigation of sleepiness.

*Subjective sleepiness.* Central to the application of countermeasures is the recognition by the driver of the presence of sleepiness. As Monk (2012, p. 95) has observed: "... subjective sleepiness ... is the messenger, as it were, by which we are made aware of our sleep insufficiency." The process by which drivers reach a decision that they are too sleepy to drive is not well known. It is clear that drivers are aware of some of the common signs of sleepiness including difficulty keep-ing the eyes open, yawning, more frequent eye blinks, difficulty concentrating, changing position, increased reaction time, and increased variation in speed (Nordbakke & Sagberg, 2007; van den Berg & Landström, 2006). Nordbakke and Sagberg (2007, p. 3) speculate that "difficulties to keep eyes open and entering a dreamlike state of consciousness make up the most important warnings that driv-ers should beware."

### Countermeasures

Satterfield and Van Dongen (2013, p. 123) have distinguished between counter-measures that are preventive, which aim to reduce sleepiness before it becomes a problem, and operational strategies, which aim to mitigate its effects when it may already be present.

*Preventive countermeasures.* Ideally, no driver should experience sleepiness. This presupposes an optimal conjunction of sleep quality with an appropriate point in the circadian cycle (see Figure 8.1). This can be determined only prior to driv-ing either before leaving home, by the work environment, or by taking appropriate advantage of opportunities to nap while on route. Getting sufficient sleep prior to driving is one of the most influential factors determining the degree of alertness of a driver (van den Berg & Landström, 2006). Both Satterfield and Van Dongen (2013) and Williamson and Friswell (2013) provide useful reviews of countermeasures open to employers and individuals for the management of occupational fatigue. In principle, drivers could be tested before they begin driving to ensure that they are sufficiently alert. Apart from the legal and ethical issues involved in such a proce-dure, it is the case that the tests that might be used have only a modest ability to predict inadequate driving. As Philip, Sagaspe, Taillard, et al. (2005, p. 1515) have observed: "Possibly only sleepiness at the exact time of driving has a direct correla-tion with actual driving performance."

Education of drivers is an important aspect of a sleepiness management system (Gander, Marshall, Bolger, & Girling, 2005) and employers clearly have a responsibility in this respect. Other considerations for employers are the choice of an optimal scheduling system (Knauth, 2003) or the judicious (Howard, Radford, Jackson, Swann, & Kennedy, 2009) use of naps (Garbarino et al., 2004; Hirose, 2005) to reduce sleepiness either during work-related driving or in advance of the commute to home. Another option is "for employers to consider ways of eliminating the driving risk after night shift. Some possibilities include chartering a bus to transport employees or requiring employees to sleep for a minimum period before driving" (Di Milia, 2006, p. 284; Wheaton et al., 2013, p. 3)

It is, nevertheless, the case that most drivers continue to drive even when they feel sleepy. Nordbakke and Sagberg (2007) found that the most frequently reported (endorsed by more than 30% of drivers) reasons for this behavior included a short trip, appointments to keep, and the wish to arrive home at a reasonable hour.

***Operational strategies.*** Absent the opportunity to ensure minimal physiological sleepiness before driving the driver is constrained to oppose physiological sleepiness either by taking naps en route or by increasing activation. However, it is critical to realize that no countermeasure, apart from the elimination of physiological sleepiness, can be other than temporarily successful. "Sleepiness is relentless, no matter how cleverly humans disguise the impairment it brings on when they seek to perform" (Dinges & Kribbs, 1991, p. 121).

Drivers use a wide variety of countermeasures to combat sleepiness. There is not sufficient evidence to reliably link particular categories of drivers with the choice of specific countermeasures but the choice may be due to factors including the length of the drive, the degree of sleepiness present, whether driving on urban roads or highways, and whether passengers are present (Meng et al., 2015). The countermeasures practiced most frequently, that is, by more than 40% of drivers, include turn the radio on loudly; open the window or turn on the air conditioning or fan; stop to eat, exercise, relax, but not nap or sleep; and eat or drink. The next most common, adopted by 30% or more of drivers, are drink coffee, soda, or caffeine; stop, pull over, and rest, nap, or sleep; eat candy; and move around or shake the head. Other behaviors less commonly adopted are sing along to music; smoke; pour water on the face or neck or slap or hit or punch oneself; change drivers; talk to passengers; change the radio station, CD, or tape; talk on the cell phone; drink an energy drink; do nothing and keep driving; or take a stimulant (Anund, Kecklund, Peters, & Åkerstedt, 2008; Beirness et al., 2005; Gershon, Shinar, Oron-Gilad, Parmet, & Ronen, 2011; Marcoux et al., 2012; Meng et al., 2015; Nordbakke & Sagberg, 2007; Sharwood et al., 2013; van den Berg & Landström, 2006; Vanlaar et al., 2007).

Unfortunately, the empirical evidence for the effectiveness of most of these behaviors as countermeasures is weak. The two countermeasures that have most consistently been shown to be effective are the use of caffeine and naps. Horne and Reyner (1996) found that a nap of less than 15 minutes duration and 150 mg of caffeine in coffee significantly reduced sleepiness and driving impairments on a simulated afternoon drive for about an hour in individuals whose sleep had been restricted to 5 hours on the previous night. The combination of a nap and 200 mg of caffeine was more effective and improved driving performance for up to 2 hours (Reyner & Horne, 1997). The effectiveness of naps and caffeine has been generally confirmed (Hartley et al., 2013; Léger, Philip, Jarriault, Metlaine, & Choudat, 2009; Mets, Baas, van Boven, Olivier, & Verster, 2012; Sagaspe et al., 2007; Schweitzer, Randazzo, Stone, Erman, & Walsh, 2006; Sharwood et al., 2013), although it must be borne in mind that they are effective for only moderate levels of sleepiness and the longer the nap the greater the likelihood of sleep inertia, the period following wakening "which is characterized by transitory hypovigilance, drowsiness and diminished performance" (Muzet, Nicolas, Tassi, Dewasmes, & Bonneau, 1995). In terms of the model shown in Figure 8.1 naps are effective by virtue of reducing physiological sleepiness whereas caffeine increases activation and only masks the underlying sleepiness. Spaeth, Goel, and Dinges (2014, p. 43) have observed that "It is important for caffeine consumers to understand that caffeine at any dose is not a chemical substitute for adequate healthy sleep. . . . when the pressure for sleep is high, caffeine has little effect on preventing performance deficits . . . ."

The provision of roadside safety rest areas reduces the frequency of fatigue-related crashes (McArthur, Kay, Savolainen, & Gates, 2013; Reyner, Horne, & Flatley, 2010). Chen and Xie (2014) found that taking rest breaks during a 10-hour trip reduced commercial truck drivers' crash risk. Two rest breaks were found to be optimal and 30 minutes was found to be an adequate length of break. Some apparent countermeasures can leave the driver feeling less sleepy but have no effects on actual driving. Watling, Smith, and Horswill (2014) found this after a 15-minute active rest break; possibly this is due to the temporary increase in activation that may mask underlying physiological sleepiness, without improving the underlying sleepiness.

Reyner and Horne (1998a) found that cold air or the use of a radio produced small but temporary increases in driving performance and were not effective countermeasures to moderate sleepiness. Similar effects of exposure to sound have also been reported in other studies (Landström, Englund, Nordström, & Åström, 1999; Ünal, de Waard, Epstude, & Steg, 2013). Some energy drinks have been reported to improve driving performance (Ronen, Oron-Gilad, & Gershon, 2014), possibly due to their caffeine content, but Anderson and Horne (2006) found that energy drinks with a large quantity of sugar may actually enhance sleepiness. Grandner et al. (2014) have cautioned that the use of energy drinks to compensate for insufficient sleep may perpetuate sleep disturbance.

**Implementing countermeasures.** Drivers perceive the most effective countermeasure to sleepiness to be to swap drivers (Nordbakke & Sagberg, 2007; Watling, Armstrong, Obst, & Smith, 2014), obviously possible only when a co-driver is present. The next five countermeasures perceived to be most effective are stop and get out of car, stop and take a nap, open the window or turn on the air conditioning, drink water, and drink coffee or a caffeinated drink (Gershon et al., 2011; Meng et al., 2015; Nordbakke & Sagberg, 2007; Watling, Smith, et al., 2014). It has frequently been observed that drivers appear to have reasonably accurate knowledge of the relative effectiveness of countermeasures, particularly of a nap, but do not make use of them.

For a driver to implement a countermeasure two conditions must be satisfied: the driver must recognize the presence of sleepiness and then be willing to implement a countermeasure. Reyner and Horne (1998b), making a distinction between self-rated sleepiness and the likelihood of falling asleep, found that subjects driving in a simulator were aware of being sleepy for an average of 45.5 minutes before a major driving incident occurred. Even when sleepy some subjects underestimated the likelihood of falling asleep. Several studies of both simulated and on-road driving have reached similar conclusions (Horne & Baulk, 2004; Kaplan, Itoi, & Dement, 2007; Verster & Roth, 2012). Herrmann et al. (2010), in a laboratory study, found that 61% of their participants fell asleep without first feeling sleepy on at least some occasions. However, Williamson, Friswell, Olivier, and Grzebieta (2014) concluded that drivers' ability to assess their level of sleepiness was sufficient for them to make a decision to stop driving. They argue that road safety policy has to focus on encouraging drivers to respond to their level of sleepiness.

Watling, Armstrong, et al. (2014) argue that the dual process model of decision making helps to explain why drivers continue to drive while sleepy in spite of knowing of effective countermeasures. This model postulates two modes of information processing: cognitive and affective. The former is rational and analytical and comparatively slow whereas the latter is experiential, intuitive, influenced by affect, and fast. Watling, Armstrong, et al. (2014) argue that the motivation to reach the intended destination could be an antecedent of affective processes (p. 264). "The lack of associations between these effective counter-measures and self-reports of continuing to drive while sleepy suggests the perceived effectiveness of stopping driving, napping, swapping drivers, and caffeine have little effect on self-reported sleepy driving behaviors. As such, attitudinal and behavior change is sorely needed to encourage drivers to utilize the more effective countermeasures" (p. 266). The responsibility for such changes is shared among individual drivers, employers, and governmental and policy-making agencies to increase education concerning effective countermeasures, change attitudes toward their implementation, and provide environments in which they can be practiced.

## CONCLUSIONS

Sleepiness is a major factor in the occurrence of work-related vehicle crashes with substantial human and financial costs. Much of this is avoidable. Mitigation of sleepiness by drivers and employers requires an understanding of the powerful underlying neurobiological mechanisms regulating sleep and circadian rhythms. Drivers have to be sensitive to the danger that is signaled by the presence of sleepiness and be prepared to take effective countermeasures. Employers have a responsibility to provide working conditions that will minimize the occurrence of sleepiness.

Although research must continue into technological developments that can aid the detection of sleepiness and identify more effective countermeasures, much can be done to optimize work schedules, educate drivers and employers, and change the attitudes of drivers to the use of effective countermeasures to sleepiness while driving.

## REFERENCES

Abe, T., Komada, Y., Nishida, Y., Hayashida, K., & Inoue, Y. (2010). Short sleep duration and long spells of driving are associated with the occurrence of Japanese drivers' rear-end collisions and single-car accidents. *Journal of Sleep Research, 19*(2), 310–316.

Abe, T., Mollicone, D., Basner, M., & Dinges, D. F. (2014). Sleepiness and safety: Where biology needs technology. *Sleep and Biological Rhythms, 12*(2), 74–84.

Åkerstedt, T. (2011). Shift work disorder and sleepiness. In M. J. Thorpy & M. Billiard (Eds.), *Sleepiness: Causes, consequences and treatment.* Cambridge, UK: Cambridge University Press.

Åkerstedt, T., Peters, B., Anund, A., & Kecklund, G. (2005). Impaired alertness and performance driving home from the night shift: A driving simulator study. *Journal of Sleep Research, 14*, 17–20.

Al-Houqani, M., Eid, H. O., & Abu-Zidan, F. M. (2013). Sleep-related collisions in United Arab Emirates. *Accident Analysis and Prevention, 2013*, 1052–1055.

Anderson, C., & Horne, J. A. (2006). A high sugar content, low caffeine drink does not alleviate sleepiness but may worsen it. *Human Psychopharmacology, 21*(5), 299–303.

Anund, A., Kecklund, G., Peters, B., & Åkerstedt, T. (2008). Driver sleepiness and individual differences in preferences for countermeasures. *Journal of Sleep Research, 17*(1), 16–22.

Arnedt, J. T., Wilde, G. J. S., Munt, P. W., & MacLean, A. W. (2000). Simulated driving performance following prolonged wakefulness and alcohol consumption: Separate and combined contributions to impairment. *Journal of Sleep Research, 9*(3), 233–241.

Aworemi, J. R., Abdul-Azeez, I. A., Oyedokun, A. J., & Adewoye, J. O. (2010). Efficacy of drivers' fatigue on road accident in selected Southwestern states of Nigeria. *International Business Research, 3*(3), 225–232.

BaHammam, A. S., Alkhunizan, M. A., Lesloum, R. H., Alshanqiti, A. M., Aldakhil, A. M., Pandi-Perumal, S. R., & Sharif, M. M. (2014). Prevalence of sleep-related accidents among drivers in Saudi Arabia. *Annals of Thoracic Medicine, 9*(4), 236–241.

Bajraktarov, S., Novotni, A., Manusheva, N., Nikovska, D. G., Miceva-Velickovska, E., Zdraveska, N., . . . Richter, K. S. (2011). Main effects of sleep disorders related to shift work-opportunities for preventive programs. *EPMA J, 2*(4), 365–370. doi:10.1007/s13167-011-0128-4

Barger, L. K., Cade, B. E., Ayas, N. T., Cronin, J. W., Rosner, B., Speizer, F. E., & Czeisler, C. A. (2005). Extended work shifts and the risk of motor vehicle crashes among interns. *New England Journal of Medicine, 352*(2), 125–134.

Barrett, P. R., Horne, J. A., & Reyner, L. A. (2004). Sleepiness combined with low alcohol intake in women drivers: Greater impairment but better perception than men? *Sleep, 27*(6), 1057–1062.

Beirness, D. J., Simpson, H. M., & Desmond, K. (2005). The Road Safety Monitor 2004: Drowsy driving (pp. 16). Ottawa, Ontario, Canada.

Bonnet, M. H., Balkin, T. J., Dinges, D. F., Roehrs, T., Rogers, N. L., & Wesensten, N. J. (2005). The use of stimulants to modify performance during sleep loss: A review by the Sleep Deprivation and Stimulant Task Force of the American Academy of Sleep Medicine. *Sleep, 28*(9), 1163–1187.

Borbély, A. A. (1982). A two-process model of sleep regulation. *Human Neurobiology, 1,* 195–204.

Broadbent, D. E. (1953). Noise, paced performance and vigilance tasks. *British Journal of Psychology, 44,* 295–303.

Brown, T., Lee, J., Schwarz, C., Dary Florentino, D., & McDonald, A. (2014). *Assessing the feasibility of vehicle-based sensors to detect drowsy driving.* Washington, DC: U.S. Department of Transportation.

Carskadon, M. A., & Dement, W. C. (1982). The multiple sleep latency test: What does it measure. *Sleep, 5,* S67–72.

Cassidy, W. B. (2014, Sep 11). Fatal U.K. accident, long jail term spotlight truck driver fatigue. *Journal of Commerce* Retrieved from http://search.proquest.com/docview/1561386981?accountid=6180

Chen, C., & Xie, Y. (2014). The impacts of multiple rest-break periods on commercial truck driver's crash risk. *Journal of Safety Research, 48,* 87–93.

Clarke, D. D., Ward, P., Bartle, C., & Truman, W. (2009). Work-related road traffic collisions in the UK. *Accident Analysis and Prevention, 41*(2), 345–351.

Czeisler, C. A. (2015). Duration, timing and quality of sleep are each vital for health, performance and safety. *Sleep Health: Journal of the National Sleep Foundation, 1,* 5–8.

Dawson, D., & Reid, K. (1997). Fatigue, alcohol and performance impairment. *Nature, 388*(6639), 235.

Dawson, D., Searle, A. K., & Paterson, J. L. (2014). Look before you (s)leep: Evaluating the use of fatigue detection technologies within a fatigue risk management system for the road transport industry. *Sleep Medicine Reviews, 18*(2), 141–152.

Dijk, D.-J., & Lazar, A. S. (2012). The regulation of human sleep and wakefulness: Sleep homeostasis and circadian rhythmicity. In C. M. Morin & C. A. Espie (Eds.), *The Oxford handbook of sleep and sleep disorders* (pp. 38–60). Oxford, UK: Oxford University Press.

Di Milia, L. (2006). Shift work, sleepiness and long distance driving. *Transportation Research Part F: Traffic Psychology and Behaviour, 9*(4), 278–285.

Dinges, D. F., & Kribbs, N. B. (1991). Performing while sleepy: Effects of experimentally induced sleepiness. In T. H. Monk (Ed.), *Sleep, sleepiness and performance* (pp. 97–128). Chichester, UK: John Wiley & Sons.

Dingus, T. A., Klauer, S. G., Neale, V. L., Petersen, A., Lee, S. E., Sudweeks, J., . . . Knipling, R. R. (2006). The 100-car naturalistic driving study. Phase II—Results of the 100-car field experiment. National Highway Traffic Safety Administration.

Drake, C. (2011). Subjective measures of sleepiness. In M. J. Thorpy & M. Billiard (Eds.), *Sleepiness: Causes, consequences and treatment* (pp. 60–71). Cambridge, UK: Cambridge University Press.

Ellis, E., & Grunstein, R. R. (2001). Medico-legal aspects of sleep disorders: Sleepiness and civil liability. *Sleep Medicine Reviews, 5*(1), 33–46.

Elzohairy, Y. (2007). *Fatal and injury fatigue-related crashes on Ontario's roads: A 5-year review.* Paper presented at the Working together to understand driver fatigue: Report on symposium proceedings, Toronto, Ontario, Canada.

Folkard, S., & Åkerstedt, T. (1992). A three-process model of the regulation of alertness-sleepiness. In R. J. Broughton & R. D. Ogilvie (Eds.), *Sleep, arousal and performance* (pp. 11–26). Boston, MA: Birkhäuser.

Ftouni, S., Sletten, T. L., Howard, M., Anderson, C., Lennè, M. G., Lockley, S. W., & Rajaratnam, S. M. W. (2013). Objective and subjective measures of sleepiness, and their associations with on-road driving events in shift workers. *Journal of Sleep Research, 22*(1), 58–69.

Gander, P. H., Marshall, N. S., Bolger, W., & Girling, I. (2005). An evaluation of driver training as a fatigue countermeasure. *Transportation Research Part F: Traffic Psychology and Behaviour, 8*(1), 47–58.

Garbarino, S., Mascialino, B., Penco, M. A., Squarcia, S., De Carli, F., Nobili, L., . . . Ferrillo, F. (2004). Professional shift-work drivers who adopt prophylactic naps can reduce the risk of car accidents during night work. *Sleep, 27*(7), 1295–1302.

Garbarino, S., Nobili, L., Beelke, M., De Carli, B., & Ferrillo, F. (2001). The contributing role of sleepiness in highway vehicle accidents. *Sleep, 24*(2), 203–206.

Gates, J., Dubois, S., Mullen, N., Weaver, B., & Bedard, M. (2013). The influence of stimulants on truck driver crash responsibility in fatal crashes. *Forensic Science International, 228*(1–3), 15–20.

George, C. F. P. (2011). Medico-legal consequences of excessive sleepiness. In M. J. Thorpy & M. Billiard (Eds.), *Sleepiness: Causes, consequences and treatment* (pp. 92–97). Cambridge, UK: Cambridge University Press.

Gershon, P., Shinar, D., Oron-Gilad, T., Parmet, Y., & Ronen, A. (2011). Usage and perceived effectiveness of fatigue countermeasures for professional and nonprofessional drivers. *Accident Analysis and Prevention, 43*(3), 797–803.

Goodman, A. (2013). Walking, cycling and driving to work in the English and Welsh 2011 census: Trends, socio-economic patterning and relevance to travel behaviour in general. *PloS One, 8*(8), e71790. doi:10.1371/journal.pone.0071790

Grandner, M. A., Knutson, K. L., Troxel, W., Hale, L., Jean-Louis, G., & Miller, K. E. (2014). Implications of sleep and energy drink use for health disparities. *Nutrition Reviews, 72*(Suppl 1), 14–22.

Gulevich, G., Dement, W. C., & Johnson, L. C. (1966). Psychiatric and EEG observations on a case of prolonged (264 hours) wakefulness. *Archives of General Psychiatry, 15*(1), 29–35.

Harrison, Y., & Horne, J. A. (1998). Sleep loss impairs short and novel language tasks having a prefrontal focus. *Journal of Sleep Research, 7*(2), 95–100.

Harrison, Y., & Horne, J. A. (1999). One night of sleep loss impairs innovative thinking and flexible decision making. *Organizational Behavior and Human Decision Processes, 78*(2), 128–145.

Harrison, Y., & Horne, J. A. (2000). The impact of sleep deprivation on decision making: A review. *Journal of Experimental Psychology Applied, 6*(3), 236–249.

Hartley, S. L., Barbot, F., Machou, M., Lejaille, M., Moreau, B., Vaugier, I., . . . Quera-Salva, M. A. (2013). Combined caffeine and bright light reduces dangerous driving in sleep-deprived healthy volunteers: A pilot cross-over randomised controlled trial. *Neurophysiologie Clinique, 43*(3), 161–169.

Herrmann, U. S., Hess, C. W., Guggisberg, A. G., Roth, C., Gugger, M., & Mathis, J. (2010). Sleepiness is not always perceived before falling asleep in healthy, sleep-deprived subjects. *Sleep Medicine, 11*(8), 747–751.

Hetland, A., & Carr, D. B. (2014). Medications and impaired driving. *Annals of Pharmacotherapy, 48*(4), 494–506.

Hirose, T. (2005). An occupational health physician's report on the improvement in the sleeping conditions of night shift workers. *Industrial Health, 43*(1), 58–62.

Horne, J. A., & Baulk, S. D. (2004). Awareness of sleepiness when driving. *Psychophysiology, 41*(1), 161–165.

Horne, J. A., & Reyner, L. A. (1995). Sleep related vehicle accidents. *British Medical Journal, 310,* 565–567.

Horne, J. A., & Reyner, L. A. (1996). Counteracting driver sleepiness: Effects of napping, caffeine, and placebo. *Psychophysiology, 33*(3), 306–309.

Horne, J. A., Reyner, L. A., & Barrett, P. R. (2003). Driving impairment due to sleepiness is exacerbated by low alcohol intake. *Occupational and Environmental Medicine, 60,* 689–692.

Howard, M. E., Jackson, M. L., Kennedy, G. A., Swann, P., Barnes, M., & Pierce, R. J. (2007). The interactive effects of extended wakefulness and low-dose alcohol on simulated driving and vigilance. *Sleep, 30*(10), 1334–1340.

Howard, M. E., Jackson, M. L., Swann, P., Berlowitz, D. J., Grunstein, R. R., & Pierce, R. J. (2014). Deterioration in driving performance during sleep deprivation is similar in professional and nonprofessional drivers. *Traffic Injury and Prevention*, *15*(2), 132–137.

Howard, M. E., Radford, L., Jackson, M. L., Swann, P., & Kennedy, G. A. (2009). The effects of a 30-minute napping opportunity during an actual night shift on performance and sleepiness in shift workers. *Biological Rhythm Research*, *41*(2), 137–148.

Jones, C. B., Dorrian, J., & Dawson, D. (2003). Legal implications of fatigue in the Australian transportation industries. *Journal of Industrial Relations*, *45*(3), 344–359.

Jones, C. B., Dorrian, J., & Rajaratnam, S. M. W. (2005). Fatigue and the criminal law. *Industrial Health*, *43*(1), 63–70.

Kaplan, K. A., Itoi, A., & Dement, W. C. (2007). Awareness of sleepiness and ability to predict sleep onset: Can drivers avoid falling asleep at the wheel? *Sleep Medicine*, *9*(1), 71–79.

Killgore, W. D. S., Killgore, D., Day, L. M., Li, C., Kamimori, G. H., & Balkin, T. J. (2007). The effects of 53 hours of sleep deprivation on moral judgement. *Sleep*, *30*(3), 345–352.

Klauer, S., Dingus, T., Neale, V., Sudweeks, J., & Ransey, D. (2006). *Impact of driver inattention on near-crash/crash risk: An analysis using the 100-car naturalistic driving study data*. Washington, DC: National Highway Traffic Safety Administration.

Knauth, P. (2003). Preventive and compensatory measures for shift workers. *Occupational Medicine*, *53*(2), 109–116.

Laframboise, K. (2014, July 23). Driver fatigue likened to DUI; Coroner urges stiff penalties after crash. *The Gazette*.

Landström, U., Englund, K., Nordström, B., & Åström, A. (1999). Sound exposure as a measure against driver drowsiness. *Ergonomics*, *42*(7), 927–937.

Léger, D., Philip, P., Jarriault, P., Metlaine, A., & Choudat, D. (2009). Effects of a combination of napping and bright light pulses on shift workers' sleepiness at the wheel: A pilot study. *Journal of Sleep Research*, *18*(4), 472–479.

Lim, J., & Dinges, D. F. (2010). A meta-analysis of the impact of short-term sleep deprivation on cognitive variables. *Psychological Bulletin*, *136*(3), 375–389.

Lowden, A., Anund, A., Kecklund, G., Peters, B., & Åkerstedt, T. (2009). Wakefulness in young and elderly subjects driving at night in a car simulator. *Accident Analysis and Prevention*, *41*(5), 1001–1007.

Luckhaupt, S. E., Kak, S., & Calvert, G. M. (2010). The prevalence of short sleep duration by industry and occupation in the National Health Interview Survey. *Sleep*, *33*(2), 149–159.

MacLean, A. W., Davies, D. R. T., & Thiele, K. (2003). The hazards and prevention of driving while sleepy. *Sleep Medicine Reviews*, *7*(6), 507–521.

Marcoux, K., D., Vanlaar, W. G. M., & Robertson, R. D. (2012). *The Road Safety Monitor 2011: Fatigued driving trends*. Ottawa, Ontario, Canada.

Marshall, N. S., Bolger, W., & Gander, P. H. (2004). Abnormal sleep duration and motor vehicle crash risk. *Journal of Sleep Research*, *13*, 177–178.

Mayhew, D. R., Simpson, H. M., Wood, K. M., Lonero, L., Clinton, K. M., & Johnson, A. G. (2011). On-road and simulated driving: Concurrent and discriminant validation. *Journal of Safety Research*, *42*(4), 267–275.

McArthur, A., Kay, J., Savolainen, P., & Gates, T. (2013). Effects of public rest areas on fatigue-related crashes. *Transportation Research Record*, *2386*, 16–25.

Meng, F., Li, S., Cao, L., Li, M., Peng, Q., Wang, C., & Zhang, W. (2015). Driving fatigue in professional drivers: A survey of truck and taxi drivers. *Traffic Injury and Prevention*, *16*(5), 474–483.

Mets, M., Baas, D., van Boven, I., Olivier, B., & Verster, J. (2012). Effects of coffee on driving performance during prolonged simulated highway driving. *Psychopharmacology*, *222*(2), 337–342.

Mitler, M. M., Carskadon, M. A., Czeisler, C. A., Dement, W. C., Dinges, D. F., & Graeber, R. C. (1988). Catastrophes, sleep, and public policy: Consensus report. *Sleep*, *11*(1), 100–109.

Monk, T. H. (2012). Sleep and human performance. In M. Morin Charles & C. A. Espie (Eds.), *The Oxford handbook of Sleep and sleep disorders* (pp. 95–109). Oxford, UK: Oxford University Press.

Mullen, N., Charlton, J., Devlin, A., & Bédard, M. (2011). Simulator validity: Behaviours observed on the simulator and on the road. In D. L. Fisher, M. Rizzo, J. K. Caird, & J. D. Lee (Eds.), *Handboodk of driving simulation for engineering, medicine, and psychology* (pp. 1–18). Boca Raton, FL: CRC Press.

Mullins, H. M., Cortina, J. M., & Drake, C. L. (2014). Sleepiness at work: A review and framework of how the physiology of sleepiness impacts the workplace. *Journal of Applied Psychology, 99*(6), 1096–1112.

Muzet, A., Nicolas, A., Tassi, P., Dewasmes, G., & Bonneau, A. (1995). Implementation of napping in industry and the problems of sleep inertia. *Journal of Sleep Research,* 4(Suppl 2), 67–69.

National Sleep Foundation. (2012). *2012 Sleep in America Poll: Planes, trains, automobiles and sleep.* Washington, DC: National Sleep Foundation.

Nordbakke, S., & Sagberg, F. (2007). Sleepy at the wheel: Knowledge, symptoms and behaviour among car drivers. *Transportation Research Part F: Traffic Psychology and Behaviour, 10*(1), 1–10.

Nordin, R. B. (2014). Rising trend of work-related commuting accidents, deaths, injuries and disabilities in developing countries: A case study of Malaysia. *Industrial Health, 52*(4), 275–277.

Noy, Y. I., Horrey, W. J., Popkin, S. M., Folkard, S., Howarth, H. D., & Courtney, T. K. (2011). Future directions in fatigue and safety research. *Accident Analysis and Prevention, 43*(2), 495–497.

Obst, P., Armstrong, K., Smith, S., & Banks, T. (2011). Age and gender comparisons of driving while sleepy: Behaviours and risk perceptions. *Transportation Research Part F: Traffic Psychology and Behaviour, 14*(6), 539–542.

Ozer, C., Etcibaşı, S., & Oztürk, L. (2014). Daytime sleepiness and sleep habits as risk factors of traffic accidents in a group of Turkish public transport drivers. *International Journal of Clinical and Experimental Medicine, 7*(1), 268–273.

Pérez-Chada, D., Videla, A. J., O'Flaherty, M. E., Palermo, P., Meoni, J., Sarchi, M. I., ... Durán-Cantolla, J. (2005). Sleep habits and accident risk among truck drivers: A cross-sectional study in Argentina. *Sleep, 28*(9), 1103–1108.

Philip, P., & Åkerstedt, T. (2006). Transport and industrial safety, how are they affected by sleepiness and sleep restriction? *Sleep Medicine Reviews, 10*(5), 347–356.

Philip, P., Sagaspe, P., Lagarde, E., Leger, D., Ohayon, M. M., Bioulac, B., ... Taillard, J. (2010). Sleep disorders and accidental risk in a large group of regular registered highway drivers. *Sleep Medicine, 11*(10), 973–979.

Philip, P., Sagaspe, P., Moore, N., Taillard, J., Charles, A., Guilleminault, C., & Bioulac, B. (2005). Fatigue, sleep restriction and driving performance. *Accident Analysis and Prevention, 37,* 473–478.

Philip, P., Sagaspe, P., Taillard, J., Valtat, C., Moore, N., Åkerstedt, T., ... Bioulac, B. (2005). Fatigue, sleepiness, and performance in simulated versus real driving conditions. *Sleep, 28*(12), 1511–1516.

Philip, P., Taillard, J., Léger, D., Diefenbach, K., Åkerstedt, T., Bioulac, B., & Guilleminault, C. (2002). Work and rest sleep schedules of 227 European truck drivers. *Sleep Medicine, 3*(6), 507–511.

Pilcher, J. J., & Huffcutt, A. I. (1996). Effects of sleep deprivation on performance: A meta-analysis. *Sleep, 19*(4), 318–326.

Powell, N. B., & Chau, J. K. M. (2010). Sleepy driving. Sleepiness and driving: A brief review. *Medical Clinics of North America, 94*(3), 531–540.

Radun, I., Ohisalo, J., Radun, J., & Kecklund, G. (2011). Night work, fatigued driving and traffic law: The case of police officers. *Industrial Health, 49*(3), 389–392.

Radun, I., Ohisalo, J., Radun, J., Wahde, M., & Kecklund, G. (2013). Driver fatigue and the law from the perspective of police officers and prosecutors. *Transportation Research Part F: Traffic Psychology and Behaviour, 18*, 159–167.

Rapino, M. A., & Fields, A. K. (2013). *Mega Commuters in the U.S.* Paper presented at the Association for Public Policy Analysis and Management Fall 2013 Conference.

Reyner, L. A., & Horne, J. A. (1997). Suppression of sleepiness in drivers: Combination of caffeine with a short nap. *Psychophysiology, 34*, 721–725.

Reyner, L. A., & Horne, J. A. (1998a). Evaluation of "In-Car" countermeasures to sleepiness: Cold air and radio. *Sleep, 21*(1), 46–50.

Reyner, L. A., & Horne, J. A. (1998b). Falling asleep whilst driving: Are drivers aware of prior sleepiness. *International Journal of Legal Medicine, 111*, 120–123.

Reyner, L. A., Horne, J. A., & Flatley, D. (2010). Effectiveness of UK motorway services areas in reducing sleep-related and other collisions. *Accident Analysis and Prevention, 42*(4), 1416–1418.

Robertson, R., Holmes, E., & Vanlaar, W. (2009). *The facts about fatigued driving in Ontario: A guidebook for the police.* Ottawa, Ontario, Canada: Traffic Injury Research Foundation.

Roehrs, T., Beare, D., Zorick, F., & Roth, T. (1994). Sleepiness and ethanol effects on simulated driving. *Alcoholism, Clinical and Experimental Research, 18*(1), 154–158.

Ronen, A., Oron-Gilad, T., & Gershon, P. (2014). The combination of short rest and energy drink consumption as fatigue countermeasures during a prolonged drive of professional truck drivers. *Journal of Safety Research, 49*, 39–43.

Royal Society for the Prevention of Accidents. (2007). *Driving for work: Fitness to drive.* Birmingham, UK: Royal Society for the Prevention of Accidents.

Sagaspe, P., Taillard, J., Bayon, V., Lagarde, E., Moore, N., Boussuge, J., . . . Philip, P. (2010). Sleepiness, near-misses and driving accidents among a representative population of French drivers. *Journal of Sleep Research, 19*(4), 578–584.

Sagaspe, P., Taillard, J., Chaumet, G., Moore, N., Bioulac, B., & Philip, P. (2007). Aging and nocturnal driving: Better with coffee of a nap? A randomized study. *Sleep, 30*(12), 1808–1813.

Satterfield, B. C., & Van Dongen, H. P. A. (2013). Occupational fatigue, underlying sleep and circadian mechanisms, and approaches to fatigue risk management. *Fatigue: Biomedicine, Health & Behavior, 1*(3), 118–136.

Schweirzer, P. K. (2011). Excessive sleepiness due to medications and drugs. In M. J. Thorpy & M. Billiard (Eds.), *Sleepiness: Causes, consequences and treatment* (pp. 386–398). Cambridge, UK: Cambridge University Press.

Schweitzer, P. K., Randazzo, A. C., Stone, K., Erman, M., & Walsh, J. K. (2006). Laboratory and field studies of naps and caffeine as practical countermeasures for sleep-wake problems associated with night work. *Sleep, 29*(1), 39–50.

Scott, L. D., Hwang, W. T., Rogers, A. E., Nysse, T., Dean, G. E., & Dinges, D. F. (2007). The relationship between nurse work schedules, sleep duration, and drowsy driving. *Sleep, 30*(12), 1801–1807.

Sharwood, L. N., Elkington, J., Meuleners, L., Ivers, R. Q., Boufous, S., & Stevenson, M. R. (2013). Use of caffeinated substances and risk of crashes in long distance drivers of commercial vehicles: Case-control study. *British Medical Journal, 346*(7900), 1–7.

Shechtman, O., Classen, S., Awadzi, K., & Mann, W. (2009). Comparison of driving errors between on-the-road and simulated driving assessment: A validation study. *Traffic Injury and Prevention, 10*(4), 379–385.

Smith, C. K., & Williams, J. (2014). Work related injuries in Washington state's trucking industry, by industry sector and occupation. *Accident Analysis and Prevention, 65*, 63–71.

Spaeth, A. M., Goel, N., & Dinges, D. F. (2014). Cumulative neurobehavioral and physiological effects of chronic caffeine intake: Individual differences and implications for the use of caffeinated energy products. *Nutrition Reviews*, 72(Suppl 1), 34–47.

Statistics Canada. (2011). National Household Survey in Brief: Commuting to work. Ottawa, Ontario, Canada: Statistics Canada.

Stutts, J. C., Wilkins, J. W., & Vaughn, B. V. (1999). Why do people have drowsy driving crashes? Input from drivers who just did. New York, NY: AAA Foundation for Traffic Safety.

Tefft, B. C. (2012). Prevalence of motor vehicle crashes involving drowsy drivers, United States, 1999–2008. *Accident Analysis and Prevention, 45*, 180–186.

Thiffault, P., & Bergeron, J. (2003). Monotony of road environment and driver fatigue: A simulator study. *Accident Analysis and Prevention, 35*(3), 381–391.

Ting, P. H., Hwang, J. R., Doong, J. L., & Jeng, M. C. (2008). Driver fatigue and highway driving: A simulator study. *Physiology and Behavior, 94*(3), 448–453.

Tornero, C., Ventura, A., Bourguet, M., & Poquet, I. (2012). Evaluation of driving ability among residents after the duty shift. *Accident Analysis and Prevention, 47*, 182–183.

TUC. (2013). *Transport and work related road safety hazards at work*. London, UK: Trades Union Congress.

Ünal, A. B., de Waard, D., Epstude, K., & Steg, L. (2013). Driving with music: Effects on arousal and performance. *Transportation Research Part F: Traffic Psychology and Behaviour, 21*, 52–65.

U.S. Department of Transportation, N. H. T. S. A. (2011). *Drowsy driving*. Washington, DC.

Vakulin, A., Baulk, S. D., Catcheside, P. G., Anderson, R., van den Heuvel, C. J., Banks, S., & McEvoy, R. D. (2007). Effects of moderate sleep deprivation and low-dose alcohol on driving simulator performance and perception in young men. *Sleep, 30*(10), 1327–1333.

Valent, F., Di Bartolomeo, S., Marchetti, R., Sbrojavacca, R., & Barbone, F. (2010). A case-crossover study of sleep and work hours and the risk of road traffic accidents. *Sleep, 33*(3), 349–354.

van den Berg, J., & Landström, U. (2006). Symptoms of sleepiness while driving and their relationship to prior sleep, work and individual characteristics. *Transportation Research Part F: Traffic Psychology and Behaviour, 9*(3), 207–226.

Van Dongen, H. P. A., Caldwell, J. A., Jr., & Caldwell, L. J. (2011). Individual differences in cognitive vulnerability to fatigue in the laboratory and in the workplace. In H. P. A. Van Dongen & G. A. Kerkhof (Eds.), *Human sleep and cognition. Part II: Clinical and applied research* (Vol. 190, pp. 140–153). Amsterdam, The Netherlands: Elsevier.

Vanlaar, W., Simpson, H., Mayhew, D., & Robertson, R. (2007). *Fatigued and drowsy driving—Attitudes, concerns and practices of Ontario drivers*. Ottawa, Ontario, Canada: Traffic Injury Research Foundation.

Vanlaar, W., Simpson, H., Mayhew, D., & Robertson, R. (2008). Fatigued and drowsy driving: A survey of attitudes, opinions and behaviors. *Journal of Safety Research, 39*(3), 303–309.

Verster, J. C., & Roth, T. (2012). Drivers can poorly predict their own driving impairment: A comparison between measurements of subjective and objective driving quality. *Psychopharmacology, 219*(3), 775–781.

Verster, J. C., Taillard, J., Sagaspe, P., Olivier, B., & Philip, P. (2011). Prolonged nocturnal driving can be as dangerous as severe alcohol-impaired driving. *Journal of Sleep Research, 20*(4), 585–588.

Vila, B. (2006). Impact of long work hours on police officers and the communities they serve. *American Journal of Industrial Medicine, 49*(11), 972–980.

Wang, Y., Mehler, B., Reimer, B., Lammers, V., D'Ambrosio, L. A., & Coughlin, J. F. (2010). The validity of driving simulation for assessing differences between in-vehicle informational interfaces: A comparison with field testing. *Ergonomics, 53*(3), 404–420.

Watling, C. N. (2014). Sleepy driving and pulling over for a rest: Investigating individual factors that contribute to these driving behaviours. *Personality and Individual Differences, 56*, 105–110.

Watling, C. N., Armstrong, K. A., Obst, P. L., & Smith, S. S. (2014). Continuing to drive while sleepy: The influence of sleepiness countermeasures, motivation for driving sleepy, and risk perception. *Accident Analysis and Prevention, 73C*, 262–268.

Watling, C. N., Armstrong, K. A., & Smith, S. S. (2013). *Sleepiness: How a biological drive can influence other risky road user behaviours.* Paper presented at the Proceedings of the 2013 Australasian College of Road Safety (ACRS) National Conference, Australasian College of Road Safety (ACRS), National Wine Centre of Australia, Adelaide, SA. http://eprints.qut.edu.au/63820/

Watling, C. N., Smith, S. S., & Horswill, M. S. (2014). Stop and revive? The effectiveness of nap and active rest breaks for reducing driver sleepiness. *Psychophysiology, 51*(11), 1131–1138.

Webb, W. B. (1975). *Sleep: The gentle tyrant.* Englewood Cliffs, NJ: Prentice-Hall.

Wheaton, A. G., Chapman, D. P., Presley-Cantrell, L. R., Croft, J. B., & Roehler, D. R. (2013). *Drowsy Driving—19 States and the District of Columbia, 2009–2010* (pp. 1033–1037). Atlanta, GA: Centers for Disease Control.

Wheaton, A. G., Shults, R. A. P., Chapman, D. P., Ford, E. S. M. D., & Croft, J. B. (2014). *Drowsy driving and risk behaviors—10 States and Puerto Rico, 2011–2012* (pp. 557–562). Atlanta, GA: Centers for Disease Control.

Wilkinson, R. T. (1992). The measurement of sleepiness. In R. J. Boughton & R. D. Ogilvie (Eds.), *Sleep, arousal and performance* (pp. 254–265). Boston, MA: Birkhäuser.

Williams, H. L., Lubin, A., & Goodnow, J. J. (1959). Impaired performance with acute sleep loss. *Psychological Monographs, 73*(14), 1–26.

Williams, L. R., Davies, D. R., Thiele, K., Davidson, J. R., & MacLean, A. W. (2012). Young drivers' perceptions of culpability of sleep-deprived versus drinking drivers. *Journal of Safety Research, 43*(2), 115–122.

Williamson, A. M., & Friswell, R. (2013). Fatigue in the workplace: Causes and countermeasures. *Fatigue: Biomedicine, Health & Behavior, 1*(1–2), 81–98.

Williamson, A. M., Friswell, R., Olivier, J., & Grzebieta, R. (2014). Are drivers aware of sleepiness and increasing crash risk while driving? *Accident Analysis and Prevention, 70*(0), 225–234.

Wilson, R. J., Fang, M., Cooper, P. J., & Beirness, D. J. (2006). Sleepiness among night-time drivers: Relationship to blood alcohol concentration and other factors. *Traffic Injury and Prevention, 7*(1), 15–22.

World Health Organization. *Global Plan for the Decade of Action for Road Safety 2011–2020.* Geneva, Switzerland: World Health Organization.

Zhang, H., Yan, X., Wu, C., & Qiu, T. Z. (2014). Effect of circadian rhythms and driving duration on fatigue level and driving performance of professional drivers. *Transportation Research Record: Journal of the Transportation Research Board, 2402*(1), 19–27.

Zhang, X., Zhao, X., Du, H., & Rong, J. (2014). A study on the effects of fatigue driving and drunk driving on drivers' physical characteristics. *Traffic Injury and Prevention, 15*(8), 801–808.

CHAPTER 9

# Fatigue and Safety at Work

JENNIFER H. K. WONG AND E. KEVIN KELLOWAY

## FATIGUE AND SAFETY AT WORK

It is widely accepted that sleep deprivation and the resulting fatigue have consider-able influence on general and safety-specific performance at work. Approximately 90% of U.S. citizens believe that chronic sleep deprivation has impacted their work performance and safety (National Sleep Foundation, 2002), and this common belief has empirical validity. Based on a meta-analysis of previous studies, Uehli et al. (2014) found that workers with sleep problems were 1.62 times more likely to experience an occupational injury compared to workers without sleep problems. Uehli et al. (2014) estimated that 13% of work injuries could be prevented if sleep problems were elimi-nated. To add an economic perspective, sleep-related losses in productivity have been estimated to cost organizations $1,967 per employee per year (Rosekind et al., 2010).

In this chapter we focus on the safety consequences of fatigue and related con-structs. Fatigue is defined as "a biological drive for recuperative rest" (Williamson et al., 2011, p. 499). A variety of factors are believed to influence or lead to fatigue, including characteristics of previous night's sleep, sleepiness during the day, job-related factors, and individual factors. In this chapter we review the research conducted on the influence of these factors on fatigue and safety performance. We propose that fatigue may influence safety by impairing safety performance through errors. We conclude with a discussion on research and practical implica-tions of fatigue, sleep, and workplace safety.

## CHARACTERISTICS OF SLEEP

### Sleep Duration

As a general rule, the human body requires 1 hour of rest for every 2 hours awake (Krauss, Chen, DeArmond, & Moorcroft, 2003). Restricted hours of sleep at night can increase the risk of injuries and accidents the next day, even with a difference of just 1 hour. Based on this premise, a series of studies have examined the safety implications of daylight saving time hypothesizing that a reduction in sleep duration would be associated with setting the clock ahead 1 hour and that this reduction, in turn, would result in increased safety incidents.

Barnes and Wagner (2009) used data from the National Institute for Occupational Safety and Health and the Bureau of Labor Statistics to examine the impact of daylight saving time, finding that workers slept 40 minutes less on the Monday following phase advances (i.e., when clocks were set ahead), whereas no difference was evident following phase delays (i.e., when the workers gained an hour). Extending beyond lost sleep, the Monday following phase advance coincided with significant increases in the frequency and severity of injuries, whereas the Monday following the phase delay did not exhibit such increases, suggesting that the lack of sleep attributable to daylight saving time had safety consequences.

Despite this evidence, other studies have failed to replicate these findings. A group of Finnish researchers examined injuries over a week before and after daylight saving time using data from the Federation of Accident Insurance Institutions (Lahti, Sysi-Aho, Haukka, & Partonen, 2011). Although there were no significant differences in frequency of accidents in the weeks prior to and after daylight saving time, there were significantly more accidents in the week after phase delay compared to the week after phase advance. The daylight saving effect was also not found in a study using a Canadian sample (Morassaei & Smith, 2010). Injury rates in the week following daylight saving time in phase advance and delay did not differ from the week before.

These conflicting findings suggest the sensibility of focusing on direct assessment of sleep duration as the variable of interest rather than relying on proxies such as the implementation of daylight saving time. Several studies have reported negative associations between sleep duration and accident rates, suggesting that less sleep is associated with more accidents. For example, the U.S. National Health Interview Survey revealed that short sleep duration and long working hours over a week independently increased the risk of occupational injury in the preceding year (Arlinghaus, Lombardi, Willetts, Folkard, & Christiani, 2012). Injury risk increased by 10% for each hourly decrease in night sleep, and increased by 14% for each increase of 10 hours in working hours per week. Additionally, structural equation analyses revealed that sleep duration mediated the negative relationship between long working hours and injury risk.

Although the most common advice is to get 8 hours of sleep each night, there are data that suggest that 7 hours of sleep is sufficient for safe work performance. Farm workers with less than 5 hours of sleep per night had significantly higher odds of injury compared to those who slept longer than 7 hours per night (Lilley et al., 2012). A rising sleep debt accumulated from several nights of insufficient sleep had been associated with more reported cases of traffic accidents in professional drivers (Carter, Ulfberg, Nyström, & Edling, 2003).

Collectively these studies suggest that sleep duration or the quantity of sleep is related to safety performance, yet there are other characteristics of sleep, such as sleep quality, that also play a role in workplace safety.

## Sleep Quality

Sleep quality encompasses almost every other type of sleep characteristic beyond sleep quantity—including, for example, difficulty in sleep onset, sleeping disorders, and overall sleep quality (Nakata et al., 2005). The assessment of sleep quality varies markedly across studies. Some studies (e.g., Chau et al., 2002) have relied on a single-item measure to assess sleep quality as a subjective perception whereas others have used validated and multifactorial instruments such as the Pittsburgh Sleep Quality Index (Buysse, Reynolds, Monk, Berman, & Kupfer, 1989).

Using three dichotomously scored single-item measures to assess difficulty in initiating sleep, sleep quality, and sleep sufficiency, Nakata et al. (2005) found that high difficulty initiating sleep, poor sleep, and insufficient sleep were associated with higher odds of occupational injury in workers compared to workers who did not report any poor sleep characteristics. In a follow-up study, Nakata (2011) found that workers who rated their sleep to be insufficient or poor were more likely to experience workplace injury. In both studies, sleep quality was significantly associated with occupational injury after controlling for demographic, lifestyle habits, health, and job-related control variables.

Chau and colleagues (Chau et al., 2002; Chau, Mur, Benamghar, et al., 2004) reported a series of analyses that compared workers who had been in accidents to workers who had not in two industries, construction and rail services. In these studies, workers who either slept less than 6 hours per day, self-rated their sleep quality as poor, or used sleeping pills to aid sleep were considered to have poor sleep quality. In the construction sector, poor sleep quality was significantly associated with injuries that required sick leave (Chau et al., 2002; Chau, Mur, Benamghar, et al., 2004). There was also a significant relationship between severity of sleep disorders (increasing from sleep duration, sleep quality, to consumption of sleeping pills) and the increasing strength of their associations with occupational accidents (Chau et al., 2002).

The types of injury resulting from sleep difficulties vary across industries. Construction workers with poor sleep quality had higher odds for fractures than all other types of occupational injuries combined (Chau et al., 2006). For railway workers, sleep quality was associated with accidents of disequilibrium, tripping, collision with a moving vehicle, and physical exertion and pain due to movement (Chau, Mur, Touron, Benamghar, & Dehaene, 2004; Gauchard et al., 2003). Importantly, poor sleep quality was not associated with a single type of injury, but rather with the frequency of injuries, suggesting that sleep has an influence on "accident proneness" (Gauchard et al., 2006).

Aside from injuries, sleep quality is associated with more severe safety outcomes such as occupational fatality and disability. Individuals who reported having "difficulty sleeping in the past 2 weeks" were 1.89 times more likely to have an accidental fatality at work compared to individuals without sleep difficulties (Åkerstedt, Fredlund, Gillberg, & Jansson, 2002). A longitudinal study discovered that sleep disturbance was significantly associated with workplace disabilities due to injuries or poisoning at work after 3 years while controlling for age, sex, socioeconomic status, shiftwork, health behaviors, somatic diseases, use of painkillers, anxiety, and depression (Salo et al., 2010). Sleep quality in a study by Salo et al. (2010) was assessed using four items drawn from the *Diagnostic and Statistical Manual of Mental Disorders* (*DSM-IV*; American Psychiatric Association) criterion for insomnia: frequency of difficulty falling asleep, difficulty staying asleep, early morning awakenings, and nonrestorative sleep in the past month.

Sleep quality can also be conceptualized as a composite of sleep characteristics. For instance, using Daan, Beersma, and Borbély's (1984) mathematical model of homeostasic drive toward sleep (calculated as a function of length of sleep, length of wakefulness, and the timing and duration of any daytime naps), a higher homeostasis drive (i.e., lower quality of sleep) was found to be associated with a 38% increase of accident reports among shiftwork police officers (Garbarino et al., 2004).

In summary, although the conceptualization of sleep quality varies across studies and researchers (i.e., single-item subjective sleep quality, multiitem measurement of sleep quality, the lack of sleep difficulties, or composite of sleep characteristics), there appears to be a strong negative association between sleep quality and injuries and accidents at work.

## Sleep Disorders

Insomnia is clinically defined in the *DSM-IV* as poor sleep quality that is severe enough to induce fatigue-related daytime functioning (American Psychiatric Association, 1994), and clinical insomnia is estimated to be associated with 3% of the total cost of workplace accidents (Shahly et al., 2012). A clinical review discovered that most of the studies of insomnia and workplace accidents showed a positive relationship between the two (Kucharczyk, Morgan, & Hall, 2012). Of the studies that used the *DSM-IV* criteria to identify insomniac individuals, the rate for accidents for insomniacs was found to be 8% compared to good sleepers at 1% (Léger, Guilleminault, Bader, Lévy, & Paillard, 2002). In addition, insomniacs were twice as likely to be involved in work-related incidents or falls than good sleepers (Daley et al., 2009).

Sleep disorders can include breathing-related disturbances ranging from symptoms with mild severity(i.e., snoring during sleep) to more severe disorders (i.e., diagnosed obstructive sleep apnea syndrome). As severity of the sleep symptoms increases, so does the risk of reporting subjective sleepiness at work (Ulfberg, Carter, Talbälk, & Edling, 1996). The likelihood of being involved in an occupational accident was higher for individuals who were heavy snorers or have obstructive sleep apnea syndrome, as found among patients at a Swedish sleep clinic, compared to a reference group that was a random sample of the general population of the country (Ulfberg, Carter, & Edling, 2000). In fact, obstructive sleep apnea syndrome appeared to be even more strongly associated with occupational accidents than was clinical insomnia (Shahly et al., 2012).

## SLEEP AND DAYTIME SLEEPINESS

The nature of sleep during the night (i.e., sleep duration, sleep quality, and sleep disorders) is believed to contribute to the state of sleepiness during the day. In turn, daytime sleepiness has safety implications when experienced during working hours. Daytime sleepiness is a subjective experience that can be assessed by asking workers the extent of their perceived sleepiness during the day using a single-item measure or by using relatively more valid measures such as the Epworth Sleepiness Scale (Johns, 1991a). Several studies have demonstrated that poor sleep quality is related to higher perceived daytime sleepiness. Professional drivers with poor sleep quality had higher odds of falling asleep while driving (Sabbagh-Ehrlich, Friedman, & Richter, 2005). Clinical insomniacs and workers who have insufficient amounts of sleep reported more incidents of unintentional sleep at work compared to good sleepers (Rosekind et al., 2010). Similarly, Lavie (1981) found that sleep latency of 60 minutes or longer, mid-sleep awakenings, snoring, excessive sleep movements, leg movements, and sleep talking were associated with excessive daytime sleepiness. In turn, daytime sleepiness in its various forms of assessment (i.e., single-item, Epworth Sleepiness Scale) was linked to higher rates of accidents and injuries (Erbaydar et al., 2010; Fransen et al., 2006; Lavie, 1981).

A recent meta-analysis suggests that sleep disturbances have a relatively larger impact on safety than daytime sleepiness. Using sleep medication or having a breathing-related problem was found to be the highest risk factors for workplace injuries, followed by multiple comorbid sleep disturbances (Uehli et al., 2014). Sleep quality and quantity were determined to be intermediate risk factors, and daytime sleepiness was considered to be the lowest risk factor. The meta-analysis implies that the comorbidity of poor sleep and sleepiness at work exacerbates the risk for injuries and accidents. In fact, one study found that men who reported heavy snoring and excessive daytime sleepiness were at increased odds for having an occupational injury, whereas no increased risk was found for either snorers who did not experience excessive daytime sleepiness or for excessively sleepy men who did not snore (Lindberg, Carter, Gislason, & Janson, 2001). This suggests that experiencing both poor sleep characteristics during the night and sleepiness at work can be even more detrimental to safety performances than either condition in isolation.

Despite these findings, some evidence suggests that individuals are more apt to blame their subjective sleepiness as the cause of accidents. In the study by Sabbagh-Ehrlich et al. (2005), interviews with professional truck drivers revealed that among drivers who experienced crashes with casualties, twice as many attributed the accident to driver sleepiness than to sleep disturbances. Of the sample of commercial bus drivers in Vennelle, Engleman, and Douglas's (2010) study, 25% reported having an accident or a near-miss accident during work that they personally attributed to sleepiness.

There is evidence to support the idea that poor sleep contributes not only to day-time sleepiness but also to the experience of fatigue. In a sample of seafarers working offshore, poor sleep quality and higher reported sleep disturbance were found to be associated with acute and long-term fatigue (Wadsworth, Allen, McNamara, & Smith, 2008). Fatigue may be a more significant predictor of injuries and accidents than sleepiness. When fatigue was compared to sleepiness in a sample of miners using the Piper Fatigue Scale (Piper et al., 1998) and the Epworth Sleepiness Scale, ratings of fatigue were higher in shift workers who experienced an accident at work compared to shift workers who had not been in an accident, yet there were no differences in sleepiness ratings between the two groups (Halvani, Zare, & Mirmohammadi, 2009). The data are equivocal and more evidence is required before making a conclusion about the relative impact of fatigue and sleep on safety.

## JOB-RELATED CHARACTERISTICS

The first set of job-related characteristics that contributes to the experience of fatigue is associated with shift work. A great deal of research has identified shift work as a significant contributing factor to fatigue at work, as well as three major injury trends (Folkard, Lombardi, & Tucker, 2005). First, the risk of injury increases with increasing shift length over 8 hours. Second, risk increases over the course of a shift with greater risk toward the end of the shift. Finally, risk is higher on the night shift because circadian rhythm is at a low point at night, prompting the body to seek rest and sleep.

### Long Working Hours

As long working hours cut into the sleeping hours of the day, sleep quantity is reduced and daytime sleepiness increases. Rates of injuries and accidents were found to increase 3-fold after 16 hours of work compared to after 9 hours of work (Rosa, 1995). Firefighters reported more sleep disturbances once hours worked per week exceeded 50 (Lusa, Häkkänen, Luukkonen, & Viikari-Juntura, 2002). Furthermore, once hours worked per week exceeded 70, the rate of occupational accidents increased the risk almost 4-fold compared to when the firefighters worked 50 hours per week.

Shifts longer than 8 hours are related to more incidents of occupational injuries (Nakata, 2011). In a sample of railway workers, every hour worked resulted in an 18% increase in the likelihood of reporting being extremely tired or unable to function effectively (Dorrian, Baulk, & Dawson, 2011). Fortunately, increasing the amount of sleep before the shift may offset these risks. Dorrian et al. (2011) found that each hour of sleep prior to work resulted in a 12% decrease in the likelihood of reporting extreme tiredness or complete exhaustion at work.

Similar research indicated that truck drivers tend to work between 11 and 16 hours a day (Souza, Paiva, & Reimão, 2005), and sometimes over 50 hours per week

(Braeckman, Verpraet, Van Risseghem, Pevernagie, & De Bacquer, 2011). Due to these long work hours, drivers reported sleeping less than 6 hours on a workday (Souza et al., 2005), and rated themselves as having poor sleep quality and excessive daytime sleepiness (Braeckman et al., 2011). The dangers of these long hours have resulted in legislation regulating the amount of hours that can be driven in a 24-hour period. However, one study discovered that a small proportion of long-haul drivers continued to disregard the legislation, and these drivers were significantly more likely to doze-off while driving and to report near misses (Häkkänen & Summala, 2000).

### Shift Work

It is no surprise that night and rotating shifts are associated with greater fatigue because our circadian rhythm dictates that we use nighttime to rest. Under normal light conditions, the peak for sleepiness is at 6:00 am (Lavie, 1986). Risk of occupational accident or injury from sleepiness was identified to be the highest around midnight, 2:00 am, 6:00 am, and 4:00 pm (Folkard, Lombardi, & Spencer, 2006; Krauss et al., 2003). Indeed, most sleep-related incidents and human-error catastrophes (e.g., Chernobyl, Exxon Valdez) occurred between 12:00 am and 8:00 am (Krauss et al., 2003; Phillips, 2000). In line with this, working night shifts was found to positively correlate with experiencing a work injury for both men and women, with the risk of injury being 8.2% and 14.4%, respectively (Wong, McLeod, & Demers, 2011).

Not only are occupational accidents more common among those who work the night shift, but the accidents that do occur during that time are more likely to lead to more severe injuries and fatality (Åkerstedt et al., 2002). Furthermore, Dinges (1995) speculated that emergency personnel may be less prepared to cope with accidents that happen during the night, thus making the accidents more costly. Shift work also increases the chance of accidents outside of work; those who work shifts were at an increased risk of being injured on the way home from work, typically by driving off the road due to fatigue (Monk, Folkard, & Wedderburn, 1996).

Individuals working rotating shifts are a unique shift work sample to study because they are exposed to not only the effect of circadian low point (i.e., working night shifts), but also to the adjustments from changes in circadian activity (i.e., switching from one type of shift to another). Nurses who worked night or rotating shifts reported fewer hours of sleep and irregular sleep schedules, and were more likely to fall asleep at work (Gold et al., 1992). However, nurses who rotated between shifts were more likely to report an accident at work that was related to their tiredness than nurses who worked only day shifts or only night shifts. Furthermore, Folkard et al. (2006) calculated that the peak time of accident risk for fixed shift work was not generalizable to rotating shift workers, implying that these two groups of shift workers are indeed distinct from each other.

Although the individuals who work shifts have the opportunity to sleep during the day, this opportunity is limited because complete circadian readjustment is almost never achieved (Monk et al., 1996). There are at least three factors that limit circadian readjustment (Monk et al., 1996). First, shift workers are exposed to sunlight when they are off work, which naturally prompts wakefulness. Second, other people who are awake during the day can inhibit and disrupt the shift workers' sleep. Finally, this biological clock is slow to adapt to shift work, with the body requiring over a week to fully adapt to working night shifts. This combination of both societal and biological pressures prevents shift workers from being nocturnal, which can lead to impaired performance and decreased safety at work.

### Nature of Work Tasks

Aside from the work shift, characteristics of work tasks can influence the experience of fatigue. Tasks that are monotonous and nonstimulating increase the feeling of fatigue and the risk of injuries (Williamson et al., 2011). To illustrate, professional drivers reported higher rates of fatigue-related accidents on highways compared to general accidents (Horne & Reyner, 1995). This may be because highway driving is highly monotonous and lacks stimulation from traffic lights, road signs, and other vehicles. Mental work overload and physically uncomfortable work positions are also characteristic of work tasks that have been found to increase fatigue at work for professional drivers (Chiron, Bernard, Lafont, & Lagarde, 2008).

## INDIVIDUAL CHARACTERISTICS

Previous studies that uncovered individual differences imply that certain subpopulations are more susceptible to the impact of sleep on safety performance. The purpose of identifying individual-related characteristics is to provide preventive advice and sleep hygiene education to higher-risk groups. The most frequently reported differences that relate to sleep and fatigue are age and gender, as well as certain lifestyle factors. In general, identification of individual risk factors has not been theoretically driven; these findings emerged instead from post hoc or control analyses in large-scale epidemiological studies (Horrey et al., 2011).

### Age

Older individuals require less sleep than younger individuals and are less affected by the effects of acute sleep deprivation (Gregory, 2008; Rogers, 2008). Thus, older workers appear to be more sensitive to accumulated sleep deficits and are more likely to be injured in the afternoon and midweek. To support this, a review noted that younger transport shift work drivers between the age of 18 and 20 years had more sleep-related accidents in the night, and drivers over 56 years old were more likely to have sleep-related accidents during the afternoon (Härmä, 1993). Another study also found that older professional drivers were more likely to be involved in accidents in the mid afternoon (Horne & Reyner, 1999). Younger shift workers experienced more at-work sleepiness on their first night shift of the week, and older workers experienced more tiredness midweek (Härmä, 1993).

The tendency for young workers to feel sleepy in the morning may be due to the fact that as individuals age, they become increasingly more morning oriented—being more alert and prepared to perform during the morning periods (Krauss et al., 2003). In addition, younger drivers are less likely to take breaks when tired (Braeckman et al., 2011). Among truck drivers who sleep less than 6 hours a workday, reports of accidents were positively associated with excessive daytime sleepiness but negatively associated with age (Souza et al., 2005). This may partly be due to the reluctance of younger drivers to take breaks because of external pressure to perform. These studies might also suggest that work experiences accumulated over a lifetime may protect older workers from sleep-related injuries by providing them with the self-assurance to determine when the need for rest overcomes the pressure to perform.

## Gender

Although there are studies that documented gender differences in susceptibility to sleep-related incidents, the findings may be confounded with an overall trend for men to experience more occupational accidents, injuries, and fatalities than women, but women may experience higher rates of specific injuries than men (Åkerstedt et al., 2002; Islam, Velilla, Doyle, & Ducatman, 2001). Furthermore, the relationship between sleep and safety may manifest differently for men and women. For example, Nakata et al. (2005) found that difficulty initiating sleep, poor sleep quality, and insufficient sleep were positively associated with occupational injuries for men but not for women. The odds of experiencing an occupational injury were higher for men who previously reported disturbed sleep than for men who were good sleepers, and higher for women who had difficulty initiating sleep than for women who were good sleepers (Salminen et al., 2010). In a study by Ulfberg et al. (2000) that compared patients at a Swedish sleep clinic to a random sample of the general population of the country, the odds of being involved in an accident at work were higher for workers who were heavy snorers or were suffering from obstructive sleep apnea syndrome and this effect was stronger in women than in men.

Gender effects may also be obscured due to the gendered nature of the workforce. Women and men may experience different job-related characteristics as a result of the gendered nature of work and these may affect the relationships between sleep and safety. For example, a study based on nationally representative data from Statistics Canada reported that "having trouble sleeping most of the time" was positively associated with occupational injury for both men and women (Kling, McLeod, & Koelhoorn, 2010). However, men were more likely to be injured if they worked in the transportation industry or in a trade, whereas women were more likely to be injured if they worked in processing or manufacturing jobs. Moreover, women who worked rotating shifts were most likely to experience occupational injury due to trouble sleeping (Kling et al., 2010; Wong et al., 2011). With regard to nonsleep factors, mental work overload increased fatigue at work for men who were professional drivers, whereas physically uncomfortable work positions increased fatigue at work for women in the same job (Chiron et al., 2008).

## Lifestyle

There is limited evidence showing that certain lifestyle habits are associated with increased sleep disturbances or risk of injuries. In a study examining a sample of firefighters, the risk of sleep disturbances increased with alcohol consumption and smoking (Lusa et al., 2002). In a case control study of construction workers, Chau, Mur, Benamghar, et al. (2004) found that smoking and physical disability were associated with more reports of workplace injuries that did not require hospitalization. It is unclear with these findings whether the lifestyle habits affect sleep and safety, or whether individuals with poor sleep habits or recent injuries tend to develop these lifestyle habits.

A clearer etiology emerges with the relationship between obesity and safety-related outcomes. Data from the U.S. National Health Interview Survey revealed that sleep duration of less than 7 hours a night and obesity (body mass index ≥30) were independently associated with a higher risk of injury at work compared to a referent group of 7–8 hours of sleep a night and healthy weight workers (body mass index < 25; Lombardi, Wirtz, Willetts, & Folkard, 2012). Furthermore, sleep duration mediated the negative relationship between high body mass index and injury risk (Arlinghaus et al., 2012). High body mass index can negatively affect sleep by causing breathing difficulties (Ulfberg et al., 2000), and the resulting sleep disruption may lead to the experience of occupational injury.

## THE ROLE OF HUMAN ERRORS

Although sleep characteristics, work characteristics, and individual differences all affect fatigue and, in turn, are associated with adverse safety outcomes, the mechanism through which fatigue results in impaired safety performance remains unclear. We suggest that a likely explanation is that increased fatigue results in the committal of slips, lapses, and mistakes (unintentional and intentional execution of actions that lead to undesirable consequences; Norman, 1988), and that it is these human errors that result in occupational accidents and injuries.

A common approach to examining human errors is the idea of cognitive failures, which are mistakes or failures to perform an action that an individual is normally capable of executing under normal cognitive functioning (Wallace, Kass, & Stanny, 2001). These failures can be attributed to interference in the individual's memory, attention, or motor function/actions. Work-related cognitive failures were found to be positively related to unsafe behaviors, accidents, and mishaps, and negatively related to safety behaviors and performances at work (Larson, Alderton, Neideffer, & Underhill, 1997; Wallace & Chen, 2005; Wallace & Vodanovich, 2003).

Certainly considerable data support the link between fatigue and errors, particularly perceptual and cognitive errors. Neuroimaging studies revealed that the areas of the brain affected by loss of sleep are important for memory, learning, and motor functioning (see Dawson, Ian Noy, Härmä, Åkerstedt, & Belenky, 2011 for a review). Sleepiness has been associated with impaired attentiveness and vigilance, psychomotor coordination, perceptual processing, memory, and reduced reaction times (Gregory, 2008; Krauss et al., 2003; Krueger, 1989; Montgomery, 2007; Sneddon, Mearns, & Flin, 2013). Long-term fatigue in seafarers accounted for 14% of the variance in self-reported cognitive failures (Wadsworth et al., 2008). Police officers with at least one type of sleep issue (sleep apnea, shift work disorder, or insomnia) had higher odds of committing an administrative error, making an error or safety violation, or falling asleep at work compared to those who did not have sleep disturbance (Rajaratnam et al., 2011).

Numerous reviews have been published detailing the detrimental impact of lack of sleep and sleepiness on medical errors and patient safety (see Montgomery, 2007; Mountain, Quon, Dodek, Sharpe, & Ayas, 2007; Parshuram, 2006; Rogers, 2008; Surani, Murphy, & Shah, 2007 for reviews). In a survey of emergency medical response services employees, sleepy workers compared to alert workers had significantly greater odds of being injured, committing a medical error, and engaging in safety-compromising work behaviors (Patterson et al., 2011). In a cross-sectional study of nurses, excessive daytime sleepiness was positively related to drug administration errors and the incorrect operation of medical equipment (Suzuki, Ohida, Kaneita, Yokoyama, & Uchiyama, 2005).

Although studies have found significant associations between sleep and errors and errors and safety, no studies to date have directly examined whether errors mediate the relationship between poor sleep and higher occupational injury rate. We believe that this is highly plausible, as errors committed over a 24-hour period are susceptible to the human circadian rhythm very much like the risk of accident; both peak at around 2:00 am (Hobbs, Williamson, & Van Dogen, 2010). The extent to which committing errors serves as a mechanism linking sleep to safety at work is determined to be a ripe topic for future research.

## COUNTERACTIVE MEASURES

Both individual and organizational measures have been proposed as means of counteracting sleepiness or fatigue at work (Barnes, 2012), thereby enhancing safety. Individually, the focus has been on the use of stimulants such as caffeine or on individual preventive measures such as napping. On an organizational level, policies and procedures may mitigate or reduce the risks associated with increased fatigue.

## Individual Strategies

The two most common measures used to counteract fatigue are caffeine and naps. Other measures such as distraction (e.g., rolling down the window and listening to music while driving) or exercise were not found to be effective in preventing sleepiness because they provide only a transient state of alertness (Horne & Reyner, 1999; Rogers, 2008). In contrast, sleep model simulations showed that after one night of no sleep, caffeine reduced the risk of injury up to 70%. However, the benefits of caffeine do not extend to extreme conditions (i.e., after a night of no sleep during a time of chronic sleep restriction; Gregory, 2008). To be most effective, caffeine should not be consumed when drowsy, but rather an hour before drowsiness is expected (Rogers, 2008).

There are reports of other types of stimulants being used at work other than caffeine (see Chapter 6 by Gish and Wagner in this book for a summary). In the healthcare sector, a stimulant called modafinil was approved to promote wakefulness (Tewari, Soliz, Billota, Garg, & Singh, 2011). Bright lights have been demonstrated to increase alertness for long periods of desk work or for night shift workers (Roger, 2008). However, the long-term impact of continuous use of stimulants on health, as well as bright lights on the body's natural circadian rhythm cycle, has not been examined.

Whereas stimulants increase alertness, a nap can restore some of the benefits of sleep. Napping before a night shift has been found to lead to a 48% decrease in accidents (Garbarino et al., 2004). Ten-minute naps can temporarily increase performance comparable to 5 hours of sleep, but 30-minute naps can be detrimental because sleep inertia can leave the individual drowsy upon waking up (Parshuram, 2006). Caffeine and naps are both cited as beneficial; however, they are better together than separate (Rogers, 2008). Engaging in a nap of less than 15 minutes and consuming 150 mg of caffeine were discovered to work as effective countermeasures to sleepiness while driving (Horne & Reyner, 1999).

## Organizational Strategies

Policy and legislation may serve as distal countermeasures to offset the increased risks associated with fatigue at work. For example, regulating the length of work shifts and instituting mandatory rest breaks may provide a means of countering the known effects of extended work shifts (Rogers, 2008). In a 12-hour work shift, the last 4 hours are identified as a critical point for fatigue as the extra hours combined with a circadian low point can lead to lower performance efficiency (Rosa, 1995). Therefore, in the last hours of a long shift the workload should be distributed lightly, and having a work break scheduled during those last hours would be beneficial as well.

Changes in shift scheduling practices can also be effective. Occupational drivers in Europe are allowed to drive for 9 hours per day, with the possibility of driving 10 hours per day twice per week (Philip, 2005). If a driver works for 6 consecutive days they must be given 45 hours off work. A study conducted in Iceland compared nurses who worked day shifts, nurses who worked night shifts, and those who rotated between the two and found no significant differences in sleep quality between the groups (Sveinsdottir, 2006). This was attributed to the country's legislature that requires nurses to have a minimum of 11 hours off between shifts. Therefore, organizations should allow enough time between shifts to rest to reduce the susceptibility of shift workers to sleep-related incidents at work. Fast rotating shift schedules that move clockwise are ideal, because they minimize disruptions in circadian rhythm, minimize sleep debt, and avoid the unfortunate occurrence of a morning shift and a night shift in the same day, thus allowing workers to better adjust to shift work hours (Costa, Anelli, Castellini, Fustinoni, & Neri, 2014; Kecklund Eriksen, & Åkerstedt, 2008).

Despite the evidence-based countermeasures, there are practical barriers to policy and legislation. For instance, the implementation of shorter on-call shifts would require hospital or government funding to supply the necessary amount of staff that would enable this change (Parshuram, 2006). In addition, all the factors of the fatigue framework must be carefully contemplated as a whole in order for policy and legislation to be effective. For example, legislations typically deal with the duration of shifts whereas other factors such as start time of shift, pattern of shift, amount of overtime, type of work tasks performed, and circadian factors are not regulated, even though all factors are important in determining driver sleepiness (Ferguson & Dawson, 2012; Horne & Reyner, 1999).

## OVERVIEW, LIMITATIONS, AND FUTURE DIRECTIONS

It seems clear that the experience of sleep and daytime sleepiness can impact safety at work. We have suggested that low quantity and poor quality of sleep, in addition to certain individual differences and job-related characteristics, result in increased fatigue. In turn, fatigue is suggested to be a predictor of perceptual and cognitive errors, which have been linked to safety performance in the workplace. It is through this mechanism of errors that we believe fatigue results in occupational accidents and injuries. Although this interpretation is consistent with the available data, we also note the need to address limitations in the existing research that impede our understanding of the relationships between fatigue and occupational safety.

### Standardize the Measurements of Sleep

By far the greatest weakness in this area of study is the lack of consistency in measures used to assess sleep. The root issue of this weakness is that the operational definition of poor sleep varies according to different researchers, therefore so do the items and timeframes used to assess sleep. The use of standardized self-reported measures of sleep would enhance our ability to compare findings across studies.

Future research could also benefit from employing other types of sleep measurements commonly used in the field of sleep medicine. This includes objective assessments of sleep quality and behaviors (e.g., actigraphy; Balkin, Horrey, Graeber, Czeisler, & Dinges, 2011), neurophysiological assessments such as electroencephalography and electrooculogram recordings (Papadelis et al., 2007), and biomathematical models of fatigue that incorporate circadian rhythm, resting, waking, and working hours in the calculation of the likelihood and magnitude of fatigue (see Dawson et al., 2011 for a review). These alternative assessment tools of sleep may be more valid because they have gone through rigorous development and are commonly used, thus offering a platform for consistent measurement. Although some of these measures are intrusive and require access to expensive technology (e.g., electroencephalography), others are relatively nonintrusive and are increasingly available for researchers (e.g., actigraphy). Moreover, the advent of "apps" that use a similar technology to track sleep duration and quality may make the objective study of sleep and safety even more accessible to researchers.

## Expand on the Measurements of Safety-Related Outcomes

The reports of injuries and accidents data need to have standardized measurements as well (i.e., items, timeframe) so findings can be properly compared across studies (Kucharczyk et al., 2012). The relationship between fatigue and safety performance also appears to be an underexplored area of investigation. Safety performance would include consideration of safety compliance (i.e., the act of following safety rules and regulations), safety participation (i.e., the willingness to participate in safety), as well as counterproductive safety behaviors (i.e., risk-taking behaviors; Martínez-Córcoles, Gracia, Tomás, Peiró, & Schöbel, 2013; Neal, Griffin, & Hart, 2000). Furthermore, studies have linked better safety performance to a lower risk of occupational injuries and accidents (e.g., Clarke, 2010). Therefore, discovering what types of safety performance are hindered by poor sleep can further our understanding on how fatigue leads to the increased likelihood of injuries at work.

Furthermore, now that a clear link between sleep and accidents has been established, it will aid organizational researchers in teasing apart the mechanisms through which this relationship operates. We have proposed one mechanism, cognitive errors, but also suggest that there is considerable advantage to expanding the measure of safety outcomes to include safety attitudes and behaviors. For example, considerable data have now accumulated regarding organizational safety climate—which represents workers' shared perceptions about safety in the workplace—as a predictor of safety events in organizations (e.g., Zohar, 1980). In the current context, safety climate is a plausible moderator of the relationship between fatigue and safety outcomes. In organizations with strong and positive safety climates, fatigued individuals may be more willing to raise safety concerns and ask for consideration. In contrast, organizations with cultures that do not value safety are unlikely to accommodate individuals who are fatigued as a result of sleep disruption. Similarly, subordinates with supervisors who display good safety leadership behaviors have a high sense of safety voice and trust in their leaders (Conchie, Taylor, & Donald, 2012). Therefore, these individuals may be more willing to disclose their diminished state of alertness to their supervisors rather than trying to work through the fatigue.

Most research has focused on sleep disruption as a predictor of safety outcomes, with relatively few investigations of how safety concerns might affect sleep. Occupational stress and organizational safety climate were found to be significant predictors of fatigue-related driving behaviors and near misses in transport drivers (Strahan, Watson, & Lennon, 2008). Cross-sectional surveys of offshore workers revealed that low risk perception and better safety climate (high safety prioritization, safety management, individual motivation, competence, and safety comprehension) predicted sleep quality (Hope, Øverland, Brun, & Matthiesen, 2010). Similarly, it has been demonstrated that leaders exact a strong influence over subordinates' safety behaviors (see Wong, Kelloway, & Makhan, 2015), and positive leadership behaviors have been found to improve subordinates' sleep quality (Munir & Nielsen, 2009). Having a good night's sleep without the worries of injury risk at work may be one of the mediators of safety climate and safety leadership on safety outcomes. A better understanding of the effect of safety on sleep can help improve sleep hygiene and, in turn, perhaps reduces the safety concerns that gave rise to the original sleep problem.

## Utilize Other Research Designs

The study of sleep and workplace outcomes is best examined with a field study. Laboratory studies are often subjected to methodological flaws or nongeneralizable simulations that prevent sleep from being established as a cause for declines in safety performances (Gaba & Howard, 2002). As previously mentioned, safety climate (Zohar, 1980) and safety leadership (Wong et al., 2015) may be important contextual factors that place a substantive constraint on the generalizability of laboratory studies (Johns, 1991b).

Some of the studies cited in this review reported using insurance claims, including workers' compensation claims, as the primary source of data. However, companies may underreport problems in order to keep their insurance premiums down or to avoid censure from government agencies (Probst, Brubaker, & Barsotti, 2008). Therefore, insurance claims datasets may be confounded by this restriction. Future studies can benefit more from smaller sample field studies that have the autonomy of using more standardized and stringent measurements of sleep and safety outcomes to uncover causal and predictive relationships.

## Can Too Much Sleep Be Bad?

A review by Folkard et al. (2005) proposed a U-shaped relationship between sleep and occupational injury for shift workers, suggesting that both too little (less than 6 hours) and too much (more than 9 hours) sleep can be associated with an increased risk of injury. Workers who had previously sustained a hand injury were associated with the habit of sleeping more than 8 hours a night in a matched-pair case-control study by Hertz and Emmett (1986). In addition, individuals with very short or very long sleep were found to have increased mortality due to accidents (Gregory, 2008). More research about the limitation of too much sleep may shed light on the conditions under which taking a nap is more beneficial than attempting to sleep longer at night, as both may be effective fatigue countermeasures that should enhance safety at work.

## CONCLUSIONS

With the link between sleep and injuries clearly established, future research should focus on the mechanisms linking poor sleep to increased accidents at work. Exploring the role of human errors and safety attitudes or behaviors may increase our understanding of these underlying changes. The use of more refined measures of both sleep and safety would further enhance our understanding of these relationships. We suggest that such advances would result in improved safety in the workplace.

## REFERENCES

Åkerstedt, T., Fredlund, P., Gillberg, M., & Jansson, B. (2002). A prospective study of fatal occupational accidents–relationship to sleeping difficulties and occupational factors. *Journal of Sleep Research, 11*(1), 69–71. doi:10.1046/j.1365-2869.2002.00287.x

Arlinghaus, A., Lombardi, D. A., Willetts, J. L., Folkard, S., & Christiani, D. C. (2012). A structural equation modeling approach to fatigue-related risk factors for occupational injury. *American Journal of Epidemiology, 176*(7), 597–607. doi:10.1093/aje/kws219

Balkin, T. J., Horrey, W. J., Graeber, R. C., Czeisler, C. A., & Dinges, D. F. (2011). The challenges and opportunities of technological approaches to fatigue management. *Accident Analysis & Prevention, 43*(2), 565–572. doi:10.1016/j.aap.2009.12.006

Barnes, C. M. (2012). Working in our sleep: Sleep and self-regulation in organizations. *Organizational Psychology Review, 2*(3), 234–257. doi:10.1177/2041386612450181

Barnes, C. M., & Wagner, D. T. (2009). Changing to daylight saving time cuts into sleep and increases workplace injuries. *Journal of Applied Psychology, 94*(5), 1305–1317. doi:10.1037/a0015320

Braeckman, L., Verpraet, R., Van Risseghem, M., Pevernagie, D., & De Bacquer, D. (2011). Prevalence and correlates of poor sleep quality and daytime sleepiness in Belgian truck drivers. *Chronobiology International, 28*(2), 126–134. doi:10.3109/07420528.2010.540363

Buysse, D. J., Reynolds, C. F., III, Monk, T. H., Berman, S. R., & Kupfer, D. J. (1989). The Pittsburgh Sleep Quality Index: A new instrument for psychiatric practice and research. *Psychiatry Research, 28*(2), 193–213. doi:10.1016/0165-1781(89)90047-4

Carter, N., Ulfberg, J., Nyström, B., & Edling, C. (2003). Sleep debt, sleepiness and *accidents among males in the general population and male professional drivers. Accident Analysis & Prevention, 35*(4), 613–617. doi:10.1016/S0001-4575(02)00033-7

Chau, N., Benamghar, L., Siegfried, C., Dehaene, D., Dangelzer, J. L., Français, M., . . . & Mur, J. M. (2006). Determinants of occupational fracture proneness: A case-control study in construction and railway workers. *Journal of Occupational Health*, *48*, 267–270. doi:10.1539/joh.48.267

Chau, N., Mur, J. M., Benamghar, L., Siegfried, C., Dangelzer, J. L., Français, M., . . . & Sourdot, A. (2002). Relationships between some individual characteristics and occupational accidents in the construction industry: A case-control study on 880 victims of accidents occurred during a two-year period. *Journal of Occupational Health*, *44*(3), 131–139. doi:10.1539/joh.44.131

Chau, N., Mur, J. M., Benamghar, L., Siegfried, C., Dangelzer, J. L., Français, M., . . . & Sourdot, A. (2004). Relationships between certain individual characteristics and occupational injuries for various jobs in the construction industry: A case-control study. *American Journal of Industrial Medicine*, *45*(1), 84–92. doi:10.1002/ajim.10319

Chau, N., Mur, J. M., Touron, C., Benamghar, L., & Dehaene, D. (2004). Correlates of occupational injuries for various jobs in railway workers: A case-control study. *Journal of Occupational Health*, *46*(4), 272–280.

Chiron, M., Bernard, M., Lafont, S., & Lagarde, E. (2008). Tiring job and work related injury road crashes in the GAZEL cohort. *Accident Analysis & Prevention*, *40*(3), 1096–1104. doi:10.1016/j.aap.2007.12.001

Clarke, S. (2010). An integrative model of safety climate: Linking psychological climate and work attitudes to individual safety outcomes using meta-analysis. *Journal of Occupational and Organizational Psychology*, *83*(3), 553–578. doi:10.1348/096317909X452122

Conchie, S. M., Taylor, P. J., & Donald, I. J. (2012). Promoting safety voice with safety-specific transformational leadership: The mediating role of two dimensions of trust. *Journal of Occupational Health Psychology*, *17*(1), 105–115. doi:10.1037/a0025101

Costa, G., Anelli, M. M., Castellini, G., Fustinoni, S., & Neri, L. (2014). Stress and sleep in nurses employed in "3× 8" and "2× 12" fast rotating shift schedules. *Chronobiology International*, *31*(10), 1169–1178. doi:10.3109/07420528.2014.957309

Daan, S., Beersma, D. G., & Borbély, A. A. (1984). Timing of human sleep: Recovery process gated by a circadian pacemaker. *American Journal of Physiology-Regulatory, Integrative and Comparative Physiology*, *246*(2), R161–R183.

Daley, M., Morin, C. M., LeBlanc, M., Gregoire, J. P., Savard, J., & Baillargeon, L. (2009). Insomnia and its relationship to health-care utilization, work absenteeism, productivity and accidents. *Sleep Medicine*, *10*(4), 427–438. doi:10.1016/j.sleep.2008.04.005

Dawson, D., Ian Noy, Y., Härmä, M., Åkerstedt, T., & Belenky, G. (2011). Modelling fatigue and the use of fatigue models in work settings. *Accident Analysis & Prevention*, *43*(2), 549–564. doi:10.1016/j.aap.2009.12.030

Dinges, D. F. (1995). An overview of sleepiness and accidents. Journal of Sleep Research, *4*(s2), 4–14. doi:10.1111/j.1365-2869.1995.tb00220.x

Dorrian, J., Baulk, S. D., & Dawson, D. (2011). Work hours, workload, sleep and fatigue in Australian Rail Industry employees. *Applied Ergonomics*, *42*(2), 202–209. doi:10.1016/j.apergo.2010.06.009

Erbaydar, N. P., Ilingiroglu, N., Hekimsoy, V., Kalender, E., Kurtulan, O., Oncul, U., . . . & Tac, Y. (2010). Sleepiness, sleep quality and the association with occupational accidents among a medical faculty residents. *Injury Prevention*, *16*(Suppl 1), A44–A45. doi:10.1136/ip.2010.029215.161

Ferguson, S. A., & Dawson, D. (2012). 12-h or 8-h shifts? It depends. *Sleep Medicine Reviews*, *16*(6), 519–528. doi:10.1016/j.smrv.2011.11.001

Folkard, S., Lombardi, D. A., & Spencer, M. B. (2006). Estimating the circadian rhythm in the risk of occupational injuries and accidents. *Chronobiology International*, *23*(6), 1181–1192. doi:10.1080/07420520601096443

Folkard, S., Lombardi, D., & Tucker, P. T. (2005). Shiftwork: Safety, sleepiness and sleep. *Industrial Health, 43*(1), 20–23.

Fransen, M., Wilsmore, B., Winstanley, J., Woodward, M., Grunstein, R., Ameratunga, S., & Norton, R. (2006). Shift work and work injury in the New Zealand blood donors' health study. *Occupational and Environmental Medicine, 63*(5), 352–358. doi:10.1136/oem.2005.024398

Gaba, D. M., & Howard, S. K. (2002). Fatigue among clinicians and the safety of patients. *New England Journal of Medicine, 347*(16), 1249–1255. doi:10.1056/NEJMsa020846

Garbarino, S., Mascialino, B., Penco, M. A., Squarcia, S., De Carli, F., Nobili, L., . . . & Ferrillo, F. (2004). Professional shift-work drivers who adopt prophylactic naps can reduce the risk of car accidents during night work. *Sleep, 27*(7), 1295–1302.

Gauchard, G. C., Chau, N., Touron, C., Benamghar, L., Dehaene, D., Perrin, P., & Mur, J. M. (2003). Individual characteristics in occupational accidents due to imbalance: A case-control study of the employees of a railway company. *Occupational and Environmental Medicine, 60*(5), 330–335. doi:10.1136/oem.60.5.330

Gauchard, G. C., Mur, J. M., Touron, C., Benamghar, L., Dehaene, D., Perrin, P., & Chau, N. (2006). Determinants of accident proneness: A case–control study in railway workers. *Occupational Medicine, 56*(3), 187–190. doi:10.1093/occmed/kqj016

Gold, D. R., Rogacz, S., Bock, N., Tosteson, T. D., Baum, T. M., Speizer, F. E., & Czeisler, C. A. (1992). Rotating shift work, sleep, and accidents related to sleepiness in hospital nurses. *American Journal of Public Health, 82*(7), 1011–1014. doi:10.2105/AJPH.82.7.1011

Gregory, J. M. (2008). Sleep: A good investment in health and safety. *Journal of Agromedicine, 13*(2), 119–131. doi:10.1080/10599240802125631

Häkkänen, H., & Summala, H. (2000). Sleepiness at work among commercial truck drivers. *Sleep, 23*(1), 49–57.

Halvani, G. H., Zare, M., & Mirmohammadi, S. J. (2009). The relation between shift work, sleepiness, fatigue and accidents in Iranian Industrial Mining Group workers. *Industrial Health, 47*(2), 134–138. doi:10.2486/indhealth.47.134

Härmä, M. (1993). Individual differences in tolerance to shiftwork: A review. *Ergonomics, 36*(1–3), 101–109. doi:10.1080/00140139308967860

Hertz, R. P., & Emmett, E. A. (1986). Risk factors for occupational hand injury. *Journal of Occupational and Environmental Medicine, 28*(1), 36–41.

Hobbs, A., Williamson, A., & Van Dongen, H. P. (2010). A circadian rhythm in skill-based errors in aviation maintenance. *Chronobiology International, 27*(6), 1304–1316. doi:10.3109/07420528.2010.484890

Hope, S., Øverland, S., Brun, W., & Matthiesen, S. B. (2010). Associations between sleep, risk and safety climate: A study of offshore personnel on the Norwegian continental shelf. *Safety Science, 48*(4), 469–477. doi:10.1016/j.ssci.2009.12.006

Horne, J. A., & Reyner, L. A. (1995). Sleep related vehicle accidents. *British Medical Journal, 310*(6979), 565–567. doi:10.1136/bmj.310.6979.565

Horne, J. A., & Reyner, L. A. (1999). Vehicle accidents related to sleep: A review. *Occupational and Environmental Medicine, 56*(5), 289–294. doi:10.1136/oem.56.5.289

Horrey, W. J., Noy, Y. I., Folkard, S., Popkin, S. M., Howarth, H. D., & Courtney, T. K. (2011). Research needs and opportunities for reducing the adverse safety consequences of fatigue. *Accident Analysis & Prevention, 43*(2), 591–594. doi:10.1016/j.aap.2010.01.014

Islam, S. S., Velilla, A. M., Doyle, E. J., & Ducatman, A. M. (2001). Gender differences in work-related injury/illness: Analysis of workers compensation claims. *American Journal of Industrial Medicine, 39*(1), 84–91. doi:10.1002/1097-0274(200101)39:1<84::AID-AJIM8>3.0.CO;2-T

Johns M. W. (1991a). A new method for measuring daytime sleepiness: The Epworth Sleepiness Scale. *Sleep, 14*(6), 540–545.

Johns, G. (1991b). Substantive and methodological constraints on behavior and attitudes in organizational research. *Organizational Behavior and Human Decision Processes, 49*(1), 80–104. doi:10.1016/0749-5978(91)90043-S

Kecklund, G., Eriksen, C. A., & Åkerstedt, T. (2008). Police officers attitude to different shift systems: Association with age, present shift schedule, health and sleep/wake complaints. *Applied Ergonomics, 39*(5), 565–571. doi:10.1016/j.apergo.2008.01.002

Kling, R. N., McLeod, C. B., & Koehoorn, M. (2010). Sleep problems and workplace injuries in Canada. *Sleep, 33*(5), 611–618.

Krauss, A. D., Chen, P. Y., DeArmond, S., & Moorcroft, B. (2003). Sleepiness in the workplace: Causes, consequences, and countermeasures. *International Review of Industrial and Organizational Psychology, 18*, 81–130. doi:10.1002/0470013346.ch3

Krueger, G. P. (1989). Sustained work, fatigue, sleep loss and performance: A review of the issues. *Work & Stress, 3*(2), 129–141. doi:10.1080/02678378908256939

Kucharczyk, E. R., Morgan, K., & Hall, A. P. (2012). The occupational impact of sleep quality and insomnia symptoms. *Sleep Medicine Reviews, 16*(6), 547–559. doi:10.1016/j.smrv.2012.01.005

Lahti, T., Sysi-Aho, J., Haukka, J., & Partonen, T. (2011). Work-related accidents and daylight saving time in Finland. *Occupational Medicine, 61*(1), 26–28. doi:10.1093/occmed/kqq167

Larson, G. E., Alderton, D. L., Neideffer, M., & Underhill, E. (1997). Further evidence on dimensionality and correlates of the Cognitive Failures Questionnaire. *British Journal of Psychology, 88*(1), 29–38. doi:10.1111/j.2044-8295.1997.tb02618.x

Lavie, P. (1981). Sleep habits and sleep disturbances in industrial workers in Israel: Main findings and some characteristics of workers complaining of excessive daytime sleepiness. *Sleep, 4*(2), 147–158.

Lavie, P. (1986). Ultrashort sleep-waking schedule. III. 'Gates' and 'forbidden zones' for sleep. *Electroencephalography and Clinical Neurophysiology, 63*(5), 414–425. doi:10.1016/0013-4694(86)90123-9

Léger, D., Guilleminault, C., Bader, G., Lévy, E., & Paillard, M. (2002). Medical and socio-professional impact of insomnia. *Sleep, 25*(6), 625–629.

Lilley, R., Day, L., Koehncke, N., Dosman, J., Hagel, L., & William, P. (2012). The relationship between fatigue-related factors and work-related injuries in the Saskatchewan farm injury Cohort Study. *American Journal of Industrial Medicine, 55*(4), 367–375. doi:10.1002/ajim.22003

Lindberg, E. V. A., Carter, N. E. D., Gislason, T., & Janson, C. (2001). Role of snoring and daytime sleepiness in occupational accidents. *American Journal of Respiratory and Critical Care Medicine, 164*(11), 2031–2035. doi:10.1164/ajrccm.164.11.2102028

Lombardi, D. A., Wirtz, A., Willetts, J. L., & Folkard, S. (2012). Independent effects of sleep duration and body mass index on the risk of a work-related injury: Evidence from the US National Health Interview Survey (2004–2010). *Chronobiology International, 29*(5), 556–564. doi:10.3109/07420528.2012.675253

Lusa, S., Häkkänen, M., Luukkonen, R., & Viikari-Juntura, E. (2002). Perceived physical work capacity, stress, sleep disturbance and occupational accidents among firefighters working during a strike. *Work & Stress, 16*(3), 264–274. doi:10.1080/02678370210163301

Martínez-Córcoles, M., Gracia, F. J., Tomás, I., Peiró, J. M., & Schöbel, M. (2013). Empowering team leadership and safety performance in nuclear power plants: A multilevel approach. *Safety Science, 51*(1), 293–301. doi:10.1016/j.ssci.2012.08.001

Monk, T. H., Folkard, S., & Wedderburn, A. I. (1996). Maintaining safety and high performance on shiftwork. *Applied Ergonomics, 27*(1), 17–23. doi:10.1016/0003-6870(95)00048-8

Montgomery, V. L. (2007). Effect of fatigue, workload, and environment on patient safety in the pediatric intensive care unit. *Pediatric Critical Care Medicine, 8*(2), S11–S16. doi:10.1097/01.PCC.0000257735.49562.8F

Morassaei, S., & Smith, P. M. (2010). Switching to daylight saving time and work injuries in Ontario, Canada: 1993–2007. *Occupational and Environmental Medicine, 67*(12), 878–880. doi:10.1136/oem.2010.056127

Mountain, S. A., Quon, B. S., Dodek, P., Sharpe, R., & Ayas, N. T. (2007). The impact of housestaff fatigue on occupational and patient safety. *Lung, 185*(4), 203–209. doi:10.1007/s00408-007-9010-5

Munir, F., & Nielsen, K. (2009). Does self-efficacy mediate the relationship between transformational leadership behaviours and healthcare workers' sleep quality? A longitudinal study. *Journal of Advanced Nursing, 65*(9), 1833–1843. doi:10.1111/j.1365-2648.2009.05039.x

Nakata, A. (2011). Effects of long work hours and poor sleep characteristics on workplace injury among full-time male employees of small- and medium-scale businesses. *Journal of Sleep Research, 20*(4), 576–584. doi:10.1111/j.1365-2869.2011.00910.x

Nakata, A., Ikeda, T., Takahashi, M., Haratani, T., Fujioka, Y., Fukui, S., . . . & Araki, S. (2005). Sleep-related risk of occupational injuries in Japanese small and medium-scale enterprises. *Industrial Health, 43*(1), 89–97. doi:10.2486/indhealth.43.89

National Sleep Foundation. (2002). NSF public opinion polls. Retrieved from http://www.sleepfoundation.org/publications/execsum.html

Neal, A., Griffin, M. A., & Hart, P. M. (2000). The impact of organizational climate on safety climate and individual behavior. *Safety Science, 34*(1), 99–109. doi:10.1016/S0925-7535(00)00008-4

Norman, D. A. (1988). *The psychology of everyday things*. New York, NY: Basic Books.

Papadelis, C., Chen, Z., Kourtidou-Papadeli, C., Bamidis, P. D., Chouvarda, I., Bekiaris, E., & Maglaveras, N. (2007). Monitoring sleepiness with on-board electrophysiological recordings for preventing sleep-deprived traffic accidents. *Clinical Neurophysiology, 118*(9), 1906–1922. doi:10.1016/j.clinph.2007.04.031

Parshuram, C. S. (2006). The impact of fatigue on patient safety. *Pediatric Clinics of North America, 53*(6), 1135–1153. doi:10.1016/j.pcl.2006.09.009

Patterson, P. D., Weaver, M. D., Frank, R. C., Warner, C. W., Martin-Gill, C., Guyette, F. X., . . . & Hostler, D. (2011). Association between poor sleep, fatigue, and safety outcomes in emergency medical services providers. *Prehospital Emergency Care, 16*(1), 86–97. doi:10.3109/10903127.2011.616261

Philip, P. (2005). Sleepiness of occupational drivers. *Industrial Health, 43*(1), 30–33. doi:10.2486/indhealth.43.30

Phillips, R. (2000). Sleep, watchkeeping and accidents: A content analysis of incident at sea reports. *Transportation Research Part F: Traffic Psychology and Behaviour, 3*(4), 229–240. doi:10.1016/S1369-8478(01)00007-9

Piper, B. F., Dibble, S. L., Dodd, M. J., Weiss, M. C., Slaughter, R. E., & Paul, S. M. (1998). The revised Piper Fatigue Scale: Psychometric evaluation in women with breast cancer. *Oncology Nursing Forum, 25*(4), 677–684.

Probst, T. M., Brubaker, T. L., & Barsotti, A. (2008). Organizational injury rate underreporting: The moderating effect of organizational safety climate. *Journal of Applied Psychology, 93*(5), 1147–1154. doi:10.1037/0021-9010.93.5.1147

Rajaratnam, S. M., Barger, L. K., Lockley, S. W., Shea, S. A., Wang, W., Landrigan, C. P., . . . & Czeisler, C. A. (2011). Sleep disorders, health, and safety in police officers. *Journal of the American Medical Association, 306*(23), 2567–2578. doi:10.1001/jama.2011.1851.

Rogers, A. E. (2008). The effects of fatigue and sleepiness on nurse performance and patient safety. In R. G. Hughe's (Ed.), *Patient safety and quality: An evidence-based handbook for nurses* (pp. 1036–1072). Rockville, MD: Agency for Healthcare Research and Quality.

Rosa, R. R. (1995). *Extended workshifts and excessive fatigue*. Journal of Sleep Research, 4(s2), 51–56. doi:10.1111/j.1365-2869.1995.tb00227.x

Rosekind, M. R., Gregory, K. B., Mallis, M. M., Brandt, S. L., Seal, B., & Lerner, D. (2010). The cost of poor sleep: Workplace productivity loss and associated costs. *Journal of Occupational and Environmental Medicine, 52*(1), 91–98. doi:10.1097/JOM.0b013e3181c78c30

Sabbagh-Ehrlich, S., Friedman, L., & Richter, E. D. (2005). Working conditions and fatigue in professional truck drivers at Israeli ports. *Injury Prevention, 11*(2), 110–114. doi:10.1136/ip.2004.007682

Salminen, S., Oksanen, T., Vahtera, J., Sallinen, M., Härmä, M., Salo, P., . . . & Kivimäki, M. (2010). Sleep disturbances as a predictor of occupational injuries among public sector workers. *Journal of Sleep Research, 19*(1p2), 207–213. doi:10.1111/j.1365-2869.2009.00780.x

Salo, P., Oksanen, T., Sivertsen, B., Hall, M., Pentti, J., Virtanen, M., . . . & Mika, K. (2010). Sleep disturbances as a predictor of cause-specific work disability and delayed return to work. *Sleep, 33*(10), 1323–1332.

Shahly, V., Berglund, P. A., Coulouvrat, C., Fitzgerald, T., Hajak, G., Roth, T., . . . & Kessler, R. C. (2012). The associations of insomnia with costly workplace accidents and errors: Results from the America Insomnia Survey. *Archives of General Psychiatry, 69*(10), 1054–1063. doi:10.1001/archgenpsychiatry.2011.2188

Sneddon, A., Mearns, K., & Flin, R. (2013). Stress, fatigue, situation awareness and safety in offshore drilling crews. *Safety Science, 56*, 80–88. doi:10.1016/j.ssci.2012.05.027

Souza, J. C., Paiva, T., & Reimão, R. (2005). Sleep habits, sleepiness and accidents among truck drivers. *Arquivos de Neuro-Psiquiatria, 63*(4), 925–930. doi:/S0004-282X2005000600004

Strahan, C., Watson, B., & Lennon, A. (2008). Can organisational safety climate and occupational stress predict work-related driver fatigue?. *Transportation Research Part F: Traffic Psychology and Behaviour, 11*(6), 418–426. doi:10.1016/j.trf.2008.04.002

Surani, S., Murphy, J., & Shah, A. (2007). Sleepy nurses: Are we willing to accept the challenge today? *Nursing Administration Quarterly, 31*(2), 146–151. doi:10.1097/01.NAQ.0000264863.94958.40

Suzuki, K., Ohida, T., Kaneita, Y., Yokoyama, E., & Uchiyama, M. (2005). Daytime sleepiness, sleep habits and occupational accidents among hospital nurses. *Journal of Advanced Nursing, 52*(4), 445–453. doi:10.1111/j.1365-2648.2005.03610.x

Sveinsdottir, H. (2006). Self-assessed quality of sleep, occupational health, working environment, illness experience and job satisfaction of female nurses working different combination of shifts. *Scandinavian Journal of Caring Sciences, 20*(2), 229–237. doi:10.1111/j.1471-6712.2006.00402.x

Tewari, A., Soliz, J., Billota, F., Garg, S., & Singh, H. (2011). Does our sleep debt affect patients' safety? *Indian Journal of Anaesthesia, 55*(1), 12–17. doi:10.4103/0019-5049.76572

Uehli, K., Mehta, A. J., Miedinger, D., Hug, K., Schindler, C., Holsboer-Trachsler, E., . . . & Künzli, N. (2014). Sleep problems and work injuries: A systematic review and meta-analysis. *Sleep Medicine Reviews, 18*(1), 61–73. doi:10.1016/j.smrv.2013.01.004

Ulfberg, J., Carter, N., & Edling, C. (2000). Sleep-disordered breathing and occupational accidents. *Scandinavian Journal of Work, Environment & Health, 26*(3), 237–242. doi:10.5271/sjweh.537

Ulfberg, J., Carter, N., Talbälk, M., & Edling, C. (1996). Excessive daytime sleepiness at work and subjective work performance in the general population and among heavy snorers and patients with obstructive sleep apnea. *Chest Journal, 110*(3), 659–663. doi:10.1378/chest.110.3.659

Vennelle, M., Engleman, H. M., & Douglas, N. J. (2010). Sleepiness and sleep-related accidents in commercial bus drivers. *Sleep and Breathing, 14*(1), 39–42. doi:10.1007/s11325-009-0277-z

Wadsworth, E. J., Allen, P. H., McNamara, R. L., & Smith, A. P. (2008). Fatigue and health in a seafaring population. *Occupational Medicine, 58*(3), 198–204. doi:10.1093/occmed/kqn008

Wallace, J. C., & Chen, G. (2005). Development and validation of a work-specific measure of cognitive failure: Implications for occupational safety. *Journal of Occupational and Organizational Psychology, 78*(4), 615–632. doi:10.1348/096317905X37442

Wallace, J. C., Kass, S. J., & Stanny, C. (2001). Predicting performance in 'Go' situations: A new use for the Cognitive Failures Questionnaire? *North American Journal of Psychology, 3*(3), 481–490.

Wallace, J. C., & Vodanovich, S. J. (2003). Workplace safety performance: Conscientiousness, cognitive failure, and their interaction. *Journal of Occupational Health Psychology, 8*(4), 316–327. doi:10.1037/1076-8998.8.4.316

Williamson, A., Lombardi, D. A., Folkard, S., Stutts, J., Courtney, T. K., & Connor, J. L. (2011). The link between fatigue and safety. *Accident Analysis & Prevention, 43*(2), 498–515. doi:10.1016/j.aap.2009.11.011

Wong, I. S., McLeod, C. B., & Demers, P. A. (2011). Shift work trends and risk of work injury among Canadian workers. *Scandinavian Journal of Work, Environment & Health, 37*(1), 54–61.

Wong, J. H. K., Kelloway, E. K., & Makhan, D. W. (2015). Safety leadership. In S. Clarke, T. Probst, F. Guldenmund, & J. Passmore's (Eds.), *The Wiley-Blackwell handbook of the psychology of occupational safety and workplace health*. West Sussex, UK: John Wiley & Sons Limited.

Zohar, D. (1980). Safety climate in industrial organizations: Theoretical and applied implications. *Journal of Applied Psychology, 65*(1), 96–102. doi:10.1037/0021-9010.65.1.96

# CHAPTER 10

# Sleep and Work Withdrawal

ERICA L. CARLETON AND JULIAN BARLING

## SLEEP AND WORK WITHDRAWAL

Attendance at work and engagement once at work are normative expectations. Yet simple observation tells us that neither can be taken for granted. Instead, employees withdraw from work in a variety of different ways that can be costly for organizations (Hanisch & Hulin, 1991). From an academic perspective, the construct of work withdrawal has traditionally included those visible behaviors in which individuals are absent from work in some manner, including tardiness/lateness or full-day absenteeism, and in more extreme cases, turnover (Johns, 2001). More recently, however, the view of what constitutes work withdrawal has been broadened to include less visible forms of withdrawal behaviors, in which individuals attend work, but withdraw behaviorally or cognitively once at work (LeBlanc, Barling, & Turner, 2014). These less visible forms of withdrawal include intentionally neglectful behaviors and cognitive and emotional distraction. They are potentially even more costly to organizations than the visible withdrawal behaviors, precisely because they remain hidden and as a result are more difficult both to study and to manage

Given the importance of withdrawal from work for organizations, it should come as no surprise that there is a large body of research examining withdrawal behaviors. Most of this research has investigated the work-related factors such as work attitudes (e.g., Hanisch & Hulin, 1990, 1991; Laczo & Hanisch, 2000) that influence withdrawal behaviors, but previous research has also shown that nonwork factors in the form of family demands (Hammer, Bauer, & Grandey, 2003) and stressors (LeBlanc et al., 2014) also influence withdrawal behaviors at work. The focus of this chapter is to understand how a ubiquitous nonwork experience, *sleep*, affects work withdrawal behaviors.

To do so, we will briefly review work withdrawal behaviors. This is followed by a discussion of how different aspects of sleep might be implicated in different forms of work withdrawal. Finally, we end with a look toward the future, and possible next steps in investigating the effects of sleep on work withdrawal.

## WORK WITHDRAWAL

Work withdrawal comprises a group of behaviors and intentions that have traditionally been defined as "physical removal from a particular workplace either for part of a day, an entire day, or permanently" (Johns, 2001, p. 233). Consistent with this, researchers have tended to focus on tardiness/lateness, absenteeism, and turnover, all of which are visible, measurable behaviors (LeBlanc et al., 2014). There has been two general perspectives about the relationship between these visible withdrawal behaviors. One perspective views tardiness/lateness, absenteeism, and turnover as manifestations of an overall withdrawal from work construct, arguing that each behavior is a way in which employees withdraw from work in response to unfavorable work attitudes such as job dissatisfaction and lack of organizational commitment (e.g., Hanisch & Hulin, 1991; Rosse & Hulin, 1985). Based on this, it is thought that the understanding of the withdrawal behaviors and their antecedents would be advanced by focusing on aggregate measures that combine the withdrawal behaviors (Berry, Lelchook, & Clark, 2012).

In some of the first work to examine withdrawal behaviors as a general family of behavioral outcomes, Hanisch and Hulin (1990, 1991) divided *organizational withdrawal* into two components, namely work and job withdrawal (Hanisch & Hulin, 1990, 1991). Work withdrawal included behaviors that dissatisfied individuals would use to avoid aspects of their specific work role or minimize the time spent on their specific work tasks while maintaining their current organizational and work–role memberships; this included behaviors such as *unfavorable job behaviors, lateness, and absenteeism* (Hanisch & Hulin, 1991). Job withdrawal on the other hand was defined as employees' efforts to remove themselves from a specific organization and their work role, including behaviors such as *turnover intentions, desire to retire, and intended retirement age* (Hanisch & Hulin, 1991).

The second perspective views each of the withdrawal behaviors as unique and driven by specific antecedents, and therefore different from an overall withdrawal construct (e.g., Price & Mueller, 1981; Steers & Mowday, 1981). A recent meta-analysis provides support for this second view of withdrawal behaviors, as the corrected correlations between all three withdrawal variables were small (i.e., 0.26 between lateness and absenteeism, 0.25 between absenteeism and turnover, and 0.01 between lateness and turnover; Berry et al., 2012). These small-to-moderate intercorrelations provide no support for an overall withdrawal construct that combines lateness, absenteeism, and turnover. In addition, the progression of withdrawal model was supported, in which lateness predicts absenteeism, and in turn absenteeism predicts turnover (Berry et al., 2012; Koslowsky, Sagie, Krausz, & Singer, 1997). This progression model suggests that relatively mild withdrawal behaviors, such as occasional lateness, are important predictors of more severe future withdrawal behaviors, such as frequent absenteeism or voluntary turnover.

## Withdrawal *from* Work versus Withdrawal *at* Work

Recently, researchers (LeBlanc et al., 2014) have expanded the concept of withdrawal to include less visible behaviors, arguing that a comprehensive understanding of workplace withdrawal behavior must include situations in which individuals are at work, but are not working. LeBlanc et al. (2014) distinguished between two types of withdrawal behaviors: withdrawal *from* work, which are the more visible work withdrawal behaviors, and withdrawal *at* work, which includes the less visible work withdrawal behaviors.

Withdrawal *from* work is defined as "physical removal from a particular workplace either for part of a day, an entire day, or permanently" (Johns, 2001, p. 233), thereby including previously discussed visible withdrawal behaviors such as partial absenteeism, tardiness/lateness, and absenteeism. Partial absenteeism goes beyond tardiness (i.e., arriving late for work), and includes leaving work early and taking extended breaks during the workday (Barling, MacEwen, Kelloway, & Higginbottom, 1994). Intending to leave the organization permanently would also reflect withdrawal from work (LeBlanc et al., 2014).

In contrast, withdrawal *at* work is defined as being "physically at work but not productive" (LeBlanc et al., 2014, p. 401), and includes less visible withdrawal behaviors such as work neglect and cognitive and emotional distraction. Work neglect is more deliberate, and involves exerting less behavioral effort while at work (e.g., Schat & Kelloway, 2000) and can include behaviors such as cyberloafing, that is, the personal use of the Internet by employees while at work (Liberman, Seidman, McKenna, & Buffardi, 2011). Distractions are any environmental events or stimuli that challenge our ability to maintain focus on goal-relevant information. These distractions capture attention and reallocate processing resources, and thus can impair performance (Dolcos & McCarthy, 2006; Ellis & Ashbrook, 1988). In line with the progression model of work withdrawal, it is possible that these withdrawal *at* work behaviors are precursors of withdrawal *from* work behaviors (LeBlanc et al., 2014); however, it remains for future research to investigate this possibility.

As would be expected, most research on withdrawal behaviors have focused on those behaviors included in withdrawal from work (i.e., lateness, absenteeism, and turnover). In predicting and explaining these withdrawal behaviors, focus has generally been on a variety of personal (e.g., gender; Steel & Rentsch, 1995), attitudinal (e.g., job commitment; Meyer, Stanley, Herscovitch, & Topolnytsky, 2002), and organizational variables (e.g., organizational support; Eisenberger, Fasolo, & Davis-LaMastro, 1990). Less is known about how nonwork variables impact work withdrawal behaviors, although there are exceptions to this, for example, work-related experiences such as work–family conflict (Hammer et al., 2003) or intimate partner aggression (LeBlanc et al., 2014) impact both withdrawal from and at work.

## The Costs of Work Withdrawal

Individual acts of withdrawal are highly costly for most organizations (Hanisch & Hulin, 1991). Employee withdrawal impacts organizations in both financial and nonfinancial ways (Laczo & Hanisch, 2000). Although calculating the precise cost of withdrawal is hazardous at best, one estimate suggests that employee lateness costs U.S. businesses more than $3 billion each year (DeLonzor, 2005). The direct costs of absenteeism are estimated to range from 2% to 15% of the gross annual payroll, although it is difficult to differentiate between avoidable and unavoidable absence (Dabboussy & Uppal, 2012; Navarro & Bass, 2006). The cost of replacing employees has been estimated to be between 50% and 200% of those employees' first year salaries (Fitz-Enz, 1997; Hale, 1998). As well, it is estimated that turnover costs U.S. businesses billions of dollars per year (Rosch, 2001). In terms of withdrawal at work, work neglect in the form of cyberloafing can cost corporations up to $54 billion annually and can decrease employee productivity by as much as 40% (Conlin, 2000). Taken together, Sagie, Birati, and Tziner (2002) considered the costs of withdrawal at and from work behaviors to a leading, medium-sized Israeli company to be approximately 16.5% of the company's before-tax income.

Withdrawal also affects organizations in nonfinancial ways. For example, absenteeism is linked to increases in workplace injuries (Goodman & Garber, 1988) and decreases in teammates' morale and work motivation (e.g., Eder & Eisenberger, 2008; Koslowsky et al., 1997). Because of the presumed costs of withdrawal behaviors, organizations devote vast amounts of time, energy, and resources to preventing or alleviating negative effects of withdrawal behaviors, including programs that focus on work engagement, organizational commitment, and retention (e.g., Harter, Schmidt, & Hayes, 2002; Holtom, Mitchell, Lee, & Inderrieden, 2005; Meyer et al., 2002).

## SLEEP

As we have already noted, work withdrawal behaviors are a function of both work and nonwork factors. Although most research has focused on the work-related predictors of work withdrawal (e.g., emotional labor; Scott & Barnes, 2011), research has also investigated the extent to which work withdrawal is influenced by important nonwork factors; in this respect, work–family conflict has been implicated as a key factor (e.g., Hammer et al., 2003). We now turn our attention to how sleep affects work withdrawal from work and withdrawal at work.

Most adults spend the majority of their time working (~7 hours/weekday, ~2 hours/weekend day; Basner et al., 2007) and sleeping (6.68 hours/night; Barnes, Wagner, & Ghumman, 2012). Despite this, sleep and work are incompatible bedfellows, as time spent working takes away from time spent asleep, and vice versa. Research suggests that the amount of sleep that full-time workers get has been decreasing over the past 30 years; at the same time, the number of working hours has increased (Knutson, Van Cauter, Rathouz, DeLeire, & Lauderdale, 2010). Adding to that are findings that suggest that sleep problems are quite common in adults (Knutson et al., 2010; Mullins, Cortina, Drake, & Dalal, 2014). According to a 2008 survey examining sleep, at least 65% of people experience sleep problems at least a few nights a week (Swanson et al., 2011). Therefore sleep problems have the potential to influence organizational functioning in general, and withdrawal behaviors in particular. It is important to note that the term "sleep problems" as used here is a broad construct encompassing the many different ways in which sleep may be disturbed (see Chapter 2 by Cheng and Drake for a more complete discussion). Sleep problems include reductions in quantity or quality of sleep, circadian rhythms problems, and sleep disorders (Mullins et al., 2014; Roehrs, Carskadon, Dement, & Roth, 2011). Each of these sleep constructs is important in and of itself; however, the goal of this chapter is not to disentangle these sleep constructs and their outcomes.

One of the most common and disabling immediate consequences of sleep problems is *sleepiness* (e.g., Pack et al., 2006; Swanson et al., 2011), which is defined as "a craving or desire for sleep" (Dement & Carskadon, 1982, p. S57). Sleepiness reflects a universal physiological need state that is comparable to our physiological need states of hunger or thirst (Drake, 2011; Roehrs et al., 2011). Powerful physiological mechanisms regulate sleep, so that although people can thwart sleep and stay awake for a while, the control over sleep–wake patterns is limited, and prolonged periods of waking activity lead to sleepiness and will eventually lead to sleep (Barnes, 2012; Breslau, Roth, Rosenthal, & Andreski, 1997; Porkka-Heiskanen et al., 1997). Dinges (1995) suggests that sleepiness is one of the most important and common inhibitors of performance in our daily lives. Because individuals are often unaware of the impairments resulting from sleepiness, they assume they are not affected by it, or that they have control over it (Banks & Dinges, 2007; Mullins et al., 2014; Van Dongen, Maislin, Mullington, & Dinges, 2003). Sleepiness has many negative effects on work; for example, sleep loss and the resulting sleepiness have been shown across a number of studies to have effects on employee's lateness, absenteeism, health problems, accident rates, and performance (e.g., Carskadon et al., 1986; Drake et al., 2010; Newman et al., 2000; Spiegel, Leproult, & Van Cauter, 1999; Swanson et al., 2011; Wolk & Somers, 2007). Therefore, sleepiness potentially plays an important role in work withdraw behaviors, and this relationship will be outlined below.

## SLEEP AND WORKPLACE WITHDRAWAL BEHAVIORS

To understand how sleep problems and sleepiness impact general work outcomes, Mullins and colleagues (2014) provided a comprehensive framework rooted in physiology that will be helpful in understanding how sleep impacts withdrawal behaviors specifically. The main tenet of their mediational model is that sleep problems (e.g., low levels of sleep quantity, low sleep quality, circadian rhythms, sleep disorders, or a central nervous system disorder) lead to sleepiness. Sleepiness then effects information processing and affect (i.e., psychological functioning), which

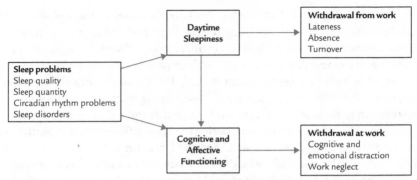

**Figure 10.1.**
Indirect paths from sleep problems to withdrawal from, and withdrawal at, work.

in turn affect work-related behavioral outcomes. They also propose that sleepiness directly influences work-related outcomes (Mullins et al., 2014) (see Figure 10.1). This model will be especially useful for understanding how sleep problems, and sleepiness, differentially influence withdrawal *from* versus withdrawal *at* work. Specifically, we expect that daytime sleepiness will have a direct effect on withdrawal *from* work. In contrast, we expect that sleepiness will indirectly influence withdrawal *at* work through psychological functioning (i.e., information processing and affective pathways) (see Figure 10.1).

It is important to note here that this is a new framework for understanding the impact of sleep on work-related outcomes. Therefore it is unclear whether sleep problems necessarily always lead to sleepiness, which then impact organizational outcomes. Potentially, some sleep problems (i.e., low levels of sleep quantity, low sleep quality, circadian rhythms, sleep disorders, or a central nervous system disorder) might have a direct effect on organizational outcomes, indicating that sleep problems may be partially mediated through sleepiness. Much of the previous research has examined the direct effect of different sleep problems on organizational outcomes, without any consideration of the role played by sleepiness. More research is needed to further investigate this relationship. In the next section we examine the differential influence that sleep problems, and therefore sleepiness, have on withdrawal *from* versus withdrawal *at* work. As well, previous research on sleep and withdrawal behaviors will be reviewed.

## Withdrawal from Work

Withdrawal from work involves physically removing yourself from work for at least some part of the day, through behaviors such as tardiness/lateness, absenteeism, arriving late, and leaving early (Barling et al., 1994; Johns, 2001), and in extreme cases, exiting the organization permanently. Sleepiness, caused by sleep problems, has the potential to directly impact individuals' withdrawal from work. Understanding the nature of sleepiness helps us understand why this is the case.

As previously stated, sleepiness reflects a physiological craving for sleep (Dement & Carskadon, 1982) and sleepiness results from a number of different sleep problems (e.g., low levels of sleep quantity, low sleep quality, circadian rhythms, sleep disorders, or a central nervous system disorder). How sleepy someone is can range from not sleepy at all and fully alert on one extreme, to a debilitating state known as excessive daytime sleepiness (Mullins et al., 2014). Although not all sleepiness is at the extreme levels, daytime sleepiness affects approximately 35% to 40% of the U.S. adult population (Drake et al., 2010; Hossain & Shapiro, 2002).

Sleepiness potentially impacts withdrawal from work in two specific ways. First, by definition sleepiness awakens the desire to sleep, and therefore reflects the desire to withdraw from whatever activities an individual is engaging in. In a work context, sleepiness is likely to make individuals withdraw *from* work. Specifically, sleepiness makes it difficult to wake up in the morning, which would impact work given that work is the first place most people go to upon awakening (Guglielmi, Jurado-Gámez, Gude, & Buela-Casal, 2014). As well, sleepiness progressively increases across the day, further increasing the desire to sleep and potentially the desire to withdrawal from work.

A second way in which sleep problems and sleepiness may impact withdrawal from work behaviors is through the negative impact that sleep has on health (e.g., Spiegel et al., 1999; Wolk & Somers, 2007). For example, sleep problems have been shown to influence many health-related outcomes such as obesity and metabolic disturbance (Spiegel et al., 1999; Wolk & Somers, 2007) as well as hypertension, heart disease, and cardiovascular mortality (Newman et al., 2000). Poor health makes work participation more challenging, and therefore influences withdrawal from work behaviors. In the next section, research examining the different withdrawal from work behaviors will be examined.

### Partial Absenteeism

Hepburn and Barling (1996) defined partial absenteeism as officially being in attendance at work on a given day, but taken unauthorized time away from work during some part of the day (e.g., by arriving late, leaving early, or taking extended breaks). There is less research on partial absenteeism than there is on absenteeism or turnover, potentially because it harder to track than these other types of withdrawal behaviors. However, there is considerable research on how sleep impacts school-related behaviors of children and adolescents, with research demonstrating that sleep problems affect tardiness at school, among other important outcomes (Wahlstrom, 2002; Wolfson, Spaulding, Dandrow, & Baroni, 2007).

Research within the work domain also indicates that sleep problems impact partial absenteeism. In a survey study 29% of respondents reported having fallen asleep or become significantly drowsy at work, 12% were late to work as a result of sleepiness, and 4% left work early as a result of sleepiness and sleep problems (Swanson et al., 2011). In separate study, Kecklund, Åkerstedt, and Lowden (1997) examined morning work and its effects on sleep and alertness. They found that early morning work was associated with more apprehension of difficulties in awakening and insufficient sleep. As is apparent, more research needs to be conducted on sleep and partial absenteeism.

### Absenteeism

In contrast to partial absence, absenteeism involves taking a full day away from work (and excludes reasons such as vacation, jury duty, or other authorized reasons). The relationship between sleep and absenteeism has attracted more research attention than other indicators of withdrawal from work behaviors. There are potentially two reasons for this. First, absenteeism is monitored by most organization and therefore data are readily available. Second, there is a clear relationship between sleep problems and physical health problems (e.g., Newman et al., 2000; Spiegel et al., 1999; Wolk & Somers, 2007), and physical health problems are a major cause of absence from work. For example, a large study conducted in the United Kingston examined the relationship between self-reported health status and sickness absence. This study demonstrated that there is a strong relationship between health measures and sickness absence from work, both in terms of short-term and long-term absences (Marmot, Feeney, Shipley, North, & Syme, 1995).

To begin the review of the literature on the relationship between sleep and absence, we first look at studies that have examined sleepiness specifically and there are a number of studies that have demonstrated this relationship. One study found that individuals who report more daytime sleepiness take more days off work for health reasons than do individuals who are not sleepy (Philip, Taillard, Niedhammer, Guilleminault, & Bioulac, 2001). Using a national sample in Sweden, Åkerstedt, Kecklund, Alfredsson, and Selen (2007) found that disturbed sleep and sleepiness/fatigue were both predictors of long-term sickness absence. Further evidence supporting the importance of sleepiness in predicting absence comes from research by Sivertsen and colleagues (2013). They examined the separate and combined effects of symptoms of insomnia and obstructive sleep apnea on long-term sick leave. Importantly, sleep apnea with no daytime sleepiness was not significantly associated with subsequent sick leave; in contrast, sleep apnea with symptoms of daytime sleepiness was strongly associated with sick leave (Sivertsen, Björnsdóttir, Øverland, Bjorvatn, & Salo, 2013).

Next we turn our attention to studies that have examined the relationship between sleep problems (e.g., disturbed sleep, sleep quality) and absenteeism that have not examined sleepiness. First, one study demonstrated that disturbed sleep is related to both long-term (90 days) and intermediate length (14–89 days) sickness leave (Åkerstedt et al., 2007). As well, Westerlund and colleagues (2008) found that self-reported sleep disturbances were associated with medically certified sickness absence from work. In another study examining poor sleep quality among Japanese white-collar employees, Doi, Minowa, and Tango (2003) found that poor sleepers were more likely to take sick leave, as well as more likely to suffer from poor physical and psychological health. Finally, in a separate study, participants reporting mediocre or poor rather than good sleep were significantly more likely to report long-term work disability during the previous 12 months (Eriksen, Natvig, & Bruusgaard, 2001).

There have been a number of studies that have investigated a specific type of sleep problem, namely, sleep disorders (e.g., insomnia, sleep apnea) and their relationship to absence from work. For example, Sivertsen et al. (2008, 2013) across two studies that used a large national sample in Norway found that having symptoms of sleep disorders was a significant risk factors for subsequent sick leave and permanent work disability. In a separate study, Swanson et al. (2011) demonstrated that absenteeism was more likely for participants who were at risk for a sleep disorder compared to respondent not at risk for any sleep disorder. Other studies have shown that individuals with a diagnosed sleep disorder (e.g., insomnia, sleep apnea) have increased sickness absence from work (e.g., Jansson, Alexanderson, Kecklund, & Åkerstedt, 2013; Lallukka et al., 2013, 2014; Sjösten et al., 2009). Lastly, Sjösten et al. (2009) found that individuals diagnosed with a sleep disorder had an increased risk for disability pension compared to controls. As demonstrated, there has been a considerable amount of research conducted on sleep and absenteeism, although it is worth noting that most of this research comes out of the sleep physiology literature.

### Turnover

Turnover is the least understood sleep outcome of all the withdrawal from work behaviors. One study examined the impact of sleep-related impairments, including sleepiness, and perceived general health on intentions to leave an organization (Blau, 2011). Using a sample of Emergency Medical Services (EMS) employees Blau (2011) found that sleep-related impairments and perceived health each accounted for an additional 2% of the variance in intent to leave, beyond background and work-related variables. However, further research is needed to examine the relationship between sleepiness and turnover to determine the precise nature of the relationship.

Even in the absence of studies, the relationship between sleep problems, sleepiness, and turnover can still be discussed. Because turnover is partially determined by job attitudes and by other withdrawal actions such as absenteeism (Hom, 2011) it is possible that sleep problems and therefore sleepiness impact turnover indirectly. Research suggests that chronically sleepy individuals have more negative attitudes regarding their jobs (Barnes, 2012). For example, in a study of workers with insomnia, participants described lower work-related self-esteem, less satisfaction with their job, as well as less efficient functioning at work (Leger, Massuel, Metlaine, & the SISYPHE Study Group, 2006). As well, sleepiness is related to increased absenteeism, which predicts intentions to leave an organization (Berry et al., 2012; Koslowsky et al., 1997). As previously indicated, turnover has been viewed as the final link in a causal chain of withdrawal behaviors (i.e., from partial absence, to absence, and then turnover), which also suggests a potential indirect effect of sleep problems, sleepiness, and turnover. However, in the absence of specific empirical studies, more research is needed to understand the relationship between sleep problems and turnover.

In conclusion, we suggest here that sleepiness would have a direct effect on withdrawal *from* work behaviors because sleepiness leads to the desire to sleep, and therefore reflects the desire to withdraw from activities in which individuals are engaged. In a work context, therefore, sleepiness would result in withdrawal from work. As well, sleep problems predict physical health, which itself is strongly associated with absenteeism. Lastly, sleepy individuals have poorer work-related attitudes, which leave people at risk for turnover. In the next section, we discuss the possible effects of sleepiness on withdrawal at work.

## Withdrawal at Work

Irrespective of how much or how well people sleep, or how sleepy they feel, the simple fact is that most individuals do not have the luxury of physically absenting themselves from work whenever they want. Attendance is a formal requirement with sanctions and punishment for noncompliance, and implicit norms further make missing work very difficult. As a result, many individuals attend work suffering from sleepiness, and it is in this state that withdrawal *at* work becomes likely. Thus, unlike withdrawal *from* work, withdrawal *at* work occurs when people attend work, but are not productive because they are distracted and/or neglect their work responsibilities (LeBlanc et al., 2014).

As is the case for withdrawal *from* work, sleep problems and therefore sleepiness are also potential antecedents of withdrawal *at* work. However, unlike the direct effects of sleepiness on withdrawal *from* work, sleepiness has its effects on withdrawal *at* work indirectly, through the impact that sleepiness has on brain functioning (e.g., cognitive and affective). The effects of sleep problems and sleepiness on brain functioning are well documented in medical research on sleep (e.g., Harrison & Horne 2000). These impairments in cognitive and affect functioning (Mullins et al., 2014) are the mechanisms through which sleepiness may impact withdrawal *at* work behaviors. This relationship is further described below.

Studies have shown that sleep problems and sleepiness have consequences on affective and cognitive functioning, including self-control processes (e.g., Barnes, 2012; Breslau et al., 1997; Lim & Dinges 2010). Specifically, sleep loss lowers brain activity by affecting the hypometabolism of glucose (e.g., Thomas et al., 2000). The areas of the brain that experience the greatest reduction in brain activity from sleepiness are located in the prefrontal cortex, the superior temporal–inferior parietal cortices, and the thalamus (Mullins et al., 2014).

Physiologically, brain imaging studies of sleep-deprived participants show that the greatest decline in cerebral metabolic rate is in the prefrontal cortex (Schnyer, Zeithamova, & Williams, 2009; Wimmer, Hoffmann, Bonato, & Moffitt, 1992). This is crucial, as the prefrontal cortex controls higher order cognitive abilities, such as self-control, planning, foresight, and problem solving (Mesulam, 1985). Other areas impacted by the hypometabolism of glucose caused by sleepiness include the superior temporal–inferior parietal cortices, which are responsible for higher order cognitive abilities such as semantic processing of auditory and visual information (Mesulam, 2000), and the thalamus, which controls the general arousal level (Mesulam, 2000).

This decrease in brain activity also affects the amygdala, the emotional center in the brain (Gujar, Yoo, Hu, & Walker, 2011). Sleep-deprived individuals experience a significant loss of functional connectivity between the amygdala and the prefrontal cortex, a region known to have strong regulatory effects on the amygdala (Sotres-Bayon, Bush, & LeDoux, 2004). As well, the decrease in metabolic activity also contributes to increased emotional activation of the amygdala following sleep deprivation (Gujar et al., 2011). Thus, sleepiness results in functional loss in areas of the brain that are responsible for higher order cognitive abilities (e.g., self-control) and in areas of the brain associated with arousal and emotions (Barnes, 2012; Mullins et al., 2014). As a result, the immediate psychological consequences of sleep loss are deficits in cognitive and affective functioning and importantly in the ability to regulate yourself.

Thus, sleep problems and sleepiness have domain-specific effects on the prefrontal cortex, which make cognitive functioning and importantly self-control as well as affective functioning vulnerable to specific failures that go beyond those expected to be caused by general low arousal (Harrison & Horne, 2000; Lim & Dinges, 2010). Therefore we suggest that individuals experiencing sleep problems and therefore sleepiness will withdraw at work. Specifically, these individuals will experience cognitive and emotional decrements at work, such as inadequate attention and increased distraction, that are beyond their control and they are also likely to experience self-control failures such as neglecting work.

### Cognitive Distraction

Decreases in activation of the brain regions responsible for higher order cognitive abilities result in substantial deficits in information processing, particularly in processing speed, attention, learning, and memory, and the ability to regulate thoughts, emotions, and action (i.e., self-control) (Baumeister, 2002). Of interest here is the effects that sleep problems and sleepiness have on attention, or stated more negatively, daydreaming and/or distraction.

Previous research suggests that sleep deprivation has a negative effect on general attention (Wimmer et al., 1992) and on selective attention, with greater deficits experienced in early stages of cognitive processing (e.g., visual processing) than in the later stages of cognitive processing (e.g., response selection; Trujillo, Kornguth, & Schnyer, 2009). This can be manifested in different ways. For example, sleepiness decreases attentional capacity through a hyperreaction to novel stimuli (Gumenyuk et al., 2010) or through lapses in attention (Drake et al., 2001; Lim & Dinges, 2010). In terms of a hyperreaction to stimuli, Anderson and Horne (2006) demonstrated that sleepiness enhanced participant distraction during the completion of a monotonous cognitive task. In terms of lapses in attention, a meta-analysis conducted by Lim and Dinges (2010) examined the effects of short-term sleep deprivation on cognitive variables, including simple and complex attention, processing speed, working memory, short-term memory, and reasoning and crystalized intelligence. They found that sleep deprivation produced significant differences in most cognitive domains; however, the largest effects were seen in tests of simple, sustained attention. Decreased attentional capabilities resulting from sleepiness therefore likely lead to cognitive distraction at work. There is some research within the work domain that supports the existence of this effect.

In a study examining commercial motor vehicle collisions, researchers showed that driver sleepiness and distraction significantly increased the severity of the incident, that is, the odds that the accident would be fatal (Bunn, Slavova, Struttmann, & Browning, 2005). Swanson et al. (2011) reported that individuals classified as at risk for sleep disorders were more likely to report cognitive impairments including difficulty with concentration. In a study of emergency physicians, researchers demonstrated that physicians were more susceptible to distractions at the end of their night shift, when they were most sleep deprived (Machi et al., 2012). Finally, a study examining the effects of reducing medical interns weekly work hours found that eliminating interns' extended work shifts (24 hours or more) in an intensive care unit significantly decreased attentional failures during night work hours (Lockley et al., 2004).

As these research findings suggests, sleep problems and sleepiness affect individuals' cognitive ability and attention, or stated more negatively, their susceptibility of distraction. Although much is known about the effects of sleep on cognitive functioning less is known about how sleep affects cognitive distraction at work specifically, leaving much room for further research in this area by organizational behavior researchers.

### Affective Decrements and Emotional Distraction

Sleepiness also affects both the recognition and experience of emotions (Mullins et al., 2014). These effects have been attributed to a sleep deprivation-induced reduction in connectivity between the amygdala (the emotion center of the brain) and the prefrontal cortices, and the resulting reduction of inhibitory input to the amygdala (Chuah et al., 2010). For example, sleep-deprived individuals have more difficulty recognizing low to moderate expressions of happy and angry emotions than do their non-sleep-deprived counterparts (van der Helm, Gujar, & Walker, 2010). Sleep-deprived individuals are more easily distracted by negative emotional stimuli (Chuah et al., 2010) and are more likely to make choices associated with higher immediate emotional valence (Bayard et al., 2011). Importantly, these findings extend to the workplace: Individuals who were classified as at risk for a sleep disorders were more likely to report mood impairments including avoiding interactions with co-workers and boredom (Swanson et al., 2011).

Although we know from previous research that sleep problems and sleepiness impact emotions, there is little research on emotional distraction specifically (for an exception, see Chuah et al., 2010). Therefore there is an even greater need for research on the effects of sleep on emotional distraction at work (see Chapter 6 for a discussion on how sleep influences emotions in general).

### Work Neglect

Work neglect is defined as exerting less behavioral effort while at work (e.g., Schat & Kelloway, 2003) or deliberately withholding effort at work (LeBlanc et al., 2014). In some respects, work neglect can be seen as a self-control failure, because self-control would normally enable employees to work even when they do not want to. Decreases in activation of the brain regions responsible for higher order cognitive abilities result in substantial deficits in all area of cognitive functioning. Importantly, sleep problems and sleepiness lead to decreases in self-control (Baumeister, 2002).

There is a considerable body of research linking deactivation in the prefrontal cortex caused by sleep problems and sleepiness to subsequent deficits in vigilance (e.g., Åkerstedt, Peters, Anund, & Kecklund, 2005; Dean et al., 2010; Durmer & Dinges, 2005) and decreased motivation (e.g., Baranski, Cian, Esquievie, Pigeau, & Raphel, 1998). For example, findings from a study examining sleep, motivation and academic performance showed that participants experiencing daytime sleepiness were more likely to procrastinate than well-rested students (Edens, 2006). A separate study examining college performance found that individuals with an eveningness preference reported lower self-control and greater procrastination (Digdon & Howell, 2008).

Research specifically within the work context suggests that sleepy individuals might neglect their work. One study documented an increase in cyberloafing in laboratory settings and in the workplace (Wagner, Barnes, Lim, & Ferris, 2012) as a result of lost and low-quality sleep. In addition, sleepiness has also been linked to a different indicator of neglectful work behavior, namely, social loafing. Specifically, sleepiness leads to an increase in social loafing in groups (Hoeksema-van Orden, Gaillard, & Buunk, 1998). Although these initial studies are interesting, additional research is required on the relationship between sleep and work neglect.

In conclusion, sleep problems and sleepiness affect withdrawal *at* work through the impact of sleepiness on brain functioning, including negatively affecting cognitive and affective functioning. Individuals experiencing sleep problems and sleepiness will experience cognitive and emotional decrements at work likely leading to inadequate attention and increased distraction, which result in self-control failures at work leading to neglect of their work duties.

## NEXT STEPS

As indicated by many of the authors in this book, organizational researchers have only recently begin to examine the meaning of sleep in the workplace, and because of this, much of this chapter is devoted to suggesting the potential for the relationship between sleep and work withdrawal. Clearly, there are many important potential avenues for this area of research in the future. In this next section, we briefly describe what we think might be a few of the most important areas in which this research could be further expanded.

First, we have offered a new way of understanding the nature of work withdrawal behaviors, specifically as withdrawal *from* and *at* work; however, more theory and research regarding this conceptualization are obviously needed, including how these different withdrawal behaviors are related to one another. Do they form a causal chain of withdrawal that starts with withdrawal at work (cognitive and emotional distraction and work neglect), moves on to withdrawal from work (partial absenteeism and then absenteeism), and culminates in turnover? Previous research does suggest that lateness predicts absence and that absence predicts turnover in a causal chain (Berry et al., 2012), and this could be a fruitful area for theorizing and investigation.

Second, as the conceptualization of withdrawal at work behaviors is in its initial stages, it is possible that other behaviors are missing from the current definition. Specifically, we suggest that work neglect should be expanded to include behaviors that involve freely available technology, over and above cyberloafing (Wagner et al., 2012). As technology is continually changing and becoming more advanced, most people have smart phones and take them to work. To what extent does cyberloafing involve smart phones, and how much of this can be attributed to sleep quality, sleep quantity, or sleepiness? With technological advances pervading the workplace, it might well be necessary to understand how the known effects of sleep on withdrawal behaviors are manifest in new ways.

Third, one of the more interesting advances in research on absenteeism in the past few years has been the focus on presenteeism (e.g., Aronsson, Gustafsson, & Dallner, 2000). Whereas absenteeism involves staying away from work when there is no valid reason to do so, presenteeism involves attending work when we probably should not (Johns, 2010), for example, attending work because of explicit or implicit pressure even though the employee has an illness that could affect others. One question, for example, is whether attending work because of external pressures when we are too tired to do so might compromise safety and/or the quality of task and contextual performance?

A fourth area of further investigation is of course looking at the relationship between sleep problems, sleepiness, and turnover. One possibility is that this effect is indirect, but research could investigate whether sleep constitutes an additional nonwork predictor of turnover. Fifth, how might different sleep problems (e.g., reductions in quantity or quality of sleep, circadian rhythms problems, the presence of a central nervous system disorder, and sleep disorders such as apnea) impact different withdrawal behaviors? For the purposes of simplicity, much of the discussion in this chapter has considered sleep problems as a homogeneous condition, even though it is not. This may limit a more in-depth understanding of the effects of sleep on withdrawal behaviors. One possibility is that clinical sleep disorders affect extreme withdrawal behaviors (for example, more than subjective sleepiness) as they are less amenable to remediation. Pursuing this route would require that we view the causes of organizational behaviors as occurring far outside the confines of a traditional organization.

Finally, we pose a question about the practical implications of research showing that in general, sleep affects withdrawal at and from work. Traditionally, management has been reluctant to engage in interventions outside of the workplace, lest it be seen as inappropriate interference in employees' private lives. This viewpoint is challenged, however, by an understanding that what happens in our private life, for example, the quality or quantity of sleep, has a significant effect on workplace behaviors. Acknowledging that the deep-seated reluctance to implement interventions outside of the workplace is unlikely to change soon, or easily, it would not be inappropriate for management to ensure in the short term that its own behaviors or expectations (such as being available on email at all hours) do not contribute to sleep problems in the first instance.

## CONCLUSIONS

Workplace withdrawal behaviors have been the focus of research for decades, and a concern for management for even longer. The research that has been conducted has primarily searched for work-related factors that result in work withdrawal behaviors. It is clear, however, that nonwork factors, including sleep, also influence withdrawal behavior, and our chapter has extended our understanding of how nonwork factors, that is, sleep, play a significant role in workplace withdrawal. The relationship between sleep problems and withdrawal behaviors is in the early stages of research, and more research on this topic is certainly needed. This is an exciting area with tremendous potential for adding to our understanding of both the effects of sleep and of withdrawal at and from work.

## REFERENCES

Åkerstedt, T., Kecklund, G., Alfredsson, L., & Selen, J. (2007). Predicting long-term sickness absence from sleep and fatigue. *Journal of Sleep Research, 16*, 341–345.

Åkerstedt, T., Peters, B., Anund, A., & Kecklund, G. (2005). Impaired alertness and performance driving home from the night shift: A driving simulator study. *Journal of Sleep Research, 14*, 17–20.

Anderson, C., & Horne, J. A. (2006). Sleepiness enhances distraction during a monotonous task. *Sleep, 29*, 573–576.

Aronsson, G., Gustafsson, K., & Dallner, M. (2000). Sick but yet at work. An empirical study of sickness presenteeism. *Journal of Epidemiology and Community Health, 54*, 502–509.

Banks, S., & Dinges, D. (2007). Behavioral and physiological consequences of sleep restriction. *Journal of Clinical Sleep Medicine, 3*, 519–528.

Baranski, J. V., Cian, C., Esquievie, D., Pigeau, R. A., & Raphel, C. (1998). Modafinil during 64-hr of sleep deprivation: Dose-related effects on fatigue, alertness, and cognitive performance. *Military Psychology, 10*, 173–193.

Barling, J., MacEwen, K. E., Kelloway, E. K., & Higginbottom, S. F. (1994). Predictors and outcomes of elder-care-based interrole conflict. *Psychology and Aging, 9,* 391–397.

Barnes, C. M. (2012). Working in our sleep: Sleep and self-regulation in organizations. *Organizational Psychology Review, 2,* 234–257.

Barnes, C. M., Wagner, D. T., & Ghumman, S. (2012). Borrowing from sleep to pay work and family: Expanding time-based conflict to the broader non-work domain. *Personnel Psychology, 65,* 789–819.

Basner, M., Fomberstein, K., Razavi, F., Banks, S., William, J., Rosa, R., & Dinges, D. (2007). American Time Use Survey: Sleep time and its relationship to waking activities. *Sleep, 30,* 1085–1095.

Baumeister, R. F. (2002). Yielding to temptation: Self-control failure, impulsive purchasing, and consumer behavior. *Journal of Consumer Research, 28,* 670–676.

Bayard, S., Abril, B., Yu, H., Scholz, S., Carlander, B., & Dauvilliers, Y. (2011). Decision making in narcolepsy with cataplexy. *Sleep, 34,* 99–104.

Berry, C. M., Lelchook, A. M., & Clark, M. A. (2012). A meta-analysis of the interrelationships between employee lateness, absenteeism, and turnover: Implications for models of withdrawal behavior. *Journal of Organizational Behavior, 33,* 678–699.

Blau, G. (2011). Exploring the impact of sleep-related impairments on the perceived general health and retention intent of an Emergency Medical Services (EMS) sample. *Career Development International, 16,* 238–253.

Breslau, N., Roth, T., Rosenthal, L., & Andreski, P. (1997). Daytime sleepiness: An epidemiological study of young adults. *American Journal of Public Health, 87,* 1649–1653.

Bunn, T. L., Slavova, S., Struttmann, T. W., & Browning, S. R. (2005). Sleepiness/fatigue and distraction/inattention as factors for fatal versus nonfatal commercial motor vehicle driver injuries. *Accident Analysis & Prevention, 37,* 862–869.

Carskadon, M. A., Dement, W. C., Mitler, M. M., Roth, T., Westbrook, P. R., & Keenan, S. (1986). Guidelines for the Multiple Sleep Latency Test (MSLT): A standard measure of sleepiness. *Sleep, 9,* 519–524.

Chuah, L. Y., Dolcos, F., Chen, A. K., Zheng, H., Parimal, S., & Chee, M. W. (2010). Sleep deprivation and interference by emotional distracters. *Sleep, 33,* 1305–1313.

Conlin, M. (2000). Workers, surf at your own risk. *Business Week, 3685,* 105–106.

Dabboussy, M., & Uppal, S. (2012). *Work absences in 2011.* (Statistics Canada Catalogue no. 75-001-X.) Ottawa, Ontario, Canada: Statistics Canada.

Dean, B., Aguilar, D., Shapiro, C., Orr, W. C., Isserman, J. A., Calimlim, B., & Rippon, G. A. (2010). Impaired health status, daily functioning, and work productivity in adults with excessive sleepiness. *Journal of Occupational and Environmental Medicine, 52,* 144–149.

DeLonzor, D. (2005). Running late: Dealing with chronically late employees who cost the company in productivity and morale. *HR Magazine,* 109–112.

Dement, W. C., & Carskadon, M. A. (1982). Current perspectives on daytime sleepiness: The issues. *Sleep, 5*(Suppl.), S56–S66.

Digdon, N. L., & Howell, A. J. (2008). College students who have an eveningness preference report lower self-control and greater procrastination. *Chronobiology International, 25,* 1029–1046.

Dinges, D. F. (1995). An overview of sleepiness and accidents. *Journal of Sleep Research, 4*(Suppl. s2), 4–14.

Doi, Minowa, M., & Tango, T. (2003). Impact and correlates of poor sleep quality in Japanese white-collar employees. *Sleep, 26,* 467–471.

Dolcos, F., & McCarthy, G. (2006). Brain systems mediating cognitive interference by emotional distraction. *The Journal of Neuroscience, 26,* 2072–2079.

Drake, C. L. (2011). Subjective measures of sleepiness. In M. J. Thorpy & M. Billiard (Eds.), Sleepiness: Causes, consequences, and treatment (pp. 60–71). New York, NY: Cambridge University Press.

Drake, C., Roehrs, T., Breslau, N., Johnson, E., Jefferson, C., Scofield, H., & Roth, T. (2010). The 10-year risk of verified motor vehicle crashes in relation to physiologic sleepiness. Sleep, 33, 745–752.

Drake, C. L., Roehrs, T. A., Burduvali, E., Bonahoom, A., Rosekind, M., & Roth, T. (2001). Effects of rapid versus slow accumulation of eight hours of sleep loss. Psychophysiology, 38, 979–987.

Durmer, J., & Dinges, D. (2005). Neurocognitive consequences of sleep deprivation. Seminars in Neurology, 25, 117–129.

Edens, K. M. (2006). The relationship of university students' sleep habits and academic motivation. Journal of Student Affairs Research and Practice, 43, 808–821.

Eder, P., & Eisenberger, R. (2008). Perceived organizational support: Reducing the negative influence of coworker withdrawal behavior. Journal of Management, 34, 55–68.

Eisenberger, R., Fasolo, P., & Davis-LaMastro, V. (1990). Perceived organizational support and employee diligence, commitment, and innovation. Journal of Applied Psychology, 75, 51–59.

Ellis, H. C., & Ashbrook, P. W. (1988). Resource allocation model of the effects of depressed mood states on memory. In K. Fiedler & J. Forgas (Eds.), Affect, cognition, and social behavior: New evidence and integrative attempts (pp. 25–43). Toronto, Canada: Hogrefe.

Eriksen, W., Natvig, B., & Bruusgaard, D. (2001). Sleep problems: A predictor of long-term work disability? A four-year prospective study. Scandinavian Journal of Public Health, 29, 23–31.

Fitz-Enz, J. (1997). It's costly to lose good employees. Workforce, 76, 50–52.

Goodman, P. S., & Garber, S. (1988). Absenteeism and accidents in a dangerous environment: Empirical analysis of underground coal mines. Journal of Applied Psychology, 73, 81–86.

Guglielmi, O., Jurado-Gámez, B., Gude, F., & Buela-Casal, G. (2014). Job stress, burnout, and job satisfaction in sleep apnea patients. Sleep Medicine, 15, 1025–1030.

Gujar, N., Yoo, S.-S., Hu, P., & Walker, M. P. (2011). Sleep deprivation amplifies reactivity of brain reward networks, biasing the appraisal of positive emotional experiences. Journal of Neuroscience, 31, 4466–4474.

Gumenyuk, V., Roth, T., Korzyukov, O., Jefferson, C., Kick, A., Spear, L.,. . . Drake, C. L. (2010). Shift work sleep disorder is associated with an attenuated brain response of sensory memory and an increased brain response to novelty: An ERP study. Sleep, 33, 703–713.

Hale, G. E. (1998). Reforming employment insurance: Transcending the politics of the status quo. Canadian Public Policy/Analyse De Politiques, 24(4), 429–451.

Hammer, L. B., Bauer, T. N., & Grandey, A. A. (2003). Work-family conflict and work-related withdrawal behaviors. Journal of Business and Psychology, 17, 419–436.

Hanisch, K. A., & Hulin, C. L. (1990). Job attitudes and organizational withdrawal: An examination of retirement and other voluntary withdrawal behaviors. Journal of Vocational Behavior, 37, 60–78.

Hanisch, K. A., & Hulin, C. L. (1991). General attitudes and organizational withdrawal: An evaluation of a causal model. Journal of Vocational Behavior, 39, 110–128.

Harrison, Y., & Horne, J. A. (2000). The impact of sleep deprivation on decision making: A review. Journal of Experimental Psychology: Applied, 6, 236–249.

Harter, J. K., Schmidt, F. L., & Hayes, T. L. (2002). Business-unit-level relationship between employee satisfaction, employee engagement, and business outcomes: A meta-analysis. Journal of Applied Psychology, 87, 268.

Hepburn, C. G., & Barling, J. (1996). Eldercare responsibilities, interrole conflict, and employee absence: A daily study. *Journal of Occupational Health Psychology, 1,* 311–318.

Hoeksema-van Orden, C. Y., Gaillard, A. W., & Buunk, B. P. (1998). Social loafing under fatigue. *Journal of Personality and Social Psychology, 75,* 1179–1190.

Holtom, B. C., Mitchell, T. R., Lee, T. W., & Inderrieden, E. J. (2005). Shocks as causes of turnover: What they are and how organizations can manage them. *Human Resource Management, 44,* 337–352.

Hom, P. W. (2011). Organizational exit. In S. Zedeck (Ed.), *APA handbook of industrial and organizational psychology: Selecting and developing members for the organization* (Vol. 2., pp. 325–375). Washington, DC: American Psychological Association.

Hossain, J. L., & Shapiro, C. M. (2002). The prevalence, cost implications, and management of sleep disorders: An overview. *Sleep and Breathing, 6,* 85–102.

Jansson, C., Alexanderson, K., Kecklund, G., & Åkerstedt, T. (2013). Clinically diagnosed insomnia and risk of all-cause and diagnosis-specific sickness absence: A nationwide Swedish prospective cohort study. *Scandinavian Journal of Public Health, 41,* 712–721

Johns, G. (2001). The psychology of lateness, absenteeism, and turnover. In N. Anderson, D. S. Ones, H. K. Sinangil, & C. Viswesvaran (Eds.), *Handbook of industrial, work, and organizational psychology: Organizational psychology* (Vol. 2., pp. 232–252). Thousand Oaks, CA: Sage.

Johns, G. (2010). Presenteeism in the workplace: A review and research agenda. *Journal of Organizational Behavior, 31,* 519–542.

Kecklund, G., Åkerstedt, T., & Lowden, A. (1997). Morning work: effects of early rising on sleep and alertness. *Sleep, 20,* 215–223.

Knutson, K. L., Van Cauter, E., Rathouz, P. J., DeLeire, T., & Lauderdale, D. S. (2010). Trends in the prevalence of short sleepers in the USA: 1975–2006. *Sleep, 33,* 37–45.

Koslowsky, M., Sagie, A., Krausz, M., & Singer, A. D. (1997). Correlates of employee lateness: Some theoretical considerations. *Journal of Applied Psychology, 82,* 79–88.

Laczo, R. M., & Hanisch, K. A. (2000). An examination of behavioral families of organizational withdrawal in volunteer workers and paid employees. *Human Resource Management Review, 9,* 453–477.

Lallukka, T., Haaramo, P., Rahkonen, O., & Sivertsen, B. (2013). Joint associations of sleep duration and insomnia symptoms with subsequent sickness absence: The Helsinki Health Study. *Scandinavian Journal of Public Health, 41,* 516–523.

Lallukka, T., Kaikkonen, R., Härkänen, T., Kronholm, E., Partonen, T., Rahkonen, O., & Koskinen, S. (2014). Sleep and sickness absence: A nationally representative register-based follow-up study. *Sleep, 37,* 1413–1425.

LeBlanc, M. M., Barling, J., & Turner, N. (2014). Intimate partner aggression and women's work outcomes. *Journal of Occupational Health Psychology, 19,* 399–419.

Leger, D., Massuel, M., Metlaine, A., & the SISYPHE Study Group. (2006). Professional correlates of insomnia. *Sleep, 29,* 171–178.

Liberman, B., Seidman, G., McKenna, K. Y., & Buffardi, L. E. (2011). Employee job attitudes and organizational characteristics as predictors of cyberloafing. *Computers in Human Behavior, 27,* 2192–2199.

Lim, J., & Dinges, D. F. (2010). A meta-analysis of the impact of short-term sleep deprivation on cognitive variables. *Psychological Bulletin, 136,* 375–389.

Lockley, S. W., Cronin, J. W., Evans, E. E., Cade, B. E., Lee, C. J., Landrigan, C. P., . . . & Czeisler, C. A. (2004). Effect of reducing interns' weekly work hours on sleep and attentional failures. *New England Journal of Medicine, 351,* 1829–1837.

Machi, M. S., Staum, M., Callaway, C. W., Moore, C., Jeong, K., Suyama, J., . . . & Hostler, D. (2012). The relationship between shift work, sleep, and cognition in career emergency physicians. *Academic Emergency Medicine, 19,* 85–91.

Marmot, M., Feeney, A., Shipley, M., North, F., & Syme, S. L. (1995). Sickness absence as a measure of health status and functioning: From the UK Whitehall II study. *Journal of Epidemiology and Community Health, 49*, 124–130.

Mesulam, M.-M. (1985). *Principles of behavioral neurology.* Philadelphia, PA: Davis.

Mesulam, M.-M. (2000). *Principles of behavioral and cognitive neurology* (2nd ed.). New York, NY: Oxford University Press.

Meyer, J. P., Stanley, D. J., Herscovitch, L., & Topolnytsky, L. (2002). Affective, continuance, and normative commitment to the organization: A meta-analysis of antecedents, correlates, and consequences. *Journal of Vocational Behavior, 61*, 20–52.

Mullins, H. M., Cortina, J. M., Drake, C. L., & Dalal, R. S. (2014). Sleepiness at work: A review and framework of how the physiology of sleepiness impacts the workplace. *Journal of Applied Psychology, 99*, 1096–1112.

Navarro, C., & Bass, C. (2006). The cost of employee absenteeism. *Compensation & Benefits Review, 38*, 26–30.

Newman, A. B., Spiekerman, C. F., Enright, P., Lefkowitz, D., Manolio, T., Reynolds, C. F., & Robbins, J. (2000). Daytime sleepiness predicts mortality and cardiovascular disease in older adults. *Journal of the American Geriatrics Society, 48*, 115–123.

Pack, A. I., Dinges, D. F., Gehrman, P. R., Staley, B., Pack, F. M., & Maislin, G. (2006). Risk factors for excessive sleepiness in older adults. *Annals of Neurology, 59*, 893–904.

Philip, P., Taillard, J., Niedhammer, I., Guilleminault, C., & Bioulac, B. (2001). Is there a link between subjective daytime somnolence and sickness absenteeism? A study in a working population. *Journal of Sleep Research, 10*, 111–115.

Porkka-Heiskanen, T., Strecker, R. E., Thakkar, M., Bjørkum, A. A., Greene, R. W., & McCarley, R. W. (1997). Adenosine: A mediator of the sleep-inducing effects of prolonged wakefulness. *Science, 276*, 1265–1268.

Price, J. L., & Mueller, C. W. (1981). A causal model of turnover for nurses. *Academy of Management Journal, 24*, 543–565.

Roehrs, T., Carskadon, M. A., Dement, W. C., & Roth, T. (2011). Daytime sleepiness and alertness. In M. H. Kryger, T. Roth, & W. C. Dement (Eds.), *Principles and practice of sleep medicine* (5th ed., pp. 42–53). St. Louis, MO: Elsevier Saunders.

Rosch, P. J. (2001). The quandary of job stress compensation. *Health and Stress, 3*, 1–4.

Rosse, J. G., & Hulin, C. L. (1985). Adaptation to work: An analysis of employee health, withdrawal, and change. *Organizational Behavior and Human Decision Processes, 36*(3), 324–347.

Sagie, A., Birati, A., & Tziner, A. (2002). Assessing the costs of behavioral and psychological withdrawal: A new model and an empirical illustration. *Applied Psychology, 51*, 67–89.

Schat, A. C., & Kelloway, E. K. (2003). Reducing the adverse consequences of workplace aggression and violence: The buffering effects of organizational support. *Journal of Occupational Health Psychology, 8*, 110–122.

Schnyer, D. M., Zeithamova, D., & Williams, V. (2009). Decision-making under conditions of sleep deprivation: Cognitive and neural consequences. *Military Psychology, 21*, 36–45.

Scott, B. A., & Barnes, C. M. (2011). A multilevel field investigation of emotional labor, affect, work withdrawal, and gender. *Academy of Management Journal, 54*, 116–136.

Sivertsen, B., Björnsdóttir, E., Øverland, S., Bjorvatn, B., & Salo, P. (2013). The joint contribution of insomnia and obstructive sleep apnoea on sickness absence. *Journal of Sleep Research, 22*, 223–230.

Sivertsen, B., Øverland, S., Glozier, N., Bjorvatn, B., Mæland, J. G., & Mykletun, A. (2008). The effect of OSAS on sick leave and work disability. *European Respiratory Journal, 32*, 1497–1503.

Sjösten, N., Vahtera, J., Salo, P., Oksanen, T., Saaresranta, T., Virtanen, M., . . . & Kivimäki, M. (2009). Increased risk of lost workdays prior to the diagnosis of sleep apnea. *CHEST Journal, 136*, 130–136.

Sotres-Bayon, F., Bush, D. E., & LeDoux, J. E. (2004). Emotional perseveration: An update on prefrontal-amygdala interactions in fear extinction. *Learning & Memory, 11*, 525–535.

Spiegel, K., Leproult, R., & Van Cauter, E. (1999). Impact of sleep debt on metabolic and endocrine function. *The Lancet, 354*, 1435–1439.

Steel, R. P., & Rentsch, J. R. (1995). Influence of cumulation strategies on the long-range prediction of absenteeism. *Academy of Management Journal, 38*, 1616–1634.

Steers, R. M., & Mowday, R. T. (1981). Employee turnover and post-decision accommodation processes. In L. L. Cummings & B. M. Staw (Eds.), *Research in organizational behavior* (Vol. 3, pp. 235–281). Greenwich, CT: JAI Press.

Swanson, L., Arnedt, J., Rosekind, M., Belenky, G., Balkin, T., & Drake, C. (2011). Sleep disorders and work performance: Findings from the 2008 National Sleep Foundation Sleep in America poll. *Journal of Sleep Research, 20*, 487–494.

Thomas, M., Sing, H., Belenky, G., Holcomb, H., Mayberg, H., Dannals, R., . . . Redmon, D. (2000). Neural basis of alertness and cognitive performance impairments during sleepiness. I. Effects of 24 h of sleep deprivation on waking human regional brain activity. *Journal of Sleep Research, 9*, 335–352.

Trujillo, L., Kornguth, S., & Schnyer, D. (2009). An ERP examination of the different effects of sleep deprivation on exogenously cued and endogenously cued attention. *Sleep, 32*, 1285–1297.

van der Helm, E., Gujar, N., & Walker, M. P. (2010). Sleep deprivation impairs the accurate recognition of human emotions. *Sleep, 33*, 335–342.

Van Dongen, H. P. A., Maislin, G., Mullington, J., & Dinges, D. F. (2003). The cumulative cost of additional wakefulness: Does-response effects on neurobehavioral functions and sleep physiology from chronic sleep restriction and total sleep deprivation. *Sleep, 26*, 117–126.

Wagner, D. T., Barnes, C. M., Lim, V. K. G., & Ferris, D. L. (2012). Lost sleep and cyberloafing: Evidence from the laboratory and a daylight saving time quasi-experiment. *Journal of Applied Psychology, 97*, 1068–1076.

Wahlstrom, K. (2002). Accommodating the sleep patterns of adolescents within current educational structures: An uncharted path. In M. A. Carksadon (Ed.), *Adolescent sleep patterns: Biological, social, and psychological influences* (pp. 172–197). New York, NY: Cambridge University Press.

Westerlund, H., Alexanderson, K., Åkerstedt, T., Hanson, L. M., Theorell, T., & Kivimaki, M. (2008). Work-related sleep disturbances and sickness absence in the Swedish working population, 1993–1999. *Sleep, 8*, 1169–1177.

Wimmer, F., Hoffmann, R. F., Bonato, R. A., & Moffitt, A. R. (1992). The effects of sleep deprivation on divergent thinking and attention processes. *Journal of Sleep Research, 1*, 223–230.

Wolfson, A. R., Spaulding, N. L., Dandrow, C., & Baroni, E. M. (2007). Middle school start times: The importance of a good night's sleep for young adolescents. *Behavioral Sleep Medicine, 5*, 194–209.

Wolk, R., & Somers, V. K. (2007). Sleep and metabolic syndrome. *Experimental Physiology, 92*, 67–78.

# CHAPTER 11

# Ready to Retire? Work, Stress, and Sleep Quality among Older Adults[1]

PETER BAMBERGER AND RONA CAFRI

## READY TO RETIRE? WORK, STRESS, AND SLEEP QUALITY AMONG OLDER ADULTS

In the majority of Organisation for Economic Co-operation and Development (OECD) countries, older adults (i.e., those 55+) account for an ever increasing proportion of the workforce. In the European Union (EU), the number of people aged 55 and over is expected to grow by more than 15% between 2010 and 2030 (Van der Heijden, Schalk, & van Veldhoven, 2008). In the United States, while those over 55 accounted for 13.1% of the workforce in 2000 and 19.5% of the workforce in 2010, it is projected that by 2020, about 25% of the workforce will be composed of older workers (Chosewood, 2012). Despite the growing proportion of older adults in the workplace, research on how work, work conditions, and impending workforce disengagement affect the well-being of older adults is still in the early stages with most research focusing on the impact of work on older employees' emotional well-being (Belogolovsky, Bamberger & Bacharach, 2012; Potonik & Sonnentag, 2013), health complaints (Foley, Ancoli-Israel, Britz, & Walsh, 2004), and mortality (Mallon, Broman, & Hetta, 2000). Interestingly, despite the fact that sleep-related problems are common among older adults (Schubert et al., 2002), can have significant safety and productivity implications (Kamel & Gammack, 2006), and may underlie the emotional and physical health outcomes just noted (Kamel & Gammack, 2006), the impact of work on sleep among older adults remains—to the best of our knowledge—unexamined.

Research on the association between work and sleep in the general workforce has focused primarily on the implications of sleep and sleep problems on employee health and performance. For example, studies have found that sleep problems are associated with decreased performance and safety at work (Barnes & Wagner,

2009), lower job satisfaction (Barnes, Ghumman, & Scott, 2013), a higher rate of sick leave (Stoller, 1994), reduced workplace productivity, and an increased use of both physical and mental healthcare services (Chevalier et al., 1999; Kuppermann et al., 1995); the full extent of the social and health problems associated with sleep can be gleaned from the other chapters in this book. These problems may be exacerbated among employed older adults as research suggests that among older adults, poor sleep quality is linked to decreased memory and concentration, poor attention and slower reaction times, and impaired executive function and performance on psychomotor tests, as well as an increased risk of falls and overall cognitive decline (Crowley, 2011).

A smaller set of studies has examined how particular work conditions may affect sleep quality, with a large body of research indicating that those working nonstandard or variable shifts are at heightened risk for sleep problems (Åkerstedt, 2003). Other studies have examined the impact of emotional labor (Wagner, Barnes, & Scott, 2014) as well as a long working week, exposure to vibrations, and a rapid work pace (Ribet & Derriennic, 1999) on sleep problems. Yet how these and other conditions, such as the uncertainties of impending workforce disengagement, affect the sleep quality of older workers is uncertain. On the one hand, consistent with attraction–selection–attrition and person–environment fit theories (Schneider, Smith &, Goldstein, 2000), it is possible that with experience, older employees adjust to such conditions, with those unable to adjust either leaving the workforce or shifting to less risky jobs. Accordingly, work and workplace conditions may pose less of a risk to the sleep quality of older adults than to their younger peers. On the other hand, research on how the physiology of aging may heighten the vulnerability of older adults to a wide range of sleep problems (Eikermann et al., 2007) suggests that the effect of these same risk factors may be amplified among older workers.

In the current study, we examine how a number of work-related conditions and factors associated with impending workforce disengagement may link to older adults' sleep quality. In particular, as shown in Figure 11.1, we focus on their

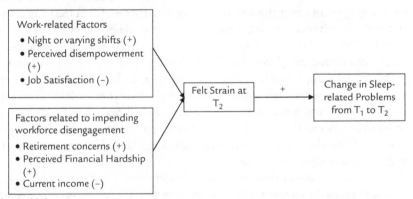

**Figure 11.1.**
A strain-mediated model of work-related risk factors for older workers' sleep problems.

possible stress-mediated effects in that a large body of research has established a strong link between stress and sleep quality. For example, studies indicate that felt strain may result in rumination, making it difficult for individuals to fall asleep (Berset, Elfering, Lüthy, Lüthi, & Semmer, 2010). Additionally, research on the experience of older adults employed beyond traditional retirement age suggests that beyond being more vulnerable to the same stressors to which their younger peers are exposed, they may also be exposed to a unique set of stressors. Accordingly, drawing from conservation of resources (COR) theory (Hobfoll, 1988), we posit a strain-mediated model of how factors relating to work and workforce disengagement may affect the sleep quality of older employees.

Our study offers several important theoretical and practical implications. First, our study offers an important contribution to theories of work and sleep by proposing and demonstrating the central role played by stress in linking work-related risk factors to sleep problems among older adults. Second, our model demonstrates that it is not merely the nature of work itself that can affect older employees' sleep quality, but also older workers' concerns about the economics of impending workforce disengagement. From a more practical perspective, our study highlights a number of potential domains for employer and/or policymaker intervention. To the extent that sleep problems may be linked to older adults' cognitive decline (Crenshaw & Edinger, 1999), sickness absence (Stoller, 1994), and longer-term retention (Jamal, 1990), gaining insight into how work-related factors affect older adults' sleep quality may offer significant returns not only to the older worker, but to employers and the broader labor market as a whole.

## Effects of Aging on Sleep Quality

Sleep problems are widespread among older adults, with insomnia—the subjective report of insufficient or nonrestorative sleep despite adequate opportunity to sleep (Woodward, 1999)—being among the most prevalent of sleep problems. Whereas insomnia affects between 4% and 11% of the general population (with a higher prevalence among women), studies estimate an incidence rate of 40% or higher among those aged 65+ (Foley et al., 2004; Schubert et al., 2005). Research suggests that underlying the heightened prevalence of sleep problems among older adults are aging-related changes in the sleep architecture that, when taken together, have led to the characterization of sleep among older adults as being "more fragile" than that of younger adults (Crowley, 2011, p. 49). Such changes include more labored sleep initiation, reduced total sleep time and efficiency [i.e., less of the key restorative phases of sleep known as the slow wave sleep (SWS) phases], and greater sleep fragmentation (i.e., disturbed or "light" sleep and increased nighttime wakefulness) (Crowley, 2011; Kamel & Gammack, 2006). Indeed, a meta-analysis of over 60 overnight sleep studies including over 3,000 adults of varying ages found that the percentage of lighter sleep phases increased with age, whereas the percentage of SWS phases decreased (Ohayon et al., 2004). Additionally, research suggests that aging is associated with a shift in the circadian rhythm, with many older people going to bed (and rising) earlier (Neubauer, 1999). One consequence of such shifts is that older adults tend to be more somnolent than those younger than them, finding it more difficult to stay awake during the day and resorting to more frequent and longer daytime naps (which, if excessive, can adversely affect the sleep–wake cycle and result in a downward spiral of sleep problems) (Feinsilver, 2003; Woodward, 1999).

Research has identified a number of precipitants of sleep-related problems among older adults including primary sleep disorders such as sleep apnea, restless leg syndrome and circadian rhythm disorders, acute and chronic illness (e.g., renal, cerebrovascular, gastrointestinal, and cardiovascular diseases, menopause, arthritis, and respiratory disorders), medication use and stimulant (e.g., coffee) overuse, environmental (e.g., noise, light) and temporal (e.g., jet lag; shift work) disturbances, and acute or recurring stressors (Crowley, 2011; Kamel & Gammack, 2006). Although some of these factors (i.e., acute/chronic stressors) may be related to the workplace and older adults' work roles, we are unaware of any research directly examining the potential association between older adults' work experiences and sleep quality.

## Work Stressors, Strain, and Sleep

As evident elsewhere in this book, research indicates that for the population at large, a variety of conditions and situations at work may be linked to poor sleep quality or sleep disturbance. For example, a number of scholars have identified distributive (Berset et al., 2011; Greenberg, 2006) and interactional and procedural (Elovainio, Kivimäki, Vahtera, Keltikangas-Järvinen, & Virtanen, 2003) injustice as having an adverse impact on employees' sleep quality. Similarly, research indicates that social stressors such as interpersonal conflict or marginalization (Pereira & Elfering, 2013), as well as low decision latitude (Kalimo, Tenkanen, Harma, Poppius, & Heinsalmi, 2000), may precipitate or exacerbate employee sleep disturbance.

In nearly all of these studies, the strain elicited by such stressors is presumed to serve as the mechanism linking work-based stressors to employee sleep disturbance. COR theory (Hobfoll, 1988) provides a basis for understanding how the strain-mediated process may operate. According to COR theory, all of the conditions noted above (as well as many other work-based conditions) may be deemed to pose a threat to or potentially depleting key resources and thus contributing to felt strain. From a resource ecology perspective, people strive to retain, protect, and build four main types of resources (i.e., tangible resources such as a home, psychosocial conditions such as social support, personal characteristics such as self-efficacy, and energies such as time, money, and knowledge), and engage in resource-consuming action when faced with their potential or actual loss (Hobfoll, 1988). Although such resource expenditure may be effective and result in loss prevention or minimization, it may also result in a downward spiral of resource loss with strain experienced as resources become depleted.

Research suggests that work-based strain may affect the sleep quality of employed adults in at least two ways. First, work-based strain may generate sleep problems by precipitating perseverative cognitions, or in other words, "the repeated or chronic activation of the cognitive representation of stress-related content" (Brosschot, Pieper, & Thayer, 2005, p. 1045). Such cognitive processing is often manifested as rumination, "a class of thoughts that revolve around a common instrumental theme and that recur in the absence of immediate environmental demands requiring the thoughts" (Martin & Tesser, 1996, p. 1). Although perseverative cognitions may be an effective means by which to mentally address a particular stressor (Pereira, Meier, & Elfering, 2013) or generate strategies to prevent threatened resource loss or develop alternatives for recouping spent resources (Brosschot, Gerin, & Thayer, 2006), they also represent an inability to "cognitively switch off" (Cropley & Purvis, 2003) and a delayed form of psychological arousal that is "incongruous with the rather relaxed state of sleep" (Berset et al., 2010, p. 72). Moreover, to the degree that such rumination is chronic, it can precipitate a downward spiral of resource drain and fatigue with physiological consequences including, but not limited to, sleep disturbance.

Second, consistent with the rumination-related effects just noted, research suggests that the strain elicited by work-related stressors may have physiological sequelae associated with sleep disturbance. More specifically, studies suggest that the resource drain associated with psychological strain is associated with the perturbation of the hypothalamic–pituitary–adrenal (HPA) axis (for a review, see Melamed, Shirom, Toker, Berliner, & Shapira, 2006), manifested by either hypercortisolism or hypocortisolism, a flattened diurnal cortisol curve, and elevated afternoon and evening cortisol levels (Melamed et al., 2006).

Although scholars have yet to test whether this strain-mediated process is more generalizable to certain groups of workers than others, there is little reason to expect that the resource-based logic underlying this model will not apply in the case of older workers. Indeed, given that sleep is more "fragile" for many older workers (Crowley, 2011, p. 49), the effects of work-based stressors are likely to be no less robust among older employees than for the workforce in general. However, the particular stressors generating such adverse sleep-related effects may be different for older workers in two ways. First, due to the physiological and social implications of aging, workplace conditions posing a more limited threat to the personal resources of younger and middle-age workers (e.g., shift work, disempowerment) may pose a heightened threat to the personal resources of older workers. Similarly, other workplace conditions that may be taken for granted by younger and middle-aged workers (e.g., job satisfaction) may facilitate resource acquisition and thus serve as significant protective factors for less mobile, older workers (Faragher, Cass, & Cooper, 2005). Accordingly, these conditions may be particularly salient in understanding how work factors precipitate or exacerbate sleep problems for older workers. Second, as workers approach retirement they are likely to be exposed to an additional set of stressors less salient to the majority of their younger colleagues, namely those relating to their financial security upon disengaging from the workforce. More specifically, although retirement may offer relief from work-based stressors, for some older adults it is likely to serve as a significant disruption in their life course or "discontinuity" (Atchley, 1989) presenting a number of potential new stressors, such as the threat of reduced income, financial insecurity, and concerns about being unable to sustain their standard of living (Wang & Shultz, 2010).

### Job-Based Factors and Older Employee Strain

From a resource ecology perspective, older workers—like their younger colleagues—are subject to a variety of job-related factors that may deplete or enhance personal resources, with the former serving as vulnerability factors for strain and the latter serving as protective factors. Here we focus on three vulnerability and protective aspects of the job that in light of the physiological and social implications of aging may have enhanced resource-related implications for older workers, and thus offer unique explanatory potential with respect to older worker strain and sleep quality. More specifically, we examine the impact of two vulnerability factors, namely shift work and disempowerment, and one protective factor, namely job satisfaction.

**Work shift and strain.** There is substantial empirical evidence (see Chapter 3) suggesting that in the general workforce, shift work (i.e., consistently working "off hours" or working according to a variable schedule) is associated with a heightened risk of disturbed sleep and fatigue (Åkerstedt, 2003). Generally, the adverse impact of shift work on sleep quality is explained on the basis of the conflict between displaced work hours and our biological clock, which for some can precipitate a disruption of the sleep cycle (Åkerstedt, 2003). However, particularly for older workers, the consequences of shift work on sleep quality may also operate via strain. More specifically, for older workers, shift work may place a particularly significant drain on a variety of personal resources. First, although shift work, by affecting sleep cycles, may place a significant drain on energy resources for employees of all ages, this drain may be particularly significant for older workers for whom sleep, as noted above, is often more "fragile." Second, the fatigue that older workers may experience as a result of shift work may take a toll on executive function, memory, and cognitive processing, thus resulting in weakened performance on the job. Indeed, Ried and Dawson (2014) found that although performance for older adults was consistently lower than for younger subjects, the change in performance between day and night shifts was significantly different for older workers, such that their performance significantly increased during day shifts and decreased across night shifts. In contrast, younger subjects were able to maintain performance across shift types. For many older workers already facing the stereotypes associated with ageism, such shift-based performance deficits may threaten self-efficacy, a key psychological resource (Hobfoll & Wells, 1998). Finally, scholars have proposed that shift work may serve as a significant stressor for workers in general by disrupting family and social activities (Harrington, 2001). However, for older workers the threat posed to social resources by shift work may be amplified in that as their work friends retire, their existing work schedules may make it difficult to maintain close social relations outside of work (Nahum-Shani & Bamberger, 2011). Research indicates that such weakened social relations can pose a significant threat to older adults' well-being (Nahum-Shani & Bamberger, 2011). By threatening and/ or depleting such resources, COR theory suggests that shift work may serve as a significant risk factor for older worker strain. Accordingly, we posit the following:

*Hypothesis 1: Relative to older employees working standard day shifts, those working atypical shifts or varying shifts experience greater strain.*

**Perceived disempowerment and strain.** Disempowerment acts are defined as any intentional or unintentional, verbal or nonverbal behavior expressed in the workplace that is interpreted by the target employee as hostile, offensive, intimidating, demeaning, or threatening (Young, Vance, & Ensher, 2003). Older workers may be disproportionately exposed to disempowerment experiences as a result of age discrimination (Yuan, 2007). More specifically, research suggests that in addition to having a more difficult time finding employment, older individuals also have difficulty retaining a job due to ageist stereotypes suggesting that older workers are less productive and cannot match the level of performance of younger workers (McCann & Giles, 2002). Ageist stereotypes may also motivate employers to reduce older workers' hours or job responsibilities. Indeed, Roscigno, Mong, Byron, and Tester (2007) found that more than 60% of the over 12,000 cases of age discrimination in employment filed with the Civil Rights Commission of the state of Ohio from 1988 through 2003 concerned job dismissal or reduction, with an additional 5% involving some form of job demotion. Particularly to the extent that such actions are deemed as based on ageist stereotypes, they may be perceived by older workers as demeaning. Moreover, to the extent that these actions are perceived as marginalizing older employees and reducing their role or status in the workplace, they may also be viewed as demeaning.

Research on older workers indicates that workers who perceive that they have been exposed to such disempowering acts are at heightened risk of suffering a decline in emotional well-being (Yuan, 2007). Underlying the adverse mental health implications of disempowerment appears to be its influence on older employees' psychosocial resources (Yuan, 2007). More specifically, research suggests that disempowerment—often manifested in terms of the reduction in work hours or responsibilities—may have a negative impact on two main resources, namely, self-efficacy and social support. Disempowerment may reduce older adults' self-efficacy by signaling to them that the organization no longer values their services, is able to rely on their judgment, or views their efforts as making a meaningful contribution. Self-efficacy may also be reduced to the extent that the reduction in hours or responsibilities results in a decline in perceived personal control or power at work (Vance, Ensher, Hendricks, & Harris, 2004). Social support resources may be adversely affected to the extent that the reduction in hours or job reassignment limits the older employee's ability to maintain relations with those work-based colleagues with whom she or he is close. Using data from the *Midlife Development in the United States* survey, Yuan (2007) found that the reduction in perceived control and social support partially mediated the adverse impact of perceived age discrimination on older adults' mental health. These findings suggest that reducing older workers' hours or diminishing their job responsibilities may be perceived as disempowering and thus threaten or directly diminish key personal resources. From a conservation of resources perspective, the perception of being subject to such disempowerment actions is likely to serve as a salient stressor for older workers, and thus potentially precipitate strain. Accordingly, we posit the following:

*Hypothesis 2: The more older workers perceive themselves as having been subject to disempowering actions, the greater the strain they experience.*

**Job satisfaction and strain**. Conversely, individuals who are endowed with greater resources or who, in the course of their daily activity, experience resource gain, are likely to be less vulnerable to strain (Hobfoll, 1988; Hobfoll & Wells, 1998). Resource gain counterbalances the drain on resources, with individuals possessing greater resource armamentaria able to employ other resources to offset resource loss. A significant body of literature suggests that in general, a greater resource armamentaria is associated with enhanced well-being. A greater resource armamentaria would likely reduce individuals' vulnerability to stressors by allowing them to use certain resources such as social support to buffer or compensate for the actual or threatened decline or depletion of other valued resources (Pearlin, 1999).

At work, job satisfaction may reflect a situation of enhanced resources and represent a basis for resource mobilization. Recent research suggests that state engagement, a concept closely related to job satisfaction, is more likely to occur when individuals have higher levels of work-based resources (Halbesleben, Harvey, & Bolino, 2009). To the extent that job satisfaction, like state engagement, reflects a more positive resource state, according to COR theory, job satisfaction may also create a situation in which individuals are able to invest resources to obtain additional resources (Hobfoll, 1988). For example, to the extent that job satisfaction reflects a positive state of social relations at work, individuals may use their social networks to acquire other resources such as additional network links that may be instrumental for enhanced performance, and thus promote resource gain (e.g., pay). In this way, job satisfaction may serve as a proxy for excess work resources that, as suggested by COR theory, would buffer employees from strain precipitated by various work-based stressors. In turn, this could explain why meta-analytic findings (Faragher et al., 2005) indicate an inverse association between job satisfaction and a number of strain-related outcomes including depression ($r = -0.43$) and anxiety ($r = -0.42$). Although these strain-related aspects of job satisfaction are likely significant for workers of all ages, because older workers, due to age discrimination, are often less able than their younger colleagues to secure alternative employment when faced with job dissatisfaction (Roscigno et al., 2007), the beneficial effects of job satisfaction with respect to strain may be particularly salient for them. Accordingly, we posit the following:

*Hypothesis 3: The greater older workers' job satisfaction, the lower the level of felt strain.*

## Factors Associated with Impending Workforce Disengagement and Older Employee Strain

As noted above, pending workforce disengagement and related perceptions of postdisengagement economic security may also serve as salient stressors for older workers. In particular, several finance-related aspects of impending workforce disengagement may serve as significant stressors for older adults, namely finance-related retirement concerns as well as current income and perceptions of financial hardship.

**Finance-related retirement concerns and strain.** Survey evidence indicates that many older workers are uncertain about the degree to which income from retirement sources (e.g., pension, social security) will cover their daily living expenses (Keith, 1993; Shultz, 1985). Indeed, the majority of older workers in the United States are either not at all confident or only somewhat confident about having enough money for retirement, whereas only 29% of workers are very confident in their ability to pay for basic expenses (Employee Benefit Research Institute, 2014).

Such retirement concerns may precipitate strain among older workers in a variety of ways (Higginbottom, Barling, & Kelloway, 1993). First, to the extent that such concerns reflect a sense that the resources older employees expected to be available to them in retirement will in fact be unavailable, the expression of such concerns may represent the loss of key energy resources and the threatened loss of key object resources (such as your home). Continuity theory (Atchley, 1989) suggests that the loss of such resources may be particularly salient to older workers in that it threatens their ability to maintain consistent life patterns after they disengage from the workforce (Wang, 2007). Second, the perception that they have not achieved a basic level of savings to provide for their family in retirement may have a negative impact on older worker's sense of self-efficacy. Finally, from a COR theory perspective, a sense that such resources are at risk may drive older adults to adopt maladaptive strategies aimed at protecting these resources (Hobfoll, 1988). For example, such concerns may lead older adults to disregard the health-related risks that continued employment may pose, or even take on extra work in order to compensate for any perceived shortfall in expected retirement income. As such strategies could result in a downward spiral of resource loss (Aldwin, Sutton, & Lachman, 1996) in the longer term, their adoption may exacerbate the strain precipitated by basic concerns regarding financial security in retirement. Accordingly, we posit the following:

*Hypothesis 4: The greater older workers' retirement concerns, the greater the level of strain experienced.*

**Current perceptions of financial hardship and strain**. Individuals perceive a sense of financial hardship to the extent that they feel unable to make ends meet and provide for the basic life needs of themselves and their families (Krause, 1987). Although several studies (e.g., Macfadyen, Macfadyen, & Prince, 1996; Peirce, Frone, Russell, & Cooper, 1994) have linked a sense of financial stress to felt strain in the workforce in general, for older workers approaching retirement, such perceptions may be particularly troubling and, for several reasons, serve as an even more salient precipitator of strain. First, due to age discrimination, many older workers may believe that they lack mobility and thus are unable to secure alternative, higher paying employment (AARP, 2013). This sense of being unable to escape their perceived economic hardship may thus serve as a drain on self-efficacy. Second, those perceiving themselves to be in current economic hardship are also likely to view valued tangible resources (e.g., home, car) as potentially threatened, and experience difficulty engaging in social activities, thus heightening a sense of social marginalization.

Finally, as in the case of retirement concerns, the perception that key tangible resources are threatened may motivate older workers to adopt maladaptive strategies. Although intended to secure these resources or stem resource outflows, such strategies have the potential to result in a downward spiral of more intensified resource loss. Empirical findings have generally supported the notion of an amplified effect of financial hardship on felt strain among older adults. For example, Krause (1987) found that older adults expressing financial hardship were more likely to be depressed than peers with fewer financial problems. Similarly, Whelan (1992) found that the deprivation of socially defined necessities was associated with increased psychological distress. Accordingly, we posit the following:

*Hypothesis 5: The greater older workers' perceived financial hardship, the greater their level of experienced strain.*

**Current income and strain**. Lower levels of income may be associated with diminished self-efficacy, and the threat to key object resources posed by a lower income may elicit the same sort of maladaptive strategies noted above. Moreover, particularly for the large proportion of older workers who view age discrimination as affecting their ability to secure a raise or promotion (AARP, 2013), a lower income level may elicit a sense of distributive or procedural injustice. To the extent that older workers believe that they are unable to correct such an injustice (AARP, 2013), there may be a further insult to self-efficacy. Research on justice perceptions and employee strain supports such a linkage, finding that feelings of injustice are associated with a variety of strain-related outcomes including emotional exhaustion, cynicism, and health complaints (Kalimo, Taris, & Schaufeli, 2003).

In contrast, as with job satisfaction, higher incomes may suggest a larger inventory of resources, and thus serve as protective factors. Older adults with higher levels of income may be able to secure resource surpluses, which, in turn, facilitate upward spirals of resource gain (Hobfoll, 1998). Prior research suggests that resource surpluses are linked to positive well-being and overall happiness (Boodoo, Gomez, & Gunderson,

2014). This may occur for a number of reasons. First, higher levels of income allow individuals to afford better healthcare and physical well-being, a key resource for older adults (Whelan, 1992). Second, higher income may provide individuals with greater social opportunities, thus enhancing older adults' network of support providers (Mansyur, Amick, Harrist, & Franzini, 2008). Finally, higher income would allow individuals greater respite opportunities, which serve as significant resource boosters, thus limiting the potential for resource drain and deprivation, and accordingly, reducing strain (Westman & Eden, 1997). Hence, we posit the following:

*Hypothesis 6: The greater older workers' income, the lower the level of felt strain.*

## Experienced Strain and Sleep Disturbance

Research suggests that strain serves as a primary mechanism through which a variety of work-related factors may affect the sleep quality of older adults. For example, Theorell et al. (1988) found that sleep disturbance increased as a function of occupation-specific levels of job strain. Similarly, Karasek et al. (1998) found that workers who belonged to the high strain group in his demand–control model suffered from sleep disorders and exhaustion more often than others, whereas Kalimo et al. (2000) found significant main effects of two key stressors (job demands and control) on insomnia, sleep deprivation, and daytime fatigue.

The link between strain and sleep quality stems from the fact that, as noted above, strain is a manifestation of resource drain and depletion, with sleep problems often serving as an important consequence of resource depletion (Vela Bueno et al., 2008). Two mechanisms underlie the means by which such resource depletion may precipitate these types of problems. The first mechanism concerns strain-precipitated perseverative cognitions, with several studies demonstrating the link between strain and rumination. For example, Cropley and Purvis (2003) and Cropley, Dijk, and Stanley (2006) showed that job strain (as manifested in terms of high demands and low control) precipitated work-related rumination. Others have demonstrated that the strain associated with time pressure and uncertainty is associated with (Hoge, 2009) and precipitates (Garst, Frese, & Molenaar, 2000) worrying and rumination. Moreover, such rumination is predictive of insomnia and poor sleep quality (Thomsen et al., 2004). For example, Cropley et al. (2006) found that compared to low strain teachers, high strain teachers took longer to unwind after work, ruminated more about work-related issues over the evening and bedtime, and reported poorer sleep quality.

The second mechanism deals with the physiological sequelae associated with strain (i.e., activation of the HPA axis, hypercortisolism or hypocortisolism, a flattened diurnal cortisol curve, and elevated afternoon and evening cortisol levels) and their impact on sleep quality. Several studies support a link between the activation of the HPA axis and insomnia (Roth, Roehrs, & Pies, 2007), as well as between sleep disturbance and elevated evening cortisol levels (Rodenbeck, Huether, Ruther, & Hajak, 2002; Vgontzas et al., 2003). Such physiological sequelae may themselves be linked to perseverative cognitions to the extent that if, as is often the case, such cognitions become self-reinforcing, they may over time precipitate a dysfunction of the neuroendocrine regulation of sleep, which, in turn, can lead to severe sleep disturbances (Van Reeth et al., 2000).

Based on the discussion above, we therefore posit the following:

*Hypothesis 7a: The greater the level of strain experienced by older workers, the poorer their sleep quality.*

Additionally, given the hypothesized links between the job and work disengagement stressors and older employees' felt strain, and between such strain and older employees' sleep quality, we suggest that felt strain mediates the link between job and work disengagement stressors and sleep quality. In other words:

*Hypothesis 7b: Strain mediates the relationships between job and work disengagement stressors on the one hand, and sleep quality on the other.*


## METHODS

### Sample

We tested our hypotheses using data from a broader longitudinal study of the implications of work and retirement on older adults' health and well-being. This sample was drawn from members of nine local and national unions (representing transportation, manufacturing, and construction workers) in the United States who, at the time of initial data collection ($T_0$ in 2000), were within 6 months of being eligible to retire with full retirement benefits. Of the 2,812 individuals in this target sample, 1,279 agreed to participate (i.e., 46% response rate), with all data collected from telephone interviews. Approximately half of the 1,279 participants chose to retire upon becoming eligible for these benefits (i.e., within a year of the initial interview). For the purposes of the current study, we examined a subset of participants who in 2008 (i.e., at $T_1$) had either deferred their retirement despite their eligibility for a full pension, or despite "retiring" (i.e., leaving their career job and drawing a pension), reported being employed for 30 or more hours per week. Of the 276 individuals meeting these criteria, 57% were female, 4% were widowed, and 13% were divorced. The mean age of those meeting these criteria at the time of initial contact (i.e., 2000) was 60.5 years ($SD = 4$).


### Measures

*Sleep-related problems* were measured at Times 1 (2008) and 2 (2009) using the Pittsburgh Sleep Quality Index (PSQI; Buysse, Reynolds, Monk, Berman, & Kupfer, 1989). This self-administered questionnaire assesses quality of sleep during the previous month and contains 19 self-rated questions covering seven components including subjective sleep quality, sleep duration and disturbance, and daytime dysfunction. Each component is scored from 0 to 3, with summated components yielding a global score between 0 and 21 (higher scores = greater sleep-related problems).

*Strain* was assessed at Time 2 (2009) on the basis of a 15-item somatic complaints measure adopted from Caplan, Cobb, French, Harrison, and Pinneau (1975). Participants were asked about how often (1 = never, 5 = frequently) in the last month they experienced strain symptoms such as fatigue, loss of appetite, and headaches. Cronbach's was 0.79.

All of the job-based and work disengagement-related factors were measured at Time 1 (2008). To assess *variable/night shift work*, participants were asked to indicate their usual hours of work, specifying their usual start and finish times or indicating that they work varying shifts.

*Perceived disempowerment* was operationalized in terms of a single item drawn from the Life Stressors and Social Resources instrument developed by Moos and Moos (1997). Participants indicated how much in the past year their lives have been troubled (1 = not troubled at all, 5 = most troubled you have ever been) by any decrease in responsibilities or hours of work. *Job satisfaction* was measured using a four-item index adopted from Pond and Geyer (1991). Cronbach's was 0.79. Subjects responded using a five-point scale (1 = "not at all" to 5 = "very much so"). *Finance-related retirement concerns* were measured with a four-item measure developed specifically for this study. Participants reported on a five-point scale how concerned they are (1 = not at all concerned, 5 = very concerned) about their ability to afford (1) prescription drugs, (2) long-term healthcare, (3) a reasonable standard of living, and (4) pay property taxes, after they retire. Cronbach's was 0.82. *Perceived financial hardship* was assessed on the basis of five items from Ilfeld's (1976) financial stressors measure. Participants reported on a five-point scale how often in the past year (1 = never, 5 = often) they did not have enough money to afford necessities (e.g., the kind of food they or their family should have, the kind of medical care they or their family should have). Cronbach's was 0.79. To assess current income, participants reported their earnings in the prior year.

To take into account several of the individual difference factors that may precipitate sleep disturbance, we controlled for age (in years), gender (0 = Male, 1 = Female), widowed (0 = No, 1 = Yes), or divorced (0 = No, 1 = Yes). Additionally, we also accounted for participant ill-health and recent hospitalization. *Ill-health* was measured with the Lifetime History of Physician-Diagnosed Illnesses measure (11 items). This instrument has been used in a wide variety of epidemiological studies focusing on the health-related problems of older populations (e.g., Colsher & Wallace, 1990), and has strong predictive validity (e.g., Salive et al., 1992). Participants reported whether they "had ever been diagnosed by a physician" with a variety of chronic illnesses (yes or no). As for *hospitalization*, participants indicated (0 = No, 1 = Yes) whether they had been hospitalized in the past month. Finally, to account for the possible impact of baseline values of sleep-related problems to capture any change in such problems from Time 1 to Time 2, we followed Venables and

Ripley's (2002) approach and used the $T_1$ outcome as a covariate in all the models explaining sleep-related problems.

## RESULTS

### Descriptive Statistics

Compared to their peers who opted to retire, those remaining at work reported a significantly higher mean level of sleep problems ($M$ for retirees = 4.80, $SD$ = 3.23; $M$ for those continuing to work = 5.33, $SD$ = 3.42), $t(997)$ = -2.43, $p$ = 0.02. Means, standard deviations, and correlations among the variables for those continuing to work are displayed in Table 11.1. These results indicate that sleep problems decreased slightly from $T_1$ to $T_2$ ($M$ = 5.95, $SD$ = 3.49 vs. $M$ = 5.52, $SD$ = 3.41, respectively). Being female was associated with a higher PSQI score in $T_1$ and $T_2$. Notable are the significant positive correlations between working variable shifts at $T_1$ and strain at $T_2$, $r(276)$ = 0.21, $p \leq 0.01$, perceived financial hardship in the past year at $T_1$ and strain at $T_2$, $r(276)$ = 0.25, $p \leq 0.01$, and retirement concerns at $T_1$ and strain at $T_2$, $r(276)$ = 0.23, $p \leq 0.01$, and the inverse correlation between job satisfaction and strain, $r(276)$ = -0.18, $p \leq 0.01$. Finally, the findings show a positive correlation between strain at $T_2$ and PSQI at $T_2$, $r(276)$ = 0.53, $p \leq 0.01$.

### Hypotheses Testing

Results of the general linear model (GLM) regression analyses used for testing our hypotheses are shown in Table 11.2 (for the job-based stressors) and Table 11.3 (for the disengagement-related stressors). In both cases, we began our analysis by testing a baseline, control model, followed by the analysis of the strain models (in order to test Hypotheses 1–3 and 4–6). Model 2 of Table 11.2 indicates partial support for Hypotheses 1–3. More specifically, consistent with Hypothesis 1, after taking the control variables into account, we found a positive association between working variable shifts at Time 1 and older worker strain by Time 2 (estimate = 0.23, $p \leq 0.01$). No support was found for the hypothesized association between night shift work and a change in strain. Support was also found for Hypothesis 2, which posited that perceived disempowerment at Time 1 would be associated with higher levels of felt strain by Time 2 (estimate = 0.11, $p \leq 0.05$). No support was found for a link between job satisfaction and older worker strain.

Partial support emerged for the impact of factors relating to impending workforce disengagement (Hypotheses 4–6). As shown in Model 2 of Table 11.3, after taking the control variables into account, older workers' retirement concerns and perceived financial hardship predicted experienced strain at Time 2 (estimate = 0.08, $p \leq 0.05$; estimate = 0.18, $p \leq 0.01$, Hypotheses 4 and 5, respectively). No support was found for Hypothesis 6, which suggested that older workers' objective income at Time 1 would be inversely associated with the level of felt strain.

**Table 11.1** MEANS, STANDARD DEVIATIONS, AND INTERCORRELATIONS OF THE VARIABLES ($N = 276^{*}$)

| Measure | Mean | SD | (1) | (2) | (3) | (4) | (5) | (6) | (7) | (8) | (9) | (10) | (11) | (12) | (13) | (14) | (15) |
|---|---|---|---|---|---|---|---|---|---|---|---|---|---|---|---|---|---|
| (1) PSQI $T_1$ | 5.95 | 3.49 | — | | | | | | | | | | | | | | |
| (2) PSQI $T_2$ | 5.53 | 3.41 | .63[b] | — | | | | | | | | | | | | | |
| (3) Age | 60.53 | 3.99 | .06 | .05 | — | | | | | | | | | | | | |
| (4) Gender (0 = Male, 1 = Female) | 0.57 | 0.50 | .09 | .14[a] | -.03 | — | | | | | | | | | | | |
| (5) Widowed (0 = No, 1 = Yes) | 0.04 | 0.20 | -.03 | -.05 | .10 | .10 | — | | | | | | | | | | |
| (6) Divorced (0 = No, 1 = Yes) | 0.13 | 0.34 | .01 | .07 | -.003 | .22[b] | -.08 | — | | | | | | | | | |
| (7) Ill-health $T_2$ | 1.30 | 1.26 | .16[b] | .17[b] | .10 | -.14[a] | -.005 | .03 | — | | | | | | | | |
| (8) Hospitalized (0 = No, 1 = Yes) | 0.10 | 0.30 | .12[a] | .02 | -.03 | .04 | .06 | .09 | .19[b] | — | | | | | | | |
| (9) Perceived disempowerment $T_1$ | 1.26 | 0.77 | .17[b] | .22[b] | -.05 | .03 | -.02 | .05 | .07 | .17[a] | — | | | | | | |
| (10) Job Satisfaction $T_1$ | 3.63 | 1.11 | -.18[b] | -.24[b] | .12 | -.31[b] | -.01 | -.06 | .07 | .01 | -.19[b] | — | | | | | |
| (11) Variable Shift $T_1$ | 0.36 | 0.48 | .10 | .16[b] | .01 | .43[b] | .12[a] | .06 | -.09 | -.02 | .06 | -.21[b] | — | | | | |
| (12) Night Shift $T_1$ | 0.06 | 0.23 | .14[a] | .15[b] | -.05 | -.04 | -.05 | -.05 | -.01 | .03 | .16[b] | -.16[b] | -.18[a] | — | | | |
| (13) Perceived Financial Hardship $T_1$ | 1.28 | 0.48 | .19[b] | .15[b] | -.01 | .08 | .03 | .07 | .04 | -.005 | .07 | -.11 | .18[b] | .01 | — | | |
| (14) Current Income $T_1$ | 10.61 | 2.16 | -.12[a] | -.13[a] | -.13[a] | -.17[b] | -.1 | -.35[b] | .04 | .05 | .05 | .09 | -.05 | -.12[a] | -.14[a] | — | |
| (15) Retirement Concerns $T_1$ | 3.21 | 1.12 | .12[a] | .17[a] | -.07 | .22[b] | -.004 | .16 | -.12[a] | -.01 | .16[b] | -.31[b] | .17[b] | .03 | .34[b] | -.2[b] | — |
| (16) Strain $T_2$ | 1.69 | 0.48 | .42[b] | .53[b] | .02 | .16[b] | -.07 | .06 | .20[b] | .03 | .18[b] | -.18[b] | .21[b] | .06 | .25[b] | -.11 | .23[b] |

[a] $p \le 0.05$.
[b] $p \le 0.01$.
[*] Due to pairwise deletion, individual correlations have between 269 and 276 observations.

Table 11.2.

**Table 11.2.** OLDER WORKERS' SLEEP PROBLEMS AND JOB-RELATED FACTORS ($N = 234$)

| | Model 1 | | Model 2 | | Model 3 | | Model 4 | |
|---|---|---|---|---|---|---|---|---|
| | Control Model DV = PSQI $T_2$ | | Strain Model DV= Strain | | Main Effect Model DV = PSQI $T_2$ | | Mediation Model DV = PSQI $T_2$ | |
| | Estimate | SE | Estimate | SE | Estimate | SE | Estimate | SE |
| Intercept | −1.44 | 2.92 | 1.46[b] | 0.51 | −1.22 | 2.91 | −4.16 | 2.78 |
| PSQI $T_1$ | 0.59[b] | 0.05 | – | – | 0.53[b] | 0.05 | 0.44[b] | 0.05 |
| Age | 0.02 | 0.04 | 0.00 | 0.01 | 0.04 | 0.04 | 0.04 | 0.04 |
| Gender (0 = Male, 1 = Female) | 0.72[a] | 0.37 | 0.07 | 0.07 | 0.18 | 0.40 | 0.06 | 0.38 |
| Widowed (0 = No, 1 = Yes) | 0.56 | 0.84 | 0.28[a] | 0.14 | 0.70 | 0.82 | 0.20 | 0.77 |
| Divorced (0 = No, 1 = Yes) | −0.21 | 0.50 | −0.03 | 0.09 | −0.23 | 0.49 | −0.14 | 0.46 |
| Ill-health $T_2$ | 0.25 | 0.14 | 0.07[b] | 0.02 | 0.27[a] | 0.14 | 0.16 | 0.13 |
| Hospitalized (0 = No, 1 = Yes) | 1.15 | 0.65 | −0.26[a] | 0.11 | 0.93 | 0.63 | 1.42[a] | 0.60 |
| Variable Shift $T_1$ (0 = No, 1 = Yes) | | | 0.23[b] | 0.07 | 0.81[a] | 0.41 | 0.39 | 0.39 |
| Night Shift $T_1$ (0 = No, 1 = Yes) | | | 0.14 | 0.15 | 0.75 | 0.87 | 0.73 | 0.82 |
| Perceived Disempowerment $T_1$ | | | 0.11[a] | 0.05 | 0.51[a] | 0.26 | 0.33 | 0.25 |
| Job Satisfaction $T_1$ | | | −0.05 | 0.03 | −0.37[a] | 0.17 | −0.31[a] | 0.16 |
| Strain $T_2$ | | | | | | | 2.12[b] | 0.38 |
| $R^2$ | 0.43 | | 0.19 | | 0.47 | | 0.53 | |
| Change in $R^2$ | | | | | 0.04 | | 0.06 | |

[a] $p \leq 0.05$.
[b] $p \leq 0.01$.

To test the strain-mediated effects of these same stressors on sleep problems, following Baron and Kenny (1986), we first tested the main effect of both sets of stressors on sleep problems (Model 3 in Tables 11.2 and 11.3), and then added strain to this model (Model 4 of Tables 11.2 and 11.3). As shown in Table 11.2, consistent with Hypothesis 7a, strain at Time 2 had a significant positive association with the change in sleep problems from Time 1 to Time 2 (estimate = 2.12, $p < 0.01$). Moreover, when controlling for sleep problems at Time 1, three job-related stressors at Time 1 were associated with sleep problems in Time 2, namely working variable shifts, perceived disempowerment, and job satisfaction (estimates = 0.81, 0.51, and −0.37, respectively, $p \leq 0.05$ in all three cases). However, when strain was

**Table 11.3.** OLDER WORKERS' SLEEP PROBLEMS AND FACTORS RELATED TO IMPENDING WORKFORCE DISENGAGEMENT ($N$ = 271)

| | Model 1 | | Model 2 | | Model 3 | | Model 4 | |
|---|---|---|---|---|---|---|---|---|
| | Control Model DV = PSQI $T_2$ | | Strain Model DV = Strain | | Main Effect Model DV = PSQI $T_2$ | | Mediation Model DV = PSQI $T_2$ | |
| | Estimate | SE | Estimate | SE | Estimate | SE | Estimate | SE |
| Intercept | −1.25 | 2.79 | 0.89 | 0.52 | −2.25 | 3.03 | −4.14 | 2.88 |
| PSQI $T_1$ | 0.59[b] | 0.05 | – | – | 0.58[b] | 0.05 | 0.47[b] | 0.05 |
| Age | 0.02 | 0.04 | 0.001 | 0.01 | 0.02 | 0.04 | 0.03 | 0.04 |
| Gender (0 = Male, 1 = Female) | 0.70[a] | 0.34 | 0.15[b] | 0.06 | 0.56 | 0.34 | 0.33 | 0.32 |
| Widowed (0 = No, 1 = Yes) | 0.55 | 0.81 | 0.25 | 0.14 | 0.60 | 0.82 | 0.19 | 0.77 |
| Divorced (0 = No, 1 = Yes) | −0.45 | 0.48 | 0.06 | 0.09 | −0.20 | 0.51 | −0.25 | 0.48 |
| Ill-health $T_2$ | 0.32[a] | 0.13 | 0.09 | 0.02 | 0.35[b] | 0.13 | 0.21 | 0.13 |
| Hospitalized (0 = No, 1 = Yes) | 1.21[a] | 0.58 | −0.11 | 0.10 | 1.32[b] | 0.59 | 1.56[b] | 0.56 |
| Retirement Concerns $T_1$ | | | 0.08[a] | 0.03 | 0.32[a] | 0.16 | 0.18 | 0.15 |
| Perceived Financial Hardship $T_1$ | | | 0.18[b] | 0.06 | −0.01 | 0.35 | −0.28 | 0.33 |
| Current Income $T_1$ | | | −0.01 | 0.01 | −0.05 | 0.08 | −0.04 | 0.08 |
| Strain $T_2$ | | | | | | | 2.11[b] | 0.36 |
| $R^2$ | 0.44 | | 0.18 | | 0.45 | | 0.51 | |
| Change in $R^2$ | | | | | 0.01 (NS) | | 0.06 | |

[a]$p \leq 0.05$.
[b]$p \leq 0.01$.

added to this model as a mediator, the estimates for variable shift (estimate = 0.39) and perceived disempowerment (estimate = 0.33) both decreased and were no longer significant. Although the estimate for job satisfaction also declined (to −0.31), it remained statistically significant. This, combined with the lack of a significant association between job satisfaction and strain, suggests that of the four job-based stressors examined, only the effects of variable shift work and perceived disempowerment on the change in sleeping problems were mediated by strain. Sobel test results offer further evidence that strain (as posited by Hypothesis 7a) mediates the effects of these two job-based stressors on sleep problems ($z$ = 2.83, $p$ < 0.01 and $z$ = 2.35, $p$ < 0.05, respectively). Results from an analysis of the significance of the indirect effects on the basis of bootstrapped (5,000 bootstrap draws) confidence intervals (Preacher, Rucker, & Hayes, 2007) confirm the significance of the indirect effects (via strain) of variable shifts (total effect = 0.87; indirect effect = 0.48, CI = 0.24, 0.82) and perceived disempowerment (total effect = 0.58; indirect effect = 0.24, CI = 0.09, 0.49) on sleep problems. Moreover, despite the absence of a significant effect of job satisfaction on strain, results of the bootstrap analysis indicate a small, but significant indirect effect (total effect = −0.42; indirect effect = −0.10; CI = −0.22, −0.01).

Partial support also emerged for strain as a mediator of the effects of disengagement-related stressors on older workers' sleep problems. As shown in Model 3 of Table 11.3, after taking the control variables into account, retirement concerns at $T_1$ were significantly related to change in PSQI (estimate = 0.32, $p \leq 0.05$). Neither of the other two disengagement-related stressors had a direct effect on sleep problems. Moreover, as shown in Model 4, when added to this model, strain was again (as posited by Hypothesis 6) positively associated with the change in older employees' sleep problems (estimate = 2.11, $p < 0.05$), and weakened the effect of retirement concerns on the change in sleep problems (from 0.32, $p < 0.05$ to a nonsignificant 0.18). Further evidence of the indirect effect of retirement concerns on older employee's sleeping problem via strain is provided by the results of the Sobel test ($z = 2.55$, $p < 0.01$), and an analysis of the significance of the indirect effects on the basis of confidence intervals determined on the basis of 5,000 bootstrap draws (Preacher et al., 2007) confirms the significance of the indirect effects (via strain) of retirement concerns (total effect = 0. 34; indirect effect = 0.16, CI = 0.07, 0.28).

## DISCUSSION

We examined sleep problems among a cohort of older workers employed in a variety of sectors who were eligible for retirement 8 years earlier. Compared to their retired peers, those opting to remain at work reported significantly higher levels of sleep problems. Moreover, consistent with our hypotheses, among the older workers deferring retirement and continuing to work, several self-perceived, employment-related factors were associated with sleep problems assessed 1 year later. Specifically, sleep was adversely affected by a variable shift work. Indeed, the effect of a variable shift was the most robust among the work-related factors examined. Perhaps more importantly, our analyses indicated that the influence of a variable shift is largely explained by the strain it generates for older workers. Such strain may stem from the more fragile nature of sleep for many older adults (Crowley, 2011), with problematic adjustment to shifting sleep cycles inducing the kind of perseverative cognition (rumination) that makes sleep initiation even more difficult. This, in turn, may result in a downward spiral of increasingly severe sleep problems. However, no evidence emerged of an adverse effect of working night shifts for the older workers that we studied. The absence of such an effect may be explained by the unionized nature of our sample. In many unionized workplaces, employees bid for alternative work schedules with more veteran workers having greater bidding rights. Accordingly, it is likely that for the older workers in our sample, night shift scheduling was volitional, with those working this shift actively opting to do so because of the utility they deemed it afforded them.

Our data also lent support to the hypothesized association between disempowerment and sleep problems. More specifically, those who were more troubled by a decrease in responsibilities or hours of work reported more severe sleep problems. These effects were also explained by felt strain, supporting the COR-based notion that by diminishing older adults' psychological resources such as self-efficacy, disempowerment generates a basis for both rumination and the kind of physiological sequelae conducive to sleep problems.

Notable, however, was the limited support found for the role of impending workforce disengagement in explaining older workers' sleep problems. Of the parameters investigated, only retirement concerns had the expected adverse impact. Here too, the data indicate that the impact of such concerns is indirect, mediated by felt strain.

## Implications for Theory and Practice

These findings have several important implications for both management theory and practice. First, our study offers an important contribution to the literature linking work and sleep by expanding the set of work-related risk factors associated with sleep disturbance. More specifically, our findings suggest that in addition to the shift-related factors that have been widely examined to date (see Chapter 3), our understanding of the etiology of sleep problems may be enhanced by taking work-based stressors into account. Additionally, our findings suggest that the stressors likely to affect employee sleep behavior may be age or cohort specific, with disempowerment and workers' concerns about the economics of impending workforce disengagement playing a particularly important role in explaining sleep problems among older employees. Second, our findings suggest that in trying to understand the mechanisms underlying the link between work shift and employee sleep problems, it is important to look beyond the direct effect of circadian rhythm adjustment. More specifically, our findings suggest that a stress-based mechanism may play no less of a role, with felt strain setting off a potential cascade of physiological sequelae ultimately affecting older adults' sleep. Finally, our findings suggest that job satisfaction for older adults may serve as an important countervailing force to the adverse effect of work-related stressors on older adults' sleep. The fact that job satisfaction was inversely associated with sleep problems and that its effects on sleep problems were largely unmediated by strain suggests that, consistent with a push–pull perspective on retirement (suggesting that those forced into retirement have very different adjustment experiences than those opting to do so on their own volition; Bacharach et al., 2008), employee volition in remaining at work beyond retirement eligibility plays a key role in determining the degree to which work in advanced age adversely affects sleep.

From a more practical perspective, our study raises several important issues for employers and policymakers. For employers, our findings suggest that sleep problems may not necessarily be a problem some older employers bring to the workplace, but rather one *precipitated* by the job or broader employment context. Understanding how work characteristics serve as risk factors for older adults' sleep problems offers employers important insights into how such problems could be prevented. For example, given the often fragile nature of older adults' sleep, employers may benefit from offering older workers positions defined by a steady (as opposed to variable) shift. In doing so, however, our findings also suggest that employers take such steps carefully, avoiding job-related changes that may be viewed as marginalizing or disempowering in nature. To the degree that such steps are experienced as disempowering, they may serve as stressors that rather than resolving sleep problems, exacerbate them.

For policymakers, although working into older age may be associated with enhanced physical and emotional well-being (Sahlgren, 2013), our findings suggest that for some, it may also be associated with heightened sleep problems. To the extent that poor or limited sleep is costly not only for employees but also for their peers, employers, and the economy at large, greater consideration may need to be given to employment laws and policies that although facilitating retirement deferral, also encourage employers to adopt work scheduling and deployment practices that are less harmful to older adults' sleep.

## Limitations

The implications noted above should be considered in the context of the study's limitations, several of which may offer opportunities for future research. First, although our analyses were based on longitudinal data, measures of felt strain and PSQI were taken at the same time. Accordingly, ambiguity exists as to the causal relations between these two constructs. Just as strain may predict sleep problems, so may sleep problems also be predictive of felt strain. Indeed, the correlations between Strain at Time 1 and PSQI at Time 2 ($r = 0.49$) and that of PSQI at Time 1 and Strain at Time 2 ($r = 0.42$) are quite similar and in all probability not statistically different from one another. Accordingly, future research should collect sufficient data to run the kind of cross-lagged model needed to fully understand the causal nature of this relationship. We also encourage scholars to adopt study designs (such as experience sampling) that allow for testing more immediate effects of work on sleep among older workers.

Second, the individuals studied in the current sample were all union members in largely blue- and pink-collar occupations, and future research should examine the degree to which our findings are generalizable to older workers in these same occupations in the nonunion sector, as well as to older white-collar workers. Finally, our study examined only a small number of job and workplace characteristics, focusing on shift- and stress-based mechanisms. To more fully understand the work-based etiology of older adult sleep problems, a wide range of other potential work-related risk factors and mechanisms remains to be explored.

## CONCLUSIONS

Although scholars are paying greater attention to the relationship between work and sleep, the great majority of the research to date has focused on the implications of sleep, sleep deprivation, and sleep-related problems on organizational behavior. In contrast, research examining the impact of work on sleep remains limited, with most of this research focusing on the impact of work schedules. The study reported in this chapter aimed at addressing this gap in the research. Despite our focus on older workers, our findings regarding the role of work-based strain as a primary mechanism linking employment and sleep is likely generalizable to younger workers as well. In that regard, we hope that our framework and findings will provide a platform for the further exploration of how work and employment relations affect sleep.

## NOTE

1. Data for this study were collected in the context of a broader study supported by the National Institute of Alcoholism and Alcohol Abuse (Grant number 5 R01 AA011976). The analyses reported in this chapter were further supported by the Smithers Institute for Alcohol-Related Workplace Studies of Cornell University and the Henry Crown Institute for Business Research, Recanati Business School.

## REFERENCES

AARP. (2013). *Staying ahead of the curve 2013: AARP multicultural work and career study. Perceptions of age discrimination in the workplace—ages 45–74.* Washington, DC: AARP.

Åkerstedt, T. (2003). Shift work and disturbed sleep/wakefulness. *Occupational Medicine, 53*(2), 89–94.

Aldwin, C. M., Sutton, K. J., & Lachman, M. (1996). The development of coping resources in adulthood. *Journal of Personality, 64,* 837–871.

Atchley, R. C. (1989). A continuity theory of normal aging. *The Gerontologist, 29*(2), 183–190.

Bacharach, S., Bamberger, P., Biron, M., & Horowitz-Rozen, M. (2008). Perceived agency in retirement and retiree drinking behavior: Job satisfaction as a moderator. *Journal of Vocational Behavior, 73*(3), 376–386.

Barnes, C. M., Ghumman, S., & Scott, B. A. (2013). Sleep and organizational citizenship behavior: The mediating role of job satisfaction. *Journal of Occupational Health Psychology, 18,* 16–26.

Barnes, C. M., & Wagner, D. T. (2009). Changing to daylight saving time cuts into sleep and increases workplace injuries. *Journal of Applied Psychology, 94,* 1305–1317.

Belogolovsky, E., Bamberger, P. A., & Bacharach, S. B. (2012). Workforce disengagement stressors and retiree alcohol misuse: The mediating effects of sleep problems and the moderating effects of gender. *Human Relations, 65*(6), 705–728.

Berset, M., Elfering, A., Lüthy, S., Lüthi, S., & Semmer, N. K. (2011). Work stressors and impaired sleep: Rumination as a mediator. *Stress and Health, 27*(2), 71–82.

Boodoo, U. M., Gomez, R., & Gunderson, M. (2014). Relative income, absolute income and the life satisfaction of older adults: Do retirees differ from the non-retired? *Industrial Relations Journal, 45*(4), 281–299.

Brosschot, J. F., Gerin, W., & Thayer, J. F. (2006). The perseverative cognition hypothesis: A review of worry, prolonged stress-related physiological activation, and health. *Journal of Psychosomatic Research, 60*(2) 113–124.

Brosschot, J. F., Pieper, S., & Thayer, J. F. (2005). Expanding stress theory: Prolonged activation and perseverative cognition. *Psychoneuroendocrinology, 30*(10), 1043–1049.

Buysse, D. J., Reynolds, C. F., Monk, T. H., Berman, S. R., & Kupfer, D. J. (1989). The Pittsburgh Sleep Quality Index: A new instrument for psychiatric practice and research. *Psychiatry Research, 28*(2), 193–213.

Caplan, R. D., Cobb, S., French, J. R. P., Jr., Harrison, R. V., & Pinneau, S. R., Jr. (1975). *Job demands and worker health: Main effects and occupational differences.* Ann Arbor, MI: Institute for Social Research.

Chevalier, H., Los, F., Boichut, D., Bianchi, M., Nutt, D.J., Hajak, G., . . . Crowe, C. (1999). Evaluation of severe insomnia in the general population: Results of a European multinational survey. *Journal of Psychopharmacology, 13,* 21–24.

Chosewood, L. C. (2012). CDC—NIOSH Science Blog—Safer and Healthier at Any Age: Strategies for an Aging Workforce. National Institute for Occupational Safety and Health. Retrieved July 25, 2012.

Colsher, P. L., & Wallace, R. B. (1990). Elderly men with histories of heavy drinking: Correlates and consequences. *Journal of Studies on Alcohol, 51,* 528–535.

Crenshaw, M. C., & Edinger, J. D. (1999). Slow-wave sleep and waking cognitive performance among older adults with and without insomnia complaints. *Physiology & Behavior, 66,* 485–492.

Cropley, M., Dijk, D. J., & Stanley, N. (2006). Job strain, work rumination, and sleep in school teachers. *European Journal of Work and Organizational Psychology, 15*(2), 181–196.

Cropley, M., & Purvis, L. J. (2003). Job strain and rumination about work issues during leisure time. *European Journal of Work and Organizational Psychology, 12*(3), 195–207.

Crowley, K. (2011). Sleep and sleep disorders in older adults. *Neuropsychology Review, 21,* 41–53.

Eikermann, M., Jordan, A. S., Chamberlin, N. L., Gautam, S., Wellman, A., Lo, Y. L., & Malhotra, A. (2007). The influence of aging on pharyngeal collapsibility during sleep. *Chest Journal, 131*(6), 1702–1709.

Elovainio, M., Kivimäki, M., Vahtera, J., Keltikangas-Järvinen, L., & Virtanen, M. (2003). Sleeping problems and health behaviors as mediators between organizational justice and health. *Health Psychology, 22*(3), 287.

Faragher, E. B., Cass, M., & Cooper, C. L. (2005). The relationship between job satisfaction and health: A meta-analysis. *Occupational and Environmental Medicine, 62*(2), 105–112.

Feinsilver, S. H. (2003). Sleep in the elderly. What is normal? *Clinical Geriatric Medicine, 19,* 177–188.

Foley, D., Ancoli-Israel, S., Britz, P., & Walsh, J. (2004). Sleep disturbances and chronic disease in older adults: Results of the 2003 National Sleep Foundation Sleep in America Survey. *Journal of Psychosomatic Research, 56,* 497–502.

Garst, H., Frese, M., & Molenaar, P. (2000). The temporal factor of change in stressor– strain relationships: A growth curve model on a longitudinal study in East Germany. *Journal of Applied Psychology, 85*(3), 417.

Halbesleben, J. R. B., Harvey, J., & Bolino, M. C. (2009). Too engaged? A conservation of resources view of the relationship between work engagement and work interference with family. *Journal of Applied Psychology, 94*(6), 1452–1465.

Harrington, J. M. (2001). Health effects of shift work and extended hours of work. *Occupational and Environmental Medicine, 58*(1), 68–72.

Higginbottom, S., Barling, J., & Kelloway, E. K. (1993). Linking retirement experiences and marital satisfaction: A mediational model. *Psychology and Aging, 8,* 508–516.

Hobfoll, S. E. (1988). *The ecology of stress.* Washington, DC: Hemisphere.

Hobfoll, S. E., & Wells, J. D. (1998). Conservation of resources, stress, and aging: Why do some slide and some spring? In J. Lomranz (Ed.), *Handbook of aging and mental health: An integrative approach* (pp. 121–134). New York, NY: Plenum.

Höge, T. (2009). When work strain transcends psychological boundaries: An inquiry into the relationship between time pressure, irritation, work–family conflict and psychosomatic complaints. *Stress and Health, 25*(1), 41–51.

Jamal, M. (1990). Relationship of job stress and Type-A behavior to employees' job satisfaction, organizational commitment, psychosomatic health problems, and turnover motivation. *Human Relations, 43*(8), 727–738.

Kalimo, R., Taris, T. W., & Schaufeli, W. B. (2003). The effects of past and anticipated future downsizing on survivor well-being: An equity perspective. *Journal of Occupational Health Psychology, 8*, 91–109.

Kalimo, R., Tenkanen, L., Harma, M., Poppius, E., & Heinsalmi, P. (2000). Job stress and sleep disorders: Findings from the Helsinki Heart Study. *Stress Medicine, 16*(2), 65–75.

Kamel, N. S., & Gammack, J. K. (2006). Insomnia in the elderly: Cause, approach, and treatment. *American Journal of Medicine, 119*(6), 463–469.

Karasek, R., Brisson, C., Kawakami, N., Houtman, I., Bongers, P., & Amick, B. (1998). The Job Content Questionnaire (JCQ): An instrument for internationally comparative assessments of psychosocial job characteristics. *Journal of Occupational Health Psychology, 3*, 322–355.

Keith, V. M. (1993). Gender, financial strain, and psychological distress among older adults. *Research on Aging, 15*(2), 123–147.

Krause, N. (1987). Chronic financial strain, social support, and depressive symptoms among older adults. *Psychology and Aging, 2*, 185–192.

Kuppermann, M., Lubeck, D. P., Mazonson, P. D., Patrick, D. L., Stewart, A. L., Buesching, D. P., & Filer, S. K. (1995). Sleep problems and their correlates in a working population. *Journal of General Internal Medicine, 10*(1), 25–32.

Macfadyen, A., Macfadyen, H., & Prince, N. (1996). Economic stress and psychological well-being: An economic psychology framework. *Journal of Economic Psychology, 17*(3), 291–311.

Mallon, L., Broman, J. E., & Hetta, J. (2000). Relationship between insomnia, depression, and mortality: A 12-year follow-up of older adults in the community. *International Psychogeriatrics, 12*(3), 295–306.

Mansyur, C., Amick, B. C., Harrist, R. B., & Franzini, L. (2008). Social capital, income inequality, and self-rated health in 45 countries. *Social Science & Medicine, 66*(1), 43–56.

Martin, L., & Tesser, A. (1996). Some ruminative thoughts. *Advances in Social Cognition, 9*, 1–47.

McCann, R., & Giles, H. (2002). Ageism in the workplace: A communication perspective. In T. Nelson (Ed.), *Ageism: Stereotyping and prejudice against older persons* (pp. 163–199). Cambridge, MA: MIT Press.

Melamed, S., Shirom, A., Toker, S., Berliner, S., & Shapira, I. (2006). Burnout and risk of cardiovascular disease: Evidence, possible causal paths, and promising research directions. *Psychological Bulletin, 132*, 327–352.

Moos, R., & Moos, B. (1997). Life Stressors and Social Resources Inventory: A measure of adults' and youths' life contexts. In C. P. Zalaquett & R. J. Wood (Eds.), *Evaluating stress: A book of resources* (pp. 177–190). Lanham, MD: Scarecrow Education.

Nahum-Shani, I., & Bamberger, P. A. (2011). Work hours, retirement and supportive relations among older adults. *Journal of Organizational Behavior, 32*, 345–369.

Neubauer, D. N. (1999). Sleep problems in the elderly. *American Family Physician, 59*, 2551–2560.

Ohayon, M. M., Carskadon, M. A., Guilleminault, C., & Vitiello, M. V. (2004). Meta-analysis of quantitative sleep parameters from childhood to old age in healthy individuals: Developing normative sleep values across the human lifespan. *Sleep*, 27, 1255–1273.

Pearlin, L. I. (1999). Stress and mental health: A conceptual overview. In T. L. Scheid (Ed.), *A handbook for the study of mental health: Social context, theories, and systems* (pp. 161–175). New York, NY: Cambridge University Press.

Peirce, R. S., Frone, M. R., Russell, M., & Cooper, M. L. (1994). Relationship of financial strain and psychosocial resources to alcohol use and abuse: The mediating role of negative affect and drinking motives. *Journal of Health and Social Behavior*, 35(4), 291–308.

Pereira, D., Meier, L. L., & Elfering, A. (2013). Short-term effects of social exclusion at work and worries on sleep. *Stress and Health*, 29(3), 240–252.

Pond, S. D., & Geyer P. D. (1991). Differences in the relation between job satisfaction and perceived work alternatives among older and younger blue collar workers. *Journal of Vocational Behavior*, 39, 251–262.

Potočnik, K. & Sonnentag, S. (2013), A longitudinal study of well-being in older workers and retirees: The role of engaging in different types of activities. *Journal of Occupational and Organizational Psychology*, 86: 497–521.

Ribet, C. & Derriennic, F. (1999)., Age, working conditions, and sleep disorders: a longitudinal analysis in the French Cohort E.S.T.E.V. *Sleep*, 22. 491–504.

Rodenbeck, A., Huether, G., Ruther, E., & Hajak, G. (2002). Interactions between evening and nocturnal cortisol secretion and sleep parameters in patients with severe chronic primary insomnia. *Neuroscience Letters*, 324, 159–163.

Roscigno, V. J., Mong, G., Byron, R., & Tester, S. (2007). Age discrimination, social closure and employment. *Social Forces*, 86(1), 313–334.

Roth, T., Roehrs, T., & Pies, R. (2007). Insomnia: Pathophysiology and implications for treatment. *Sleep Medicine Reviews*, 11, 71–79.

Sahlgren, G. H. (2013). *Work longer, live healthier: The relationship between economic activity, health and government policy*. London, UK: Institute of Economic Affairs.

Salive, M. E., Cornoni-Huntley, J., LaCroix, A. Z., Ostfeld, A. M., Wallace, R. B., & Hennekens, C. H. (1992). Predictors of smoking cessation and relapse in older adults. *American Journal of Public Health*, 82, 1268–1271.

Schneider, B., Smith, D. B., & Goldstein, H. W. (2000). Attraction–selection– attrition: Toward a person–environment psychology of organizations. In W. B. Walsh, K. H. Craik, & R. H. Price (Eds.), *Person-environment psychology: New directions and perspectives* (2nd ed., pp. 61–85). Hillsdale, NJ: Lawrence Erlbaum.

Schubert, C. R., Cruickshanks, K. J., Dalton, D. S., Klein, B. E., Klein, R., & Nondahl, D. M. (2002). Prevalence of sleep problems and quality of life in an older population. *Sleep*, 25, 889–893.

Shultz, J. H. (1985). *The economics of aging*. Belmont, CA: Wadsworth.

Stoller, M. K. (1994). Economic effects of insomnia. *Clinical Therapeutics*, 16(5), 873–897.

Theorell, T., Perski, A., Åkerstedt, T., Sigala, F., Ahlberg-Hultean, G., Svensson, J., & Eneroth, P. (1988). Changes in job strain in relation to changes in physiological state: A longitudinal study. *Scandinavian Journal of Work, Environment, and Health*, 14, 189–196.

Thomsen, D. K., Mehlsen, M. Y., Hokland, M., Viidik, A., Olsen, F., Avlund, K., ... Zachariae, R. (2004). Negative thoughts and health: Associations among rumination, immunity, and health care utilization in a young and elderly sample. *Psychosomatic Medicine*, 66(3), 363–371.

Van der Heijden, B., Schalk, R., & van Veldhoven, M. J. (2008). Ageing and careers: European research on long-term career development and early retirement. *Career Development International*, 13(2), 85–94.

Van Reeth, O., Weibel, L., Spiegel, K., Leproult, R., Dugovic, C., & Maccari, S. (2000). Physiology of sleep—Interactions between stress and sleep: From basic research to clinical situations. *Sleep Medicine Reviews*, 4(2), 201–219.

Vance, C. M., Ensher, E. A., Hendricks, F. M., & Harris, C. (2004). Gender-based vicarious sensitivity to disempowering behavior in organizations: Exploring an expanded concept of hostile working environment. *Employee Responsibilities and Rights Journal, 16*(3), 135–147.

Vela-Bueno, A., Moreno-Jimenez, B., Rodriguez-Munoz, A., Olavarrieta-Bernardino, S., Fernandez-Mendoza, J., Jose De la Cruz-Troca, J., . . . Vgontzas, A. N. (2008). Insomnia and sleep quality among primary care physicians with low and high burnout levels. *Journal of Psychosomatic Research, 64*(4), 435–442.

Venables, W. N., & Ripley, B. D. (2002). *Modern applied statistics with S-PLUS* (4th ed.). New York, NY: Springer-Verlag.

Vgontzas, A. N., Zoumakis, M., Bixler, E. O., Lin H. M., Prolo, P., Vela-Bueno, A., . . . Chrousos, G. P. (2003). Impaired nighttime sleep in healthy old versus young adults is associated with elevated plasma interleukin-6 and cortisol levels: Physiologic and therapeutic implications. *Journal of Clinical Endocrinology and Metabolism, 88*, 2087–2095.

Wagner, D. T., Barnes, C. M., & Scott, B. A. (2014). Driving it home: How workplace emotional labor harms employee home life. *Personnel Psychology, 67*(2), 487–516.

Wang, M. (2007). Profiling retirees in the retirement transition and adjustment process: Examining the longitudinal change patterns of retirees' psychological well-being. *Journal of Applied Psychology, 92*(2), 455–474.

Wang, M., & Shultz, K. S. (2010). Employee retirement: A review and recommendations for future investigation. *Journal of Management, 36*(1), 172–206.

Westman, M., & Eden, D. (1997). Effects of vacation on job stress and burnout: Relief and fade out. *Journal of Applied Psychology, 82*, 516–527.

Whelan, C. T. (1992). The role of income, life-style deprivation and financial strain in mediating the impact of unemployment on psychological distress. Evidence from the Republic of Ireland. *Journal of Occupational and Organizational Psychology, 65*(4), 331–334.

Woodward, M. (1999). Insomnia in the elderly. *Australian Family Physician, 28*, 653–658.

Young, A. M., Vance, C. M., & Ensher, E. A. (2003). Individual differences in sensitivity to disempowering acts: A comparison of gender and identity-based explanations for perceived offensiveness. *Sex Roles, 49*, 163–171.

Yuan, A. S. V. (2007). Perceived age discrimination and mental health. *Social Forces, 86*, 291–311.

# PART III

# Management and Educational Implications

CHAPTER 12

# Sleep and Other Energy Management Mechanisms

*The Engines for Sustainable Performance at Work*

GRETCHEN M. SPREITZER,[1] CHARLOTTE FRITZ,
AND CHAK FU LAM

## SLEEP AND OTHER ENERGY MANAGEMENT MECHANISMS: THE ENGINES FOR SUSTAINABLE PERFORMANCE AT WORK

Employee health and well-being are declining (American Psychological Association, 2014), and employee engagement is at historical lows according to the Gallup—13%, an all-time low in 2013. A lack of engagement at work is associated with reduced productivity while presenteeism is on the rise (Johns, 2010). At the same time, many work organizations are trying to do more with less (Ton, 2014), which increases workloads even more, adding more demands on employees and reducing hours available for recovery from work on evenings and weekends. As a result, as employees feel more and more depleted, some become more proactive in seeking out mechanisms for energy management that are within their own sphere of control (Fritz, Lam, & Spreitzer, 2011). In this chapter, we explore the impact of a number of strategies for energy management (including healthy sleep habits, which is the focus of this handbook) to help employees not only cope with work demands but also thrive amid the challenges. We also provide a tool that employees may find helpful in managing their energy across the workday—the Energy Audit (Spreitzer & Grant, 2012).

Human energy is an affective experience that includes a sense of positive arousal, eagerness to act, and the capability of acting (Quinn & Dutton, 2005). It is a "reinforcing experience that people enjoy and seek" (Dutton, 2003a, p. 6). One way that energy is manifested in the doing of work is through the experience

of vitality (Thayer, Newman, & McClain, 1994). Vitality refers to having significant energetic resources and is captured in the experience of enthusiasm and
feeling alive at work (Ryan & Frederick, 1997). An employee high in subjective vitality feels alert, energized, and spirited (Bostic, Rubio, & Hood, 2000;
Spreitzer, Sutcliffe, Dutton, Sonenshein, & Grant, 2005). Thus, within the work
context, human energy is a "fuel" that helps organizations run successfully (Bruch
& Vogel, 2011). It is an important, renewable resource (Hagger, Wood, Stiff, &
Chatzisarantis, 2010) that fosters high performance and sustainability in employees and organizations (Dutton, 2003b; Pfeffer, 2010; Spreitzer & Porath, 2012).

This chapter focuses on ways in which employees can "refuel their engines" or
"recharge their batteries." Specifically, we examine strategies that are within the
employee's own sphere of control rather than more macroorganizational policies or
practices (Fritz, Lam, & Spreitzer, 2011). Loehr and Schwartz (2003) suggest four
domains of strategies for managing human energy that we believe are helpful for
employees when managing their energy at work:

1. Physical energy management strategies: These emphasize the physiological
   foundation of human energy and include eating healthily, taking regular breaks
   every 90 minutes (Trougakos, Hideg, Cheng, & Beal, 2014), exercising (including
   cardiovascular and strength training), and adequate sleep (Barnes, 2012).
2. Emotional energy management strategies: These emphasize the quality of the
   relationships with others at work (Dutton, 2003a). They focus on the emotional
   connections and include the reciprocal nature of giving and receiving social support (Baker & Bulkey, 2014).
3. Mental energy management strategies: These emphasize the ability of individuals to focus their attention and concentrate on the work at hand. They focus
   on being mindful and in the present moment so work can get done (Dane &
   Brummel, 2014).
4. Spiritual energy management strategies: These emphasize work that has a clear
   sense of purpose/meaning (Quinn & Thakor, 2014). Spiritual strategies focus
   on what individuals find to be inspiring in their work including work that has a
   sense of purpose to it.

Loehr and Schwartz (2003) suggest that people will experience the most
sustainable levels of energy when they regularly renew across all of the four
domains of energy rather than in just one or two of the domains. Energy in
each domain needs to be fueled, not just outside of work during leisure time,
but, given how much of our day is spent working, during the workday itself
(Schwartz, 2010).

Interestingly, although these strategies make sense intuitively, they have not
been examined empirically in tandem with one another. Thus, we do not know if
they positively reinforce each other or if some strategies are more impactful than
others. In Study 1, we seek to provide empirical support for the positive relationship between these domains of energy management and employees' perceptions of
energy at work.

## STUDY 1

### Validating the Four Domains of Energy Management Strategies

In Study 1, we examine the relationship between engagement in the four domains of energy management and feelings of energy at work. We hypothesize that each type of strategy will be related to higher levels of energy in the doing of work:

Hypothesis 1: Engagement in physical energy management strategies will be related to higher levels of experienced energy.

Hypothesis 2: Engagement in emotional energy management strategies will be related to higher levels of experienced energy.

Hypothesis 3: Engagement in mental energy management strategies will be related to higher levels of experienced energy.

Hypothesis 4: Engagement in spiritual energy management strategies will be related to higher levels of experienced energy.

### RESEARCH DESIGN

#### Sample

The sample was composed of 410 young professionals in a variety of industries (e.g., consulting, financial services, healthcare, manufacturing, and nonprofits). The data were collected using an on-line assessment completed approximately 1 month prior to starting an MBA program at a large Midwestern university. Three hundred and twenty-four employees completed the survey (response rate = 79%) and respondents (66% male; mean age = 28.3 years; average of 5.6 years of work experience) did not differ significantly from nonrespondents with regard to demographic background. Feedback was provided to individual participants for their own development, and they were each assured that their responses would remain confidential.

#### Measures

Because we were not able to find readily available, short, validated scales for each of the energy management strategies of Loehr and Schwartz (2003), in several cases we created our own. Each energy management strategy was measured on a six-point frequency scale (1 = almost never to 6 = almost always).

*Physical energy management strategies.* We created a list of 17 items capturing physical energy management strategies. Specifically, we measured nutrition with seven items (e.g., "Eat breakfast everyday"; $\alpha$ = 0.80), taking breaks with two items (e.g., "Get up and take a break every 90–120 minutes"; $\alpha$ = 0.70), sleep with three items (e.g., "Get 7–8 hours of sleep each night; $\alpha$ = 0.64), and exercise with five items (e.g., "Do some form of physical activity daily"; α = 0.86). The full list of items can be found in Appendix A.

*Emotional energy management strategies.* Emotional energy management strategies were assessed through two items measuring support received from others (α = 0.64) and three items measuring support given to others (α = 0.74).

*Mental energy management strategies.* Mental energy management strategies were measured using Brown and Ryan's (2003) mindfulness scale. The scale included 12 items with a sample item being "I tend not to notice feelings of or physical tensions" (reverse-coded; α = 0.84).

*Spiritual energy management strategies.* Spiritual energy management strategies were measured through items indicating a sense of mission (α = 0.50) and a sense of meaning (α = 0.74). The items for mission were developed for this study and included "I am guided more by my internal vision than by external pressure," "I follow a clear set of principles or beliefs that governs my actions," and "My purpose in life is as much focused on others as it is on me." A sense of meaning (Spreitzer, 1995; only available to a subset of individuals collected 6 months later) was measured with three items (e.g., "The work I'm doing is meaningful to me").

*Energy.* We assessed energy at work using Ryan and Frederick's (1997) seven-item subjective vitality scale. Sample items included "I feel alive and vital at work" and "I have energy and spirit at work." Cronbach's alpha was 0.92.

## FINDINGS

In each case, and in support of Hypotheses 1–4, we found a positive and significant relationship between each of the energy management strategies and the experience of energy in the doing of work (see Table 12.1). Thus, engaging in physical, emotional, mental, and spiritual energy management strategies was associated with a sense of energy and vitality. Interestingly, the strongest relationship was found for mental strategies followed by emotional and then spiritual strategies. Thus, Study 1 provides support for all four domains of energy management. In support of the popular ideas on energy management developed by Loehr and Schwarz (2003), people can address their energy needs by moderating the use of physical, emotional, mental, and spiritual strategies (Table 12.2). In Study 2, we continue to examine the role of energy management but will examine how sleep is related to the experience of energy at work in more depth.

## STUDY 2

### Exploring the Relationship between Sleep and Energy

Sleep as a universal way to replenish human energy and ensure everyday functioning and productivity has received limited attention from organizational researchers so far (Barnes, 2012, has been a leader in this realm of work). This is surprising

**Table 12.1.** RELATIONSHIPS BETWEEN STRATEGIES AND ENERGY
AT WORK

| Energy Management Practice | Correlation with Energy at Work |
|---|---|
| *Physical* | |
| Nutrition | 0.23** |
| Breaks | 0.12* |
| Sleep | 0.16** |
| Exercise | 0.25*** |
| *Emotional* | |
| Support given | 0.36*** |
| Support received | 0.29*** |
| *Mental* | |
| Mindfulness | 0.40*** |
| *Spiritual* | |
| Mission | 0.31*** |
| Meaning | 0.29* |

***$p < 0.001$.
**$p < 0.01$.
*$p < 0.05$.

given the high prevalence of chronic sleep disorders in American adults (National Institute of Neurological Disorders and Stroke, 2014). Sleep deprivation, even from a single night of too little sleep, is associated with drowsiness, lower concentration, impaired memory, and impaired physical performance (see Barnes, 2012, for a review). On a neurological level, sleep allows neurons to repair themselves. Without sleep, neurons may become so depleted in energy or so polluted with byproducts of normal cellular activities that they begin to malfunction (National Institute of Neurological Disorders and Stroke, 2014). Some sleep researchers suggest that sleep may be more influential for our well-being than diet or exercise (e.g., Dement & Vaughan, 1999). Vitality at work, as an aspect of high well-being, indicates that the "fuel tank" is full and that the employee has the capacity to engage in a variety of performance-related behaviors (Baumeister, Muraven, & Tice, 2000).

Therefore, in Study 2, we aimed to replicate the findings from Study 1 regarding sleep and energy at work as well as exploring relationships between sleep and other work-related outcomes. Specifically, based on Barnes' (2012) proposition, we hypothesize that sufficient sleep is associated with fewer missed workdays as an indicator of work withdrawal. In addition, we hypothesize that sufficient sleep is associated with better health behaviors such as engaging in exercise and less caffeine consumption.

*Table 12.2.*

|  |  | 1 | 2 | 3 | 4 | 5 | 6 | 7 | 8 | 9 |
|---|---|---|---|---|---|---|---|---|---|---|
| 1. | Nutrition |  |  |  |  |  |  |  |  |  |
| 2. | Breaks | 0.27*** |  |  |  |  |  |  |  |  |
| 3. | Sleep | 0.23*** | 0.27*** |  |  |  |  |  |  |  |
| 4. | Exercise | 0.24*** | 0.28*** | 0.18** |  |  |  |  |  |  |
| 5. | Support given | 0.09+ | 0.15** | 0.06 | 0.17** |  |  |  |  |  |
| 6. | Support received | 0.05 | 0.07 | 0.02 | 0.11* | 0.47*** |  |  |  |  |
| 7. | Mindfulness | 0.05 | 0.11* | 0.20*** | 0.02 | 0.15** | 0.17** |  |  |  |
| 8. | Mission | 0.07 | 0.05 | 0.09 | 0.11* | 0.36*** | 0.25*** | 0.20*** | 0.37** |  |
| 9. | Meaning | 0.10 | -0.03 | 0.15 | 0.04 | 0.33* | 0.07 | 0.23+ | 0.49*** | 0.43*** |

***$p < 0.001$.
**$p < 0.01$.
*$p < 0.05$.

Hypothesis 5: Sufficient sleep is associated with higher energy at work.

Hypothesis 6: Sufficient sleep is associated with lower absenteeism.

Hypothesis 7: Sufficient sleep is related to healthy practices. Specifically, sufficient sleep is associated with (1) increased exercising and (2) decreased caffeine consumption.

## RESEARCH DESIGN

### Sample

Study participants ($N = 214$) worked in a variety of professional and clerical positions at a U.S. software company. They were on average 45 years old, 53% were male, and 63% had a college degree. Participants had worked at the company an average of 11 years. Respondents indicated working 40.50 hours per week on average ($SD = 8.10$) and came from a variety of departments including quality, finance/accounting, human resources, general administration, information technology, sales/marketing, legal, and customer relations. About 81% of respondents were in supervisory positions of some kind.

### Measures

**Sleep.** Sleep was measured by asking respondents to report the average amount of hours of sleep they had that week.

***Energy.*** We again assessed energy with a measure of subjective vitality at work using Ryan and Frederick's (1997) seven-item subjective vitality scale. Cronbach's alpha was 0.90. We also assessed energy with the seven-item vigor subscale of the POMS (Profile of Mood States; McNair et al., 1981). Sample items included "full of pep" and "alert." Cronbach's alpha was 0.95.

***Absenteeism.*** Absenteeism was measured by asking respondents to report the number of missed days of work due to illness in the past month.

***Healthy practices.*** Exercising was measured by asking respondents to indicate the average number of times they exercise each week. Caffeine consumption was measured as the average servings of caffeine per day.

## FINDINGS

Participants reported sleeping on average 6.6 hours per night ($SD$ = 1.1). Incidentally, this is the national average of sleep reported in other studies (Schwartz, 2010). They reported having missed 0.38 on average due to illness in the past month ($SD$ = 0.98). Furthermore, they reported exercising 3.3 time per week on average ($SD$ = 2.0) and on average drinking 2.1 servings of caffeine per day ($SD$ = 2.2)

In support of hypotheses 5–7, the findings suggest that sleep quantity is positively and significantly associated with each outcome (see Table 12.3). Specifically, sleep quantity is associated with higher levels of energy (i.e., both subjective vitality and vigor), thereby confirming findings form Study 1. Results also indicate that similar to Study 1, sleep quantity is related to health behaviors such as increased exercise and lower caffeine consumption. Finally, sleep quantity was also associated with lower absenteeism due to illness. Building on Study 1, these results help in producung a clearer picture of how sleep matters for human energy at work, missing workdays, and engaging in healthy behaviors (i.e., increased exercise and decreased caffeine consumption).

### Supplemental Analysis on Sleep and Energy

In both Study 1 and Study 2, we examined sleep somewhat differently. Whereas in Study 2 we assessed sleep quantity (i.e., the hours of sleep on average per night),

***Table 12.3.*** CORRELATIONS BETWEEN SUFFICIENT SLEEP
AND ENERGY/ENERGY STRATEGIES

|  | Vigor | Subjective Vitality | Absenteeism | Exercising | Caffeine Consumption |
|---|---|---|---|---|---|
| Sleep quantity | 0.15* | 0.14* | −0.23** | 0.17* | −0.25** |

\*\*$p$ < 0.01.
\*$p$ < 0.05.

Study 1 included a three-item measure that indicated sleep quality. For this supplemental analysis, we return to the Study 1 sample and scale. Specifically, we will explore the relationship between each of the three sleep items with each other (each taking a slightly different angle on sleep) as well as with the experience of energy.

When we think about sleep, we often think first about the quantity of sleep (i.e., consistent with our measure in Study 2). Is a person getting enough sleep each night to avoid sleep deprivation? Most experts suggest that healthy adults need 7–8 hours. To this end, one of our sleep items (Item 1) refers to sleep quantity with a target of 7–8 hours of sleep per night.

A second item (Item 2) asks employees to indicate to what extent they go to bed at a set time each night and get up at about the same time each morning, which is distinct from the quantity of sleep. In other words, a person could go to bed and wake up at consistent times but get significantly less than 7–8 hours of sleep per night. Loehr and Schwartz (2003) suggest that consistent waking and sleep times create a sleep habit that not only enables a person to more easily fall asleep at night but also makes it easier to wake up in the morning. Disrupting this schedule may make it more difficult to fall asleep in the evening and can create sleep inertia in the morning when it becomes difficult to wake up from a deep sleep. Similarly, "sleeping in" on weekends makes it harder to wake up early on Monday morning because it resets sleep cycles for a later awakening (Dement & Vaughan, 1999). Along with other sleep-regulation behaviors, this can be described as an aspect of "sleep hygiene."

A third item (Item 3) asks employees to indicate how often they go to bed early and wake up early. A recent study comparing "morning people" (i.e., those early birds who like to get up at dawn) and "evening people" (i.e., night owls who prefer to stay up late and sleep in) found that morning people tend to be more persistent (Preckel, Lipnevich, Schneider, & Roberts, 2011). Morning people are also more resistant to fatigue, frustration, and difficulties, which can translate into lower levels of anxiety, lower rates of depression, higher life satisfaction, and a lower probability of substance abuse. This is in tune with the old adage attributed to Benjamin Franklin, "Early to bed and early to rise, makes a man healthy, wealthy and wise." It is also consistent with circadian research on "morningness" and "eveningness" (Tankova, Adan, & Buela-Casal, 1994), which demonstrates that morning people achieve more academically.

Our data further indicate that these three healthy sleep items are related, suggested by moderate correlations ranging from 0.4 to 0.6. However, the patterns of relationships between individual sleep items and the experience of energy at work are somewhat different. Specifically, Item 1 ("Do you get 7–8 hours of sleep each night?") was not significantly related to the experience of energy at work ($r = 0.02$, ns). However, Item 2 ("Do you go to bed early and wake up early?," $r = 0.18$) and Item 3 ("Do you go to bed and wake up consistently at the same time?"; $r = 0.15$) were both significantly associated with a sense of energy. Just to be sure the pattern of correlations was not by chance, we also examined the three sleep items in relation to a measure of positive emotions that also included some energy items. Results were similar, indicating no relationship with Item 1 but significant relationships with Items 2 and 3. This suggests that sleep habits such as consistent and early waking/sleeping times may be just as important, or even more important, for energy at work than the actual amount of sleep.

In some ways, getting 7–8 hours of sleep may be the easier sleep practice to implement than the other two (particularly the practice of getting to bed at a relatively early time). Employees may argue that it is too difficult to get to bed at a reasonable time each night given the demands of work and life (Barnes, Wagner, & Ghumman, 2012; Perlow, 2012). However, one additional reason for going to bed late may be the consumption of caffeine (even in the late afternoon). Therefore, one strategy for better sleep would be to avoid drinks that contain caffeine, which acts as a stimulant and keeps people awake after mid-afternoon (Dement & Vaughan, 1999). Sources of caffeine include coffee, chocolate, soft drinks, nonherbal teas, diet drugs, and some pain relievers. Some research further points to the importance of mentally disconnecting from work at least an hour to two before bedtime. This is increasingly hard with the tether of technology and smartphones (Perlow, 2012). Recent research also demonstrates that artificial light from electronics in the bedroom can make it difficult to fall asleep in a timely manner (Gooley et al., 2011). All of these things make it more difficult for employees to develop healthy sleep practices, thereby potentially impacting energy at work.

In the next section of this chapter, we will describe a tool called the Energy Audit (Spreitzer & Grant, 2012), which can be helpful to employees in managing their energy throughout their day, at work as well as at home. Although not directly related to sleep, it can be a useful tool for individuals to manage their energy for higher performance and quality of life.

## INTRODUCING THE ENERGY AUDIT: A TOOL FOR MANAGING ENERGY

The goal of the energy audit is to increase the awareness of energy levels throughout the day and to offer insight on how to better mobilize energy for high performance. Participants should complete an energy audit for two or more workdays so that they can begin to see patterns across weekdays. We do not recommend doing the audit on weekends because activities and sleep practices may be quite different then. Rather, participants should choose days that best represent normal sleep patterns and daily work schedules. To complete the audit, participants track their energy level each hour, starting with the time they wake up. Then participants should note what they were doing at that point in time. For example, a person who woke up at 8:00 am should write down 8 am, their energy level, and that they "had breakfast." The table provided in Appendix B can be helpful in tracking energy levels across the workday. Figure 12.1 provides an example of what this kind of tallying should look like.

## Energy Audit – Awareness and Action
### Traci Grant and Gretchen Spreitzer

What is energy? Think of energy as the amount of vigor, vitality or zest you have, or your quantity of "get up and go." The goal of this energy audit is to increase your awareness of your changing energy levels throughout the day and to offer insights on how to regulate your energy.

This audit should be done for at least two week-days. Please choose days that represent your usual sleep pattern and daily schedule.

Track your energy level each hour, starting with when you wake up. Make a note of any specific factors that might be relevant to your energy in the column to the right. For example, if you woke up at 8:00 a.m., and your energy is low, write "woke up". If, at 8:30 a.m., you eat your breakfast and your energy spikes up, write "ate breakfast."

It may be difficult to mark your energy every hour. You can set a cell phone alarm or set up email reminders. If you do miss a time, write down the time and mark your energy as soon as you remember. Then, try to get back on track. For example, if you remember at 11:30 a.m., but were supposed to log at 11, write in 11:30 a.m. with a corresponding energy level. Then also log your energy at 12 noon to get back on track.

Please use the following scale to audit your energy each hour:

1-2:  Very Low
3-4:  Low
5:    Neutral
6:    Moderate
7-8:  High
9-10: Very High

Please bring your completed audits to class for discussion and to be turned in.

| TIME | ENERGY LEVEL | WHAT WERE YOU DOING? |
|------|------|------|
| 9:00 | 1 | Woke up first time/ hit snooze |
| 10:00 | 5 | Walked to class |
| 11:00 | 4 | In class |
| 12:00 | 3 | Still in class |
| 1:00 | 7 | Walked home from class/made lunch |
| 2:00 | 4 | E-mailing |
| 3:30 | 6 | Doing work/emailing |
| 4:00 | 8 | Talking to friends |
| 5:00 | 7 | Drove home to see dog |
| 6:00 | 4 | Taking care of dog |
| 7:00 | 2 | Ate ramen noodle dinner |
| 8:00 | 6 | Drove back to campus |
| 9:00 | 7 | More e-mails/computer work |
| 10:00 | 9 | Getting ready to go out |
| 11:00 | 9 | Out at friends house |
| 12:00 | 8 | At the bar |
| 1 am | 8 | At the bar |
| 2 am | 6 | Walking home |
| 3 am | 2 | In Bed |

**Figure 12.1.**
Energy audit energy tracking.

It may be difficult to track energy hour by hour. To help with this, participants can set a cell phone alarm or set up email reminders. If they miss a time, they can write down the time and rate their energy retrospectively as soon as they remember. They can then try to get back on track for the next upcoming assessment. For example, a participant who remembers the 11:00 am time slot at 11:30 am should write in 11:30 am with a corresponding energy level. Then the participant can also report his or her energy at 12 pm to get back on track. In addition, participants should be sure to note the number of hours they slept the previous night. This is important because we know from Study 1 and Study 2 that sleep quantity can affect energy levels.

Once participants have tracked their energy at hourly points across the workday, the next step is to plot their energy levels. Participants can plot their energy levels on the graph in Appendix C so they can see how their energy ebbs and flows over the course of the day. To do this, participants should put an "x" in the box that reflects their score at each hour increment. Then participants can connect the "x's" to produce their energy profile in the form of a plot. See Figure 12.2 for an example of what this plot should look like.

Once participants have plotted their energy profiles, they are then asked to answer three questions. First, when during the course of their day did their energy tend to be the highest? What were they doing at those times? Second, when during the course of their day did their energy tend to be the lowest? What were they doing at those times? Finally, as participants observe the things they were doing when their energy was the highest and the things they were doing when their energy was most depleted, what new insights do they now have about how to better manage their energy?

The idea here is to help employees see which energy management practices they may already be using to regulate their energy during their workday. If they see patterns regarding what they are doing each time their energy is high, then perhaps they can find ways to integrate more of those activities into their workday, especially if they notice regular times in their energy profile when their energy is low (such as right after lunch or right after a task requiring high concentration). If they see patterns regarding activities they tend to be doing when their energy is low, then perhaps they can find ways to reduce the frequency of those activities during their usual workday. It may even be that some of those low energy activities can be delegated to others who might find those activities more energizing. These are all examples of job crafting (Berg, Wrzesniewski, & Dutton, 2010) in which individuals make small changes in their work tasks, responsibilities, or relationships to make their job more fulfilling.

The last step of the energy audit is to identify one or two energy management interventions (see Appendix D). The idea in this last step is to ask employees to make a commitment to a behavioral change to create a habit for better energy management. Participants can select among physical, emotional, mental, or spiritual

## Energy Audit Worksheet

Plot your energy levels on the following graph so you can track your energy across the course of the day.
Hours slept previous night: 6 hours

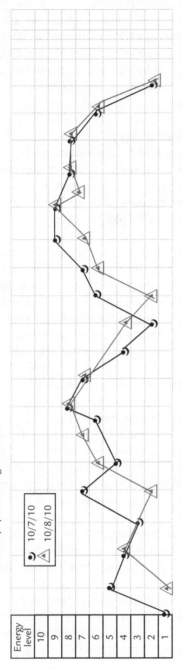

| Energy level | | | | | | | | | | | | | | | | | | |
|---|---|---|---|---|---|---|---|---|---|---|---|---|---|---|---|---|---|---|

Legend: ● 10/7/10 △ 10/8/10

Energy levels: 10, 9, 8, 7, 6, 5, 4, 3, 2, 1

| Time | 9am | 10am | 11am | 12am | 1pm | 2pm | 3pm | 4pm | 5pm | 6pm | 7pm | 8pm | 9pm | 10pm | 11pm | 12pm | 1am | 2am | 3am |
|---|---|---|---|---|---|---|---|---|---|---|---|---|---|---|---|---|---|---|---|

### When was your energy the highest? What were you doing at those times?

My energy was the highest towards the evening when I was with my roommate and friends getting ready to go out.

### When was your energy the lowest? What were you doing at those times?

My energy was lowest when I was getting up/going to bed and right after eating a meal. I tend to get sleepy after eating a really filling meal.

### What new insights do you have about how to better manage your energy?

Don't try to do non-stimulating tasks immediately after lunch.

**Figure 12.2.**
Energy audit energy plotting.

interventions listed on the worksheet or come up with one of their own. The hope is to create a new habit that will help create more energy or reduce experiences that deplete energy.

## PRACTICAL IMPLICATIONS

In this chapter we provided some empirical evidence regarding how sleep is related to human energy. Specifically, in Study 1 we found that sleep can be described as a physical energy management strategy that indeed is associated with employees' sense of energy during the day. Thus, our data suggest that sleep can help increase employees' sense of energy at work, something that individual employees as well as work organizations should be reminded off. For example, supervisors should be aware that asking their subordinates to work overtime may reduce opportunities for sufficient sleep, thereby impacting their levels of energy in the short term as well as potentially in the long term.

Furthermore, our results indicate positive relationships between sleep and the different forms of physical energy management strategies (nutrition, taking breaks, exercise), suggesting that the different strategies may positively reinforce each other while fostering employee energy. In other words, sleep can help employees engage in other healthy behaviors while healthy behaviors at the same time may allow for better sleep. These findings are supported by results from Study 2, which indicate that sleep quantity was positively associated with exercise and negatively related to caffeine consumption. Therefore, organizations may benefit from encouraging employees to engage in physical energy management strategies to boost their energy at work. Specifically, supervisors may point to the importance of taking time to eat healthy meals, take breaks, exercise, and get sufficient and restful sleep. Even more so, supervisors may increase the probability of employees engaging in these behaviors by being a positive role model.

Study 1 further indicated positive relationships between sleep and employee mindfulness. Examining the role of mindfulness in employee sleep and energy is a promising avenue for future research. So far, research focusing on mindfulness, sleep, and employee outcomes is still in its infancy, but Hulsheger et al. (2014) provide some evidence that regular mindfulness practices contribute to higher sleep quality. We propose that mindfulness is associated with a mental and physical "down-regulation" that can be achieved through meditation and mindfulness practices (e.g., Kabat-Zinn, 1990), potentially translating into better employee sleep (Allen & Kiburz, 2012). Furthermore, it is possible that sufficient and restful sleep will enhance mindfulness and employee energy during the workday. Work organizations may therefore benefit from providing employees with opportunities to learn and practice mindfulness at work.

Our results further indicate the role of the type of sleep assessment when examining relationships with employee energy at work. Specifically, as discussed earlier, our results suggest that going to bed and getting up at the same time consistently and going to bed and getting up early seem to be more relevant for employee energy than the amount of hours slept. This is helpful information for employees that can be part of sleep hygiene training provided by work organizations. Furthermore, this information can be integrated into the Energy Audit, thereby helping employees monitor and increase their energy throughout the workday.

Finally, our data show relationships between sleep quantity and absenteeism due to illness. This is an important finding for organizations to consider given that employee absenteeism is associated with lost productivity and possibly increased healthcare costs. Therefore, there seem to be direct financial benefits for organizations by ensuring that their employees get sufficient sleep.

We hope that these preliminary cross-sectional findings will spark interest in more rigorous research that can establish causal relationships between sleep, energy management practices, and human energy. Longitudinal or experimental/interventional research would be a step in the right direction. Future research can also track actual sleep patterns rather than focusing on self-reports of sleep that may be less accurate than using sleep monitoring technology. We therefore encourage future research to further establish empirical support for the importance of sleep in enhancing human energy at work and beyond. Future research should also examine how organizational practices and leadership may affect the sleep quality of employees. For example, sleep supportive leadership behaviors such as not expecting employees to be on call at all hours of the day, even virtually, has been shown to contribute to improved sleep quality (Barnes & Spreitzer, 2015).

## NOTES

1. We thank Susan Ashford and Kim Cameron, our colleagues at the Ross School of Business, for their collaboration in collecting the data used in Study 1.
2. Czeisler, C. (2006). Sleep deficit: The performance killer. *Harvard Business Review*, October.
3. Field, A. (2008). Why you need sleep in order to succeed. *Harvard Management Update*, January.
4. Loehr, J., & Schwartz, J. (2001). The making of a corporate athlete. *Harvard Business Review*, January.
5. Schwartz, T., & McCarthy, C. (2007). Manage your energy, not your time. *Harvard Business Review*, October.
6. Rubenstein, J., Meyer, D., & Evans, J. (2001). Executive control of cognitive processes in task switching. *Journal of Experimental Psychology: Human Perception and Performance*, 27(4), 763–787.
7. Schwartz, T., & McCarthy, C. (2007). Manage your energy, not your time. *Harvard Business Review*, October.
8. Gelles. D. (2012). The mind business. *Financial Times*, August 24.
9. Fredrickson, B. (2001). The role of positive emotions in positive psychology: The broaden-and-build theory of positive emotions. *American Psychologist, 56*, 218–226.
10. Danner, D., Snowdon, D, & Friesen, W. (2001). Positive emotion in early life and longevity: Findings from the nun study. *Journal of Personality and Social Psychology, 80*, 804–813.

11. Neuhoff, C. C., & Schaefer, C. (2002). Effects of laughing, smiling, and howling on mood. *Psychological Reports, 91*, 1079–1080.
12. Grant, A. (2013). *Given and take: A revolutionary approach to success.* New York, NY: Penguin Books.
13. Haidt, J. (2000). The Positive emotion of elevation, *Prevention & Treatment, 3*(1).
14. Baker, W., Cross, R., & Parker, A. (2003). What creates energy in organizations? *Sloan Management Review, 44*(Summer), 51–56.
15. http://www.centerforpos.org/the-center/teaching-and-practice-materials/teaching-tools/job-crafting-exercise/.
16. Emmons, R. A., & Crumpler, C.A. (2000). Gratitude as a human strength: Appraising the evidence, *Journal of Social & Clinical Psychology, 19*, 56–69.
17. King, L. (2001). The health benefits of writing about life goals. *Personality and Social Psychology Bulletin, 27*(7), 798–807.

## REFERENCES

Allen, T. D., & Kiburz, K. M. (2012). Trait mindfulness and work–family balance among working parents: The mediating effects of vitality and sleep quality. *Journal of Vocational Behavior, 80*, 372–379. doi:10.1016/j.jvb.2011.09.002

Baker, W., & Bulkey, N. (2014). Paying it forward versus rewarding reputation: Mechanisms of generalized reciprocity. *Organization Science, 25*(5), 1493–1510.

Barnes, C. (2012). Working in our sleep: Sleep and self-regulation in organizations, *Organizational Psychology Review, 2*, 234–257.

Barnes, C., & Spreitzer, G. (2015). Why sleep is a strategic resource. *Sloan Management Review, 56*(2), 19–21.

Barnes, C. M., Wagner, D. T., & Ghumman, S. (2012). Borrowing from sleep to pay work and family: Expanding time-based conflict to the broader nonwork domain. *Personnel Psychology, 65*, 789–819.

Berg, J. M., Wrzesniewski, A., & Dutton, J. E. (2010). Perceiving and responding to challenges in job crafting at different ranks: When proactivity requires adaptivity. *Journal of Organizational Behavior, 31*(2), 158–186.

Bostic T. J., Rubio, D. M., & Hood, M. (2000). A validation of the subjective vitality scale using structural equation modeling. *Social Indicators Research, 52*, 313–324.

Brown, K. W., & Ryan, R. M. (2003). The benefits of being present: Mindfulness and its role in psychological well-being. *Journal of Personality and Social Psychology, 84*, 822–848.

Bruch, H., & Vogel, B. (2011). *Fully Charged: How great leaders boost their organization's energy and ignite high performance.* Boston, MA: Harvard Business School Press.

Dane, E., & Brummel, B. J. (2014). Examining workplace mindfulness and its relations to job performance and turnover intention. *Human Relations, 67*, 105–128.

Dement, W., & Vaughan, C. (1999). *The promise of sleep.* New York: Dell.

Dutton, J. E. (2003a). *Energize your workplace: How to build and sustain high-quality connections at work.* San Francisco, CA: Jossey-Bass Publishers.

Dutton, J. E. (2003b). Fostering high quality connections through respectful engagement. *Stanford Social Innovation Review, Winter*, 54–57.

Fritz, C., Lam, C. F., & Spreitzer, G. M. (2011). It's the little things that matter: An examination of knowledge workers' energy management. *Academy of Management Perspectives, 25*(3), 28–39.

Gallup Corporation. (2013). State of the American Workplace. http://www.gallup.com/strategicconsulting/163007/state-american-workplace.aspx.

Gooley, J., Chamberlain, J., Smith, K., Khalsa, S., Rajaratnam, S., Van Reen, . . . Lockley, S. 2011. Exposure to room light before bedtime suppresses melatonin onset and shortens melatonin duration in humans. *The Journal of Clinical Endocrinology & Metabolism, 96*(3), E463–E472.

Hagger, M. S., Wood, C., Stiff, C., & Chatzisarantis, N. L. D. (2010). Ego depletion and the strength model of self-control: A meta-analysis. *Psychological Bulletin, 136*(4), 495–525.

Hülsheger, U. R., Lang, J. W. B., Depenbrock, F., Fehrmann, C., Zijlstra, F., & Alberts, H. J. E. M. (2014). The power of presence: The role of mindfulness at work for daily levels and change trajectories of psychological detachment and sleep quality. *Journal of Applied Psychology, 99*, 1113–1128.

Johns, G. (2010). Presenteeism in the workplace: A review and research agenda. *Journal of Organizational Behavior, 31*(4), 1099–1379.

Kabat-Zinn, J. (1990). *Full catastrophe living: Using the wisdom of your body and mind to face stress, pain, and illness.* New York, NY: Bantam Dell. doi:10.1037/032287

Loehr, J. (2008). *The power of story: Change your story, change your destiny in business and in life.* New York, NY: Free Press.

Loehr, J., & Schwartz, T. (2003). *The power of full engagement.* New York, NY: Free Press.

Perlow, L. (2012). *Sleeping with your smartphone: How to break the 24/7 habit and change the way you work.* Cambridge, MA: Harvard Business Press.

Pfeffer, J. (2010). Building sustainable organizations: The human factor. *Academy of Management Perspectives, 24*(1), 34–45.

Preckel, F., Lipnevich, A., Schneider, S., & Roberts, R. (2011). Chronotype, cognitive abilities, and academic achievement: A meta-analytic investigation. *Learning and Individual Differences, 21*, 483–492.

Quinn, R., & Dutton, J. E. (2005). Coordination as energy-in-conversation: A process theory of organizing. *Academy of Management Review, 30*, 36–57.

Quinn, R., & Thakor, A. (2014). Imbue the organization with a higher purpose. In J. Dutton & G. Spreitzer (Eds.), *How to be a positive leader.* San Francisco, CA: Berrett-Koehler.

Ryan, R. M., & Frederick, C. M. (1997). On energy, personality and health: Subjective vitality as a dynamic reflection of well-being. *Journal of Personality, 65*, 529–565.

Schwartz, T. (2010). *The way we're working isn't working.* New York, NY: Free Press.

Spreitzer, G. M. (1995). Psychological empowerment in the workplace: Dimensions, measurement, and validation. *Academy of Management Journal, 38*(5), 1442–1465.

Spreitzer, G., & Grant, T. (2012). Helping students manage their energy: Taking their pulse with the energy audit. *Journal of Management Education, 36*(2), 239–263.

Spreitzer, G., and Porath, C. (2012). Creating sustainable performance. *Harvard Business Review, January-February*, 92–99.

Spreitzer, G., Sutcliffe, K., Dutton, J., Sonenshein, S., & Grant, A. M. (2005). A socially embedded model of thriving at work. *Special Issue: Frontiers of Organization Science, 16*, 537–549.

Tankova, I., Adan, A., & Buela-Casal, G. (1994). Circadian typology and individual differences: A review. *Personality and Individual Differences, 16*(5), 671–684.

Thayer, R. E., Newman, R., & McClain, T. M. (1994). Self-regulation of mood: Strategies for changing a bad mood, raising energy, and reducing tension. *Journal of Personality and Social Psychology, 67*, 910–925.

Ton, Z. (2014). *The good jobs strategy: How the smartest companies invest in employees to lower costs and boost profits.* Boston, MA: Houghton Mifflin.

Trougakos, J., Hideg, I., Cheng, B., & Beal, D. (2014). Lunch breaks unpacked: The role of autonomy as a moderator of recovery during lunch. Academy of Management Journal, 48(5), 764–775.

Work and Well-being Survey. (2014). American Psychological Association. http://www.apaexcellence.org/assets/general/2014-work-and-wellbeing-survey-results.pdf

## APPENDIX A

Nutrition

- Eat three meals daily
- Eat two snacks limited to 100–150 calories
- Eat breakfast everyday
- Never go longer than 4 hours without food
- Eat 40% grains, 40% fruits/vegetables, and 20% protein in a typical meal
- Keep the size of protein to no greater than the palm of your hand
- Eat until you are satisfied, not full

## BREAKS

- Routinely move every 30–45 minutes to reduce tension
- Get up and take a break every 90–120 minutes

## SLEEP

- Go to bed early and wake up early
- Go to bed and wake up consistently at the same times
- Get 7–8 hours of sleep each night

## EXERCISE

- Do some form of physical activity daily
- Do at least strength training workouts per week
- Do at least two cardiovascular interval workouts per week
- Push yourself to discomfort when you work out
- Exercise at moderate to high intensity

## APPENDIX B: ENERGY AUDIT ENERGY RATING

Please use the following scale to measure your energy during each waking hour:

    1–2: Very Low
    3–4: Low
    5–6: Neutral
    7–8: High
    9–10: Very High

Use the table below to track in hourly intervals your energy level and what you were doing at each point in time.

| TIME | ENERGY LEVEL | WHAT WERE YOU DOING? |
|------|--------------|----------------------|
|      |              |                      |
|      |              |                      |
|      |              |                      |
|      |              |                      |
|      |              |                      |
|      |              |                      |
|      |              |                      |
|      |              |                      |
|      |              |                      |
|      |              |                      |
|      |              |                      |
|      |              |                      |
|      |              |                      |
|      |              |                      |
|      |              |                      |

## APPENDIX C: PLOTTING YOUR ENERGY PROFILE

*Plotting Your Energy Profile*

**Energy Level**

10

9

8

7

6

5

4

3

2

1

**Time**

## APPENDIX D: ENERGY AUDIT PART 2: ENERGY INTERVENTION WORKSHEET

Now that you have completed the energy audit, it is time to learn how to better mobilize your energy for high performance. Reflect on any patterns you noticed in your energy profile. You might think about how you can (1) do more of something that gives you energy or (2) reduce doing what depletes your energy. Below we provide some evidence-based strategies (using the physical, mental, emotional, or spiritual categories) for increasing your energy.

### PHYSICAL ENERGY INTERVENTIONS

The body is our fundamental source of energy—sleep, nutrition, and exercise are the fuel.

### Sleep

According to Charles Czeisler, a leading sleep researcher at Harvard, "24 hours without sleep or a week of sleeping 4–5 hours induces cognitive impairment equivalent to "being drunk."[2] Sleep deprivation causes slower cognitive and social processing, problems with memory, and difficulty concentrating.[3] Get 7–8 hours of sleep. Go to bed and get up at about the same time each day.

### Nutrition

Always eat breakfast and eat five or six smaller meals to speed up your metabolism. Eat a balanced diet. Reduce empty calories such as sugary snacks and soda. Moderate caffeine and drink more water.[4]

### Exercise

Get active. Exercise to get your heart beating intensely three or four times a week for 20–30 minutes. Engage in strength training at least once a week. Take the stairs. Go for a walk.[5]

### MENTAL ENERGY INTERVENTIONS

Mental energy is about focus and concentration. Some refer to this as executive function.

### Stop Multitasking

Multitasking slows us down, makes us more likely to make mistakes, and increases our risk of health problems.[6] For important tasks that require full attention, avoid distractions by finding a quiet space to work. Turn off your phone and email.

### Take a Break

Not only should you try to take a short break every 90–120 minutes, you can take a mental break from individual tasks by switching to a different task as you feel fatigue.[7]

### Mindfulness

Being more fully present in the moment has been shown to help you focus, make better decisions, feel more connected to others, and reduce stress. More companies offer mindful practices including Google, General Mills, and Aetna.[8]

## EMOTIONAL ENERGY INTERVENTIONS

Create excitement and enthusiasm about what you do each day.

### Be Positive

Positive emotions can "undo" negative emotions and be the building blocks of resilience that combats physical illness.[9] People who report more positive emotions live longer and healthier lives.[10] Both smiling and laughter have been found to boost your mood.[11] Check out more proven ideas for creating positive emotions at http://www.happinessprojecttoolbox.com/.

### Help Someone

It is better to give than receive. At least this is true for helping others.[12] You can offer to assist a friend or co-worker with a task. Hold open a door or give a genuine compliment. Pass along a resource you know someone has an interest in. It is even contagious when others witness an act of kindness.[13] Download the "Do Good" app for your I-phone. It was developed by Michigan undergrads.

## Spend More Time with Energizers

Energy (positive or negative) can be contagious.[14] So seek out interactions with those who are positive energizers and minimize those who sap your energy through "job crafting."[15]

## SPIRITUAL ENERGY INTERVENTIONS

Your spirit provides a powerful source of motivation, determination, and intensity in your everyday life.

## Show Gratitude

Keep a gratitude journal—write down three things you are grateful for at the end of each day. Even better, write a gratitude letter to someone who has made a difference to you. Research has shown that gratitude is associated with better life satisfaction and increased social support and may help prevent stress and depression.[16]

## Reinforce Meaning

Writing about what's meaningful in your life for 20 minutes a day can increase well-being and health. Think about your life goals and write them down.[17] Or write about what is meaningful in your daily life—what matters most to you. If you have a faith tradition, consider adding more prayer into your everyday life.

**What Single Intervention(s) Can You Commit to Doing for the Next Week?** Be as specific as you can in terms of who, what, where, when, and why. Try to select something that is out of your normal pattern of activity.

CHAPTER 13

# Management Educators Are Asleep at the Wheel

*Integrating the Topic of Sleep into Management Education*

CHRISTOPHER M. BARNES, MAARTJE E. SCHOUTEN,
AND EVELYN VAN DE VEEN

**MANAGEMENT EDUCATORS ARE ASLEEP AT THE WHEEL:
INTEGRATING THE TOPIC OF SLEEP INTO MANAGEMENT
EDUCATION**

Many employees are not getting sufficient amounts of sleep. One large-scale representative study in the United States indicates that 29.9% of survey respondents had less than 6 hours of sleep the previous night (Luckhaupt, Tak, & Calvert, 2010). A growing literature is uncovering a variety of negative effects of sleep deprivation, such as cognitive errors, poor performance, distorted risk analyses, and negative interpersonal behavior (for reviews, see Harrison & Horne, 2000; Lim & Dinges, 2010; Pilcher & Huffcutt, 1996). As noted by Barnes (2012), this topic has recently crossed over into the management literature. In the past few years, management researchers have empirically linked a lack of sleep to work outcomes including deviant behavior (Christian & Ellis, 2011), unethical behavior (Barnes, Schaubroeck, Huth, & Ghumman, 2011), cyberloafing at work (Wagner, Barnes, Lim, & Ferris, 2012), workplace injuries (Barnes & Wagner, 2009), poor work attitudes (Scott & Judge, 2006), and problems with concentration, organization, and patience (Swanson et al., 2011). Moreover, a lack of sleep has been linked to lowered creative and innovative thinking, a lowered ability to incorporate new information into action plans (Harrison & Horne, 1999), and poorer processes in work teams (Barnes & Hollenbeck, 2009). These are highly relevant outcomes in an increasingly dynamic society in which work is often organized in teams.

Despite this prevalence of employees working on insufficient levels of sleep, and the litany of negative outcomes associated with this, management education largely ignores the issue of sleep. Sleep is a topic that is almost totally ignored in management textbooks, management case studies, classroom activities, and other tools associated with management curricula. This oversight is problematic, given that ignoring the issue of sleep results in a failure to prevent many of the negative outcomes associated with people working with insufficient amounts of sleep. Recent articles (Barnes, 2011; Caldwell, 2012; Caldwell, Caldwell, & Schmidt, 2008) provide an initial framework for helping management educators understand the issues surrounding sleep—including how to manage employees who may not get enough sleep. However, it is important that management educators take this further, by advancing their tools for management education about sleep issues and by increasing the amount of attention devoted to this topic in management programs. It is the responsibility of management educators to develop the best possible leaders. Such leaders understand at a concrete level that sleep deprivation has a negative impact on short-term and long-term performance and employee well-being.

Accordingly, the purpose of this chapter is twofold. First, we advocate for management education to include content on sleep and its relevance to the workplace. Second, we provide recommendations about the ways in which management educators can utilize this literature to add value to the education of management students. This includes suggestions for how to most effectively teach this topic, which calls for a pedagogical approach geared toward dealing with existing misconceptions and one that deviates from more traditional pedagogical approaches.

## EMPLOYEES WORKING ON SHORT SLEEP: A CLOSER LOOK

One reason that management education has fallen short on the topic of sleep is that managers and management educators likely underestimate the prevalence of employees working while short on sleep. Recently, sleep physiologists have allocated considerable resources to investigating the prevalence of short sleep in a variety of people and contexts. Luckhaupt and colleagues (2010) conducted an analysis of a large-scale National Institute of Health survey of Americans. They found that among civilians who were employed, 29.9% averaged less than 6 hours of sleep per night. This was especially prevalent for managers, of whom 40.5% slept on average less than 6 hours per night. Swanson and colleagues (2011) conducted an analysis of the Sleep in America study of employed individuals working at least 30 hours per week, and found that 26% of participants reported difficulty falling asleep a few nights per week or more, 42% reported frequent awakenings at night a few nights per week or more, and 29% reported extreme sleepiness or falling asleep at work in the past month. Thus, it appears that many Americans sleep so little that they actually fall asleep at work. Other studies show similar results in Great Britain (Groeger, Zijlstra, & Dijk, 2004), Finland (Salminen et al., 2010), and Korea (Joo et al., 2009; Park et al., 2010).

Although historically absent from the management literature, the sleep physiology literature has a rich body of research examining the effects of low levels of sleep (cf. Harrison & Horne, 2000). Recently, management and applied psychology scholars have devoted an increasing amount of research attention to the topic as well. These literatures provide a considerable foundation of knowledge on the effects of working while short on sleep that can be integrated into management education. The effects of sleep deprivation can be broadly divided into effects on motor functioning (e.g., work injuries, response times), cognitive functioning (e.g., risk analysis, creative thinking), and affect (e.g., job satisfaction, mood).

Barnes (2012) and Mullins, Cortina, Drake, and Dalal (2014) summarize much of this literature, drawing from sleep physiology as well as management and applied psychology. A partial list of the effects of lost sleep and poor quality sleep on employee outcomes includes poor self-control, high levels of unethical behavior, cyberloafing, social loafing, and work injuries, as well as low levels of motivation, effort, organizational citizenship behavior, work engagement, and task performance. As Barnes (2012) notes, the variety of effects of a lack of sleep can occur even when missing small amounts of sleep. Going a single night without sleep (Harrison & Horne, 1999), missing a few hours of sleep in a given night (Christian & Ellis, 2011), missing 40 minutes in a single night (Barnes & Wagner, 2009), or restricting sleep to 5 hours a night for 4 consecutive nights (Elmenhorst et al., 2009) can elicit the negative effects of a lack of sleep. In other words, levels of sleep that are quite common among employees will lead to the cognitive, affective, and behavioral outcomes noted in this section.

Moreover, the effects of lost sleep accumulate over time. Researchers use the term "sleep debt" to highlight this effect, noting the clear effects of sleep debt on individual functioning (Banks, Van Dongen, Maislin, & Dinges, 2010; Rupp, Wesensten, & Balkin, 2010). Thus, even if an employee had a full night of sleep on a given night, a short night the previous night can have carryover effects that hinder the employee on that day. What makes this especially dangerous is that people often do not realize that they are impaired by a lack of sleep (Dorrian et al., 2003), or may even outright deny that a lack of sleep hinders their work (Helmreich, 2000; Zeitlin, 1995).

The effects of a lack of sleep mentioned throughout this book have been widely studied across the fields of management and applied psychology. Moreover, many of them, such as job satisfaction, decision making, motivation, affect, conflict, and working in teams, are core to even introductory Organizational Behavior courses. Neglecting the topic of sleep in management education would mean neglecting a driver of important effects in the workplace.

## Solutions for Managers

The literature makes it clear that it is very common for people to work on short sleep, that working on short sleep creates a multitude of problems, and that organizations are often the source of the problem. Therefore, it is imperative that we as management educators seek and disseminate solutions to these issues. There are at least four articles that provide guidance on this topic. Caldwell and colleagues (2008) and Caldwell (2012) provide recommendations for managing fatigue and sleepiness that focus primarily on aviators and other vigilance-based occupations. Barnes (2011) provides similar recommendations, focusing on the context of management. Barnes and Spreitzer (2015) provide suggestions for senior level managers in managing the sleep of their employees. By providing a broad set of recommendations for managing employees who are short on sleep, management educators can give future managers a set of tools that they can use in their specific contexts. Not every tool will work in every context, but managers can match their strategy to the constraints of their work environment. In the following section, we discuss some of these strategies.

Barnes (2011) organizes these into prevention-based strategies and mitigation-based strategies. Prevention strategies aim to avoid situations in which employees are working on low levels of sleep by increasing the amount of sleep that they get, whereas mitigation strategies aim to minimize the negative effects of sleepy employees. Prevention strategies draw largely from the recommendations of Caldwell et al. (2008) about work schedules, including limiting shift lengths, keeping regular work schedules (rather than rotating schedules), and scheduling work to coincide with portions of the circadian rhythm that are high in alertness. Caldwell (2012) recommends going a step beyond this and actively assessing fatigue. Sleep can be measured objectively with actigraph devices worn on the wrist (van de Water, Holmes, & Hurley, 2011) or through sleep diaries (Monk, Buysee, Rose, Hall, & Kupfer, 2000). Computer models such as the Fatigue Avoidance Scheduling Tool use sleep and waking activity schedule data to estimate task effectiveness at a given moment (Hursh et al., 2004). By assessing or estimating how impaired an employee might be, a manager can make a more informed decision about task assignment. As Barnes (2011) recommends, tasks requiring creativity and especially critical tasks should not be assigned to sleepy employees. Thus, one way to avoid the issue of having sleepy employees engaged in these tasks is to assign the tasks to other more rested employees.

An additional prevention strategy provided by Barnes (2011) is to schedule slack personnel resources. Although slack personnel resources increase payroll costs, they provide a buffer against sudden increases in work demands that may occur from unexpected increases in product orders, sudden crises in organizations, or other issues that may leave a work staff conducting a greater than normal level of work. Slack personnel resources can help ensure that employees do not work extended shifts that cut into sleep. In addition, they provide managers with flexibility in how tasks are assigned to personnel, such that creative or critical tasks are not assigned to sleepy employees. Without slack personnel resources, managers have fewer degrees of freedom in task assignment decisions.

Another prevention strategy intended to aid the sleep of employees is to decrease work-related stress (Barnes, 2011; Caldwell et al., 2008). Work-related stress and anxiety undermine employee sleep (Wagner, Barnes, & Scott, 2014). Addressing this would be a natural way to increase the amount of sleep for employees. Designing jobs to have lower cognitive or emotional demands and decreasing workload would likely decrease stress and thus ameliorate sleep difficulties associated with stress. Interpersonal sources of stress, such as injustice and incivility, have been linked to difficulties sleeping (Greenberg, 2006; Niedhammer, David, Degioanni, Drummond, & Philip, 2009). Generating and following fair organizational policies should help minimize the occurrence of workplace injustice. Workplace incivility can be decreased either through training (Leiter, Laschinger, Spence, Day, & Oore, 2011) or through hiring/firing decisions, and should result in lower levels of stress.

One prevention-focused training intervention that can help to maximize employee sleep is to educate employees about proper sleep hygiene (Caldwell et al., 2008). Sleep hygiene refers to the behaviors and context associated with falling and staying asleep (Mastin, Bryson, & Corwyn, 2006). Research indicates that poor sleep hygiene leads to difficulties sleeping (Gellis & Lichstein, 2009; Mindell, Meltzer, Carskadon, & Chervin, 2009). Caldwell et al. (2008) provide specific advice regarding sleep hygiene: use consistent bedtimes and wake times; use the bedroom for sleep and sex only (no television, reading, or smartphone use); exercise, but not within at least a few hours of bedtime; avoid caffeine late in the day and in the evening; do not use alcohol as a sleep aid; and do not use nicotine near bedtime.

Naps are a hybrid tool that can be used either to prevent sleepiness or to treat it as it occurs, but are generally used to mitigate the effects of sleepiness after the fact (Barnes, 2011). Recent narrative and quantitative reviews indicate the efficacy of naps in aiding performance in a variety of tasks (Driskell & Mullen, 2005; Milner & Cote, 2009). This research indicates that the longer the nap, the more restoration occurs. However, long naps increase the odds that the end of the nap will coincide with a portion of the sleep cycle that will leave the naper groggy upon awakening, hindering performance initially. Nevertheless, even short naps can result in significant recovery; Lahl, Wispel, Willigens, and Pietrowsky (2008) found that a 6-minute nap led to significant improvement in declarative memory, as compared to a control condition in which the same amount of time elapsed but no nap occurred. Keeping naps to 30 minutes or less reduces the risk of grogginess upon awakening, while still capturing the benefits of recovery from napping (Barnes, 2011). Nap timing is also important (Caldwell et al., 2008). Generally speaking, naps should be aligned with the nadirs in the circadian rhythm; 3–5 pm and 4:30 am are times that are especially well-suited for a nap, given that people tend to be low in alertness and feeling sleepy in those periods anyway.

Another set of mitigation strategies ties back to scheduling. Caldwell et al. (2008) recommend limiting the amount of time spent on tasks for an individual working while sleepy. Providing frequent breaks will help employees stay fresher than they otherwise would be. Barnes (2011) recommends rotating tasks among employees to achieve a similar effect. Task rotation will not allow for recovery, but will decrease monotony that can push sleepy people into falling asleep. Barnes (2011) also recommends scheduling tasks to be conducted by groups. Ideally, at least one person in the group will be able to detect errors in the work of the sleepier team members. Moreover, rested members can engage in backing up behavior to help sleepy members finish their tasks (Barnes, Hollenbeck, Wagner, Nahrgang, & Schwind, 2008). Scheduling sleepy employees to conduct work in teams adds a layer of complexity (Barnes & Hollenbeck, 2009), but can provide opportunities for team members to collaborate with team members or leaders to improve their declining performance.

A final strategy for mitigating the effects of lost sleep is the use of pharmaceutical aids (Caldwell et al., 2008). Caffeine is the most commonly used pharmaceutical aid. Research indicates that caffeine, modafinil, and dextroamphetamine can each partly offset some of the negative effects of lost sleep (Killgore et al., 2008). However, there are important limitations to this strategy. These substances may have effects that persist longer than the desired period; an individual may consume caffeine to stay awake for an hour or two remaining in a work shift, but then have difficulty falling asleep for multiple hours thereafter. Long-term use of these substances can create dependency issues. Finally, usage of these aids masks the problem of insufficient sleep, which may lower the possibility of having the employee address the more important underlying issue of why he or she is not sleeping enough. Nevertheless, in certain contexts, especially those in which people may be harmed if an employee makes a mistake, aids such as caffeine can be effective when used strategically.

Beyond these specific prevention and mitigation strategies, Barnes and Spreitzer (2015) recommend creating an organizational culture that values sleep. This is done both explicitly, through leader statements, and more tacitly, through the examples set by senior managers and other leaders. Creating a norm for immediately responding to emails sent at 3 am is sure to shape an organization's culture in a manner that devalues and deprioritizes sleep; managers should seek to do the opposite.

The recommended workplace tactics here are the best currently available, but they provide a limited set of options that might not be practical in all contexts. Examples of such limitations could be a limited amount of control over day-to-day assignments, environmental pressures not to schedule slack personnel resources, or norms regarding napping in the office. Below we highlight contexts in which the recommended tactics might be more or less useful.

For example, in times of economic hardship, freeing up already limited resources to hire "extra" personnel might provoke resistance from stockholders and other stakeholders of the organization. However, if this were instigated during periods of growth, perhaps companies might be better able to deal with changes in demands and ultimately function better. Similarly, if there are strong norms against taking naps during work time in an organization, this recommendation might not be well received. There are examples of organizations—especially international governmental organizations—that already have implemented the availability of so-called "nap rooms" to accommodate international travelers.

With regard to scheduling issues, the suggestions are especially useful for organizations that do not operate on a 24-hour cycle. But they might also help organizations that do operate on a 24-hour cycle, such as hospitals or some production companies, to make smarter scheduling decisions. Organizations not operating on a 24-hour cycle will have the flexibility to commence work at different times during the day, thus accommodating varying circadian rhythms. However, even if organizations are constrained by their 24-hour cycle, paying attention to circadian rhythms and the time it takes to adjust to new sleep patterns might enable managers to limit shift lengths to 8 hours, start work shifts at smarter times, and rotate the shifts at a slower pace.

Although it is unlikely that managers can mandate employees to wear an actigraph device or keep a sleep diary, making the issue of sleep deprivation open for discussion, potentially with data to back up an employee's story, could enhance feelings of trust and psychological safety that may enable an employee to voice his or her limitations when sleep loss has occurred (Detert & Burris, 2007). If this topic is approached in a positive manner as a means of improving the quality of life of the employee, it is bound to be better received than a forceful approach.

As much work in contemporary organizations is organized around team efforts, rotating tasks might be especially worth considering for teams that are low in skill differentiation—"the degree to which members have specialized knowledge or functional capacities to make it more or less difficult to substitute members" (Hollenbeck, Beersma, & Schouten, 2012, p. 84)—because these team members often share the same knowledge with which they can complete tasks. However, in teams with high skill differentiation, task rotation might not be practical as the skills and knowledge of each team member are different.

Second, with regard to the sleepy team leaders mentioned earlier, leadership and power could be shared depending on the level of fatigue of the team member. Shared leadership is a team property whereby leadership is distributed among team members rather than focused on a single designated leader (Carson, Tesluk, & Marronne, 2007; Pearce & Sims, 2002). This concept of shared leadership has received much attention recently and one of the great benefits of sharing leadership in teams is that the team members are more proactive and more engaged in the decision making of the team (Wang, Waldman, & Zhang, 2014). This means that mistakes can be caught by multiple members. One sleepy team leader, or even a sleepy team member in a self-managed team, might have less of an impact on the team performance when there are checks and balances within the team.

In a related recent study, Aime, Humphrey, DeRue, and Paul (2014) discuss the benefit of shifting power among team members. This is different from shared leadership as this is specifically not about sharing responsibility between members, but about shifting responsibility to the most appropriate team member for that portion of the task. Under such a team structure, decision-making responsibility may be shifted away from the sleepy team member toward a more well-rested one. However, in teams high in authority differentiation, sharing leadership or shifting power among team members will probably not result in the desirable effects because of the differentiation in decision-making responsibility among team members. This could result in a situation in which a well-rested team member low in the team hierarchy needs to take over the work of the team leader, without having actual authority to make any decisions. Moreover, this could upset the existing hierarchy in the team resulting in competition for higher positions in the team, which is generally associated with poor team outcomes (Bendersky & Hays, 2012; Greer & Van Kleef, 2010).

It is possible that the context of a given organization will limit the degree to which any of these strategies are feasible. However, by providing a menu of options, management educators can arm future managers with the capability of selecting the set of solutions that is most practical in their context. One of the responsibilities of management education is to teach students to be critical and creative in their assessment of problems and solutions (Baker & Baker, 2012). One of the hallmarks of critical assessment and creative problem solving is to have the appropriate knowledge to assess the situation (Amabile, 1996). Thus, it is the responsibility of management education to offer the content on which to base these decisions. When management students become managers, they need to be able to recognize not only the cause and the effect, but also be able to choose the best solution from a menu of options most appropriate for the situation.

## STRATEGIES FOR MANAGEMENT EDUCATION

The sections above clearly indicate that the management literature provides useful guidance for managers with regard to the topic of sleep. It is disappointing that this content is not currently included in management education. This is especially problematic given the aim of most business schools to develop leaders, both through their undergraduate as well as their graduate education. Leaders typically have the greatest ability to address the causes of sleep loss in the workplace. Therefore, the first aim of management education related to sleep should be to enhance the understanding of the effects of sleep loss on the bottom line functioning of a company, be it through increased injuries and turnover, lowered motivation and creativity, or increased levels of conflict in teams.

The second aim of management education should be to understand the workplace-related causes of sleep loss, such as shift cycles and stress, in order to effectively tackle these causes. In addition, an understanding of these causes of lost sleep will give managers the opportunity to intervene in a manner that improves employee sleep and therefore improves employee effectiveness. The final aim of management education should be to enable students to effectively understand, evaluate, and apply relevant workplace tactics to prevent or mitigate the effects of sleep loss. First and foremost, this requires knowledge about sleep deprivation, but second, this requires the ability to think creatively and independently rather than to accept solutions at face value (Baker & Baker, 2012). As the literature on sleep and management grows, management educators have the opportunity to address the historically neglected topic of sleep in a scientifically grounded manner. Beyond developing better leaders, teaching students about the topic of sleep might result in the additional benefit of having them apply it to their own lives immediately. As sleep deprivation affects processes such as memory (Walker & Stickgold, 2006), effort, and motivation (Baranski, Cian, Esquievie, Pigeau, & Raphel, 1998;

Engle-Friedman et al., 2003), a well-rested management student might also be a better performer in the classroom.

The goals of getting students to understand and appreciate the importance of sleep in the context of work may actually be the most difficult. Most people have a general understanding at the abstract level that they feel worse and probably perform worse when they are short on sleep than when they are well rested. However, despite this general understanding, the data clearly indicate that people often do not apply this abstract idea to concrete behavior in their everyday lives; people often either decide explicitly—or implicitly through their behavioral choices—that sleep is less important than other activities in their lives (Barnes, Wagner, & Ghumman, 2012). Thus, although it is essential to educate students to a point at which they can answer on an examination that a lack of sleep leads to poor performance, cognitive errors, and decrements in mood, this alone will likely be insufficient to change how they manage issues surrounding sleep.

Students need to understand on a more concrete level how this applies to the choices they make in their lives and in the context of their future jobs. They need to understand that even small amounts of lost sleep impact employees and organizations in significant ways. They need to understand that attitudes about sleep being "only for the weak," ideas that caffeine is the cure for lost sleep, or shared beliefs that dedicated workers should be willing to trade sleep for work are dangerous for employees and organizations. Such beliefs will typically cause much more harm than good. Students need to understand how their job demands and supervisors may push them to cut into their sleep, and that they will face temptations to trade the short-term benefits of working when they should be sleeping for the cumulative and often longer-term costs of sleep deprivation. A reasonable analogy is hand washing for medical personnel; telling medical personnel that they really should wash their hands often is much less effective in eliciting actual hand washing behavior than is a focus on real world outcomes of hand washing and how it aids the health and well-being of patients (Grant & Hofmann, 2011).

Once students appreciate the importance of sleep for work outcomes, it is important to give them tools to address the issue. We should educate them on both how to prevent sleep loss in the first place as well as how to mitigate the effects of sleep loss after they have occurred. This perspective will allow these future managers to take action on the issues rather take than a fatalistic view. Recent summaries provide an overview of the research literature that should offer helpful tools in addressing these two goals (Barnes, 2012; Harrison & Horne, 2000; Lim & Dinges, 2010). Practitioner-focused articles provide guidance both for what happens when people are short on sleep and for what managers can do to manage employees who are short on sleep (Barnes, 2011; Barnes & Spreitzer, 2015; Caldwell, 2012; Caldwell et al., 2008). This content gives educators the information they need to convey the causes, effects, and prevalence of employees working on low levels of sleep, as well as what managers can do about these issues. Thus, the time is ripe to integrate the topic of sleep into management education.

An obvious way to include the topic of sleep in management education is to include it as a topic in management textbooks and lectures. However, we argue that the strong misconceptions surrounding this topic as detailed above require a specific pedagogical approach that goes above and beyond inclusion in textbooks and lectures, with teachable moments created before new knowledge is taught. Teachable moments arise spontaneously or can be created on purpose to confront people with the limitations of their currently held views and as a result enhance their willingness and ability to learn. Research on learning shows that people need to encounter the limits or the incorrectness of their initial idea before they are able to fully incorporate the new idea (Bransford, Brown, & Cocking, 2000). However, this finding is still rarely applied in actual teaching practice. Many educators are unaware of this principle, and even if they are aware of it, they tend to think that it is enough to simply inform students that their view is wrong, rather than devising a way in which students are really confronted with this discovery.

One of the great benefits of teachable moments is that they strongly encourage double-loop learning in which both the underlying assumptions are challenged as well as the resultant actions (compared to single-loop learning in which only the actions are changed without modification of the underlying assumptions; Argyris, 2002). The topic of sleep is surrounded by many prejudices that predominantly advocate that those who forego sleep in favor of work are better employees and that sleeping healthy amounts is for the weak. Furthermore, people have strong misconceptions about the immediacy of the effects of sleep loss. To address these prejudices and misconceptions, people need to be confronted in some way with the incorrectness of their ideas—it is not enough to simply tell them. This again is associated with the concept of creating "teachable moments." Thus, we advocate a pedagogical approach that revolves around creating powerful teachable moments targeted at the central misconceptions mentioned above.

A sleep audit[1] paired with an in-class discussion to compare experiences would be one way to create such a teachable moment. As an educational exercise, management students can keep a diary of their sleep over the period of a week or two. At a minimum, this can help make salient the fact that they often end up trading sleep for other activities; this awareness can help them make more purposeful choices. A more ambitious version of the exercise would entail including other measures, such as their mood at the time of each diary entry, or even having them engage in a cognitive task that can be objectively scored. Another option would be to have students note in each entry why they slept the amount indicated; this might make it clear that they chose to stay up late studying (or engaging in various social events), or that stress made it hard to sleep. The more the sleep audit ties into their personal lives, the more effective it will be in personalizing the topic of sleep. If the sleep audit is paired with an in-class discussion students are given the opportunity to convince each other of the effects of sleep (loss) and to be aware of more than just their own experiences. A limitation to the sleep audit is that it may not confer the direct experience of negative effects as it strongly depends on the student's circumstances during the audit.

Another option to create a teachable moment would be to give a quiz on the assumptions about sleep deprivation in class. This is a more cognitive and less experiential exercise, but it will challenge many assumptions. A simple set of multiple choice or true/false questions will give students an opportunity to voice their currently held assumptions, essentially tapping their lay theories of sleep. Some examples are "Most people do not actually need 8 hours of sleep to perform at their best," "Missing 40 minutes of sleep on a single night will not significantly impact work the next day," and "People's ability to assess risks is not impaired by sleep loss." These statements are false, as indicated by the research literature. To the degree that students get any or all of these questions wrong, their assumptions will be called into question. This should leave them more open to appreciating the topic of sleep and sleep-related content that management educators provide.

After students' assumptions have been challenged in this way, we suggest teaching the relevant content in more traditional ways, with a combination of textbooks, lectures, and case studies. Currently, sleep is almost completely ignored in management textbooks. Although we would be excited to see a stand-alone section on sleep in popular management textbooks, this may not be realistic the given other demands on management curricula. However, sleep could be integrated with other material in sections that have ties to sleep. We think there are several such topics that are both commonly covered in management textbooks and that link well to the topic of sleep, including, affect, work attitudes, motivation, stress, work design, decision making, safety and well-being, ethics, creativity, leadership, and teams. To fully get the message across concerning both how important and how tricky the topic of sleep is for managers, we would recommend that students are able to apply their knowledge in a simulation of a company that struggles with sleep deprivation and its effects and causes. Ideally this would reveal the difficulties they will experience as a manager in scheduling employees for long shifts, scheduling employees for night shifts, and minimizing slack personnel resources. Short-term financially oriented goals will push students to squeeze maximum labor from the minimum number of employees in a cost-effective manner, despite the fact that this will often result in work schedules that create sleep problems.

## CONCLUSIONS

Management educators have remained silent about the topic of sleep for too long. However, the time is ripe to end that silence. There is a growing scientific basis in the management literature from which to draw, both to understand the issues surrounding sleep and to actively manage them. There is a growing zeitgeist in the popular press about sleep evidenced by many recent reports regarding sleep on outlets such as CNN, the *Wall Street Journal*, and the *New York Times*. Management educators should harness this interest in the topic and include the topic of sleep in management education. Anything less is irresponsible, and will lead us to produce future managers who harm the performance of their organization and the well-being of their employees.

This chapter focused on the existing literature on the effects, causes, and workplace strategies relevant for sleep deprivation that can be found in the work domain. However, we recognize that other effects, causes, and strategies for sleep deprivation exist outside of the work domain. Work–family conflict, family demands (e.g., a sick child), and household demands (Barnes et al., 2012) can all in various ways be causes for and can be affected by sleep deprivation, whereas recovery activities such as exercise and relaxation can prevent sleep loss outside of the workplace (Sonnentag, Binnewies, & Mojza, 2008). Throughout the chapter we have created explicit linkages to management education in order to highlight why and how the topic of sleep should be included in management education. Finally, we provide suggestions for a specific pedagogical approach especially geared toward challenging existing assumptions. However, one article with a few suggestions from a few authors is only a start. Management textbook authors should consider including sleep content in their work. Case study authors should consider designing cases in which sleep is a relevant issue. Other management educators should collaboratively develop and test teaching strategies that will help meet the goals of having management students understand and appreciate the issues surrounding sleep, and give them the tools to manage these issues. Through these cumulative efforts, we can add tremendous value to the education of management students, which will eventually benefit a broad range of organizations and employees. We should begin these efforts now.

## NOTE

1. This idea is analogous to the Energy Audit exercise conducted by Gretchen Spreitzer at the University of Michigan.

## REFERENCES

Aime, F., Humphrey, S., DeRue, D. S., & Paul, J. B. (2014). The riddle of heterarchy: Power transitions in cross-functional teams. *Academy of Management Journal, 57*, 327–352.

Amabile, T. M. (1996). *Creativity in context.* Boulder, CO: Westview Press.

Argyris, C. (2002). Double-loop learning, teaching, and research. *Academy of Management Learning & Education, 1*, 206–218.

Baker, D. F., & Baker, S. J. (2012). To catch a sparkling glow: A canvas for creativity in the management classroom. *Academy of Management Learning & Education, 11*, 704–721.

Banks, S., van Dongen, H. P. A., Maislin, G., & Dinges, D. F. (2010). Neurobehavioral dynamics following chronic sleep restriction: Dose response effects of one night for recovery. *Sleep, 33*, 1013–1026.

Baranski, J. V., Cian, C., Esquievie, D., Pigeau, R. A., & Raphel, C. (1998). Modafinil during 64 hr of sleep deprivation: Dose-related effects on fatigue, alertness, and cognitive performance. *Military Psychology, 10*, 173–193.

Barnes, C. M. (2011). I'll sleep when I'm dead: Managing those too busy to sleep. *Organizational Dynamics, 40*, 18–26.

Barnes, C. M. (2012). Working in our sleep: Sleep and self-regulation in organizations. *Organizational Psychology Review, 2*, 234–257. doi:10.1177/2041386612450181

Barnes, C. M., & Hollenbeck, J. R. (2009). Sleep deprivation and teams: Burning the midnight oil or playing with fire? *Academy of Management Review, 34*, 56–66.

Barnes, C. M., Hollenbeck, J. R., Wagner, D. T., DeRue, D. S., Nahrgang, J. D., & Schwind, K. M. (2008). Harmful help: The costs of backing up behavior in teams. *Journal of Applied Psychology, 93*, 529–539. doi:10.1037/0021-9010.93.3.529

Barnes, C. M., Schaubroeck, J. M., Huth, M., & Ghumman, S. (2011). Lack of sleep and unethical behavior. *Organizational Behavior and Human Decision Processes, 115*, 169–180. doi:10.1016/j.obhdp.2011.01.009

Barnes, C. M., & Spreitzer, G. (2015). Managing the strategic resource of sleep—The key to human sustainability. *MIT Sloan Management Review, 56*, 19–21.

Barnes, C. M., & Wagner, D. T. (2009). Changing to daylight saving time cuts into sleep and increases workplace injuries. *Journal of Applied Psychology, 94*, 1305–1317. doi:10.1037/a0015320

Barnes, C. M., Wagner, D. T., & Ghumman, S. (2012). Borrowing from sleep to pay work and family: Expanding time-based conflict to the broader non-work domain. *Personnel Psychology, 65*, 789–819. doi:10.1111/peps.12002

Bendersky, C., & Hays, N. A. (2012). Status conflict in groups. *Organization Science, 23*, 323–340.

Bransford, J. D., Brown, A. L., & Cocking, R. R. (2000). *How people learn: Brain, mind, experience, and school*. Washington, DC: National Academy Press.

Caldwell, J. A. (2012). Crew schedules, sleep deprivation, and aviation performance. *Current Directions in Psychological Science, 21*, 85–89.

Caldwell, J. A., Caldwell, J. L., & Schmidt, R. M. (2008). Alertness management strategies for operational contexts. *Sleep Medicine Reviews, 12*, 257–273.

Carson, J. B., Tesluk, P. E., & Marronne, J. A. (2007). Shared leadership in teams: An investigation of antecedent conditions and performance. *Academy of Management Journal, 50*, 1217–1234.

Christian, M. S., & Ellis, A. P. J. (2011). Examining the effects of sleep deprivation on workplace deviance: A self-regulatory perspective. *Academy of Management Journal, 54*, 913–934.

Detert, J. R., & Burris, E. R. (2007). Leadership behavior and employee voice: Is the door really open? *Academy of Management Journal, 50*, 869–884.

Dorrian, J., Lamond, N., Holmes, A. L., Burgess, J. H., Roach, G. D., Fletcher, A., & Dawson, D. (2003). The ability to self-monitor performance during a week of simulated night shifts. *Sleep, 26*, 871–877.

Driskell, J. E., & Mullen, B. (2005). The efficacy of naps as a fatigue countermeasure: A metaanalytic integration. *Human Factors, 47*, 360–377.

Elmenhorst, D., Elmenhorst, E. M., Luks, N., Maass, H., Mueller, E. W., Vejvoda, M., . . . Samel, A. (2009). Performance impairment during four days partial sleep deprivation compared with acute effects of alcohol and hypoxia. *Sleep Medicine, 10*, 189–197.

Engle-Friedman, M., Riela, S., Golan, R., Ventuneac, A. M., Davis, C. M., Jefferson, A., & Major, D. (2003). The effect of sleep loss on next day effort. *Journal of Sleep Research, 12*, 113–124.

Gellis, L. A., & Lichstein, K. L. (2009). Sleep hygiene practices of good and poor sleepers in the United States: An internet-based study. *Behavior Therapy, 40*, 1–9.

Grant, A. M., & Hofmann, D. A. (2011). It's not all about me: Motivating hand hygiene among health care professionals by focusing on patients. *Psychological Science, 22*, 1494–1499.

Greenberg, J. (2006). Losing sleep over organizational injustice: Attenuating insomniac reactions to underpayment inequity with supervisory training in interactional justice. *Journal of Applied Psychology, 91*, 58–69.

Greer, L. L., & Van Kleef, G. A. (2010). Equality versus differentiation: The effects of power dispersion on group interaction. *Journal of Applied Psychology, 95*, 1032–1044.

Groeger, J. A., Zijlstra, F. R. H., & Dijk, D. J. (2004). Sleep quantity, sleep difficulties and their perceived consequences in a representative sample of some 2000 British adults. *Journal of Sleep Research, 13*, 359–371.

Harrison, Y., & Horne, J. A. (1999). One night of sleep loss impairs innovative thinking and flexible decision making. *Organizational Behavior and Human Decision Processes, 78*, 128–145.

Harrison, Y., & Horne, J. A. (2000). The impact of sleep deprivation on decision making: A review. *Journal of Experimental Psychology: Applied, 6*, 236–249.

Helmreich, R. L. (2000). Culture and error in space: Implications from analog environments. *Aviation Space and Environmental Medicine, 71*(9, Suppl.), A133–A139.

Hollenbeck, J. R., Beersma, B., & Schouten, M. E. (2012). Beyond team types and taxonomies: A dimensional scaling conceptualization for team description. *Academy of Management Review, 37*, 82–106.

Hursh, S. R., Redmond, D. P., Johnson, M. L., Thorne, D. R., Belenky, G., Balkin, T. J., . . . Eddy, D. R. (2004). Fatigue models for applied research in warfighting. *Aviation Space and Environmental Medicine, 75*, A44–A53.

Joo, S., Baik, I., Yi, H., Jung, K., Kim, J., & Shin, C. (2009). Prevalence of excessive daytime sleepiness and associated factors in the adult population of Korea. *Sleep Medicine, 10*, 182–188.

Killgore, W. D. S., Rupp, T. L., Grugle, N. L., Reichardt, R. M., Lipizzi, E. L., & Balkin, T. J. (2008). Effects of dextroamphetamine, caffeine and modafinil on psychomotor vigilance test performance after 44 h of continuous wakefulness. *Journal of Sleep Research, 17*, 309–321.

Lahl, O., Wispel, C., Willigens, B., & Pietrowsky, R. (2008). An ultra short episode of sleep is sufficient to promote declarative memory performance. *Journal of Sleep Research, 17*, 3–10.

Leiter, M. P., Laschinger, H. K., Day, A., & Oore, D. G. (2011). The impact of civility interventions on employee social behavior, distress, and attitudes. *Journal of Applied Psychology, 96*, 1258–1274.

Lim, J., & Dinges, D. F. (2010). A meta-analysis of the impact of short-term sleep deprivation on cognitive variables. *Psychological Bulletin, 136*, 375–389.

Luckhaupt, S. E., Tak, S., & Calvert, G. M. (2010). The prevalence of short sleep duration by industry and occupation in the National Health Interview Survey. *Sleep, 33*, 149–159.

Mastin, D. F., Bryson, J., & Corwyn, R. (2006). Assessment of sleep hygiene using the sleep hygiene scale. *Journal of Behavioral Medicine, 29*, 223–227.

Milner, C. E., & Cote, K. A. (2009). Benefits of napping in healthy adults: Impact of nap length, time of day, age, and experience with napping. *Journal of Sleep Research, 18*, 272–281.

Mindell, J. A., Meltzer, L. J., Carskadon, M. A., & Chervin, R. D. (2009). Developmental aspects of sleep hygiene: Findings from the 2004 National Sleep Foundation Sleep in America Poll. *Sleep Medicine, 10*, 771–779.

Monk, T. H., Buysse, D. J., Rose, L. R., Hall, J. A., & Kupfer, D. J. (2000). The sleep of healthy people: A daily study. *Chronobiology International, 17*, 49–60.

Mullins, H. M., Cortinia, J. M., Drake, C. L., & Dalal, R. S. (2014). Sleepiness at work: A review and framework of how the physiology of sleepiness impacts the workplace. *Journal of Applied Psychology, 99*, 1096–1112.

Niedhammer, I., David, S., Degioanni, S., Drummond, A., & Phillip, P. (2009). Workplace bullying and sleep disturbances: Findings from a large scale cross-sectional survey in the French working population. *Sleep, 32*, 1211–1219.

Park, S., Cho, M. J., Chang, S. M., Bae, J. N., Jeon, H. J., Cho, S., . . . Hong, J. P. (2010). Relationships of sleep duration with sociodemographic and health-related factors, psychiatric disorders and sleep disturbance in a community sample of Korean adults. *Journal of Sleep Research, 19*, 567–577.

Pearce, C. L., & Sims, H. P. (2002). Vertical versus shared leadership as predictors of the effectiveness of change management teams: An examination of aversive, directive, transactional, transformational, and empowering leader behaviors. *Group Dynamics: Theory, Research, and Practice, 6,* 172–197.

Pilcher, J. J., & Huffcutt, A. I. (1996). Effects of sleep deprivation on performance: A meta-analysis. *Sleep, 19,* 318–326.

Rupp, T. L.,Wesensten, N. J., & Balkin, T. J. (2010). Sleep history affects task acquisition during subsequent sleep restriction and recovery. *Journal of Sleep Research, 19,* 289–297.

Salminen, S., Oksanen, T., Vahtera, J., Sallinen, M., Harma, M., Salo, P., . . . Kivimaki, M. (2010). Sleep disturbances as a predictor of occupational injuries among public sector workers. *Journal of Sleep Research, 19,* 207–213.

Scott, B. A., & Judge, T. A. (2006). Insomnia, emotions, and job satisfaction: A multilevel study. *Journal of Management, 32,* 622–645.

Swanson, L. M., Arnedt, J. T., Rosekind, M. R., Belenky, G., Balkin, T. J., & Drake, C. (2011). Sleep disorders and work performance: Findings from the 2008 National Sleep Foundation Sleep in America Poll. *Journal of Sleep Research, 20,* 487–494.

van de Water, A. T. M., Holmes, A., & Hurley, D. (2011). Objective measurement of sleep for non-laboratory settings as alternatives to polysomnagraphy—a systematic review. *Journal of Sleep Research, 20,* 183–200.

Wagner, D. T., Barnes, C. M., Lim, V., & Ferris, D. L. (2012). Lost sleep and cyberloafing: Evidence from the laboratory and a Daylight Saving Time quasi-experiment. *Journal of Applied Psychology, 97,* 1068–1076. doi:10.1037/a0027557

Wagner, D. T., Barnes, C. M., & Scott, B. A. (2014). Driving it home: How workplace emotional labor harms employee home life. *Personnel Psychology, 67,* 487–516.

Walker, M. P., & Stickgold, R. (2006). Sleep, memory, and plasticity. *Annual Review of Psychology, 57,* 139–166.

Wang, D., Waldman, D. A., & Zhang, Z. (2014). A meta-analysis of shared leadership and team effectiveness. *Journal of Applied Psychology, 99,* 181–198.

Zeitlin, L. R. (1995). Estimates of driver mental workload: A long-term field trial of two subsidiary tasks. *Human Factors, 37,* 611–21.

# AUTHOR BIOGRAPHIES

**Peter Bamberger** is Associate Dean for Research and Professor of Organizational Behavior at the Recanati School of Business Administration, Tel Aviv University, and Research Director of the Smithers Institute, Cornell University. Current research interests include prosocial organizational behavior and occupational health psychology. Recent publications include *Human Resource Strategy* (Routledge, 2014) and *Retirement & the Hidden Epidemic: The Complex Link Between Aging, Work Disengagement and Substance Misuse . . . and What to Do About It* (Oxford University Press, 2014).

**Larissa K. Barber** earned her Ph.D. from Saint Louis University in 2010. She is currently an Assistant Professor in the Social/Industrial-Organizational Psychology program at Northern Illinois University. Her research focuses on the topics of sleep, employee stress and health, personality, and counterproductive work behavior. Her research has been published in a variety of outlets, including the *Journal of Occupational Health Psychology, Stress & Health, Applied Psychology: Health and Well-Being, Organizational Research Methods*, and the *Journal of Organizational Behavior*.

**Julian Barling** is the Borden Chair of Leadership at the Smith School of Business, and author of *The Science of Leadership: Lessons from Research for Organizational Leaders* (Oxford University Press, 2014). His research focuses on the effects of leaders' psychological well-being on the quality of their leadership behaviors and the development of leadership behaviors. He was formerly the editor of the *Journal of Occupational Health Psychology*. He was elected as a Fellow of the Royal Society of Canada in 2002, and is a Fellow of several other international associations.

**Christopher M. Barnes** is an Associate Professor of Management in the Foster School of Business of the University of Washington. He received a Ph.D. in Organizational Behavior from Michigan State University. His research interests focus primarily on the relationship between sleep and work, including both the effects of sleep deprivation on work outcomes as well as the effects of work phenomena on sleep. His research has been published in a variety of top management and applied psychology journals, such as *Academy of Management Journal, Journal of Applied Psychology*, and *Organizational Behavior and Human Decision Processes*. He has also published in the *Journal of Sleep Research*. His research has been covered by media outlets such as *BBC World News, Wall Street Journal, Harvard Business Review, New York Times*, and many others.

**Christopher J. Budnick** is a Ph.D. student in the Social/Industrial-Organizational Psychology program at Northern Illinois University. His research focuses on the topics of social cognition, evaluative situations, self-regulation, and social anxiety. His research has been published in *Anxiety, Stress, & Coping*, and *Journal of Employment Counseling*.

**Rona Cafri** is completing her M.Sc. in Organizational Behavior at the Recanati School of Business Administration, Tel Aviv University. She holds a B.A. in Psychology from the University of Michigan Ann Arbor. Her research focuses on the impact of work on sleep among older adults.

**Erica L. Carleton** received her Ph.D. in Organizational Behavior from the Smith School of Business at Queen's University. Her research interests include: leadership, sleep and well-being. She has received external government funding to conduct her Ph.D. research examining sleep and its impact on leadership and well-being. Erica is currently a post-doctoral fellow at the Ian O. Ihnatowycz Institute for Leadership at the Ivey School of Business, Western University.

**Anne Casper** is a Ph.D. Candidate of Work and Organizational Psychology at the University of Mannheim. She studied Psychology at the University of Jena, Germany and the Pennsylvania State University. Her dissertation focuses on employees' cognitive and behavioral reactions to job stress.

**Philip Cheng**, Ph.D., is a postdoctoral fellow at the Henry Ford Hospital Sleep Disorders and Research Center in Michigan. He received his Ph.D. in clinical psychology from the University of Michigan.

**Tori Crain** is an incoming assistant professor in the Psychology Department at Colorado State University. She received her Ph.D. in industrial/organizational psychology with a minor in occupational health psychology from Portland State University. Her research interests include both positive and negative aspects of the work–nonwork interface, in addition to the interplay among work, nonwork, and sleep.

**Christopher Drake**, Ph.D., is Director of Sleep Research at the Henry Ford Hospital Sleep Disorders and Research Center in Michigan. He is also an Associate Professor of Psychiatry and Behavioral Neurosciences at Wayne State University. Dr. Drake received his Ph.D. in clinical psychology from Bowling Green State University. He is a licensed clinical psychologist and is certified in behavioral sleep medicine.

**Helen S. Driver** obtained a Ph.D. in Physiology from the University of the Witwatersrand, Johannesburg, South Africa and completed a postdoctoral fellowship in Zurich, Switzerland. Her research interest is in women's sleep. She trained in sleep medicine in Canada and manages a sleep disorders laboratory at Kingston General Hospital and Queen's University. From 2008 to 2011 she served as President of the Canadian Sleep Society (CSS) and is a Director of the Board of Registered Polysomnographic Technologists (BRPT).

**Charlotte Fritz,** Ph.D., is an Associate Professor in Industrial and Organizational (I/O) Psychology at Portland State University. Her research focuses on what keeps employees happy, healthy, engaged, and productive. Specifically, she examines phenomena around recovery from work, work–life balance, and interruptions in the workplace. She has published in journals such as the *Journal of Applied Psychology, Journal of Management, Journal of Organizational Behavior,* and the *Journal of Occupational Health Psychology.*

**J. Jeffrey Gish** is a Ph.D. student and graduate teaching fellow in the department of management at the University of Oregon's Lundquist College of Business. Transitioning to academics after several years as a small business owner, his research focuses on the psychological and sociological aspects of entrepreneurship including sleep, status, optimism, and new venture dynamics.

**E. Kevin Kelloway** is the Canada Research Chair in Occupational Health Psychology and a Professor of Psychology at Saint Mary's University. As a prolific researcher, he is a Fellow of the Association for Psychological Science, the Canadian Psychology Association, the International Association for Applied Psychology, and the Society for Industrial-Organizational Psychology.

**Chak Fu Lam** is an assistant professor of Management and Entrepreneurship at Sawyer School of Business of Suffolk University. He graduated with a Ph.D. in Management and Organizations at Ross School of Business of the University of Michigan in 2013. His research focuses on citizenship behaviors and well-being at work. He has published his research in top-tier academic journals, including *Organizational Behavior & Human Decision Processes, Academy of Management Annals, Journal of Applied Psychology,* and *Journal of Personality.* He teaches organizational behavior, negotiation, and cross-cultural management.

**Alistair W. MacLean,** Ph.D., was educated at the University of Aberdeen, Queen's University at Kingston, where he is currently a Professor in the Department of Psychology, and the University of Edinburgh. In addition to clinical work he has carried out research on a number of aspects of sleep. Most of his recent work has been on the effects of sleep loss on performance and, in particular, the effects of prolonged wakefulness on sleepiness and driving performance.

**Anna Sophia Pinck** is a Ph.D. student at the chair of Work and Organizational Psychology of the University of Mannheim, Germany, supervised by Professor Sabine Sonnentag. She studied at the University of Freiburg and the University of Heidelberg. In her research, she investigates the role of mindfulness for well-being and social interactions at the workplace. She is especially interested in the role of leaders.

**Maartje E. Schouten** is a visiting assistant professor of management at Michigan State University's Eli Broad College of Business. She received her Ph.D. in Organizational Behavior from Erasmus University Rotterdam in The Netherlands. Her research examines the roles social hierarchy and theory of mind play in interpersonal and team processes and outcomes.

**Sabine Sonnentag** is a full professor of Work and Organizational Psychology at the University of Mannheim, Germany. Her research addresses the question of how employees can achieve sustainable high job performance and remain healthy at the same time. She studies recovery from job stress, proactive work behavior, and self-regulation at work. In her research she uses a multimethod approach with a strong emphasis on quantitative diary data and within-person analysis.

**Gretchen M. Spreitzer,** Ph.D., is the Keith E. and Valerie J. Alessi Professor of Business Administration at the Ross School of Business at the University of Michigan (RSB). Her research focuses on employee empowerment and leadership development, particularly within a context of organizational change and decline. Her most recent research examines how organizations can enable thriving. This is part of a new movement in the field of organizational behavior known as Positive Organizational Scholarship (www.bus.umich.edu/positive).

**Evelyn van de Veen** trains faculty in the areas of teaching and assessment. She works as an independent trainer for her own company *evandeveen*. Her main concern is translating pedagogical insights into practical advice. She has a degree in Classics from the University of Groningen (The Netherlands) and an M.Sc. in Artificial Intelligence from the University of Edinburgh (UK).

**David T. Wagner** is an assistant professor of management at the University of Oregon's Lundquist College of Business and is a graduate of the Management Department at Michigan State University. His research examines moods and emotions in the workplace, the impact of sleep and fatigue on workplace outcomes, and the interface between work and life domains. His research has been published in the *Academy of Management Journal, Journal of Applied Psychology, Personnel Psychology*, and *Journal of Sleep Research* and has appeared in popular outlets including the *Harvard Business Review, Wall Street Journal*, and CBS nationwide radio.

**Jennifer H. K. Wong** is currently pursuing her Ph.D. in Industrial-Organizational Psychology at Saint Mary's University. She completed her M.Sc. in Applied Psychology from the same university in 2012. She takes on a multidisciplinary approach to occupational health and safety by incorporating methods and theories from related areas of research.

# INDEX

Mueller, J.S., 113
Mullen, N., 157
Mullins, H.M., 197–198, 265
Multiple Sleep Latency Test, 26
Muraven, M., 133–134
Mur, J.M., 180
Murray, G., 105

Nakata, A., 173, 179
nap(s)
    in counteracting fatigue at
        workplace, 182
    optimal duration of, 109, 182
    in sleep loss management, 108–109
napping
    types of, 108–109
narcolepsy
    characteristics of, 43
    sleepiness while driving due to, 157
National Institute for Occupational Safety
        and Health
    on impact of daylight saving
        time, 172
National Institute of Health
    on sleep, 264
National Sleep Foundation (2012) study
    on truck drivers' work shifts, 156
Navy SEALS
    caffeine for sleep loss in, 107–108
negative affect
    sleep deprivation and, 22, 110
negative mood
    lack of sleep and, 102
neglect
    work, 195
        defined, 205
        sleepiness and, 198f, 205
neurobiological arousal
    sleep-related effects of, 85
New York Times
    on sleep, 273
Ng, T.W.H., 82
Niedhammer, L., 88–89
Nielsen, M.B., 80
night shift(s)
    permanent, 13
        rotating shifts vs., 15–16
night-shift work
    assessment of, 225
    prevalence of, 13
night-shift worker(s)
    circadian misalignment
        in, 12–13, 12f
    reverting to night time sleep on
        off-shift day, 16

Nishida, Y., 155
Nixon, A.E., 79, 80
non–24-hour sleep-wake rhythm
        disorder, 45
non-rapid eye movement (NREM)
        parasomnias, 45
nonwork experiences and activities
    described, 56
    employee sleep and
        processes underlying relationships
            between, 57–59, 58f
    sleep and
        relationship between, 55–76
nonwork-related thoughts
    employee sleep effects of, 64
Nordbakke, S., 158, 159
Nordin, M., 86
Notelaers, G., 63
Nowicki, G.P., 113
NREM parasomnias. see non-rapid eye
        movement (NREM) parasomnias
nutrition
    guidelines for, 257

obesity hypoventilation syndrome
        (OHS), 43
Obst, P., 155
obstructive sleep apnea (OSA), 39–43
    absenteeism due to, 41–42
    accidents related to, 42
    burnout syndrome and, 42
    characteristics of, 39
    cognitive impairments related to, 41
    comorbidity of, 40–41
    costs related to, 42–43
    CPAP for
        costs related to, 43
    defined, 39
    effects of, 32, 41
    prevalence of, 40
    sleepiness while driving due to, 157
obstructive sleep apnea hypopnea
        syndrome, 39
obstructive sleep apnea syndrome (OSAS),
        39, 174–175
    type 2 diabetes with, 40
occupational fatigue
    driving and
        legal and policy implications,
            149–150
OECD countries. see Organisation for
        Economic Co-operation and
        Development (OECD) countries
OHS. see obesity hypoventilation
        syndrome (OHS)